*Our book is dedicated to our wives,
Judith and Susan*

Personal Issues In Human Sexuality

Sol Gordon, Ph.D.

Director, The Institute for Family Research
and Education, Syracuse University

Craig W. Snyder, Ph.D.

Marriage and Family Therapist, Onondaga Pastoral
Counseling Center

Allyn and Bacon, Inc.
Boston London Sydney Toronto

Series editor: Judith Shaw
Production Administrator: Jane J. Schulman
Editorial Production: Kailyard Associates
Interior Design/Photo Research: Kailyard Associates
Cover Coordinator/Designer: Linda K. Dickinson

Photo Credits:
Part One, pg. 1. © Mark Antman/The Image Works
Part Two, pg. 31. © Alan Carey/The Image Works
Part Three, pg. 105. © Joel Gordon, 1978
Part Four, pg. 157. © Joel Gordon, 1983
Part Five, pg. 182. © John Running/Stock Boston
Part Six, pg. 173. © Gale Zucker

Library of Congress Cataloging in Publication Data

Gordon, Sol, 1923
    Personal issues in human sexuality
     1. Sex instruction. 2 college students—Sexual behavior. 3. Hygiene, Sexual. I. Snyder, Craig W. II. Title. (DNLM: 1. Sex. 2. Sex. Behavior.
HQ 21 G665p
HQ35.2.G67   1986   613.9'5   85-27499
Bibliography: p.
Includes index.

  ISBN 0 205 08736 1

Printed in the United States of America
10 9 8 7 6 5 4 3 2 1   92 91 90 89 88 87 86

Contents

Preface

After reading one of the conventional textbooks in human sexuality, students often end up feeling unsatisfied. Although it is important for people to learn the latest facts and research findings, these do not often lend insight into the inherently personal issues of one's own sexual behavior. The abundance of competently written texts available fulfill the academic requirements; our focus is on the more personal, philosophical, and ethical issues in people's lives.

We are acutely aware that our book is controversial. The perspective taken within these pages is not always an unbiased presentation; although differing viewpoints on a number of issues are acknowledged, the tone at times reflects the authors' support for egalitarian relationships (and generally speaking, the women's movement) and loving fidelity, and opposition to sexual exploitation, harassment, and abuse. Many widely debated areas are covered, and some readers will disagree with our orientation, which is based on years of clinical work with families, and educational work with students. The idea is that in the process of disagreeing, opinions are clarified, and personal feelings are openly examined in a realistic manner. This approach reveals our respect for the reader's ability to decide for him or herself.

Yesterday's female orgasm was vaginal. Then came the clitoral variety, which in turn yielded to G Spot- and multi-orgasms. Will tomorrow's be a mammary orgasm? Trends such as these highlight one of our main theses: we are not living in the age of sexual revolution so much as in an era of *anti*sexual revolution, in which sexuality at times is akin to a gymnastic performance. What constitutes some of the data on human sexuality is a series of false assumptions carefully documented by research. Within this framework, too little attention has been devoted to the loving and caring and intimacy that comprise the heart of people's sexual relationships.

If the innermost reaches of people's uncertainties about their sexuality were probed, the question that would surface most often is, Am I normal and adequate and lovable? The nature of self-esteem affects a number of other questions concerning how love and sexuality emerge in our lives: How will you educate your own children? In what manner will you relate to those with whom you become intimately, perhaps sexually, involved? How accepting of your own sexual impulses, fantasies, behavior, and orientation can you be? In the process of working through these personal issues, societal trends, research findings, and a whole constellation of knowledge take on new meaning.

Nearly all individuals harbor insecurities and doubts about themselves—few are comfortable with their sexuality. Hardly a person reaches adulthood without having some traumatic experience, making mistakes, or suffering from guilt and/or misinformation. When these issues have not been resolved effectively, sexuality tends to become overly important and out of perspective. Each person, though unlike any other, shares to some extent in the common reservoir of difficulties, and perhaps joys, that sexuality encompasses. We hope readers will find in the following chapters some ideas and wisdom that will be helpful in understanding themselves.

S.G.
C.W.S.

PART ONE
Coming to Terms with Our Own Sexuality First

CHAPTER 1

The Sexual Revolution and Intimacy

Has there in fact been a sexual revolution over the past twenty years? Few rhetorical questions have aroused such heated debate or passion. If there has been one, has it been for better or for worse, and what have been its major accomplishments?

Undeniably, there has been a revolution in the amount of sexual messages one finds in the media and in personal conversations. The explosion in sexually related themes in the public consciousness, however, has both positive and negative elements associated with it. The term *revolution*, though often used synonymously with progressive reform, is far from *the* answer to people's sexual concerns.

Many aspects of the alleged sexual revolution appear actually to be a part of an *antisexual* revolution. Among its main characteristics are the following:

- People have sex shortly after meeting, and then consider getting to know each other. But the possibility of a relationship is already sabotaged by the morning after. It's as if the old fairy tale of the frog and the princess has been rewritten with a contemporary twist: Today, the princess kisses the prince, and he turns into a frog and hops away.

- People use sex as a test or a proof of love, by saying in effect, If you really love me, you'll have sex with me or, Since our sex together isn't so great, we must not love each other.

- There is a widespread failure to understand that individuals get hurt because they don't feel loved, *not* because they don't know how to make love.

3

- Sexuality is perceived as a gymnastic performance; that is, orgasms and sexual techniques, rather than love and intimacy, are the focus of attention.
- Sexist, violent, exploitative media programs reach the top of the ratings charts.

Within the antisexual revolution, people use sex as an avoidance of, rather than an expression of, caring and intimacy. Sam Keen, a well-known psychologist and author, has commented, "When our eros is limited to genital sexuality it becomes obsessive, and boring, and finally destructive." The negative side of our heralded sexual revolution offers little comfort to millions of lonely, alienated people needing love but getting laid instead. Arthur Schlesinger, Jr., suggested that if sexual repression failed to produce happiness in the nineteenth century, sexual liberation appears to have done little better in the twentieth. Ironically, some of the most unhappy people are "sexually liberated."

The antisexual revolution failed to distinguish between sex and sexuality and at times glorified the former at the expense of the latter. *Sex* refers specifically to genitally oriented behaviors. *Sexuality* encompasses a broad spectrum of sexual thoughts, feelings, fantasies, dreams, values, and behaviors: it relates more to who we are than what we do. Whenever the sexual revolution embraced such concepts as, if it feels good, do it, do your own thing, and free love, it deteriorated into a game of flesh and disassociated itself from the moral and ethical frameworks within which most people wish to operate.

Within America's confused escape from sexual repression, however, are kernels of an enlightened sexual revolution. Some progress has occurred. In general people today have the number of children they want and are able to plan births. Adult sexual relations for pleasure, as opposed to sex for reproduction, is more of the accepted cultural norm. Many physicians and health-care workers are required to attend courses in human sexuality as part of their education, something that even fifteen years ago was unheard of in professional schools. Women have begun to affirm their sexual identities and are making progress toward being accepted and treated as equals. Some men are forsaking sex per se in favor of sensuality, love, and intimacy.

When compared with other developed nations, however, the United States does not fare well in some important respects. Teenage pregnancy, which is contraindicated for numerous medical and psychological reasons, is significantly more common in the United States than in such countries as Sweden, France, Canada, England, and the Netherlands (in fact, our rate is more than double that of any of these other nations). The authors of the study that reported these findings (Jones, 1985) found the lowest rates of teenage pregnancy in countries with relatively liberal attitudes toward sexuality, easily accessible contraceptive services for young people without parental notification, and perhaps most important, such nations had comprehensive programs in sex education in their schools. Though the United States resembles these other countries in socioeconomic and cultural characteristics, in some ways it lags far behind in its level of sexual maturity.

Clearly, the authentic sexual revolution has far to go. If asked, most individuals would be able to describe (or recognize) a deviate, dysfunctional, or unhealthy sexual adaptation in another person. Would the same individuals, however, be capable of describing or recognizing a model of mature, healthy adult sexuality? What does the sexually healthy person look, act, or feel like? When this vision of a healthy sexual adaptation is part of most people's consciousness, the sexual revolution will have achieved perhaps its greatest goal.

THE DEVELOPMENT OF INTIMACY

In the end, the sexual revolution has meaning mainly insofar as it is able to enhance the growth of genuine intimacy between people in their relationships. Intimacy grows from, and is rooted in, real trust. Without this trust, the sharing, communication, and love that comprise intimate relationships are impaired. Intimacy requires a trust that partners will not be hurt and need not fear attack when they reveal vulnerabilities to each other.

The link between sex and intimacy is not as straightforward as is sometimes assumed. Two people can be sexually involved and yet engage each other on a superficial, nonintimate level. Sex itself can be very intimate, somewhat intimate, or alienating at the extreme. The two people may not even like (or know) each other. Some people make sex out to be the most cherished, loving thing, but real intimacy occurs between two people exchanging their ideas and feelings with each other.

This point was observed by Shere Hite in her book *The Hite Report* in which hundreds of women generally concurred that what they enjoyed the most about physical closeness was touching, cuddling, and caressing, more than sexual intercourse itself. Early in 1985, Ann Landers, the syndicated national columnist, asked her female readers which they preferred, and whether they'd be willing to give up "the act" in order to be held close and treated tenderly. Of the more than 90,000 women who responded, 72 percent said yes—they'd forsake intercourse for the cuddling. It must be acknowledged that this was a biased sample, since *dissatisfied* women would more likely be motivated to answer this question printed in a newspaper. It was clear from the women's answers that they would still like to have intercourse as long as they could have the cuddling as well. The findings illustrate how closeness and sensuality are the main ingredients in a mutually intimate relationship and that many men have been socialized to dissociate sex from intimacy.

The interrelationships among love, intimacy, and friendship are not always appreciated to their full extent. For instance, regardless of expectations beforehand, somehow sex invariably changes things in a relationship. It's rarely a simple matter: it's one with which close friends sometimes wrestle. Once two people have had a sexual experience with each other, it changes their feelings toward each other. People's moods change, and reactions after-the-act range from feeling the encounter was very bad to very good. Sexual interaction, even with the same person, can elicit a wide variety of responses in ourselves from time to time. The fact that sex changes things forces individuals to think through the meaning of sex for themselves. The quality of love and intimacy may be better or worse after sex is initiated, but it will not be the same.

Intimate relationships tend to be tolerant of the different moods and interests that people express. In loving interactions, two people don't always feel the same. Sometimes you're loving and caring, and sometimes you're irritable and upset. There's a flow back and forth in which you care for the other person just a little bit more than you care for yourself. You are sensitive and responsive to the needs of your partner. Equilibrium is achieved not through a static balance in which things are always equal but rather through a shifting imbalance in which first you care for someone *else's* needs, then he or she cares for yours; sometimes you're active, sometimes you're passive.

The timing in intimate relationships is also critical, and this is especially true in the area of honesty. Lovers, spouses, and even friends often wonder, How much should I tell about myself, and when is a good time? Although honesty is often a good policy, strangely enough people sometimes regret telling the truth. A partner may not be ready for the truth and perceives being told as a hostile act (which, consciously or unconsciously, it may be). It's not always appropriate to tell all about past sexual liaisons or even fantasies that people experience. A marvelous cartoon that appeared in a national magazine pictured a couple in bed together; they had obviously just finished making love, and the man looked dejected. The woman in the cartoon said: "Would you have preferred that I was having sex with Burt Reynolds and fantasizing about you?"

Intimacy typically does not thrive in the cathartic exchange of nitty-gritty details concerning one's sexual past. The strong desire to learn of all past loves and sexual encounters of one's partner may be a sign of jealousy and, most likely, insecurity. The person worries, Am I as good a lover as his other lovers? Are there things I should be doing that I'm not? Does she secretly still love this other person? Complete honesty about the past creates fertile ground for comparisons such as these and leads to conflict that can be avoided through exercising a little discretion. Even when no specifically sexual interactions take place with past loves, present loves may still anxiously search for signs that the flame has not gone out. Even some of the best intimate relationships cannot sustain total openness.

The timing of sex and the expectations related to it strongly influence the quality of intimacy that people share. For instance, one expectation often is that men should want sex most of the time; women thus may feel rejected when men don't feel like it. One woman whose husband worked nights complained that he came home tired and wasn't interested in sex with her. He was, however, interested in cuddling up with her and going to sleep. She thought, If he really loved me, he'd want sex with me. Their sense of timing was skewed, and made even more problematic through the time-honored but false idea that men are primed for "it" any time of the day or night.

Other couples wrestle with these issues in terms of who initiates their sexual activity. Traditionally, the man was "supposed" to be the aggressor, and the woman was "supposed" to wait for him to ask. With one couple, the husband stated that he was very turned on by his wife but steadfastly refused to accept her invitations to sex. His exaggerated notions of masculinity and femininity prevented this couple from establishing the intimacy they wanted and enjoying the full range of attraction they had for each other.

Intimacy is a metaphor for the limitless verbal and nonverbal forms of communication that transpire between two people. Gazing into each other's eyes, holding hands, lying together in front of a fire, massaging or bathing each other, cooking favorite meals, or simply sensing each other's presence in a crowded room, are a few of the many nonverbal intimacies that people exchange. Often, these carry more weight than the words that accompany them. One woman said of her past relationship, "I could always tell when he was angry with me by the way he'd wrinkle his face and walk stiffly. He'd deny that he was upset and force a smile, but he was pretending, and I was very good at 'reading' him not by what he said, but by what he did and how he did it."

Closeness is created and maintained not only through the sharing of endearments and loving gestures. In intimate relationships, there needs to be ample room for anger and arguments, bad moods, and short tempers. These emotions are among the most difficult for lovers to accept and understand in each other. The use of "I messages" can enhance the level of understanding, however, and defuse some of the toxic anger that grows in conflicts when accusations, past hurts, and nearly anything is fair game.

For example, instead of saying, Your stupid habit of picking lint off my clothes in public has got to stop, say, I feel embarrassed and childish when I'm not treated like an adult. I'd like you to stop picking lint off my clothes in public. Instead of saying, You drive me crazy with your nagging and constant talking—I can't get a word in edgewise, say, I feel that often I don't get much chance to speak my mind when we're talking. I don't like to compete for talking time. In both of these instances, the speaker reveals his or her feelings, and takes responsibility for them, rather than accusing the other of being a bad person who "caused" him or her to feel a certain way.

In intimate relationships, it may help to agree beforehand that when conflicts do arise, both partners will make an effort to restrict the argument to the issue at hand. Past hurts and arguments from six months ago will not be added as fuel to the fire. By limiting conflicts this way, an effective resolution is more likely. This acceptance of conflicts will be facilitated by the understanding that it is not possible to go through life without making mistakes, feeling depressed, getting angry. Though pop psychologists sometimes create the erroneous impression that occasional depression, etc. is unhealthy, such "negative" emotion actually is part of the repertoire of most healthy people.

How can two people together work toward achieving intimacy? One way of approaching this question is to ask, Who among the people you know are the most happy. Are they necessarily the best looking? Have you ever wondered why, for instance, a short fat woman and a skinny unattractive man seem to be so entranced with each other? When two people love each other, sexual attractions and intimacy can emerge.

It's not that short, fat, or unattractive people can't find a mate. It's that people who hate themselves and express it in *being* (not looking) unattractive, shortsighted, or fatuous tend to repel rather than attract others. Believing that certain perfumes, hair tonics, hygienic sprays, or selected sexual techniques will make you attractive gets you nowhere. Being a real person is what is attractive to some other people. People who have good self-esteem are attractive to some other people—period.

It is somewhat unusual, but not unheard of these days, for people to be virgins on their wedding day. For them, intimacy and love require that they not be sexually experienced before marriage. This is certainly a healthy, acceptable choice for some couples, and in some ways society, because of the so-called sexual revolution, has failed to support those who wish to remain virgins. An unfortunate variation on this scenario occurs among some men who say, "I'll screw around all I want before marriage, but I'll only marry a woman who is a virgin." This sort of hypocrisy hardly enhances the quality of intimacy that is likely to develop. Men (or women) may legitimately wish to marry a virgin only if they themselves remain virgins. Our answer to those who advocate this double standard is: it is better for you to marry a person, not a hymen.

Working toward intimacy can be hampered in a number of other ways. There exists, for example, the elusive search for a true aphrodisiac that will make even unwilling people sexually available. Powder from ground-up beetles (known as Spanish Fly), powdered rhinoceros horn (which, because it is highly sought after, is leading to the extinction of the rhinoceros), ginseng, and a host of other supposedly magical substances have been touted for their sexually stimulating properties. The truth about these things is that some have no effect, and some are physically dangerous, Spanish Fly for example. Some people consider alcohol, marijuana, or cocaine as aphrodisiacs, but these tend to cause people to withdraw into themselves and their private thoughts and fantasies. There may be a subjective sense that physical pleasure is increased, but the loving communion between the partners will be characterized by alienation and a drugged detachment.

Although the nature of intimacy may be fragile and easily damaged, it can be nourished through the efforts of those in love. Erich Fromm wrote that love thrives on four distinct qualities. First is caring in a profound way about your partner's welfare and growth. Next is respect for your partner's identity, respect for his or her right to be who he or she is, rather than how you would like them to be. Another quality is taking responsibility to care for the other person in an involved, active way. Last is knowledge of the other person—his or her values, needs, wants, dreams, foibles—without which love may feel empty.

A great gift that lovers can give each other and that will enhance the qualities Fromm describes is the gift of listening. In our hectic, complex world there often appears to be precious little time, or interest, for listening. Listening to another involves quieting our own thoughts and concentrating on the message we are receiving. To be listened to is an act of love, a process that communicates, Your inner being is valued and important; please share it with me.

If intimacy is both a strong togetherness and a distinct separateness, a person can say, When I am free to be myself, and also to merge with you in the marvelous union we create, no threat exists when either of us wishes to be alone or to be together. Love thus becomes a delicate balance between dependence and independence, between giving and receiving. Intimacy suffers among individuals who fear the fusion and closeness that love might "impose" on them, as well as among those who fear solitude and cling desperately to their lover as if to a piece of driftwood from a shipwreck.

Commitment of some degree is ultimately required for intimacy to flourish. It may not be a lifelong intention to remain together, but without some statement to the effect that We're very involved with, and interested in, each other, and intend to explore together the meaning of our feelings for each other for the foreseeable future, it is easy for feelings of insecurity to arise. Reluctance to open oneself up is understandable when it is uncertain whether next week or next month may bring the end of the relationship.

Though this book is largely about human sexuality, the real excitement and meaning between people is found in the quality of intimacy they share. Sexual techniques and experiences can contribute to intimacy, but they are only the how-tos in a mutually responsive relationship. Perhaps the greatest value of the sexual revolution can be found in the dialogues it provoked in society concerning these issues. The revolution heightened people's awareness that the dilemmas existed and opened the way for love, sexuality, and spirituality to be understood anew. The real turn-on, in the parlance of the sexual revolution, is love and intimacy.

REFERENCES

Jones, E. S., et al. "Teenage Pregnancy in Developed Countries: Determinants and Policy Implications." *Family Planning Perspectives*, **17** (2), March-April, 1985.

CHAPTER 2

Coming to Terms with Your Own Sexuality

Sexual intercourse, as an aspect of our sexuality, is greatly overrated. If some people's public persona were to be believed, however, it would often appear that only nuclear war is a more important issue in their lives.

Sexual intercourse is, at best, number nine on our list of the ten most important characteristics of a relationship. This is our sense, in order of importance, of what it's all about:

1. Love, caring, and intimacy together
2. A sense of humor and playfulness
3. Honest communication and interesting conversation
4. A passionate sense of mission or purpose
5. Friends together and separately
6. Commitment to one's own identity and ideals
7. Tolerance for occasional craziness, irritableness, conflict, error
8. Acceptance of each other's style
9. Sexual fulfillment
10. Sharing household tasks

Occasionally, when this list is presented to an audience, an outraged male will suggest that it is nonsense (no female ever has); how could sex be number nine? The reply is always, Because there are eight things more important. And besides, of the 3243 really important aspects of a relationship, sex is one of the top ten. Not bad.

It is fashionable these days for some professionals to attribute major evils of our times to the excesses of the women's liberation movement. The following is typical of what is being *attributed:*

- The human male is committing sexual suicide.
- Motherhood, rooted in biology and history (or eternity), is being prostituted by women who expect men to share in household and parenting responsibilities, especially when preschool children are involved.
- Professionals are treating an alarmingly large number of men who are impotent as a result of their relationships with aggressive women.
- Bisexuality is only a *cover* for innate or latent homosexuality.
- Children are growing up confused to the point of needing psychiatric treatment because they are not sure of their roles in life. This is especially true of girls who join the Little League, boys who study ballet.
- The increase in the number of women who commit criminal acts is due to their wanting to act like men.

It is possible to come up with these findings by

- Reporting on a small sample to an uninformed journalist.
- Creating the impression in the media that society is in imminent danger because everybody is doing it (*it* being, for example, experimenting with bisexuality or women forcing men to change diapers, thus reversing an historic role).
- Creating nonexisting polarities: for example, if you are not heterosexual, you must be a homosexual.
- Setting up straw men or women by citing isolated incidents or extreme examples or excesses as being typical of the women's movement.

It is becoming clear that for every impotent man, suicidal woman, or confused child there are now, as a result of the influence of the women's liberation movement, thousands of liberated people who are finding themselves in a life they can celebrate. Instead of *observing* trends, some people are good at trying to *create* them as a consequence of their personal insecurities and limited experiences.

A strange alliance of forces in our society has conspired to debase the meaning, intent, and value of sexuality. Some well-intentioned ministers claim that if you have sex before marriage, you'll have nothing to look forward to in marriage, or there will be no surprises after you marry. This might be countered with the claim that if you are expecting sexual intercourse to be the only surprise in marriage, don't marry. It's not worth it. There are also supersophisticated researchers who would have us believe that sex is something you can quantify, all of which contributes to the disastrous illusion that sex is akin to a gymnastic performance. Some researchers actually want us to take seriously the absurd notion that men reach their sexual peak at age nineteen and women at twenty-nine. Where did they get data like this, from a random sample of eighty-five-year-old men and women? A distraught young man once came to me (Sol Gordon) and sadly revealed his fate: "I'm twenty years old and already past my prime, and I haven't even started yet."

Nevertheless, the fact that human sexuality has become an area of scholarly research in a wide variety of disciplines is a sign of progress. A great deal of knowledge has been generated through research efforts, which collectively have established sexuality as a legitimate academic discipline. At times, however, an overly scientific approach to sexuality has depersonalized the essence of sexuality and fueled a conceptualization of sex that is performance- and competition-oriented. Thus, we encourage readers not to develop an antiresearch bias, but rather to question the validity of the procedures and findings of the research they encounter.

What has all this to do with coming to terms with one's own sexuality? It's the introduction. A way of putting sex into a perspective along with other aspects of your existence.

Sexual intercourse is one aspect but not the overwhelmingly important part of a relationship. This is not to say that in some families sex isn't number one. It is often number one when there is a problem or a hangup. It is number one when couples are more preoccupied with performance or orgasms than they are with the relationship. It assumes enormous proportions if a couple believes that if we really love each other, we will have great sex or simultaneous orgasms. The fact is that some couples really love each other, yet have sexual relations that appear less than adequate, even dysfunctional. On the other hand, there are couples who hate each other and have great sex together. Sex is neither a test nor a proof of love. Sexual intercourse can be and often is an enjoyable aspect of well-adjusted couples; *well-adjusted* being operationally defined as people who like each other and who enjoy being married to each other (and includes those living together in committed relationships).

It is in this context that some crucial aspects of sexuality are elaborated on below as an aid in exploring and evaluating your own sexual behavior, knowledge, and feelings. As will be evident, certain ideas and biases will not coincide with your own. The process of disagreement and debate in our pluralistic society is an excellent medium for personal growth and education. Our bias is toward common sense and respect for individual differences. This is preferable to "hard data," biblical injunctions, or moralistic imperatives. Nevertheless, consider this quote from Virginia Woolf: "At any rate, when a subject is highly controversial—and any question about sex is that—one cannot hope to tell the truth. One can only show how one came to hold the opinion one does hold. One can only give one's audience the chance of drawing their own conclusions as they observe the limitations, the idiosyncrasies of the speaker."

Appreciating Our Sexuality: Some Concepts

These concepts are particularly important in appreciating our own sexuality:

Normal and abnormal. Normal sexual behavior *among adults* is defined as being voluntary, nonexploitative, and consensual. Generally, this behavior is not only pleasurable and guilt-free, but also enhances self-esteem. Abnormal sexual behavior is characterized by being compulsive (involuntary), exploitative, (often) nonconsensual, guilt-ridden, and rarely pleasurable. It generally lowers self-esteem. Provided sex meets these general criteria and does not seriously conflict with the participants' values, it does not matter how and where it takes place; the mouth, the anus, the vagina, and it does not matter who does what. (We are, of course, taking for granted that all sexual behavior should occur in a private setting.)

Select, don't settle. Human beings are not like animals. Animal sex is biologically programmed, but even animals "make do" with their own if the opposite sex is not available. It appears that no sensible person need worry that heterosexuality, as a primary lifestyle, will disappear. The real concern in most of the world is overpopulation, not whether more people are bi-, auto-, or homosexual, or simply don't want to have children.

It also seems evident that one's sexuality is not rigidly fixed even though there is evidence to believe that what is termed *constitutional homosexuality,* is a sexual orientation and not readily subject to change (the same is true of *constitutional heterosexuality*). People do go through stages, make mistakes, and experience different feelings at varying times of their lives. Those cycles can include long or short periods of fidelity or infidelity, homosexual incidents, a brief encounter, a weird indiscretion or a "perversion" here and there. People can grow and profit from both good and bad experiences.

It's even okay to feel that you are naturally attracted only to members of the opposite sex, for whatever reason, and not care how open or modern you are supposed to be. Other possibilities and attractions are boundless, but it's not okay to exploit people and abuse them for your own pleasure.

This does not mean, select one thing and that's it. What makes sense in one period of your life makes no sense in another period. Nor does it mean that people don't have to work for and toward what they want most from their lives. Furthermore, not every meal has to be a gourmet feast.

All thoughts are normal. Sexual thoughts, wishes, dreams, and daydreams and turn-ons are normal, no matter how "far out." Behavior can be wrong, but ideas cannot be. Thoughts, images, and fantasies cannot, in themselves, hurt you. Guilt is the energy for the repetition of fantasies that are unacceptable to you.

Anybody with some degree of imagination has, from time to time, a range of thoughts, from murderous, sadistic, incestuous, or rape fantasies, to heroic escapades and undying love. That does not mean that they are going to come true, or that people are going to act them out. As a matter of fact, accepting as normal one's "unacceptable" thoughts is the best way of keeping them under voluntary control. People who constantly repress their fantasies or become preoccupied with them, because of guilt, are the ones most likely to be harmful to themselves and others.

Guilt is a good thing to feel if you've done something wrong. There are, however, two types of guilt: mature and immature. The former type helps you organize yourself and enables you to respond in a more rational manner to a similar situation or temptation in the future. Mature guilt can enhance your self-image provided you don't overdo it and let it degenerate into immature guilt, which disorganizes and overwhelms a person. You can usually tell if your guilt is immature because it is an overreaction to something you did wrong, more commonly, from something you didn't do but just thought about. More often than not it is a way of expressing hostility toward yourself and results in feelings of depression. Almost everyone at one time or other suffers from immature guilt. This is not to be confused with normal bad/upset feelings or with grieving and mourning in response to real events in a person's life.

Sexual arousal. The popular culture, especially its mass media, creates the notion that there are standard stimuli for getting aroused. Men, for example, are supposed to be aroused by the pretty girl selling automobiles or by *Playboy* Bunnies. That's all right except that men who aren't aroused by the current fashion often feel compelled to fake it. The fact is that human beings are sexually aroused by a variety of stimuli. *Not* knowing that *all* forms of arousal are all right is what causes trouble.

Some people feel guilty if they are sexually aroused when playing with children, roughing it with dogs, being attracted to their parents, sitting in moving vehicles, having sadistic fantasies, or looking at pornography. If you can accept the arousal experience without guilt, no harm is done. And why not enjoy some of it? A problem exists if you act out the sexual arousal, or if you can get excited only or mainly by thoughts or acts you or your partner find unacceptable and exploitative.

Women's liberation. The women's liberation movement is probably the best single force for the liberation of men. Men, in the long run, will profit the most from being *forced* to relate to liberated women. Men who are free of the pressures of the double standard and aggressive behavior will be able to share responsibilities and bring harmony to the most disquieting, sexist aspects of our society.

Some people have come to associate the women's liberation movement only with specific issues, such as abortion on demand, day care, and equal opportunities in employment. But liberation is more than this. Liberation means that both men and women are attempting to discover themselves in a realistic, rather than an idealistic or culturally stereotyped, manner and are then acting on these discoveries. Explaining these new feelings and actions may be one of the most important bridges that men and women can build.

Masturbation. Nearly all professionals these days say that masturbation is all right and that it is a normal developmental stage. Then there is a pause: It's all right if you don't do it too much. And nearly everyone is asking, How much is too much?

Masturbation is a good, healthy sexual expression for all people, no matter at what age or stage in life they happen to be: child, teenager, young adult, middle-aged, or elderly who are either single or married. Masturbation is best when it is voluntary (as opposed to compulsive) and is accompanied by a range of fantasies.

A lot of men and women don't often admit it, but they achieve their best orgasms by masturbating. Married people with satisfactory sex lives masturbate. Some people masturbate rarely or not at all. That's all right, too. Guilt about masturbation is about the only thing that's not desirable.

Telling the truth about your sexual past. This may be a good thing, but you should make sure that you are telling the truth for the right reasons. Sometimes people reveal their past to hurt or express hostility toward their partner. Others want to know the past for abusive purposes. Don't let it all hang out. There is a great need for privacy in some aspects of our lives.

Coitus. Many myths are perpetuated by some "sexperts" who write sensuality and sex manuals. There is no special amount of time a man's penis is supposed to stay in a woman's vagina to guarantee satisfaction. For some, it's seconds; for others, a couple of minutes. As a matter of fact, it can vary from time to time and each time. There just are no standards for everyone. Find out by experimenting with what is most enjoyable for the two of you. Intercourse is not essential for sexual pleasure, nor is having an orgasm each time or even most of the time, and certainly not having simultaneous orgasms.

Female orgasms. More nonsense has been written about this subject than any other area of sexuality. Women have been made to feel so insecure that some need a *Good Housekeeping* seal to certify their orgasms. Often they pose the question in a serious way to a professional: How can I tell if I have an orgasm? And just as often the professional will respond with an uninformed answer, If you had one, you'd know it. This response only reinforces the insecurity.

Orgasm is mainly a psychological phenomenon—with associated physical sensations. We define orgasm as a very brief, intensely pleasurable sensual experience accompanied by a series of contractions. Orgasm is not always necessary to enjoy sexual intimacy and a mature relationship with another human being. It's just another dimension of pleasure that is good to experience.

Most women who enjoy their own bodies, have good feelings about themselves, and like the idea of sexual intimacy have orgasms:

- If they are not intent on having one each time.
- If their partner doesn't ask each time, Did you have one? (What kind of conversation is that, anyway?)
- If they don't take seriously some of the research, especially that which suggests the type of father you should have had to achieve orgasm.
- If they feel comfortable about masturbating.

Male orgasms. The best-kept male secret is that every time a man ejaculates he has an orgasm. This is simply not true. Any man who denies it either is not telling the truth or can't be trusted. Sometimes a man will ejaculate and feel nothing at all. At times there is a little pleasure and at times a great deal. Orgasms vary in strength and pleasure, during masturbation, intercourse, and all sexual acts. Men sometimes fake orgasms. Men are better programmed to experience orgasm than women, but this is changing.

Size. An all American hangup! Men worry whether their penis is *big* enough. Freud got it wrong. It's men who have penis envy. Size has nothing to do with giving or receiving sexual pleasure. Besides, one cannot tell the size of a penis by looking at it when it is not erect. Some hang long; some appear quite small but erect to sizes larger than those that appear huge.

Women needlessly worry that their partner's penis is either too small for satisfaction or too big (painful) for their vagina. When we recall that the vagina accommodates the birth of a baby, it is difficult to believe genital size is a factor in pleasure or pain. On the other hand, tension and an inability to relax can be related to both pleasure and pain.

Breast size or shape has nothing to do with sexual or personal adequacy. In the early stages of puberty, girls often worry because of uneven or late breast development compared to their friends. This is sad, because there is a wide range of perfectly healthy, normal stages of growth. Many females with large breasts are as self-conscious as those with small ones. The most current style is the larger the better. At other times, preferences dictated the smaller the better.

Sublimation. People used to think (and some still do) that sex could be sublimated or propelled into "higher channels" without direct expression by being creative, athletic, doing charitable work, or becoming a priest or a nun. Adult sexuality can only be: expressed, repressed, suppressed, but it cannot be sublimated!

The individuals with the greatest potential for problems are those who repress significant aspects of their sexuality. Repressed sexuality is often revealed by means of: physical disorders, immaturity, revulsion in response to natural bodily functions, meanness, obsessive-compulsive neurosis, fears of homosexuality, and failure to achieve orgasm, among others. Some people who are emotionally mature never have had sexual intercourse. They are usually able to acknowledge, but suppress, impulses toward sexual relations or masturbation. Many people are emotionally immature but have highly satisfactory sexual experiences. Many people are emotionally mature who enjoy an active, vigorous sex life. The range of sexual expressions in its relationship to maturity is infinite.

Normal sex problems. Just about everybody is sexually dysfunctional sometimes. In other words, they are unable to "perform" despite wishing they could. An occasional experience of being impotent, having premature ejaculation, not reaching orgasm, or being turned off from sex altogether is not uncommon. If you don't panic or become fixated into what could be merely a temporary out-of-sorts state of mind, the situation will improve. If you attach too much importance to what could have been a temporary problem, it can get worse.

Role playing (positions and techniques). Every sexual relationship can be enhanced by varying roles during encounters. One can be active or passive, both can be active or both passive. One can care for and be taken care of, bathe someone or be bathed, massage or be massaged, and relate similarly in bed.

When you get down to it, no one need be frozen in an assigned role. Traditional concepts of what is supposed to be maleness and femaleness (or active and passive) no longer apply, if they ever really did. What counts is communication and intimacy, which translate into sexual rapport. Roles, positions, and techniques are only the mechanical "how-to's" in a mutually responsive relationship.

On being horny. Feeling horny is not mainly physiological, biological, constitutional, or hereditary. It is primarily a psychological phenomenon. If you feel horny and your spouse or lover has a headache (which is lasting for days), masturbate. If you have a mature (not guilt-ridden) attitude toward masturbation, you will feel better afterward. In any case, don't go around telling everybody you feel this way since it is terribly boring and sometimes even burdensome to be with a person who is complaining that he or she is horny.

Homosexuality. It is no longer believed that homosexuality is caused by any one thing or a special combination of factors. Homosexuals exist in every culture and society. Ancient Greek culture found homosexuality acceptable. Our culture has frowned upon it.

It is a false assumption that a person who has homosexual thoughts or dreams must be a homosexual. Mature people are aware of the fact that they have both homosexual and heterosexual feelings, even though the majority of them prefer sexual activities with members of the opposite sex. In this connection, it might be helpful to point out that it is not easy to judge a person's sexual orientation by appearance. Some feminine-looking men or masculine-looking women are heterosexual; and some highly masculine, so-called macho all-American, types are homosexual.

The gay liberation movement together with notable research, such as that conducted recently at the Kinsey Institute, has made it abundantly clear that homosexuals are just as healthy or unhealthy as heterosexuals. Sexual orientation does not determine whether a person is mature or normal. Saying a person is a homosexual tells us as much about a person as saying a person is heterosexual. If we're going to sex-identify each other, let's start out with the idea that we are all *human sexuals*.

People have the right, without stigma or coercion, to be what they are. If some 90 percent of the population are heterosexual, that's their business. If perhaps 10 percent express themselves by homosexual, bisexual, or by no overt sexual behavior, that's their business as well. Certainly it is cruel and immoral for government to have anything to say about sexual relations between two consenting adults. It is hoped a time will come when people's sexual orientation will be of little or no legislative interest and certainly none of anybody's business (unless that body is an unwilling partner).

Perversion. This is an old-fashioned word used to describe what some people find revolting. For example, there are still some people who consider anal or oral sex perverted. Fancy names for perversions are exhibitionism, masochism, sadism, fetishism, voyeurism, necrophilia, and bestiality. There is nothing wrong with any kind of sex between consenting adults in private, if each partner is nonexploitative and the act is voluntary. Anal and oral sex are enjoyable for many people and are also ways to have sexual pleasure for those who don't want, or can't, have sexual intercourse.

The more accepted term is sexual deviation. Perversion probably should be restricted to sexual arousal behaviors that are harmful to another person or animal. This refers to sexual activity that is usually compulsive and guilt-ridden. Examples might be a male who gets his kicks from displaying his penis to a woman in a public place or a woman who enjoys intercourse only when she causes physical pain to her partner. We all have "perverted" feelings at times. They are neurotic if they are one's main way of getting sexually satisfied.

Fear of other people's preferences. It's all right to have sexual preferences. It is not necessary to enjoy or "be into" anal, oral, auto-, homo-, or group sexuality to be "with it." But having fixed powerful emotions, such as, revolting, disgusting, perverse, obscene, or unnatural, in response to behavior that is enjoyable *to others*, usually means that you have a problem. Males are occasionally heard to say, If any faggot so much as comes near me, I'll kill him. This may mean that the person who makes the threat is immensely threatened by his own homosexual impulses, which, of course, we all have. It does not necessarily suggest that the person is, in fact, a homosexual.

Sexual addictions. Compulsive masturbation means you do it not because you like it but because you can't help it. (However troublesome, it is still "safer" than compulsive eating or drinking.) Compulsive heterosexual or homosexual behavior (even if not forced on the other person) takes place outside an interest in a relationship. It does not enhance or enrich the person, and it rarely provides gratification beyond momentary relief. A person who is always "on the make" is rarely capable of a sustained relationship and despite boasting to the contrary, usually does not enjoy sex. Sexual molestation of children is always a compulsion. Being talked into having sex when you really don't want to, before you feel ready for it, with someone you really don't care about, and without using birth control are kinds of compulsive responses.

When your main drive to achieve some sexual outlet is transferring your attachments to a thing (shoe, undergarment, leather, dress) or when other forms of indirect behavior such as exposing yourself, stealing, or viewing others (Peeping Tom) become compulsive sexual expressions, you may have a sexual addiction.

First experiences of sexual intercourse. Many first experiences of sex are not pleasurable despite stories to the contrary. This is especially true if they occur when you are too young, too immature, or on your honeymoon. It is especially important not to diagnose yourself on the basis of these experiences. Men sometimes think they are sexual freaks if they are impotent or ejaculate prematurely on their first encounters. Women may feel that they are not sexual or feminine if they don't have an orgasm the first time around.

It is surprising how many people have acknowledged that their first sexual experiences were empty, flat, and even repulsive. Yet, sex can become a beautiful experience if two people care about each other and give priority to their relationship. On the other hand, sex can become a nightmare if the two don't care about each other or concentrate on position games and simultaneous orgasms, or if they have to sneak, hide, and hurry.

On being sexually attractive. People who are self-accepting are sexually attractive to *some* other individuals! It doesn't matter what the cosmetics and toothpaste industries have to say about it.

As the above list illustrates, people experience pressures to be healthy and well adjusted in many areas of their lives. We are not suggesting that we have to be completely comfortable with our sexuality, only that we not be hung up or pervasively neurotic about it. We are suggesting that once we put our own sexuality into perspective, we will be making fewer mistakes as we relate to our friends, family, and children.

There exists no such thing as complete comfort or self-actualization with regard to one's sexuality. Such mythical comfort represents a self-defeating goal for people who might otherwise be content with their own level of growth.

REFERENCES

Woolf, V. *A Room of One's Own.* New York: Harcourt, Brace, Jovanovich, 1929, 1957.

CHAPTER 3

How Can You Tell If You're Really in Love and Whom Not to Marry

How can I tell if I'm really in love? For most people, no question is more exciting and compelling than this one. Of course, no one has *the* answer to the myriad of other questions that exist:

- Why do so many people feel insecure about love?
- Why, if a teenager is in love, adults (often parents) are quick to say: It's puppy love, You'll get over it, Wait until you're older.

(Yet, so many of these same adult critics often recall with nostalgia, and sometimes despair, that the best and most marvelous love experiences in their life occurred during their own adolescence or young adulthood.)

Other questions that arise as people explore their feelings may be, Can people fall truly in love only once? Is the best love love at first sight? Why do so many people seem to fall in and out of love—often? And finally the ultimate question, Is it true that love is blind? (In practice, if love is blind, it had better not remain so for more than twenty-four hours. After that, open your eyes and see with whom you are in love.)

Although there are many different kinds of love and loving relationships (one can love many people in different ways), being *in love* usually refers to a powerful desire to be with, and to win the respect and affection of, just one other person. Our view is that this primary relationship has priority in a basic way, and thus it is not possible to be in love with more than one person at the same time. Within these primary relationships, the quality of love may be either mature or immature.

It's not that difficult to tell the difference between mature and immature love. Immature love is exhausting to the people involved and tends to detract from their overall levels of energy and enthusiasm. They may boast, I'm in love! I'm in love!, and yet it's even tiresome watching them. When love such as this is immature and perhaps obsessional, people are too preoccupied with themselves to find time to shower, study adequately for their courses, or keep the apartment clean. How can I do the dishes? I'm in love!

Immature lovers often have what is called a hostile-dependent relationship. That means that they don't enjoy being with the person they are supposed to be in love with, and they can't stand to be away from them. When they're together they fight, argue, feel jealous, but when they're apart they miss each other desperately. One partner may frequently ask, "Do you love me? Do you love me?" (If the other person says No, the couple could have their first meaningful conversation.)

Mature love, on the other hand, is energizing. You have time for most of the things you want to do, and when you are with your loved one, you feel happy, joyous, secure. That doesn't mean you never argue, but most of the time you really want to please each other. In general, your caring about the other person seems just a bit more important than that person caring for you. You can tell whether your love is mature or immature by becoming aware of how much energy you have, and of the overall quality of your spirit and emotional state. People who are maturely in love will be intent on making themselves the best possible (not perfect) partner for their loved one. This will involve actively supporting the other person in his or her work and aspirations and understanding the occasional stresses that accompany most relationships.

A concept we'll develop further into the book states that there is a difference between sex and love: they are best when they accompany each other, but they are by no means synonymous. Erich Fromm (1957), in his classic book *The Art of Loving*, suggests that sexual desire is just one of the many manifestations of the need for love. You can have sex with someone you don't love, and you can be sexually dysfunctional with a person you love a great deal. It is possible to be turned on by a person you're unable to abide; it's not unusual to be turned on by a part of a person, such as breasts, legs, chest, or ass. But you can't have a conversation with an ass—even a smart ass.

This difference makes an authentic dilemma for many people in their choices of whom to love. One young woman who exemplifies this conflict stated, "I really care about John. . . . He's a great friend, and we have a lot of fun together, but he doesn't turn me on sexually. But then there's Robert. He's not that smart, and we have practically nothing in common, but I find him very desirable and sexually exciting." Chances are that if she marries Robert, the relationship will be a disaster. The fact is that people have distorted ideas of what constitutes "chemistry" between individuals. How much do you remember from high school chemistry class? That's about how long chemistry in love lasts.

One example of what caring for another person in a loving relationship means can be seen in the following anecdote. A man approaches his fiancée for a sexual encounter and she responds, "Oh honey, I'd love to have sex with you, but not right now. I have a headache."

"You have a headache on my day off? You have a lot of nerve." In a mature love relationship, his response might be: "Oh, I'm sorry you're not feeling well. Let me get you some aspirin. There's always tomorrow."

People are often troubled by the intriguing question, What is the difference between love and infatuation? In the first month or so (two months during the summer), they are essentially indistinguishable from each other. The symptoms of this ecstatic period—a pounding heart, trouble sleeping, euphoria—become a kind of alternate reality for a while as one focuses intensely on this other person. Beyond this initial period of excitement, signs begin to emerge that help to differentiate between love and infatuation. Either love or infatuation can start out as mature or immature, and then develop into either a mature or immature relationship.

At this stage, it's not unusual for people to realize that they are deeply in love with someone who doesn't return the feeling with equal commitment. When this happens to mature people, they will make a reasonable effort to evoke affection from the other person. Sometimes, just assuming that the other person does or will love you can help affection to grow. If these efforts fail, there is a natural disappointment, perhaps even a period of mourning for the failed love affair. But after a time, people who are unable to abandon their lost hopes begin to appear tragically pathetic to their friends and families as they continue trying to make the person love them.

One disturbing piece of folklore that has circulated over the years implies that there is only one true love on earth for each person—this is a variation of the "match made in heaven" theme. Thus, when people's love relationships end, they may fear that they will never again experience the feelings of love they enjoyed. Quite the contrary is often the case: People tend to grow and mature even through broken relationships and often find that the following love relationships are more deeply rooted and more emotionally satisfying.

Others, conversely, make the same mistakes over and over again and fall in love with the wrong person.

Why do some people fall in and out of love? If that has been your experience, you may be aware of the pattern: An initial period of great love and excitement yields rather quickly to disillusionment. There is some truth to the observation that people who fall easily into love fall easily out of it. Repetitive patterns such as these may reflect an underlying fear or anxiety concerning intimacy (brief-lived relationships, after all, preclude the possibility that intimacy will develop). There are other reasons as well for why destructive cycles such as these repeat themselves. It's not unusual to encounter individuals who are so desperate for love, they're willing to take all kinds of risks. Thus, their own self-esteem and happiness may yield to the powerful need to be attached, whatever the cost. Peer pressure, or the ingrained attitude that going out with someone is always better than sitting alone on Saturday night, can seduce people into making unwise decisions in their choice of partners.

Love, when confused with sexual gratification, can become part of an addictive process. Both men and women sometimes use sex to relieve intolerable feelings of anxiety. This creates a temporary illusion of love.

For many individuals, a striking difference exists between their public image of love and their private experience of it. This creates internal conflict, since people are influenced by images in the media, which tend to depict love as sensational and glamorous. These Hollywood-type images do not even remotely resemble most people's private experience of love, and thus feelings of inadequacy develop: Why does my relationship seem so boring when compared to what everybody else seems to have? The answer is that life in reality isn't like the images that appear in the media.

Consider the often-confused difference between love and hate. They would appear to be opposites, easily told apart, and yet one often masquerades for the other in people's lives. One young woman appeared for her counseling appointment wearing a pair of dark sunglasses and a turtleneck sweater. Underneath the turtleneck were bruises where she had been struck by her lover. Her initial comment was, "I was really scared when it happened, and for a while I wouldn't even talk to him. He felt terrible, and kept telling me how much he loved me and didn't want to lose me. I believe him and I really love him, too. And after all, he's a hot-blooded Latin, they're just like that." She failed to understand that such behavior in relationships is not love and is not Latin—it's hate.

It's not love when people abuse each other physically or emotionally. It's not love when partners chronically fight and selfishly disregard the other's needs. Hatred is exhausting, and yet since there may be calm periods between the explosions, partners may fool themselves into believing that, We hurt each other so much because underneath it all, we really love each other.

Some men and women hope to escape the difficulties involved in establishing and maintaining loving relationships by acting on the well-worn dictum that opposites attract. There are easily recognized examples of this in our folklore: The obsessive and compulsive man who needs everything organized, neat and under control, paired with his histrionic, spontaneous woman; the homebody and the socialite; the emotionally expressive partner and the shy, withdrawn partner. It may be true that opposites occasionally do attract, but this may not be the basis for a satisfying relationship. People sometimes find themselves frustrated with the frequent conflicts that develop as they cope with the same opposite qualities in their mate that attracted them in the first place. Some couples, however, discover a kind of complementarity in their differentness that gives each other something unique.

If being taken care of is your main motivation for entering into a relationship, that is not the basis for mature love. If you feel that you're nobody unless somebody loves you, you're not likely to amount to much after somebody loves you. Nobody can validate who you are. The better you feel about yourself, the easier it is to develop a meaningful relationship. People who have a high level of self-esteem are not available for exploitation and don't exploit other people. Remember what Eleanor Roosevelt said: "Nobody can make you feel inferior without your consent."

THE PROCESS OF MATURE LOVE

Can one person ever know love as another person experiences it? Love is a personal statement of the self and does not lend itself easily to generalizations. Everyone knows love in a particular way; first the way I love myself, and then at least one other human being. We love objects, trees, the sun, ballet, books. Love for these inanimate things may be intellectual or aesthetic, but is essentially one-sided and involves no interaction.

Loving another person involves elements of intellect, emotion, and activity. It is fullest when voluntarily expressed in many varied aspects of life. Loving your partner becomes more than just the pleasure of being together; it includes active concern for each other's emotional, material, and bodily needs. It may be perceived as a responsibility, but seldom as a burden because you have consciously chosen to act in this way and are not merely reacting to the demands of your partner.

To love someone, you must like the person also. Some couples become unhappy when they discover that they are involved with someone they initially loved, but whose interests and mannerisms bother them! The time you spend together will exhaust you if this is the case, and you'll begin seeking diversions outside the relationship. Love creates its own balance, at times ecstatic, at other times boring, most of the time somewhere in between.

Any ideal of love needs to be seen as a goal for ourselves without unrealistic expectations. To love responsibly is to be fully human. We let others know us, for only then are our relationships and communication real. This happens when we speak honestly of our own feelings and behavior. As we've already described, honesty means *saying what you mean*, not revealing every detail. Otherwise, we remain a facade to spouse, relatives, children, and friends. Other people's guesses and intuitions regarding our character can differ greatly from our own impressions. Vulnerability accompanies self-disclosure, and the risk of being attacked on those points that are most sensitive to us.

Love does not simply establish itself and then go on existing with no further care. Life changes and people change with it. Your own lifestyle and experiences as well as those of the people you love evolve at unknown rates you cannot predict or control.

Myths and illusions surround traditional, loving, marital relationships. For some people who've been influenced by the women's movement, marriage and marital love have become more realistic, though some lament the passing of romantic illusions. It has led to the realization that when people marry they aren't wedding a composite fantasy of an *ideal* person. Since love will not last in unchanging intensity, there is a compelling need for two people to work together through the difficult periods that are inevitable.

Love often undergoes periods of indifference and animosity. The couple whose feelings do not change radically is rare indeed. Many people continue to marry with the notion that marriage will not substantially alter the texture of their relationship. That notion is bound to be a source of major disappointment and frustration. Society, friends, and relatives all perceive people differently once they are married. Even couples who once married believing that it was nothing more than "a piece of paper" discover afterwards that the contract changed expectations—their expectations of themselves and those from the outside world.

Marriage, even though it may last for fifty years, unfolds as a combination of memorable episodes connected by the passage of uneventful time. Consider the things you enjoy most—orgasms, sunsets, your lover's smile, or any joyful occasion. How long do they last? Imagine how disillusioned you might be attempting to prolong unnaturally any of these events, which, though repeatable, are brief.

Many couples complain that their intimacies and feelings for each other have become *monotonous*. Perhaps they have fallen into the routine of substituting making love for being in love or having sex at certain times and with fixed frequency. For some *the act* loses its imaginative qualities and becomes a repetition of techniques mainly because the focus has been on sexual intercourse rather than a sexual relationship.

The myth of *togetherness and exclusivity* may qualify as the most tiresome aspect of traditional relationships. This myth suggests that love and companionship with one person should satisfy an individual's *every* emotional, physical, social, and intellectual need. It often happens that couples share the same friends and discard those unacceptable to their mates. Perhaps they give up activities and interests that the partner dislikes, or even worse, suffer the losses in silence. They maintain a "couple front" wherever they go. These signals warn all outsiders that each partner is off limits unless the other is agreeable. Possessiveness in the name of love produces two results. First, it stifles individual expression and creativity. At the same time, it grossly limits a couple's range of experience. At the other extreme, many couples share no interests and spend little time together.

One reason that marriage itself *seems* less appealing these days comes from a sense that it is too constraining. The woman who spends all her time at home and the man who feels pressured to make money may begin to resent their "traps" and their partners who seem responsible for keeping them there. As men and women develop options to these stereotyped sex roles, there promises to be greater variety in marriage. Most males still may be preoccupied with their work and most females may continue to regard the caretaker's role as paramount. Yet, there is beginning to emerge a male population that helps out around the house and an increasing number of women who work outside the home. The traditional husband-and-wife, two-children, one-breadwinner, self-contained family is all but disappearing. The quality of love and marriage, however, is *not* determined by the mere facts of what people do. In other words, "traditional" roles can be egalitarian provided that they are volitional. Conversely, a woman who works outside the home because her husband wants her to and not because she wants to, is not part of an egalitarian relationship despite the apparently "modern" situation.

Sexual relations and love combined make a great recipe, but they are essentially different ingredients. Sex can reflect the health of relationships in one sense, but it doesn't necessarily serve as the barometer of the overall success of marriage. Sexual intimacy occupies a very small percentage of time in the average week. In fact, there is no relationship between the number of times a couple has sex and the viability or strength of their relationship. If sex is the most important part of your relationship, you probably aren't communicating well about other, more vital aspects of your marriage. For instance, can you sense and empathize with each other's moods? Can you be comforting? Can you take care of each other without worrying about who did it last?

Marriage and family therapists have been saying for years that harmony must be based on a mutual desire to please and fulfill the other's needs. If you feel that the needs of your lover are demands, then you aren't likely to enjoy fulfilling them. If one is asked to please a lover in a favorable manner and made to feel that one is doing so because of love, both partners will feel fulfilled. Pleasing each other thus becomes a mutual giving, not giving in.

It's easy to be cavalier and say that people *should* communicate, but learning new ways is not so easy. First there needs to be careful consideration of the ways communication is inhibited. People living together often fall into behavior patterns in which certain things are not discussed. Consequently, each partner feels frustrated, and neither accepts the responsibility for not trying earlier or at all.

One of the more common problems for couples is the desire not to hurt the other's feelings. Suffering anything from bad breath to unimaginative sex because one or both of the partners cannot bring themselves to risk constructive criticism reflects a fear of inflicting pain. Silence at this level may be sincerely motivated but eventually becomes transformed into emotional problems and underlying anger.

Timing is also important. Couples know that if they bring up sensitive matters when either is tired, tense, irritable, or angry, the message gets lost or misunderstood.

Sometimes a person doesn't say what's really on his or her mind: an effort at communication is made, but the message remains unclear. Or each speaks his mind and nothing happens. The situation remains the same, even after a sizeable expenditure of emotions in a dramatic encounter. In such cases, the participants' unrealistic expectations lead them to believe that things would improve just by becoming conscious of them. For instance, a wife may complain, "I want you to show me more affection. I need caring and attention in addition to sexual intercourse," and there may not be any follow-through, even though her husband wants to please her. Later, the conversation might run, "You still don't show me any affection" (meaning pats, caresses, praise, and kisses).

"But you never reminded me to."

"I shouldn't have to remind you—you should want to do it without being asked."

Sometimes communication and change initially require mechanical efforts until we internalize the change and the desired goals are achieved in a spontaneous manner. In the early stages of the process, it would be *desirable* to have built-in reminders to get the improvements on the road. It is admitted that this is role-playing behavior. Developing spontaneous behavior often *requires* a reservoir of experimental and self-conscious efforts first.

Indecisiveness also hinders communication. We ask, Should I or shouldn't I talk about it? The fear of consequences and of impending disaster and an intense preoccupation at this level are an enormous waste of time. A lot of energy may be expended in the decision-making process. Our advice is to take the chance and try communication as an alternative to repression and avoidance.

Many people are so desperately indecisive that they avoid confrontation by discussing the problem with friends, relatives, and neighbors instead of their partners. These sympathetic ears prevent the issue from reaching the partner by relieving tension and anxiety and without getting at the real nature of the problem. When and if you do get around to discussing the problem directly, the person may resent the fact that he or she was the last to know.

An excellent review of marital communication and happiness appeared in the *New York Times* (Goleman, 1985). One of the major findings of the research reviewed in this article reveals that how well a couple communicates before marriage is one of the strongest predictors of success once married. Premarital counseling programs are now being designed with this guiding concept, which also is a sensible caution to those who are considering a lifetime together with someone with whom communication is poor.

Use what we say to evaluate your present or future relationship and expectations. You may gain insight and be able to exercise more control over your decisions. Long-standing differences in priorities often provide the source of greatest unhappiness. If you do try to communicate and meet irreconcilable differences, seek a marriage counselor, or participate in encounter groups, which often present better opportunities for understanding.

When bombarded with suggestions and advice such as this, people often become unsure about what love and caring are, and hence their efforts to do so become very cumbersome and self-conscious. In effect they are *too aware* of what, how, and when they do something simply to enjoy it. At these times the needs of both partners become very confusing and we seem to forget all we ever knew about pleasing ourselves. It might be essential to learn or relearn what these desires are. We often forget our all-too-human reluctance to follow even the best advice: Your partner may know that smoking or overeating habits are harmful but irrationally repeats the behavior anyway. Any approach to self-exploration and change should allow for frustration and errors. Strive to see advice as a process in which you develop insight into your ability, or lack of it, to follow what is recommended.

Many contemporary commentators offer criticisms of marriage and the marital relationship. Some claim that the duration of meaningful relationships is shortening as we become more mobile, hold jobs for shorter periods of time, and experience accelerated shifts in values and interests. Short-term relationships that introduce sex immediately to get the "barrier" out of the way proliferate. Thus, sex becomes a means of getting close, but the intimacy it generates remains handily disposable.

Despite the criticisms of marriage and the family, millions of married people are faithful to each other, yet wonder, Can it last? Can it remain interesting and exciting? Perhaps it can if people can feel free, for example, to go off for a day or evening with a friend (male or female) without guilt, suspicion, resentment, or jealousy. This attitude can enhance relationships: You and your spouse can construct a framework for a creative fidelity. Sometimes, however, we need to be reminded that fidelity is not boring—it is a continuing creative striving to enrich your relationship.

Elsewhere, we made use of a list referring to what's important in a marriage. The list ran: love, laughter, talk, involvement, friendship, integrity, tolerance, adaptability, sex, sharing. It might be thought-provoking for you to think this through for yourself. Then make up your own list of the ten most important things in a marriage. Ask your partner to do the same and then discuss the surprises or similarities.

How can you tell if you're really in love? M. Scott Peck, in his best-selling book *The Road Less Traveled*, states that genuine love does not grow out of an emotional impulse but is rather, volitional—an intellectual decision to love and to commit oneself to another person. There may still exist romance and powerful feelings of attractions, but the fundamental "glue" holding the relationship together will be a thoughtful, conscious choice to love and remain involved with another person.

WHOM NOT TO MARRY

We admit this is a backhanded approach to an area where the usual advice concerns whom *to* marry. This advice, however well-intentioned, most often doesn't have much impact. Conventional wisdom dictates that certain personality characteristics in a potential spouse can guide one's decision. Our somewhat untraditional approach, instead, will be to describe those traits and situations that should signal a warning.

Imagine that you are involved with someone, and that the topic of marriage has arisen, or, if you are presently involved in a serious relationship, use the following criteria to evaluate your potential for marriage with your present partner.
Don't get married

- if you are both still young (roughly, under twenty-one). Most marriages in this age group end in divorce or separation.
- if you don't have a good relationship with either your mother or father, and your prospective spouse seems to be "just like" your troublesome parent.
- if you don't know or understand each other very well, or don't accept each other's ideas, even though you may spend a lot of time together.

- if you spend most of your time together disagreeing and arguing.
- if one or both of you asks frequently, Do you really love me? Are you sure it's me you love?
- if your decision to get married has been heavily influenced by your future in-laws. Ironically, many people find themselves at the altar, having been seduced by the warm acceptance, flattery, wealth, and even the cooking of a potential in-law.
- if you often think maybe things will get better after we're married, or if your partner keeps promising, I'll straighten out after we're married. The troubling area may be careless use of money, sex with other people, or an alcohol problem. Marriage usually makes such problems worse, not better, since once you're married your expectations are higher.
- if your partner doesn't respect your intelligence.
- if your prospective partner has traits that you abhor (such as a violent temper, unclean grooming habits) and you avoid raising the issue for fear of giving offense.
- if your partner insists that you both forsake all your old friends and agree to have only those friends that are mutual.
- if your partner cannot tolerate time alone and resents the time that you wish to spend alone reading, pursuing a hobby, meditating.
- if you are unable to spend an entire day with your partner, without turning the television on once, and still enjoy yourselves.
- if, after doing some soul searching, you discover that you're marrying a sex object. The appeal of a centerfold or beefcake wears disturbingly thin if there are few other things about the person that appeal to you.
- if there has been an experience of violent behavior between yourself and your partner, and you believe there's a possibility that it could happen again. Some people (both men and women) may promise, I'll never hit you after we're married, but such vows are not usually kept.
- if, though you enjoy some of your time together, you feel in significant ways that your partner is selfishly motivated and seems to consider his or her own welfare more than your own in most situations.
- if you are unable to agree on where you are going to live or under what circumstances you would move, e.g., what if one of you got a job in another city?
- if you are considering an intermarriage (marriage to someone of another religious faith or race) and are unable to agree on how the children should be raised (or are unable to agree on whether or not to have children).
- if your materialistic values are radically different. Couples often have tremendous conflicts because, for instance, one spouse is comfortable with a modest, middle-

class standard of living and the other insists on lavish furnishings, fancy vacations, and a steady ascent up the ladder of success.

The above is far from an exhaustive list. Some of the conditions listed may exist and you may still enjoy a well-adjusted, interesting married life. The flaw in some unhappy marriages isn't that the spouses are bad people, but rather that they neglected to examine carefully the many key elements that would significantly influence their lives in the future.

REFERENCES

Fromm, E. *The Art of Loving*. Boston: Unwin Paperbacks, 1957.

Goleman, D. "Marriage Research Reveals Ingredients of Happiness." *New York Times*, April 16, 1985, p. C1, C4.

Peck, M. S. *The Road Less Traveled*. New York: Simon & Schuster, 1978.

PART TWO
Personal Dilemmas

CHAPTER 4
Religion and Sexuality

"Pollster Says Religion Up But Morality Down." This was the headline for a report on a 1984 poll entitled "1984 Religion in America." The report discovered a "giant paradox" between people's beliefs and behavior. In sum, it stated that ". . . very little difference is found in the behavior of the churched and unchurched on a wide range of items including lying, cheating and pilferage." Though this is not true for a small percentage of "highly spiritually committed," for most people the growing religious emphasis of the past few years has not altered their morality.

For most people whose religious beliefs are important to them, the personal issue concerning sexuality has to do with resolving the discrepancy between their sexual behavior and their religion's teachings. For example, in our research at Syracuse University, at least 90 percent of the students in a human sexuality class believe that premarital sex is acceptable to them. The class, which divides roughly into equal thirds of Protestants, Jews, and Catholics, has answered in these percentages for the past ten years. And yet, all three of these major religions disapprove of premarital sexual experiences. Though many people accept the wisdom and counsel of their church or synagogue in a variety of areas, in the area of sexuality many people have been finding their own way. For them, this can be a great personal dilemma, for they wish both to express their religious convictions *and* engage in sexual relationships that suit their own consciences.

Most religious educators and theologians agree that in the area of sexuality, organized religions have traditionally assumed a sex-negative posture. Historically, sex has been seen as a necessary evil despite the fact that Old Testament scholars have maintained that the Bible presents the basis for joyous acceptance of sex. A marvelous celebration of sexuality can be found in the "Song of Songs," though it has been subject to widely differing interpretations. In modern times most major religious denominations have adopted positive, enlightened views, and the more liberal churches and synagogues stress compassion and understanding toward a wide range of differences in the human sexual condition.

Without advancing any particular creed we are nevertheless writing from our own religious persuasions. We believe that a major malaise in society today stems from a spiritual void. Whether one embraces organized religion or has one's own personal communion with God or the cosmos, it is apparent that various religious forces are taking an increasingly active role in the area of human sexuality.

Widespread interest in sexuality and religion was rekindled by a remarkable book entitled *Embodiment* by James B. Nelson, a Professor of Christian Ethics at United Theological Seminary from Minnesota. Professor Nelson's amazing clarity and grace shines out at the start when he makes a distinction between sex and sexuality:

> Sex is a biologically-based need which is oriented not only toward procreation but, indeed, toward pleasure and tension release. It aims at genital activity culminating in orgasm. While sex usually is infused with a variety of human and religious meanings, the focus is upon erotic phenomena of a largely genital nature.
>
> Sexuality, on the other hand, is a much more comprehensive term associated with more diffuse and symbolic meanings, psychological and cultural orientations. While it includes sex and relates to biological organ systems, sexuality goes beyond this. To be sure, sexuality is not the whole of our personhood, but is a very basic dimension of our personhood. While our sexuality does not determine all our feelings, thoughts, and actions, in ways both obvious and covert it permeates and affects them all.
>
> Sexuality is our self-understanding and way of being in the world as male and female. It includes our appropriation of attitudes and characteristics which have been culturally defined as masculine and feminine. It involves our affectional orientation toward those of the opposite and/or the same sex. It includes our attitudes about our own bodies and those of others. Because we are "body-selves," our sexuality constantly reminds each of us of our uniqueness and particularity: we look different and we feel differently from any other person.
>
> Sexuality is a sign, a symbol, and a means of our call to communication and communion. This is the most apparent in regard to other human beings, other body-selves. The mystery of our sexuality is the mystery of our need to reach out to embrace others both physically and spiritually. Sexuality thus expresses God's intention that we find our authentic humanness in relationship. But such humanizing

relationship cannot occur on the human dimension alone. Sexuality, we must also say, is intrinsic to our relationship with God.

Ironically, sexuality, including the physical and psychic pleasures it provides, has been the source of great anxiety and controversy. The associations of sex with the Fall of Mankind and the resulting feelings of sin and guilt it engenders color many people's attitudes toward their own sexuality. The human conscience has wrestled with these moral issues since before Christ. Should the adulteress be stoned? Is the "spilling of one's seed on the ground" reprehensible? Increasingly, the populace has pressed theologians to answer these and other questions concerning contraception, abortion, and the ethics of premarital sex. In a way, contemporary religious thought has become intrinsically linked with the issues revolving around human sexuality.

Gradually, religions are moving beyond the absolute, genitally oriented view of sex per se. For some clergy and laity alike, the mere fact of premarital sex may not seem condemnable. If sexual behaviors occur in the context of loving and mutual sharing, sometimes the interpretation is more one of acceptance than automatic condemnation. Marital sex itself, once considered the only valid means of expression, is no longer automatically accepted as being good: it can be exploitive, hurtful, and unloving, even though the church blessed the marital convenant.

In the last several decades, pre- and extramarital sex have been widely discussed, as has sex for the never-married. A major study of the United Church of Christ titled *Human Sexuality: A Preliminary Study* (1977) went beyond the debate of exactly which behaviors are acceptable and which are not by seeking to establish one morality consistent with all forms of human sexual expression:

> *First, love's justice requires a single standard* rather than a double standard. This should mean there is not one ethic for males and another for females, one for the unmarried and another for the married, one for the young and another for the old, nor one for those who are heterosexually oriented and another for those oriented toward their same sex. The same basic considerations of love ought to apply to all.
>
> *Second, the physical expression* of one's sexuality in relation to another ought to be *appropriate to the level of loving commitment* in the relationship. Human relationships exist on a continuum—from the fleeting and casual to the lasting and intense, from the relatively impersonal to the deeply personal. So also, physical expressions exist on a continuum—from varied types of eye contact and casual touches, to varied forms of embraces and kisses, to bodily caresses and genital petting, to foreplay and genital intercourse. In some way or another, we inevitably express our sexuality in every relationship. The morality of that expression, particularly its more physical expression will depend upon its appropriateness to the shared level of commitment and the nature of the relationship.
>
> *Third, genital sexual expression* ought to be evaluated in terms of the basic elements of a moral decision, informed by love.

Motive (why should I do, or not do, this?). Each genital act should be motivated by love. This means love for one's partner. It also, however, means a healthy love of oneself. Infusing both of those loves is love for God whose good gift of sexuality is an invitation to communion.

Intention (at what am I aiming in this act?). Each genital act should aim at human fulfillment and wholeness, which are God's loving intentions for all persons. In marriage the procreation of children may also be the intent of certain times of intercourse, but statistically those times will be in a small minority, and even then the desire for children is part of our quest for wholeness, for wholeness is known in relationships. Fulfillment also requires sexual pleasure. Good genital sex is highly erotic, warm, intimate, playful, and immensely pleasurable. At times it can also be almost mystical in its possibilities of communication and communion. In each of these ways it can contribute to wholeness, a deep sense of being at one with oneself, with the other, and with God.

The Act. (Are certain sexual acts inherently right and good, and are certain others inherently wrong and bad?) It is notoriously difficult to label whole classes of acts as inherently right or wrong, since the moral quality of any act hinges so heavily upon what is being communicated by it in the particular context. What are our intentions and what are their effects? We can surely say that sexual acts which are characterized by loving motives and intentions will exclude all acts which are coercive, debasing, harmful, or cruel to another.

Consequences. (What will most likely result from this act, and in what ways will I be willingly accountable?) Responsibility for the results of a sexual act is also a mark of love. This involves responsibility to the ongoing relationship, its commitments, and its promises. It means responsibility to the partner's emotional health insofar as that is linked with a given sexual act. If a child is conceived and born, it means responsibility for nurture. Responsibility also means that this particular act must be weighed in terms of its effect on the well-being of the wider human community. Will it endanger the love and justice by which communities must exist?

The issues of artificial methods of contraception remain a controversy even today. Only in the past century have religious leaders been forced to proclaim their official positions; before that, such methods simply didn't exist. Generally, the counterargument has been that they interfere with God's will in placing new life on earth, and that the sacred union between husband and wife becomes profaned.

In *Human Sexuality—New Directions in American Catholic Thought,* the Catholic Theological Society said that artificial means of contraception may at times be "both morally responsible and justified."

This important document authored by some of the leading Catholic theologians in the United States generally supports the view that many forms of sexual behavior could be considered acceptable as long as they are "honest, faithful, socially responsible, life-serving and joyous."

The report goes on to list vital medical, psychological, personal, and religious considerations involved in the decision of which, if any, method of birth control should be used. The official hierarchy of the church did not endorse this report. These findings were decidedly more liberal than the official proclamations of Pope Paul VI, who wrote in his encyclical *Humane Vitae* (1968):

> That teaching, often set forth by the magisterium, is founded upon the inseparable connection, willed by God and unable to be broken by man on his own initiative, between the two meanings of the conjugal act: the unitive meaning and the procreative meaning. Indeed, by its intimate structure, the conjugal act, while most closely uniting husband and wife, capacitates them for the generation of new lives, according to laws inscribed in the very being of man and woman. By safeguarding both these essential aspects, the unitive and the procreative, the conjugal act preserves in its fullness the sense of true mutual love and its ordination towards man's most high calling to parenthood.
>
> To use this divine gift destroying, even if only partially its meaning and its purpose is to contradict the nature both of man and woman and of their most intimate relationship, and therefore it is to contradict also the plan of God and His will.

This view was reaffirmed by Pope John Paul II in his historic visit to the United States in 1979, and again in statements made in 1984.

The growing influence of the women's liberation movement in the past two or three decades has fueled the conviction that there is no divine, religious, or biological reason that men should hold the monopoly on church leadership. The churches thus find themselves confronted by demands for equality by female priests.

Neither the Catholic nor Mormon churches allow women to become priests or ministers (nor do the Orthodox Jews permit women to become rabbis). However, the Episcopal church has begun ordaining women priests amidst a storm of controversy that has caused some congregations to secede. (And recently Conservative congregations have ordained women rabbis as have the Reforms before them.) The role of women in the church increasingly has become a legitimate theological issue. Writing in *Religion and Sexism*, Joan Arnold Romero noted:

> In much the same way as blacks have experienced the white Jesus in a white church preaching an alienating message, a number of women, too, are becoming conscious of the alienation from a masculine God, a masculine Church, and a masculine theology. For women the situation has in many ways been worse, for they form the bulk of the population of the Church, while in the structures of authority as represented both theologically and institutionally, it is men who have had the role of representing God to the people.

Religions are encountering the same questioning of traditional sex roles with which other institutions have come face to face. The patriarchal societies where men were the providers and also attended to intellectual and political concerns are passing. In a society in which making a living no longer depends mainly on physical strength and where women are learning the lessons of equality and opportunity, even the essence of canon law and spiritual enlightenment have come under the influence of women's liberation.

Certainly, some people are horrified by these developing trends in contemporary religious doctrines. They continue to look back to a time when behaviors and rituals were enforced with no viable alternatives. Unfortunately, people who were raised to fear sex often have difficulty giving free rein to their desires and imaginative sex play once married. The guilt and conditioned fear of sex are not suddenly erased by taking a spouse. The woman's lifelong fear of pregnancy and sex is not neutralized by marriage, and the notion of divine retribution for sins does not disappear after the wedding day. By taking a more accepting view of people's sexuality, religions are slowly communicating that sex *is* a joyous, wonderful experience rather than a cause for shame.

Religion is an intensely personal part of life, and it can become an issue in people's lives in a number of ways. Certainly a major aspect, which this chapter discusses in detail, are the ways in which people's sexual values and behavior are shaped by religious influences. Religion often becomes central in relationships as well, as partners wrestle with whether or not their beliefs and practices are compatible. People of the same faith often disagree on such matters, but often interfaith relationships confront religious differences to a greater extent.

A Catholic student at a small college fell in love with a Jewish male student, and initially they gave little thought to their differing religious heritages. As the relationship deepened and prospects for meeting each other's family arose, tension began to develop. The young man's parents had told him that he was free to date whomever he wished but was to marry only a Jewish woman—otherwise he would be betraying his faith and his family and would be disowned. The young woman's family was less vehement in their objections but insisted that if they were to marry, the children would have to be raised Catholic. The impending holiday season precipitated a crisis for this couple and rather than face their families together, they broke off the relationship with a sense that things would never work out.

People are sometimes able to resolve religious differences between themselves, only to discover that families remain opposed even for years after the wedding. Although some couples are able to endure these stresses, others cannot: demographers have found that in interfaith marriages there is a greater likelihood of divorce. People who are in, or who are contemplating entering into, interfaith relationships need to consider their own and their families' responses. In a sense a person marries not only another person but another family as well.

Sometimes families open their arms to a child's fiancé of the same religion only to discover later that a shared faith was hardly a guarantee that the person would make a good spouse. One family rejoiced when their youngest daughter married a man who, like themselves, was Jewish. It wasn't long after the marriage, however, that the man was found to be hostile and exploitive. A while after her divorce this daughter remarried, this time outside her own faith, and the second husband emerged as a true mensch.

Among couples from different religious backgrounds, the question of conversion sometimes arises. It's not unusual for one of the partners to have much stronger religious feelings than the other, in which case the one with less involvement may agree to convert. Conversion may be less successful where the one doing the changing feels that he or she is abandoning a vital tradition within one's own family or faith. Rather than conversion, among some couples the crucial element is a sensitivity to each other's differing beliefs and rituals.

The religious upbringing of children may be an issue in both interfaith and same-faith relationships. One partner may consent to marry a person of another faith only if the children are raised in his or her own religion. Or, it may occur that a wife wishes to send the children to parochial school, or Sunday school, and the husband strongly opposes this. These are the seeds of virulent marital conflict, and *everyone* would do well to discuss these issues *before* getting married. It is ironic that religion may not seem significant at the time of the wedding but suddenly attains great power at the birth of a child.

Many progressive religious groups have pronounced that sexuality is an inherently good, enriching part of life and that there exists the right of individual choice, whether or not in the context of organized religious doctrines. People will ultimately be judged by their God. Some people are deists, who deny that God rules the world and tells humankind what to do, but who nonetheless cherish their own special relationship with God. Others, atheists and agnostics, might deny the validity of any religion or belief, or they may simply be apathetic to the whole affair; nonetheless they enjoy a wholly moral and loving sexuality. There are also many people who are religious but whose sexual behavior is unaffected by that fact. The possibilities for individual interpretations and expressions, with a variety of religious and moral orientations, are infinite.

The churches and synagogues have a difficult time of it. They compete for attention with the mass media, television chief among them. Young people watch about six hours of TV daily, sexual violence, permissiveness, and exploitation being major themes. Popular magazines and advertisements purvey the sensational aspects of sexuality, implying that by using the right cologne, toothpaste, wardrobe, etc., love will come. Organized religion faces a challenge in turning these young people around and trying to convince them that sexuality can be a state of loving grace and fulfillment between two people. So much in society contradicts the message that the sanctity of sexuality is often lost in a sea of hype.

Some religions are still out of touch with contemporary lifestyles, and there is often a discrepancy between the dictates of church officials and the way people actually behave. Though most denominations no longer unconditionally condemn premarital sex, they still believe that sexual relations' proper place is within marriage (yet less than 10 percent of couples are both virgins on their wedding night). For this and other reasons it is popular to fault religions for failing to meet the needs young people have for faith, love, and the celebration of sex.

To enter the brotherhood of religious community, young people have turned increasingly to cults and certain mystic sects from the East. It is difficult not to have misgivings regarding the proliferation of many of these cults, if only for the reason that they tend to alienate children from their parents. This is a tragic development and has given rise to charges of brainwashing and manipulation. The names of cults are far too numerous to list here, but in general they advance the following characteristics:

- There is a leader who is *always* right. You give up your right to make up your own mind.
- The cult has a philosophy that the end justifies the means.
- You are expected to believe and not think.
- They often encourage you to break off relations with your parents (who represent the old, unenlightened past that threatens to destroy your newfound faith).

In matters of the spirit, churches and synagogues can offer people guidance in understanding and accepting their sexuality in a positive way. Beyond this, they can also provide education and instruction in how to handle intimate relationships, as well as some of the more factual areas of sexuality. Schools that attempted to institute adequate sex education programs have tended to come up against the issue of values: what values should be taught, in which religious perspective? Churches by nature do not have to resolve this dilemma. The crisis of values in schools often means that nothing but the basic, mechanical facts about sex are presented. Churches, however, can offer information within the context of their own spiritual and religious beliefs without worrying that parents or taxpayers will object. It can also be done with the understanding that churches are supplementing, not replacing, parents' primary role as the sex educators of their own children. Some of today's parochial schools have excellent sex education programs, and some of the finest work in the field of human sexuality comes from traditionally conservative churches.

Rabbi Robert Gordis (1978) has presented the Jewish perspective on sexuality:

Since God created man with his entire complement of impulses, sex is a manifestation of the Divine. It is not to be glorified as an end in itself, as is paganism, or in the exaggerations of romantic love. Hence, the Bible and the Talmud are frank and outspoken in dealing with the sexual component of human experience. The pages of our classic literature are free from both obscenity and false modesty, from pornography and prudishness, which are essentially two sides of the same coin.

Rabbi Gordis goes on to describe how Judaism has traditionally celebrated the sexual relationship between husband and wife:

> . . . sexual relations between husband and wife, while naturally private and intimate, are held to be a perfectly legitimate form of pleasure which justifies itself as such, even without the goal of procreation. . . . The marriage relationship between a man and a woman is not a concession to the lower instincts, but, on the contrary, the ideal human state. . . . This healthy-minded, affirmative attitude toward sex, which is recognized as an essential and legitimate element of human life, is rooted in a religious world view.

Some churches and synagogues have already developed good programs in sex education but to date have done little to prepare parents to sex-educate their children. Rarely does the minister, priest, or rabbi use his or her sermon as an opportunity to translate current theological thought into terms of behavior in human relationships and sexuality. Surveys have demonstrated that congregations would welcome this kind of guidance and involvement with their churches.

But just in the same way as religion can be a source of guidance and inspiration, it can also be used as deception and as a vehicle for political influence.

In our country, where the separation of church and state is the law of the land, religious groups are increasingly entering the political scene. Many religious leaders feel that basic religious beliefs are being undermined by secular policies and profaned by liberal, godless forces. They see the solution in more religious influence in public schools and government. The concern revolves around such issues as the Equal Rights Amendment, abortion, prayer in schools, gay rights, contraceptive availability to minors, and governmental policies, which religions see as detrimental to the family unit. Collectively, they are expressing the need for organized religion to support their own declared views on sexuality.

There is a danger of these desires for morality turning into a kind of moralistic war, with different groups attempting to impose their own beliefs on the rest of society. There is a particular concern about the upsurge of reactionary elements who disguise hatred, fear, and bigotry with religious arguments. History is replete with incidents in which "religion" has been used to persecute Jews and other religious groups, to justify slavery, and to deny civil rights to homosexuals. In this light, it is unwise to confuse reactionary politics with religion.

The John Birch Society, the Moral Majority, and even the Ku Klux Klan parade religion as the justification for their views. They are against the reintroduction of the Equal Rights Amendment, and against gay-rights ordinances in any city that proposes them. These and other issues fundamentally affecting sexuality and the quality of life should not be decided on the bases of fear or distorted interpretations of the Bible. Selectively quoting from the Bible and imposing literal interpretations on the passages is a dangerous, self-serving enterprise. One could, for example, take literally the Bible's pronouncement that a menstruating woman is "unclean," or one could hold, as stated in Deuteronomy, that a virgin who is raped must marry her rapist. Similarly, one could endorse incest by quoting the story of Lot and his daughters.

Such literal interpretations of the Bible gave rise to the "blue laws" that still exist on most states' books. Though rarely if ever enforced, the laws generally prohibit such acts as oral-genital relations, anal intercourse (often lumped together with oral sex and called *sodomy*), and homosexual behaviors. It is amazing that in some states these same antiquated laws stand side by side in the books with laws that hold it is still legal for a man to rape his wife.

The First Amendment to the U.S. Constitution protects the freedom of individual and collective religious expression. No religious group has the right to impose their own beliefs or dogma on the rest of the population, even if it represents the majority in a given community (e.g., a neighborhood of 70 percent Jehovah's Witnesses or Christian Scientists could not pass a law prohibiting blood transfusions). Even within one particular congregation or denomination, the religious leaders usually cannot speak with authority for all members. Within the body of "official" church doctrines, there must remain a respect for certain individual differences of opinion.

The fervent, sometimes fanatical positions of others should not obscure the basic message that religion is a powerful, deeply moving part of human existence. In many families, and for many individuals striving to promote ideals of honesty, trust, compassion, and love of God and humanity, religion offers a sound, enriching medium for expressing these values.

For those who find little or no meaning in religion itself, sexuality has spiritual connotations that need not be identified with any recognizable religious denomination or persuasion. As Abraham Maslow points out in his book *Religious Values and Peak Experiences,* these spiritual values have naturalistic meaning and do not need supernatural concepts to support them. The sacred symbols of God, family, and country belong to everyone, regardless of each person's political or religious interpretation.

It is typical of each generation to believe that the sexual/religious issues of the day are timeless, the most crucial ever, and must be resolved for a better tomorrow. As we know, life continues and the crises of today yield to the as-yet-unknown issues of tomorrow. If we, as a society, as family members, and as sexual human beings can refrain from committing the errors of fear and repression, we can then embark on the road to a more enlightened sexuality. If we are successful in instilling this great spiritual message in our children, then our legacy to them will all be worthwhile.

REFERENCES

The Catholic Theological Society of America. *Human Sexuality: New Directions in American Catholic Thought.* New York: Paulist Press, 1977.

Gordis, R. *Love and Sex: A Modern Jewish Perspective*. New York: Farrar, Straus & Giroux, 1978.

Maslow, A. *Religious Values and Peak Experiences*. New York: Penguin, 1964.

Nelson, J. B. *Embodiment: An Approach to Sexuality and Christian Theology*. Minneapolis: Augsburn Publishing House, 1978.

Pope Paul VI. *Humanae Vitae*. Rome: 25 July 1968.

Romero, J. A. "The Protestant Principle: A Woman's-Eye View of Barth and Tillich." In R. R. Ruether (Ed.), *Religion and Sexism*. New York: Simon & Schuster, 1974.

The United Church of Christ. *Human Sexuality: A Preliminary Study*. New York: United Church Press, 1977.

CHAPTER 5

Cohabitation and Alternative Sexual Lifestyles

In American society, since marriage is the norm for approximately 90 percent of the population, anything other than marriage might be considered an *alternative*. Both within and outside marriage, however, many options exist that are nontraditional (homosexuality is covered in another chapter). The standard texts in human sexuality provide an accurate accounting of definitions, incidence, and demographics for these lifestyles; our concern will be more with how these alternatives might impact on your lives.

The major alternatives covered in this chapter are cohabitation, singlehood, childlessness, and extramarital sexuality. A host of other alternatives and permutations, which will not be discussed, include group sex, polygamy, polygyny, communes, and commuter marriages. Our focus will be on a general philosophy of alternatives rather than on the particulars of who does what to whom in these situations.

Most essential to understanding this area is the distinction between *alternative lifestyles* and *alternative sexual relationships*. The latter term infers that one's behavior is determined on the basis of sex; the former has a broader meaning. An alternative sexual relationship may mean that sex is the focus of the interaction. One might choose to cohabit, or to remain single, or to engage in extramarital sex, purely for sexual reasons, for the gratification or excitement that these may provide. Our general philosophy is: When sex per se is the prime motivation in one's relationships, regardless of the alternative or traditional form they take, the relationship is in trouble.

The term *alternative lifestyle* implies that sexuality may be only one aspect of one's life that is nontraditional. This yields a vision of life that is broader in perspective than one narrowly defined by one's sexual behavior. A person who is self-employed leads a lifestyle that is an alternative to working for someone else; being a vegetarian is an alternative to eating meat; living in a house built underground is an alternative to living on the surface as most people do. One could simultaneously be a self-employed vegetarian who lives underground and who was a virgin when he or she got married! Why does the sexual aspect of it need to dominate how the person is defined or thinks of him or herself?

COHABITATION

Cohabitation (living together) was first heralded in the 1960s as the choice for people who didn't need marriage—"just a piece of paper"—to legitimize their love for another person. Today, it is fairly common on college campuses for lovers to share an apartment, or a room in a house that is shared with other students. The depth of feeling in the relationship may range from convenience, to sexual involvement, to what is perceived as an enduring commitment.

Since it first began to make headlines some twenty to twenty-five years ago, cohabitation rates have grown more rapidly than almost all other forms of relationship patterns. In fact, in 1985, the rates of cohabitation are *triple* those of 1970. Researchers have had difficulty defining what living together actually entails. The Census Bureau (1981) defines it as a household occupied by unrelated persons, and yet many college students share houses and apartments as roommates and don't consider themselves to be cohabiting. For most people, living together exists only when there is a loving, sexual relationship that brings the two together.

The questions that people have before entering into cohabitation usually have to do with: Will this arrangement lead to marriage? Will we be monogamous, or will we be free to see other people? Should I tell my parents and what will they say or do when they find out? If the relationship ends, will the hurt I feel be worth the experience? If I decide a month after we move in together that it's all a mistake, how will I get out of it?

First, people need to be clear with each other concerning whether living together symbolizes a trial period before marriage, a meaningful way to be loving and intimate, or an economic reprieve from hard times. A college junior from Massachusetts related how she and her lover talked the whole thing over beforehand and agreed that it wouldn't necessarily lead to marriage. He was graduating a year earlier than she was anyway, and wanted to feel free to pursue his career in other cities without worrying about abandoning her. "Underneath it all, I was hoping that he'd want to marry me and would hang around for a year waiting for me to finish school. I never told him that and I was enraged when he left in June to work in another state."

There exist both public and hidden agendas, and it is mainly the hidden variety that leads to troubles. The male above could not be held responsible for her unspoken hopes; he was, on the contrary, upset over her concealing these feelings from him. He commented later that "It made me feel like the bad guy when rationally I knew I had acted in good faith."

When the question comes to monogamy versus a more open relationship, again there is often both a public and a private agenda. The overwhelming majority of couples agree together that they will not become sexually involved—even for an evening—with anyone else. The facts of people's behavior, however, reveal that during monogamous marriages, for instance, as many as half of all husbands and wives experience extramarital sex at some time. When cohabiting, the sex outside the relationship is usually kept secret; when it becomes known, it usually ends the relationship in a short time.

For young adults especially, the living together may be with a first love. The pain of jealousy and learning of one's lover's infidelity can be agonizing. Our intention here is not to pass judgment, but instead to raise the issues that people need to consider before becoming involved outside a relationship. These include: Am I having sex with another person because my lover does not satisfy me? Because I need variety? Because I'm too young/impulsive to commit myself to only one person? Because I don't believe in monogamy for myself (though I agreed to it to keep this relationship alive)?

Moving in together represents a risk, and there's no way to know beforehand how it will all turn out. Common sense dictates that it's best if couples explore their feelings extensively together before making any commitments. The real dilemma emerges for those who find themselves involved in a situation that feels disastrous and from which they wish to escape (see Chapter 3). Sometimes, from fear of hurting the other's feelings, or from fear of loneliness and never again finding someone to love, people prolong unsatisfying relationships. In a sense, the energy in their relationship is invested in moving away from something (loneliness) rather than toward something (love, togetherness).

When these ambivalent feelings (concerning whether or not to leave a relationship) fester, they often produce hostility for the other person, or guilt and/or anger directed against the self. These slowly destroy the fabric of living-together relationships and interfere with day-to-day living (quarrels, sharp words, silences may prevail). In this way the authentic meaning of the conflicts may not surface, and instead people concern themselves only with the symptoms of a bad relationship (e.g., fighting over spilt milk). It's best, although difficult, to open things up and confront what's happening between you.

Living together, of course, may be a wonderful experience. It has the potential to bring partners closer together and allow them to explore the give and take between themselves. There can be opportunities to explore the many feelings that one has concerning loving relationships. Following are a few quotes from people who felt positive about their cohabiting:

We'd been living in separate apartments and it got to the point that mine was always empty—we spent all of our time at Marsha's place. Once we moved in together, it felt so much more relaxing, like some of the questions concerning how we felt about each other weren't so unresolved. Living together just felt like the right thing to do—I've never questioned that.

Mitch and I spent the first three months of our living together trying to adjust to each other's styles of living. At first I felt angry with him, because once we were living together it seemed like he was suddenly doing things he never did before—like stay up half the night, come home from classes in a lousy mood and stay that way all evening. Gradually we started to see that we'd been hiding those things from each other, trying to present only a positive image to each other. Once that painted-on face wore away, our love for each other seemed less contrived, more involved with the real guts of our lives.

Living with Adrienne was good from the start. We had a wonderful sexual attraction for each other and a good life outside of bed, too. Even though we eventually split up and went our separate ways, there wasn't that much animosity—I still look back on that time as one of the best.

Never before in my life had anything felt as good as being loved by, and loving, Frank. Ever since I had entered my teenage years I had been wanting to have someone special to be with and living with him felt like I wasn't so alone anymore. Once we started living together, it was obvious that we wanted it to last, and we were married after about a year. And we're still together.

Nevertheless, for many students, anxiety over the response of parents consumes a great deal of energy and sometimes helps determine the fate of the relationship itself. Our clinical observations are that the male's parents are more likely to be told than are the female's; apparently the double standard, in which women are criticized more for premarital sexual experiences, influences couples in their decision of whom to tell.

When one or both sets of parents have not been told of the living arrangements, an interesting acrobatic act may ensue. One partner, for example, may never be allowed to answer the phone, or may have to move his or her clothes into the attic and take a nameplate off the mailbox when parents visit. An intricate web of deception and half-truths can grow. The alternative, as experienced by many students, is that parents react very negatively to the news, and family relationships suffer. Parents have been known to sever financial aid, disinherit, and otherwise punish their children in an attempt to force the cohabitation to end. Even after graduation, and among older people, cohabitation may elicit similar negative responses from families.

Despite the most strenuous efforts to prevent it, parents inevitably find out sooner or later (couples who are planning on marriage may hope that this occurs after the wedding). What happens next will probably be easier to bear if you have already established a reasonably good relationship with your parents, and if your parents like and approve your choice of a partner. Even when parents do not object morally to cohabitation, they usually do react angrily to having been deceived. The nature and duration of parents' responses can be roughly predicted from their behavior in stressful or crisis situations that arose in the past. If they have tended to respond with interested, caring support, or angry withdrawal, they may be expected to react similarly to the news of your cohabitation.

One recent graduate of a technical school in the midwest related to us how she handled her parents' reaction: "I decided just to let them be angry for a awhile. I knew that I would be if my child had concealed that kind of thing from me. My acceptance of their anger seemed to help them cool off. I've seen friends of mine become defensive with their parents and attack them for not approving, and the situation just lasted that much longer with more bitterness on both sides. I told them I understood that they were upset and told them why I did it; what my plans were. They never really liked the whole idea, but after a while at least we could see each other without there being a lot of tension."

Those who view living together as a possible prelude to marriage usually are curious about the effect this will have on their lives together once married. The majority of formal studies that have been conducted in this area have reported few, if any, differences in the marriages of those who cohabited versus those who did not. This means that in the areas of marital satisfaction, resolution of conflict, egalitarianism, emotional closeness, self-disclosure, and degree of commitment, there have been no differences found between those who cohabit and those who do not (among those who ultimately marry).

A number of people live together for long periods of time without ever marrying: in fact, they express the desire not to. Some of these cases have made headlines. In one instance, the actor Lee Marvin was sued by his ex-lover with whom he had lived for many years, on the grounds that he had promised to take care of her financial needs. This suit gave rise to the concept of *palimony;* it did not, however, spawn a glut of similar cases as was predicted it would. Among the elderly, there is also a significant trend toward living together since marrying at this late stage of life for many would entail the loss of pensions or social security benefits.

Cohabitation, for some couples, undoubtedly helps them learn to live with each other. It also seems true, however, that the same lessons are learned in the first year or two of marriage among those who do not live together beforehand. The key element seems to be the quality of the relationship itself (see the section "Intimacy" in Chapter 1). In other words, a good relationship has a high chance of being successful regardless of whether or not one cohabits, and a bitter, unhappy relationship will probably fail no matter what living arrangements are made (you can't save a relationship by deciding to cohabit any more than you can save a marriage by deciding to have children).

SINGLEHOOD

For the majority of readers of this book, a lifetime or prolonged period of being single is a disagreeable prospect. Within this broad category of singles are those who have never, and will never, marry (this includes homosexual couples), as well as those who are separated, divorced, and widowed. As the result of these trends, the 1980 Census reported that during the 1970s, the number of persons living alone increased by more than 60 percent, meaning that at present nearly one-quarter of all American households is composed of a single person. As is probably obvious, some of these people are single voluntarily, and others find themselves alone through no choice of their own (U.S. Bureau of the Census, 1981).

The concern in this section is with those who choose to remain single, or who are considering this decision, and those who remain involuntarily single for prolonged periods. Remaining single by choice is legitimate when the individual prefers this lifestyle and wishes to preserve his or her autonomy and independence. A fair number of people stay single because it permits them to devote their energies fully to an important cause. Single people sometimes are better able to give priority to their work, or to a vital mission that represents their life's purpose. This is true of people who devote themselves to a variety of religious orders.

Remaining single in no way means that people necessarily forego loving, intimate relationships entirely. Many singles enjoy relationships that last for years with the same person(s), though they never marry or live together (a well-known example of this would be Katharine Hepburn and Spencer Tracy). It is just as true, though, that significant numbers of people choose to remain single and in some cases, celibate, without conducting intimate relationships.

Perhaps the central questions that people need to answer for themselves are: Am I leaning toward the single life because I don't want to cope with the hassle, pain, and trauma I fear sexual involvement or marriage will bring? Or, is singlehood my preference because it best meets my needs for autonomy, dedication to my work, or adherence to my moral values? If remaining single is an expression of a fear of sexuality and intimacy, then it may be a wise decision to remain unmarried, at least until the problems are substantially resolved. For some people, this may mean that personal problems keep them apart from a loving relationship for most of their lives. There are also instances, though, where this decision, based on fear and anxiety, provides an immediate solution but is ultimately disappointing. The individuals thus may not create opportunities to work through their apprehensions and reach a level of functioning that would be more satisfying in the long run. Marriage is definitely not for everybody. On the other hand, some people deprive themselves of love and intimacy because of problems that could be alleviated.

The situation is entirely different for those who would like to marry, but who, for various reasons, are not able to obtain an acceptable partner. Society traditionally has not been kind to such people. They have been saddled with derogatory labels such as spinster and old maid; men, while enjoying the relatively innocuous label of bachelor, nevertheless may be suspected of being "latent homosexuals" if they remain single much beyond the age of forty. Although the numbers of single people have been steadily increasing, an undesirable stigma is still attached to the never-married.

It is disappointing to spend many years alone when one would prefer not to. Those who marry with the belief that this will end forever their struggle against loneliness, however, are often dismayed. Some of the loneliest people are involved in marriages that offer little in the way of companionship or shared interests. In addition, many studies have found that those who are single or divorced often report themselves to be happier than those who are living in miserable marriages. In this perspective, it's apparent that a variety of satisfying and unsatisfying lifestyles exist both within and outside marriage; those who remain single need not be the targets of sad condolences. And feeling sorry for oneself can become more destructive than the fact of being single (some singles, naturally, feel sorry for their married friends!).

EXTRAMARITAL SEXUALITY

A fair degree of inventiveness has been displayed by those wishing to remain married *and* engage in sexual relations outside the marital dyad. The ways in which extramarital sex occurs may include: *open marriage,* wherein spouses agree together that each may have outside sexual liaisons; *swinging,* in which spouses swap partners with other couples; *intimate networks,* which are similar to swingers, though with an important difference: Swinging contacts tend to be of brief duration with little or no emotional meaning. In intimate networks, couples may share sexual partners over a long period of time with varying degrees of emotional involvement; finally (and probably the most common), is extramarital sex engaged in without the spouse's knowledge or consent.

A great distinction exists between brief sexual encounters outside a marital relationship in which no emotional commitment is made, and ongoing affairs in which priorities may actually shift from the marriage to the affair. Some people manage outside sexual interactions well, in the context that they take a minimum of energy away from the marriage. Some people also report that their extramarital experiences help to keep their marriages vital and interesting. The situation is quite different when the affair progresses to the point that the marriage may no longer be the primary relationship. One woman who learned of her husband's affair was far more concerned with the quality of his emotional attachment to the other woman than she was with the fact of their sexual relations. This theme emerged in the 1984 movie "Falling in Love," in which a man tells his wife of his feelings for the other woman. He hastily adds that no sex has occurred, yet his wife replies, "It's much worse than if sex had taken place."

In keeping with this chapter's premise, a major concern with sex outside marriage is its meaning and motivation. When the main reason for open marriage, or for extramarital relations of any variety, is sex itself, the arrangements and relationships often tend not to work. Relationships of all kinds in which sex is the organizing factor tend to be disillusioning (the authors acknowledge their bias here). Even when such relationships do not violate one's morality, despite a strong wish for the situation to work out, it usually deteriorates after a relatively brief period.

Many clients have confided to us in therapy that "If my spouse or lover ever had sex with anyone else even one time, that would be the end of things between us." Two examples may serve to highlight some of the subtleties in this area.

Imagine two couples. The first couple is strictly monogamous and have what might be considered a traditional marriage. They have few shared interests: on most weeknights, he's out with his friends bowling or at the bar, and on weekends he goes hunting, fishing, or watches sporting events on television. She belongs to a women's bowling league and spends a lot of time with her friends playing bridge. Once a year for a week they go away on vacation together. The second couple has quite a different relationship. They have a passionately shared interest in working to end world hunger and take at least one night out each week together without the children. They spend their evenings conversing, reading, or watching television in each other's company and enjoy the cultural events that they attend together in neighboring cities. A couple of times each year, each of them separately may meet a friend in another town and have a sexual experience.

Where do your sympathies lie? The first couple, though monogamous, has little to recommend their marriage other than their sexual fidelity. The second couple enjoys a vitality and loving commitment to each other, though they do sometimes participate in sexual relations with other people. To whom would you rather be married? Clearly a myriad of variations exists concerning how people resolve these dilemmas in their relationships; these basic issues, however, are not easily resolved for most people with a single hard and fast rule. Some individuals, however much it may conflict with societal values and spouses' desires for absolute fidelity, are not able to fulfill their needs for love, intimacy, and sexual involvement with just one other person, no matter how much they may love that person. This by no means implies that their spouses or lovers are inadequate—it simply means that their needs are not satisfied within conventional marriage.

One can also engage in sex outside a primary relationship to inflict revenge, hurt, and jealousy on one's partner. This hardly constitutes an "alternative lifestyle," but represents instead the failure of a couple to communicate meaningfully about their needs and discontents within the relationship. A twenty-five-year-old man said of his affair: "We hadn't been getting along for a few months, and I was feeling like she was being very callous toward me a lot of the time, not responsive to things I'd tell her, hardly enthusiastic when I'd want to make love. So when I had this opportunity to make love with another woman, I remember actually thinking 'This will really get her . . . I can't wait until I can see the look on her face.' " He did indeed get a hurt response from his lover, who herself later said, "I felt like killing him because I could feel him gloating over my pain. I hated him for a while before I was even able to speak to him again."

Another woman, on learning of her husband's affair, not only entered into an affair of her own, but also hired a private detective to follow her husband and give her full reports on his behavior. Once she had sufficient evidence, she went to the police and pleaded that he had physically threatened her (he hadn't) and obtained a restraining order against her husband. He was enraged at her false accusation of his physical threats toward her and moved out of the house immediately. Both then consulted separate lawyers. As a futile attempt at reconciliation (too little, too late), they attended two marriage counseling sessions, but were too explosive even there to spend time constructively figuring out where things had gone wrong. The power of hostility, once given full rein, can be deadly effective. And it can block couples from discovering viable alternatives to ending their relationship.

CHILDLESSNESS

Marriage equals parenthood. That is the traditional dictum handed down from generation to generation: be fruitful and multiply. Couples who married and never produced children were by definition infertile; no sane, righteous person would *choose* not to bear offspring. Those spouses who, in history, have wished not to become parents have been considered sinful and deviates. Evidence for this abounds: Within the Catholic church, for instance, opposition to artificial methods of contraception is based on the belief that every conjugal act should remain open to the possibility of conception.

The pressure for compulsory pregnancy and parenthood has been diminishing gradually over the past two decades and has been accompanied by a declining rate of fertility. Those couples that do choose to have children are having fewer and fewer (the average number of children per couple in 1985 was about 1.8). Contemporary estimates vary, but in general it is believed that between 10 and 20 percent of all couples never have children; of these perhaps half do so intentionally.

Voluntary childlessness is a decision reached by some people whose self-concept is that they should not become parents. For them, this may very well be an intelligent decision—not everyone should become parents. Owing to experiences in childhood in one's family of origin, people grow up sometimes feeling that they don't wish to repeat the pain they experienced there. Though it would be difficult to prove through research, it is probably true that some of the child abuse and neglect reported each year could be prevented if people who are not good parent material decided to forego childbearing.

The option simply to remain childless is one that is chosen by a significant number of people. As with other aspects of a person's life, there are both healthy and unhealthy reasons for making such a decision. One of the most often heard reasons was articulated by a woman who had been seen in individual psychotherapy for a period of two years. She had been raised in a tremendously chaotic, unloving family, and said of her experience: "I grew up feeling that nothing was more hurtful than to be a child. Reaching out to my mother or father almost always earned me a slap, or criticism, or just no response at all, nothing. The more I look at myself today, the more I can see that I identified with some aspects of my mother. I hate to admit it, but in some ways, I'm just like her. And I'm terrified that if I become a mother, despite my best intentions, I'll repeat her mistakes and wind up being just as hurtful to my child as she was to me. So I'm never, never going to have a child. It's the safest way."

This young woman was right in believing that sometimes, despite conscious wishes not to, people unconsciously identify with undesirable aspects of parents. It is also true, however, that many aspects of these troubling similarities with parents can be brought to consciousness where they can be examined and understood. This process often gives the individual a stronger sense of control over behavior. The young woman above, for example, was afraid that she wouldn't be able to control herself with her children and would lash out at them before she was aware of what she was doing. Through therapy, however, she first developed greater control in her relationship with her parents and then in her relationship with her lover of two years. These positive experiences left her feeling confident that were she to have children, her mothering abilities might not be perfect but would certainly be adequate.

Other people, however, remain childless because their priorities differ from what is popularly assumed to be the *normal* script for married couples. As mentioned in the section above on singlehood, work or a special purpose may consume one's energies that otherwise would be spent in child-rearing. Raising a child requires an enormous investment in time, money, and love. In the financial dimension alone, current estimates state that about $100,000 (in 1981 dollars) is required to raise one child from birth until he or she graduates from a four-year public college. Even without college, the expense even for low-income families is $74,950 (*New York Times*, 1984). The pronatalist stance (every person a parent) would lead literally millions of people to abandon their own aspirations to conform to a maladaptive societal value. It is more ominous that it would lead to the birth of countless children whose lives would be characterized by neglect, abuse, and despair.

One of the most significant conversations that couples have before they decide to get married concerns their respective feelings about having children. If your prospective spouse either holds the opposite sentiment from yourself or is basically undecided, it is unwise to marry with the fantasy that he or she will "come around" to your way of thinking. Numerous clinical examples from the files of marriage and family therapists could be cited to illustrate the conflict, acrimony, and ultimate demise of marriages in which disagreements over childbearing could not be resolved.

Those couples who are involuntarily childless have several options. Progressive research over the past number of years has yielded successful scientific techniques that are able to restore fertility to women and men whose reproductive systems have not functioned properly. In vitro fertilization has captured the most media attention. In this procedure, an egg is extracted surgically from a woman's ovary and then fertilized in a petri dish with sperm from her husband. The fertilized embryo is then implanted in her womb where, it is hoped, a fetus develops to which the woman eventually gives birth.

When the couple themselves are unable by any means to conceive, they may consider adoption. This is a big problem for those who would like a healthy infant: In 1970, the number of adoptions per year hit about 175,000, but in 1983 the number had declined to only about 100,000 per year (Strong et al., 1983). Far more unwed young mothers have been choosing to keep their babies, and thus the supply for adoption has dwindled. Couples who are willing to adopt a minority child, a child over the age of three or four, or one who has a disability, will find that their wait is far shorter than the five to ten years wait of those who desire a white infant.

People undergo many changes in their feelings, attitudes, and behaviors as they grow and mature. What makes sense in one period of life may at a later time seem strange or uncharacteristic. Witness the experiences of people who return to their hometowns for ten- or twenty-year high school reunions. The high school dummy has become a successful businessman, or the brain of the senior class has floundered from one meaningless job to the next.

In their sexual lives as well, people report that feelings and preferences undergo evolution with the passing years. In many areas of their lives, people do not typically select one thing (divorce, singlehood, extramarital, or open relationships), which then remains unchanged for the remainder of their lives. People who get divorced often remarry after a while; people who thought they'd remain single suddenly find themselves getting married in their fifties for the first time; people who experienced a period of extramarital sex may spend years being monogamous.

However much we, the authors, favor the freedom of people to have options in their lives and not to be trapped in unsatisfying relationships or situations, it still seems that the better alternative is for people to make the right choice of partners or lifestyles in the first place. For most people, having an enduring, loving relationship and a stable home in which to raise children (if they want them) makes the most sense.

REFERENCES

New York Times. "Outlays for the Raising of Children Are Linked to Family Size." June 20, 1984, p. C15.

Strong, B., DeVault, C., Suid, M., & Reynolds, R. *The Marriage and Family Experience*. New York: West Publishing Co., 1983.

U.S. Bureau of the Census (1981). "Marital Status and Living Arrangements: March 1980." *Current Population Reports*, Series P-20, No. 365. Washington, DC: Government Printing Office.

CHAPTER 6

Masturbation or Self-Pleasuring

Thirty to forty years ago masturbation was no problem. You simply got tired blood, mental illness, acne, and blindness from it. Even though no one believes these myths about masturbation anymore, our society still retains much of the historical baggage that has accumulated about the evils of "self-abuse."

The paradox: Masturbation is one of the most indulged in, but least talked about, human behaviors. Try to imagine yourself having a conversation about your own masturbatory practices with a trusted friend, counselor, or spouse. Most people respond with anxiety, guilt, shame, or fear of this exercise, even if they believe that there is nothing wrong with it. If it is discussed, among males it is referred to jokingly, disparagingly as "jerking off"; outside some women's groups where it may actually be celebrated, masturbation among women may be discussed in hushed tones.

The word *masturbate* is derived from the Latin verb *masturbare:* to defile by hand. *Onanism* is another term for masturbation, so designated in the mistaken belief that Onan in the Book of Genesis was struck dead for masturbating. Most biblical scholars now accept the view that Onan's fate resulted from his refusal to impregnate his dead brother's widow, according to the custom of the time.

Masturbation is not mentioned anywhere in the Old Testament. Some New Testament statements made by Saint Paul, as well as the pronouncements of early church fathers such as Saint Augustine, have led to an interpretation that considered masturbation in the same category as sex with animals. One influential medieval Christian theologian made distinctions between "acts in accordance with nature" and "acts contrary to nature." The former had to do with procreative possibility: fornication, adultery, incest, and rape constituted lesser violations, though they were deemed sinful. Acts considered a greater evil than any of the above included masturbation, homosexuality, and bestiality.

Erroneous notions about the waste of semen led to early Christian concerns about masturbation. At no time did there seem to be a great concern about women masturbating. People apparently made the assumption that women just didn't do it.

In 1710 a pamphlet appeared in England with the title "Onania, or the Heinous Sin of Self Pollution and All Its Frightful Consequences for Both Sexes, Considered with Spiritual and Physical Advice." This pamphlet was followed by many others authored by the most respected physicians of the time. Even Benjamin Rush, the father of American psychiatry, published an article in 1812 describing the terrible consequences of masturbation. According to him, it caused insanity, vertigo, epilepsy, impotence, loss of memory, and perhaps even death.

This grim view of masturbation was accepted by almost the entire medical profession during the nineteenth and the early twentieth centuries. One book dealing with the subject of masturbation during this time was called *Safe Counsel* by B. G. Jefferis, M.D., Ph.D. First published in 1893, it went through thirty-nine editions, the last of which was printed in 1928 and was read by millions of people. Jefferis makes the following comments about the evils of masturbation:

> The glands that are a part of the organs of sex have a similar part to perform in the development of the body. They secrete fluids which are absorbed into the blood and there take a chief part in developing the body in its strength and in what we call its virility. You know the difference between boys who are manly and strong, tingling with life and action, and those who are weak and tired and lolling around. As this wonderful fluid is secreted by the testes and works its way to the blood vessels and is carried to all parts of the body, where it performs its part in building it or so furnishing it that we discover this particular strength, virility. And as the fluids are drawn off through the friction or rubbing of the organs, the whole body suffers the loss of the fluids that it must have in order to be made strong and able to endure strain. So here lies all the folly and sin of self-abuse; it is depriving the body of what it needs for its own strengthening. The boy who forms the habit of self-abuse is as unwise as a man would be if he were to break into his own house, rob it of its most precious goods, and throw them into the fire at the end.

The author goes on to implore boys to desist from masturbating, warning that if they don't it will result in high-strung temper, physical damage, a constant tired feeling, moral loss, damaged nerves, etc. Jefferis continues: "The best friends of boys know that cowardness, deception and general shiftiness almost always go along with sexual excess."

What can we do about it? *Safe Counsel* offers the following advice:

> . . . the more the habit is indulged the weaker the will grows; the weaker the will becomes the less power it has to control the habit. So a boy goes on robbing himself of the very weapons that he ought to have in his hands to conquer the evil habit. But there is always some power left; and the way to increase that is to use it to the limit. . . .

> . . . physical help is open-air exercise. Everyone knows that sitting quietly for a long time in cramped positions will tend to produce sexual cravings while hard exercise in the open air is useful in working off physical energy and so bringing about health habits. Fresh air under all conditions helps in the problem.

In 1917 Professor T. W. Shannon wrote a book entitled *Eugenics or the Laws of Sex Life and Heredity*. It contains some of the following gems:

> By far the worst form of venereal indulgence is self-pollution . . . It is wholly unnatural, and, in every respect, does violence to nature. It impairs the intellectual and moral faculties and debases the mind in the greatest degree . . . The sense of taste is . . . blunted . . . the eyes . . . become languid and dull, and lose their brightness and liveliness of expression. . . .

Shannon goes on to quote a physician:

> I myself have seen many young men drop into premature graves from this cause alone.

Will marriage help? Shannon replies with the following answer:

> Certainly marriage need not be recommended to the confirmed masturbator in the hope or expectation of curing him of his vice. He will most likely continue it afterwards, and the circumstances in which he is placed will aggravate the misery and the mischief of it. For natural intercourse he has little power or no desire, and finds no pleasure in it; the indulgence of a depraved appetite has destroyed the natural appetite. Besides, if he be not entirely impotent, what an outlook for any child begotten of such degenerate stock: Has a being so degraded any right to curse a child with the inheritance of such a wretched descent? Far better that the vice and its consequences should die with him.

In contrast with these prophets of gloom, Havelock Ellis (1859–1939), a lone British voice, set the stage at the turn of the century for a few brave physicians and educators who, in the 1930s and 1940s, began to question such archaic and unscientific views about masturbation. It wasn't until Alfred Kinsey (1950s) scandalized the world by reporting the almost universal masturbation practices among men and the majority of women that professionals and religious leaders began to shift their views. We went through a period of diagnosing masturbators as narcissistic, selfish, lonely, depressed, in a state of arrested development, or, at best, immature. Then we progressed through a stage of viewing masturbation as normal for teenagers. Next, it became okay if you didn't do it too much. Naturally, no one in the United States knew how much was too much. (Once a year? Twice a week? After every meal?)

Masturbation is a healthy expression of sexuality at any age. Like other behaviors, such as eating or drinking alcohol, it can become compulsive when done in response to guilt or anxiety. One overeats not because one is hungry, but because of anxiety; similarly, people drink too much liquor not because they are thirsty but in response to anxiety or other intraphysic troubles. Of all these compulsive behaviors, however, too much masturbation is surely the least harmful. Thousands die every year from excessive eating and drinking. No one, however, has ever died from overmasturbating. Thus, if you must have a compulsion, please choose masturbation.

Owing to the intense emotions and societal pressures that come to bear, this is a difficult area to place in perspective. For instance, what basis is there for claiming that people who masturbate tend to be shy and lonely? Some of our best friends are masturbators, and some people who never masturbate have no friends at all. Where's the connection?

Not a shred of scientific evidence has ever been produced proving that masturbation per se is physically harmful. Indeed, considerable evidence exists to suggest that it is healthy and therapeutic in many ways. Our own clinical experience repeatedly confirms some of the early research by René Spitz (1945). Dr. Spitz, a world-renowned child development specialist, conducted careful studies that indicated how an absence of masturbation in very young children (i.e., the first year of life) often pointed to a disturbed mother-child relationship. Follow-up studies by Spitz and others strongly support the view that genital play was seen in families with good parent-child relationships. On the other hand, emotionally deprived children had a tendency to masturbate very little and, instead, leaned toward the use of aggressive behavior to relieve stress. Furthermore, excessive masturbation (defined as more than ten times daily) may occur when a child feels suddenly deprived of a close relationship with the mother or feels the relationship threatened by the arrival of a sibling.

Beginning with infants, parents should not pull their baby's hand away from its genitals when they notice the child fondling them. Parents love the game when they say to the child, "Touch your nose," and then praise the child, "Touch your ear, your toes . . ." But parents rarely add, "Touch your penis, or vagina," and then praise the child in the same way.

Children should be allowed to masturbate without being made to feel guilty. They need only be taught the private nature of it. It represents a healthy exploration of their sexuality and a good experience of appreciating the erotic aspects of their bodies. If it is guilt-free and enjoyable, it becomes self-limiting. Any behavior, including masturbation, when it is a response to guilt or tension, can become compulsive and needs to be dealt with in the larger contexts of personality development and family interaction. The absence of any other personality problems, such as nightmares, stuttering, refusal to eat, etc., suggests that one should not pay too much attention to masturbation. Counseling help should be sought for youngsters when masturbation (and any other behaviors), really *are* extreme.

People of all ages can be helped to appreciate that masturbation is a normal way of expressing and enjoying their sexual feelings and relieving sexual tensions. Young people do feel "horny." What a neat way of enjoying themselves. Furthermore, why shouldn't adults be able to masturbate comfortably and pleasurably when opportunities for sex with their partners are not available? Trips away from home, periods of illness and/or hospitalization, or when a partner does indeed have a headache or doesn't feel like it are all opportunities. Some adults enjoy masturbating occasionally to keep in touch with their sexual feelings, or simply as a way to spend some pleasant time alone.

Society pays a big price for its still repressive views on masturbation. Clinical data and research on persons who have committed violent sexual crimes strongly suggests a relationship between feelings of guilt and punishment for childhood masturbation and the need to dominate or violate women or children. These symptoms also seem to go along with early parental rejection or deprivation of emotional sustenance.

Society has so brainwashed young men that many feel it's unmanly to masturbate once they've experienced first sexual intercourse. Consequently, our country has left a sad reservoir of unwanted children in such places as Japan, Vietnam, and Thailand. To many men, prostitution, or even rape, seem preferable alternatives to masturbation. This is no small matter.

Three brief anecdotes will illuminate the ways in which misperceptions continue to inhabit people's attitudes.

We asked a father who was worried about his teenage daughter having intercourse whether he would prefer her to masturbate or risk pregnancy and venereal disease. His reply was, "Neither."

An editor of a medical journal asked us to respond to a question posed by a seventeen-year-old boy who stated that he couldn't speak to a female or go to a dance without getting an erection. The young man had pleaded for help. He especially asked that no one make fun of him; it was a serious matter for him. He also didn't want to be told that he'd get over it, which the editor revealed was the best solution several experts had argued. We suggested to the young man that he simply go to the bathroom and masturbate before he went to a dance or a date. After an hour or so he may have to repeat the process. He should then be able to enjoy a relaxed evening without embarrassment. The editor refused to print our reply, claiming that it was not professional advice; we, however, still can't think of a better solution.

Ten years ago one of us spoke to the mental health association in an upstate New York community. Reference was made to masturbation. A reporter present accurately recorded what had been said. When the article was submitted to the editor, he refused to use the word masturbation since he felt that this was inappropriate terminology for a family newspaper. A debate then ensued among the staff members regarding a proper substitute for the word masturbation. Two were considered: self-abuse and self-pleasuring. It was to the honor and distinction of the staff that they finally agreed to use self-pleasuring.

The treatment of choice for preorgasmic women involves learning how to enjoy self-pleasuring. Often women who have been preorgasmic for many years achieve their first orgasms through masturbation and then go on to become orgasmic with their partners as well.

For some people with sexual problems masturbation can be a therapeutic tool where psychotherapy alone has failed. Men who suffer from premature ejaculation or impotence often learn greater control using masturbation. In the last few decades, attitudes concerning masturbation have done a dramatic about-face among professionals: these enlightened views are gradually filtering into the population at large.

Sure, we've come a long way. Woody Allen stated in one of his films that he enjoys masturbation—at least he's having sex with someone he loves. Some religious groups still frown on it, yet even the most extreme opponents in the Catholic church, for example, have modified their position considerably during the last twenty-five years. We predict that twenty-five years from now no one will give masturbation another thought besides its pleasurable aspects.

Regardless of such idealistic prophecies, some people will remain uncomfortable with masturbation. Some anxiety may be inevitable, but the chain can be broken by learning to understand and accept one's sexual impulses. Some may not like to use words such as masturbation or expressions such as "playing with yourself." We're indebted to our colleague, Gloria Blum, for the concept of "private touching." It rightly suggests that masturbating, like other forms of sexuality, are not public matters.

Our overall position is as follows. There is no evidence that all healthy people masturbate, or that you must masturbate to be healthy. There are some, especially adult women, who have no memory of ever masturbating and who suffer no apparent ill effects. There are mature men and women who give up masturbation entirely after they obtain regular opportunities for sexual intercourse. There are also people who enjoy masturbation more than coital sex. Most people continue to masturbate at some time or other throughout their entire lives. Once may be too much if you don't enjoy it.

REFERENCES

Jefferis, B. G. *Safe Counsel.* New York: Intext Press, 1928.

Shannon, T. W. *Eugenics, or the Laws of Sex Life and Heredity.* New York: Doubleday & Co., 1917.

Spitz, R.A. "Hospitalism: An Inquiry into the Genesis of Psychiatric Conditions in Early Childhood." *Psychoanalytic Study of the Child,* 1945, **1,** 53–74.

CHAPTER 7

The Abortion Controversy

THE POLITICAL LANDSCAPE

The United States Supreme Court's landmark decision on abortion (January, 1973) states in part:

> We recognize the right of the individual, married or single, to be free from unwarranted governmental intrusion into matters so fundamentally affecting a person as the decision whether to bear or beget a child. That right necessarily includes the right of a woman to decide whether or not to terminate a pregnancy.

Since 1973 almost all national opinion polls have indicated that a majority of the population supports this Supreme Court decision. One recent poll, the New York Times/CBS Poll (1984), found the following views on abortion.

- 63 percent oppose, and 28 percent favor, a Constitutional amendment banning all abortions
- 48 percent oppose, and 43 percent favor, a Constitutional amendment which bans all abortions, except those necessary to save the life of the mother
- 80 percent support legal abortions in the event of serious birth defects, or pregnancy due to rape

Other polls have found similar or higher percentages in support of abortion, and there is little difference in opinion according to whether people are Catholic, Protestant, or Jewish. In practice, Jews tend to have slightly fewer abortions than the other two groups. Significant differences in world views exist between those who are pro-life (anti-abortion) and those who are pro-choice (support a woman's right to decide for herself). The 1984 work of Kristin Luker paints a clear picture of the two camps.

Among those who are pro-life, there is a tendency to view men and women as distinctly different, with corresponding roles. This view reflects the traditional position of women as fulfilled most in motherhood, men most in their occupations. Mothers who work, it is felt, are possibly hurting their families' chances for health and growth. Pro-lifers tend to advocate larger-than-average families and oppose artificial methods of contraception and premarital and extramarital sex, which are seen as interfering with the procreative meaning of sexual behaviors. Sexuality is felt to be a sacred covenant between husband and wife; sexuality education for children outside the home is believed to usurp the parents' rights to control their children's formation of values. Finally, abortion itself is opposed because it violates the Commandment, Thou Shalt Not Kill.

The constellation of values among those who advocate pro-choice is virtually the opposite of these. They view parenthood as a vital part of marriage but not necessarily a woman's only life role or as excluding men from participation. They tend to believe that sex for procreation only has created a double standard that discriminates against and controls women's sexual behavior. There is an acceptance of a wide range of contraception and a general belief that sexuality education helps to prepare people for a higher quality of life. No responsible pro-choice advocate is *pro-abortion*. That is, abortion is not accepted as an alternative to birth control. In general, pro-choicers believe in planned, responsible parenting. The life of the mother, and of living members of a family, are given precedence over the embryo, which is a nonviable entity.

Even in a democratic society, a majority opinion does not necessarily prevail, nor does it have the right to impose its views on a minority. And yet, a (significant) minority view has become one of the most volatile, divisive domestic issues of our time. It is essential to respect people whose views are different from one's own; this injunction has become strained by conflicting factions who at times claim that their morality is higher and their connection with God is more sacred than other people's. This chapter will present a diversity of opinions on the subject; our view is that those who wish to make choice illegal are overstepping essential constitutional bounds, though we defend their right to differing *opinions*.

Here are a few facts. An abortion performed by a physician in the first trimester is much safer than giving birth and does not interfere with this woman's subsequent fertility. (There always exists, however, *some* risk in surgical procedures.) There is some evidence that multiple abortions (over five) may have some effect on the health of the mother and her ability to sustain a future pregnancy. This means that if you've already had two or more abortions, you'll want to consult closely with your physician about the effects of another if you find yourself unintentionally pregnant again. It is hoped the experience of one abortion will lead people to be very careful next time around.

Wherever abortion is illegal, thousands of poor women die because of backroom, nonsterile, botched-up procedures. This was true of Catholic Italy until 1980 when abortion became legalized. It still holds true for Mexico and for most of South America. On December 2, 1979, the *New York Times* reported that an official governmental agency in Mexico estimated there are 1.2 million illegal abortions each year resulting in the death of 40,000 women due to complications. On the other hand, people with money have little or no difficulty securing safe abortions whether it is legal or not.

More than 90 percent of all abortions in this country occur in the first trimester of pregnancy, when the procedure is safest, simplest, and cheapest. Nevertheless, anti-abortion organizations continually misrepresent this fact in their literature, which typically shows a photo of a mutilated fetus that is at least twice the age of those aborted in the first trimester (first three months of pregnancy). Arguments pro and con have centered at times on attempts to determine when life begins. Members of the right-to-life group assert that life begins at conception and thus should be protected by law. Pro-choice advocates do not deny that a fetus is composed of living tissue, but assert that the fetus is not viable (that is, cannot sustain itself outside the mother's body). They also argue that the woman alone has the right to make decisions about her body: no government or outside agency has the right to interfere.

Some right-to-lifers are not known to be especially sympathetic to causes that affect the life, liberty, and well-being of humans once they emerge from the womb. One need only compare voting records in Congress between those who favor a right-to-life amendment to the Constitution and those who oppose it. One then sees which group has consistently voted against measures in the interest of the impoverished people of our country. Of course, there are some exceptions. But those who are anti-abortion tend to vote for bills supporting capital punishment, against handgun regulation, and against bills for family support, school lunch and milk programs, and assistance to the aging population.

In the entire world today, the most notable example of a person who cares about the unborn as well as the born is Mother Teresa of Calcutta. On winning the Nobel Peace Prize for 1979 she declared, "To me the nations that have legalized abortion, they are the poorest nations."

This statement appears ironic to those who know that the majority of nations where abortion is illegal are the impoverished, corrupt dictatorships in South America and the Moslem countries of Asia and Africa. There, the wealth is concentrated in the hands of a few families. On the day the story about Mother Teresa was reported in the *New York Times* (December 11, 1979), the same newspaper carried a headline announcing that 35 million children in Latin America lacked basic foods. The vulnerability of these children to early death is so great that the United Nations Children's Fund estimates that one million children under the age of four will die each year. Yet, the best birth control methods are outlawed in these very same nations. How tragic it is that making birth control either illegal or unavailable and abortion illegal (which does not significantly reduce the number of abortions anywhere) literally provides a death sentence for millions and millions of mothers and young children all over the world.

Abortion is unquestionably a moral, ethical, and religious issue; yet, in this country, it has become a political issue as well. There is a tremendous difference between a personal, spiritual belief that abortion is wrong, and a belief that legislation which reflects that opposition should be enacted. Some right-wing adherents have seized on the abortion issue as a vehicle to acquire power. Of course, some prominent progressives also oppose abortion. The critical issue is whether anyone, regardless of political affiliation, is justified in lobbying to make abortion illegal.

During the 1984 presidential campaign between Ronald Reagan and Walter Mondale, abortion became a central issue. One of the key figures in this controversy was Catholic Archbishop John J. O'Connor, who advocated that candidates for public office should oppose abortion on demand and work for legislative reform to override the Supreme Court's 1973 decision. He argues, in agreement with millions of other Americans, that abortion is the taking of human life; even though a large proportion of our population accepts the morality of abortion, laws are designed to protect the common good. Thus, though there exist some people whose personal, moral beliefs permit them to commit arson, burglary, and even murder, we nevertheless legislate against such behaviors. The Archbishop asserts that abortion falls into this category, in which something that is widely accepted is wrong. Especially within the Catholic religion, where abortion is officially opposed, the church leaders face a dilemma: about 25 percent of all abortions performed in the United States each year are among Catholic women, who have abortions at rates slightly higher than their proportion of the population.

Large numbers of people oppose abortion rights out of sincere concern for the sanctity of human life. Their beliefs may also support a nuclear freeze and/or disarmament, various forms of aid to alleviate hunger and poverty, and many forms of medical, educational, and social service assistance to the disadvantaged and disabled. Some do not agree with the Archbishop when he says that even victims of rape or incest should bear their children and find in this a "rich fulfillment"—whether they keep the children or put them up for adoption. In addition, many bishops do not share John O'Connor's view that abortion is the foremost issue for voters. A statement signed by twenty-three Roman Catholic bishops believe that this narrow focus on abortion has confused Catholics into thinking that their votes should be cast for politicians solely on the basis of the person's stance on abortion. Their statement asserted that nuclear threats were equally pressing as a moral concern, and that "To claim that nuclear war is only a potential evil and that abortion is actual neglects a terrible reality" (the *Boston Globe*, 1984).

Few would deny that abortion is a moral issue, though the debate hinges on whether abortion is perceived as *public* versus *private* morality. Those who oppose abortion rights believe that this is a public issue, in the same way as murder and other crimes against persons are and thus should be subjected to laws. Others, such as Henry

Siegman, Executive Director of the American Jewish Congress, believe that abortion is essentially a matter of one's own moral conscience, a private experience of one's religious beliefs. Since there are many variations of this private conscience, they argue, it is indefensible that a pluralistic society such as ours would seek to legislate one version of this private morality for the public as a whole. Those who believe that abortion is akin to murder, however, assert that framing the issue as public versus private morality is a sort of nonsensical moral gymnastics and that abortion is simply, objectively, wrong.

In our view, individuals who exhibit the least human dignity are those who compare the holocaust, the mass murder of 6 million Jews, to abortion. There exists no comparison more immoral or depraved. It is both illogical and outrageous to suggest that the calculated murder of millions of children and adults can be equated with an individual woman's decision to terminate her pregnancy. Such action is often taken after consultation with her minister, to terminate the product of rape, incest, unwanted pregnancy due to contraceptive failure, or to prevent the birth of a child afflicted with Tay-Sachs disease, down's syndrome, etc.

THE PERSONAL DIMENSION

For most people an unintended pregnancy is more of a personal dilemma than a political issue. An emotional reaction to the news may run from depression, anger, and guilt to sadness, indecision, and fear. Since medical confirmation of the pregnancy usually comes around the fifth or sixth week, decisions of what to do need to be made relatively quickly (abortion in the first trimester occurs up until twelve weeks of pregnancy).

It is advisable for a woman to receive some form of counseling if she is not sure she wants the baby. Among unmarried women, an important consideration is: To what extent should the father be included in the decision? Should he even be told of the conception? Women can expect a range of reactions from the man. Sometimes he is vehemently opposed to either abortion or adoption and wants to get married. Sometimes he strongly favors abortion and is willing to help pay for the procedure but wants no emotional strings attached. Although some men believe that they should have an equal voice in the pregnancy-outcome decision because they, too, are the potential child's parent, many women believe that since it is their body, they alone have final say in the decision.

Women who choose abortion, according to Wassenberg and Nass's 1977 study, as opposed to those who decide to keep the child, tend to be older middle-class women who either work or attend college. Though some women experience feelings of guilt and regret after having an abortion, in most instances these feelings are not overly severe or prolonged. Reactions will vary, depending on the quality of support received from husbands, lovers, friends, and family members. In fact, feelings of depression and anxiety are likely to be stronger before the abortion: afterwards, a sense of relief is likely to prevail. Overall, a national survey by Yankelovich, Skelly, and White (see Nass et al, 1984) found that only 8 percent of women felt in retrospect that abortion had been the wrong choice for them.

Even though they would make the same decision if they had it to do over again, abortion is often remembered with some sadness. Seeing a young child accompanied by her mother may provoke the thought, My child would be about that old now if I'd not had an abortion. Some women who have abortions early in their reproductive years may reach their early thirties without having had any children and wonder if they missed their only opportunity to become a mother. Among some pro-choice advocates there is a wish to minimize the extent of these lingering negative feelings, perhaps because of fear that acknowledging them would fuel the motivation of anti-abortionists. Women and men need to consider these possibilities beforehand, however, so that an informed choice is made, based on an awareness of oneself. People involved in sexual relationships should discuss their feelings about abortion and how each would respond to an unintended pregnancy.

Women who are faced with the choice of abortion or birth sometimes feel that in choosing abortion, they are making the "selfish" decision. That is, selfish in the sense that they are opting for what is best in their own lives, rather than what will preserve the fetus. As Carol Gilligan points out in her book *In a Different Voice,* pregnancy and motherhood have until recently symbolized women's destiny; abortion entails a break from a tradition in which women have been socialized to exercise care and avoid hurt. For many women, the dilemma after an abortion, or even in the process of making the decision, is whether or not they will continue to feel that they are good persons afterwards. This is a crucial issue if you are contemplating abortion: can you live with the decision and maintain a positive self-image?

One woman who was seen at a university health center for counseling was considering getting married to her boyfriend but felt a conflict over whether to tell him about her abortion two years previously. Would he still love her? Disclosing the abortion also meant an admission that she was not a virgin when she first slept with her present lover, and she was terrified that he would leave her. The counselor was the first person ever to know of the abortion, and he had been told only because the student was in the middle of another pregnancy scare, which potentially implied another abortion. The decision reached was to bring the boyfriend in for several counseling sessions, during which he would learn of the abortion and the couple would have the opportunity to discuss whatever feelings arose. Ironically, it turned out that the boyfriend also had been involved in an abortion with a past girlfriend and was able to empathize with his present lover's fears.

The decision of whether or not to abort also has powerful implications for significant others in a woman's life. Husbands, lovers, children, and parents all have a vital stake in the potential birth of a child. Pressures to make a certain decision may be overt, as in the case of parents pushing for birth and adoption, or subtle, perhaps in a woman detecting her lover's aloofness when she announces her plans to abort. The concern over selfishness enters in here as well: will you decide in a way that pleases others and fulfills their expectations or act on your own conscience? Certainly for some women there is little internal or external conflict and their abortion is relatively painless; but for others, guilt may persist for some time.

It is equally clear that alternative decisions to abortion carry important consequences that need to be considered. Couples, especially young ones who marry to legitimize a birth, stand a far greater chance of eventual divorce. Among teenage women, birth itself is a much greater physical and psychological risk than is abortion. In addition, the life script for both mother and unwanted child is grim: poverty, curtailed education, child abuse. Close to 80 percent of teenage marriages end in divorce or desertion within five years. Even among older women, though unwanted children are sometimes loved and well cared for, the risks are greater than when the child was planned and wanted.

It is abundantly clear that abortion is a woefully poor method of contraception. Though many unintended pregnancies are the result of contraceptive failure among responsible people, most result from nonuse of any kind of birth control, or misuse of some method (such as using foam after intercourse, or taking just one pill).

In this context, abortion sometimes represents a failure of sexuality education to reach the most uninformed and vulnerable of individuals. But in the personal dimension, it reflects couples' failure to discuss sex and contraception *before* they become sexually involved. Talking about these things beforehand means that you are able to care for yourself and protect your emotional and physical well-being in a profound way. Those who are least able to care for their own needs may be at greatest risk. In addition, sometimes there is a fear that a relationship cannot sustain confronting the issue of contraception before sexual activity begins. If that's the case, you'll want to consider whether the relationship is worth the risk; in all likelihood, the relationship won't last even if you *don't* discuss these issues.

REFERENCES

Boston Globe. October 23, 1984, p. 15.

Gilligan, C. *In a Different Voice.* Cambridge, MA: Harvard University Press, 1982.

Granberg, D., & Granberg, B. W. Abortion attitudes 1965–1980: Trends and determinants. *Family Planning Perspectives,* 1980, **12** (5), 250–261.

Luker, K. *Abortion and the Politics of Motherhood.* Los Angeles: University of California Press, 1984.

Nass, G. D., Libby, R. W., & Fisher, M. P. *Sexual Choices.* Monterey, CA: Wadsworth, 1984.

New York Times. October 14, 1984, p. E3.

CHAPTER 8

Lust

Some years ago, Jimmy Carter commented, "I've looked on a lot of women with lust. I've committed adultery in my heart many times."

The famous *Playboy* interview in 1976 nearly cost Jimmy Carter the election; at least some politicians thought so. He did win despite his open acknowledgement of what most adult men feel at one time or another.

Lust in men appears to be a near-universal phenomenon, and in our society the prohibitions against it derive from Christ's pronouncement in Matthew 5:28: "But I say to you that every one who looks at a woman lustfully has already committed adultery with her in his heart." His message would seem to be clear, but contemporary theologians are now making a concerted effort to distinguish between *lust* and *fantasy*.

As usual, the dictionary provides a clue. Webster's defines lust as "a desire to gratify the senses," whereas fantasy means "imagination or fancy; especially, wild, visionary fancy." We might then interpret lust to involve a sexual desire or impulse followed by some deliberate means of consummation. Fantasy, on the other hand, connotes a wide range of thoughts that do not require the involvement of another person to satisfy one's own needs. Fantasies may become a source of energy for creative efforts and an impetus for mature relationships. The two terms (*lust* and *fantasy*) have erroneously at times been used interchangeably. A man who *lusts* after a woman (or another man) is pursuing a fantasy in an aggressive way; he meets her, his eyes scan her body, and he begins scheming ways to affect the seduction. His desire is his motivation. This is worlds apart from a developing relationship wherein sexual desire evolves in the context of the relationship itself. A man who *fantasizes* sexually about another person creates mental images in his mind and builds on the scenario as he wishes. There is often little control over the appearance or disappearance of the thought itself, which may or may not be pleasurable to the individual. Day or night dreams that we have may involve being raped, ravaged, witnessing our own funeral, or they may be surreal and disconnected messages with no definite theme. The thoughts may be primitive symbols of the unconscious or may represent personal fixation on a particular sexual situation. But they do not in themselves imply antisocial or sexist behavior nor do they mean the individual intends to live them out in real life. The theory that all dreams represent our real wishes is simply absurd. If a man accepts the fantasies as a healthy part of his personality, he will not suffer the obsessive repetition of the thoughts that are caused by guilt. For most men, the experience of both lust and fantasy can have physical as well as psychological ramifications. The stirring in the loins, quickening pulse, and other physiological responses accompany the mental process. That doesn't matter. What matters is the behavior that results.

If anything, Christ was saying that lust is a distortion of man's instinctual sexual drive. It is impersonal, a burden for women who resent being the objects of men's desire, and can become a hypnotic force to the man preoccupied with it. In his book *Embodiment: An Approach to Sexuality and Christian Theology*, James B. Nelson states, . . . if lust is untamed, inordinate sexual desire which is not only the passion for *possession* of another but which also becomes, by its centrality in the self, an expression of *idolatry*, then we are dealing here with something different from the usual erotic awareness expressed in sexual fantasy."

We recently received a letter from a friend of ours that is so remarkably honest and to the point that we have excerpted it below. He is a lawyer living in Wisconsin with his wife and three children, and his letter highlights the attempts of one man to come to terms with his own feelings of lust.

> The major issue of sexuality that I struggle with is lust. I find that there is always a sexual agenda in any interaction I have with any attractive woman. This is not that sexual desire is a secondary thought; it is a primary thought when I interact with an attractive woman. I haven't yet made any overt attempts to develop a sexual relationship with another woman. Within my marriage I have not given myself permission to ignore the fidelity clause. I think I am fixated at some level of adolescent sexuality and am not sure how to grow through it. I would like to be able to relate to women as people first and not sexual partners. I have some unresolved sexual need. I know that I am not alone by looking at the content of TV programs and advertising. I know that there is a better way, a way that leads to love and does not fixate on lust. A close friend and I have discussed the lusting we feel and he has resolved it as being man's lot in life to have those feelings and you just learn to live with them. I disagree

that they must be just lived with. I think that you learn to transcend the lust. That feeling of lust blocks power feelings which lie beyond. Feelings of Love, which transcend sexuality.

One other reason I am interested in working through the issue of lust and sexuality is the energy which I believe is generated from our sexuality. This energy is experienced as lust and is misdirected, misused and therefore drained. If it is experienced in its pure form as Love, it is synergetic producing more than was put into it. I believe that there is a great deal to be learned about the nature of human's sexuality. I learn by experiencing my own.

This man is a lawyer, but he could be a construction worker, a clerk, or a librarian. He makes several succinct points: lust negatively channels sexual energy. It stifles friendships with women and dominates any form of social interaction with them. We are reminded of a story told to us by another friend. He was entertaining a woman, who had been a friend of his for years, before she went on a date with another man. She was wearing beautiful, flowing clothes, and an alluring perfume and was looking astonishingly appealing. As they were embracing goodbye at the door, our friend said to her, "You look and smell so good. Why have we always been just friends?" She instantly replied with a playful smile, "Because it will last longer this way."

We would like to answer our friend's letter here and perhaps gain some insight into how to deal with the issue and problem of lust.

What should you do about the problem of lust? First pat yourself on the back for not pursuing your lust in a way that you would find self-destructive. Though it is a problem for you, you are well along in understanding the nature of your relationship with your own lustful feelings. It is all right to have the *thoughts* you describe, though it seems that you feel a strong sense of residual unrest at not being able to finally resolve the matter. You might discuss your feelings with your wife, who may be more compassionate and perceptive than you believe. Most or all men experience feelings similar to yours, and you can't resolve them simply by deciding you won't feel that way anymore. Feelings of lust are deeply ingrained in the psyches of men who are programmed to think this way in a sexist society. Start by telling yourself, "This is how I feel. I will consciously continue to deal with my sexual impulses in a mature way, even if it means I have to pretend in my behavior that I don't feel this way at all." In the first stages you'll have to deal with the problem mechanically until you are able to develop friendships with women outside of any sexually oriented dramas.

Now you can appreciate how women feel about sexual harassment in the marketplace, or why they resent the feelings that they must "pay off" after going out with a man. Perhaps you can also understand how men would respond if they became *sexual objects*, as some movie idols and rock stars are.

Men are "supposed" to be authentic, but you will not be betraying your real self by keeping your behavioral impulses to yourself. If you attempt to deny the feelings, they will not disappear, even if you no longer consciously experience them. They will instead emerge in other, more subtle ways that will perplex and trouble you more than the feelings of lust you describe. Only by accepting the feelings as a part of who you are can you affect changes. The "control" you say these feelings have over you is most likely a fear that you will act on them against your own best, conscious wishes. But you are bound to have sexual thoughts concerning every aspect of your life, and only by deciding that it is all right to feel them can you demystify them and become free of their dictates. That in itself will release the energy you speak of, the energy "experienced in its pure form as Love": love for your own wholeness as a human being, love for your creative impulses and sexual fantasies, love for your wife and family. You will *own* your passion, for life, for attractive women, without feeling compelled to translate it into behavior you would find demoralizing and counterproductive. You will laugh with it and move with it in grace; it will be one fundamental part of your being without overshadowing all the rest.

Historically, a woman's lustful feelings have been denied, or stereotyped as wicked, supernatural forces wielded by witches and demon-women. Lilith, the mythological seductress who destroyed men with her charms, and Circe, who enchanted Odysseus and turn his men into swine, are two examples from the literature. These accounts were written by men who undoubtedly found women's lust to be an overpowering, hypnotic source of energy.

In our own culture, women have traditionally repressed their lust and transmuted it into more socially acceptable, benign expressions. Typically, they are seen as lusting after rich husbands, diamonds and furs, security and illusions of romantic involvement (bolstered by the current popularity of Gothic novels). Women who admit to a fantasy life and who feel free to initiate sexual encounters with men (even their husbands) continue to be scrutinized as unladylike and aggressive. They are shackled with "bad reputations," labeled unfit mothers, and accused of trying to imitate a man's role.

This puts women, and men, in a double bind. Men often lament that women do not initiate sex often enough, or at all. When women actually do pursue a sexual encounter, however, men sometimes feel threatened or emasculated. Thus, women's lust becomes a threat to the man's sense of his masculinity. Marty Klein (1984) comments that men need to relinquish the adolescent model of sexuality in which sex is the main vehicle for feeling manly. Instead, better sex results when men focus on the pleasurable experience of sex. "Accepting a wider range of female sexual expression," he writes, "will, with time, certainly prove exciting and more satisfying for all concerned" (p. 29).

My Secret Garden by Nancy Friday and a number of other books by such authors as Anais Nin, Iris Murdoch, and Erica Jong have made it clear that women do indeed have fantasies and powerful sexual urges that can be expressed directly and with passion. The sexual thoughts span a broad range of ideas and experiences.

Male lust is usually more apparent and more easily observed; men's role as sexual predators creates more identifiable problems and has thus attracted more attention and social commentary. Women, however, tend to keep their lustful feelings more private; they struggle with them internally, weighing the relative benefits of expression versus repression. As such, the feelings are not often a societal problem, but they usually pose personal difficulties to the individual as compelling as the difficulties lust causes to men.

REFERENCES

Friday, N. *My Secret Garden: Women's Sexual Fantasies*. New York: Pocket Books, 1973.

Klein, M. "Do We Really Want Sexually Aggressive Women?" *Forum*, July 1984, pp. 26–29.

Nelson, J. B. *Embodiment: An Approach to Sexuality and Christian Theology*. Minneapolis: Augsburg Publishing House, 1978.

Webster's New World Dictionary of the American Language: Second College Edition. New York: Simon & Schuster, 1982.

CHAPTER 9

It's Not Okay to Be Antigay

Despite all the research done on the possible causes of homosexuality, society has still no idea what the causes are (any more than the causes of heterosexuality are known). Extensive research hasn't led to more and more understanding; in fact, it adds plausibility to the commonsense notion "the more we know, the less we know." The point is to poke fun at those researchers who "know." Once upon a time, all of us knew: if you had a weak father and a strong mother, the chances of becoming a homosexual were magnified. Most professionals in the field only recently discarded this theory. Apparently, researchers started out with the erroneous assumption that all homosexuals were in a state of arrested development. Lately, professionals have taken another look at American families: It appears that many consist of strong mothers and weak (or absent) fathers. In addition, nearly all the research on homosexuals has been done on patients in therapy. This would be analogous to concluding that heterosexuals are disturbed because about 95 percent of people in therapy are heterosexual.

Only one thing is known with reasonable certainty: Almost every homosexual was born to a heterosexual couple. The evidence of heredity, hormonal imbalance, and interactional patterns of parents is very sparse and lacking credibility.

Until the end of the nineteenth century, it was believed that people were either homosexual *or* heterosexual. Freud, however, postulated that all of us were born polymorphous perverse with a potential for bisexuality. Alfred Kinsey fairly well destroyed the either-or notion with his monumental research of the 1940s and 1950s. His work, conducted at the Institute for Sex Research in Indiana, suggests that people's sexual behavior could be categorized as follows:

0—Exclusively heterosexual behavior
1—Largely heterosexual but incidental homosexual behavior
2—Largely heterosexual but more than incidental homosexual behavior
3—Equal amount of heterosexual and homosexual behavior
4—Largely homosexual but more than incidental heterosexual behavior
5—Largely homosexual behavior but incidental heterosexual behavior
6—Exclusively homosexual behavior

Kinsey's studies found that about 4 percent of males and 2 percent of females were probably exclusively homosexual. By the time they reach middle age, about 50 percent of males and 29 percent of females have had an overt erotic experience with a member of their own sex. In addition, 37 percent of all males and 13 percent of females had at least one homosexual experience to the point of orgasm between adolescence and old age. The Institute for Sex Research defined a homosexual as anyone who has had more than six sexual experiences with members of their own gender. We don't happen to agree with this definition, but it is estimated that homosexuals constitute about 10 percent of the population of the United States. Though accuracy is uncertain, members of the homosexual community believe that less than 10 percent of the homosexual population has come "out of the closet," that is, publicly identify themselves as being gay.

Although homosexuality was accepted and even cherished by the ancient Greeks and some so-called primitive societies, in the western world it was, for the most part, both condemned and proscribed. The biblical injunctions against homosexuality resulted from the need to increase the size of the population, as well as from the limited knowledge of the subject at the time. The best, and in our judgment, the most sensitive review of religion and homosexuality may be found in Reverend John McNeill's book *The Church and the Homosexual.* Father McNeill is a Roman Catholic priest who has recently been silenced after his views became widely known and popular. His sympathetic understanding of homosexuality has also been supported by the Committee on Sexuality of the Catholic Theological Society of America, but not by either the pope or the majority of cardinals and bishops.

The 1973 decision of the American Psychiatric Association to modify homosexuality in its official "Diagnostic and Statistical Manual of Mental Disorders" provided a turning point for the professional community. The Association's declaration reads as follows:

Whereas homosexuality *per se* implies no impairment of judgment, stability, reliability or general vocational capabilities, therefore be it resolved that the American Psychiatric Association deplores all public and private discrimination against homosexuals in such areas as employment, housing, public accommodations and licensing and . . . that the American Psychiatric Association supports and urges the repeal of all legislation making criminal offenses of all sexual acts performed by consenting adults in private (1973).

This position covers only those homosexuals who accept their homosexuality. Those who are in conflict can still be diagnosed as "sexual orientation disturbance" as against the previous category "constitutional psychopathic inferior."

A majority of professionals now support the position taken by the American Psychiatric Association. Furthermore, almost all western European countries, as well as about twenty-four American states, have repealed laws that make consensual adult homosexual behavior a crime.

Though the causes of homosexuality are hotly debated, leading scholars have reached a consensus that a person's sexual orientation is largely determined by the age of four or five. Many homosexual individuals do not become aware of their homosexual orientation until long after this formative period, perhaps in their late teens or twenties (some postmenopausal widowed women become homosexual after their fifties and sixties, with no prior homosexual history). The political and personal ramifications of this are powerful, since it is often alleged that people "choose" to be homosexual, or "switch" to homosexuality as a conscious decision after a painful divorce, after being raped, etc. Choice certainly exists over with whom to engage in sexual activity, but a basic sexual orientation is not subject to such dramatic change. Much of the animosity toward homosexuals seems to be grounded in the belief that homosexuals deliberately adopt this orientation as a means of belittling heterosexual family values and flaunt themselves outrageously.

Crusades against homosexual rights ordinances in many cities are based on the popular myths about the seduction and recruitment of children into the homosexual lifestyle. Fear of this is often cited as justification for preventing the hiring of homosexuals in public schools. Yet, established research in the field documents that in less than 10 percent of the instances of child molestation, teachers actively seduced children of the same sex. In any case, more than 90 percent of all child molestation in schools involves heterosexual males and is directed at females. Should heterosexual males be barred from teaching in the public schools? Even if sexual identity were not determined by age five, it would be unrealistic to think that in a school where the teaching staff consists of 90 percent heterosexuals and 10 percent homosexuals, most of the children would flock to the latter. Can heterosexuals be so easily eliminated as role models for children?

Regarding rights and discrimination, the majority of well-informed people in the country consider people who happen to be homosexual to be entitled to the same civil rights as heterosexuals. There are those, like Jerry Falwell and others, who argue against civil rights for homosexuals. Falwell has made nonsensical statements, among them, "If God had wanted homosexuals, He would have created Adam and Steve."

Suppose we responded by saying, "If God had wanted black people, He would have created Adam and Sheba." What would you call us, religious or just plain racist?

IF YOU THINK YOU'RE HOMOSEXUAL

The period of late adolescence and young adulthood (ages 18 to 25) is a critical time for understanding one's sexuality. Sexual experiences and relationships develop, and confronting a growing awareness of one's homosexuality can be an agonizing process. Who should be told? Is it all right to act on these sexual desires? Would my friends reject me if they found out?

In our judgment, erotic desire or fantasy do not constitute the main element in determining a person's sexuality. Our definition of a homosexual is pragmatic: "A person who, in his or her adult life, has and prefers sexual relations with members of the same sex." A person could have many homosexual fantasies and experiences and still not be a homosexual. Recent Masters and Johnson (1979) studies reveal that even exclusive heterosexuals acknowledge having homosexual fantasies. The idea that thoughts and even some experiences make one a homosexual could have a devastating impact on a person's life.

If you think you're homosexual or bisexual, don't punish yourself for it because some elements of society believe it's wrong. People typically discover their homosexual orientation in an unfolding process over many years. The process may include sexual experiences with members of both sexes that help to confirm or disconfirm one's feelings about oneself. Psychotherapy may be part of this period, though it certainly is not necessary for the great majority. It is difficult to estimate the proportion of people who go on to accept their homosexual orientation versus those who adopt a more heterosexual orientation. If a person feels that he or she is gay, yet, at the same time, wants to fight it ("to be cured"), the initial rejection of homosexual feelings uses up most of the energy needed to effect the change. In a sense, one needs to say, If I am, I am, but if I could figure a way out of it, I'd prefer it.

Most psychotherapists believe that people who are 6 on the Kinsey scale are *constitutional* homosexuals and, thus, their sexual orientation cannot be changed any more than a *fixed* heterosexual's orientation (0 on the Kinsey scale) can be changed. Masters and Johnson (1979) were criticized for their claim that they "cured" around 70 percent of well-motivated homosexuals who came to them for help. Their critics suggested that these patients were not fixed homosexuals (6 on the scale), but rather more like the 2s, 3s and 4s on the Kinsey scale.

These classifications may represent those people who are bisexuals. Bisexuality is a phenomenon that is not well researched or understood. It does not mean being equally attracted to both sexes; it simply means that one is capable of being attracted to and sexually active with members of either sex. The evidence is strong that bisexuality is not just a *cover* for homosexuality. It is an authentic sexual orientation that is upsetting to some but pleasurable to others.

It is usually psychologically better if one can tell parents and friends, acknowledge one's sexual orientation, and not worry about being "found out." Today's reality, although better than the reality of even ten years ago, doesn't permit us to be heroes in somebody else's situation. Only the people who are involved suffer the consequences. Sometimes the emotional fallout doesn't settle for years, and there is a lasting discomfort during family get-togethers. One college sophomore came out to his family, and his mother and three brothers accepted this news immediately without great stress. But the father was adamant, and refused to let his son come home for visits, cut off financial support for his college education, and refused even to talk with his son on the telephone. Tension between the mother and father escalated to the point of separation.

There is no fault to be attributed to the act of coming out in this situation, and although the father's reaction was indefensible, that's the reality in some families. There exist countless other anecdotes where, despite an initial period of rejection, the family mobilized itself and eventually accepted the fact of having a homosexual member.

Some friends may drop you, some for good, others only for as long as it takes for them to accept the news. It is sad that some homosexuals end up with only other homosexuals as friends, just as often happens among other minority groups who associate only with each other, such as the disabled, or blacks. This works both ways. White heterosexuals are similarly limited by their associations with other white heterosexuals who are not disabled, or minority, or "different."

Even in this area, however, some changes can be observed. The class in human sexuality at Syracuse University we teach each semester provides data on a number of key sexual issues. Fifteen years ago only a few hands were raised in response to the question, Do you know a homosexual well? Today, almost every hand goes up, an indication that although the incidence of homosexuality has remained the same, people's (at least students') attitudes have undergone some evolution.

It is important to realize that most homosexuals manage extremely well. They are mature, healthy people who are contributing, responsible members of society. Although significant numbers are neurotic, this can be said about heterosexuals also. Perhaps one day a person's sexual orientation will be of no concern to anyone. People will be judged by their character and actions. Homosexuality is not a lifestyle—it is a sex style. Homosexuals exist in all walks of life. They espouse the same range of political and philosophical positions as found among heterosexuals.

The act of coming out and making a statement of affirmation is significant and often heroic, but only because gay men and lesbian women continue to be oppressed. Former President Carter has suggested the following train of thought:

> What has caused the highly publicized confrontation on homosexuality is the desire
> of homosexuals for the rest of society to approve and add its acceptance of homosex-

uality as a normal sexual relationship. I don't feel that it's a normal sexual relationship. (Playboy, 1976)

He then adds the following:

But at the same time, I don't feel that society, through its laws, ought to abuse and harass the homosexual.

The issue, however, is not nearly as much a desire for acceptance of homosexuality as a normal sexual relationship, as concern for civil and legal rights. Take, for example, New York City, which has a policy not to renew government sponsorship for groups that provide social services and which also discriminate against homosexuals. The Roman Catholic Diocese of the city, led by Archbishop John J. O'Connor, vowed in late 1984 to forgo tens of millions of dollars in funding rather than change its policy against the hiring of homosexuals.

It is all right to have your personal opinion about homosexuality. In our view, it's not acceptable to harass or to discriminate just because you are in a position to do so. What consenting adults do in private is no one's business. There is something wrong with people who intrude into other people's private affairs. People who inspire the least respect are those who use the Bible to justify their hatred or bigotry. God's message to all of us is to love thy neighbor as thyself.

This is of great concern in the homosexual community, where the loathing of heterosexuals combines with the self-hatred of many homosexuals to create great tension. Some straights can be heard saying such things as If a faggot so much as comes near me, I'll kill him. Why does it have to be murder? Can't no thank you suffice? Among homosexuals, the psychological and physical violence from the outside can be overwhelming, and it is very likely this violence that has given rise to large homosexual communities in such cities as San Francisco and New York. Here, living among peers serves both a protective and a social purpose. Homosexuals must fight harder to survive in, say, a midwestern industrial city than in New York City.

That is an important consideration if you are homosexual. Certainly it will be easier to resolve your own personal struggles if you don't have to cope daily with hostility from people who are threatened by your sexual orientation. It's a trade-off if you elect to remain in the closet; then there is no need to deal with people's reactions, but there is the anxiety that comes with living a life that is unauthentic to yourself.

Self-esteem and self-acceptance are major issues for homosexuals, and there exist no easy ways to achieve them. Those who are not blessed with a ready understanding and acceptance of themselves must struggle. Brian McNaught, one of the most eloquent spokespersons from the gay movement, talks of how homosexuals are raised with the same sick jokes about queers and faggots as are the rest of society. It is sad and ironic, he writes, that some homosexuals have learned to call themselves "faggots," in the same way that blacks often jokingly call each other "nigger."

Beyond the issue of public versus private identity, the crucial issue for most homosexuals concerns the nature of their intimate relationships. The script for heterosexuals is well-defined: marriage. But for gay men and lesbian women, society offers no such covenant. The public image of homosexuals, especially men, is that their relationships are consummated in restrooms and bath houses, furtively sneaked behind bushes in public parks or in back rooms of gay bars. There is little recognition of enduring love and commitment between homosexuals in the public eye. The book, *The Male Couple*, by McWhirter and Madison (1984) gives ample testimony to enduring homosexual relationships.

Ongoing relationships between homosexual partners make many heterosexuals anxious; if they can characterize all sexual activity between gays and lesbians as impersonal and "immoral" they can rigidly maintain their rejection of homosexuals themselves. The notion that loving, caring relationships might develop threatens these attitudes.

For homosexuals themselves, committed, perhaps live-together relationships represent more of an "advertisement" to the outside world of their sexual orientation. It's fair to say that much of the alleged promiscuity among homosexuals is partly a response to the hostility of straights; impersonal sex, or short-term liaisons, are most easily kept secret. Among the gay community, many voices have been raised in protest against the self-damaging nature of multiple sexual partners. Fear of AIDS (see Chapter 20) and herpes is credited in part with more conservative sexual behaviors among gays.

The AIDS scare has also served to highlight another dimension of the dilemma: casual sex undermines many people's desires for loving, intimate relationships. In truth, the degree of promiscuity among homosexuals has been grossly exaggerated by the media. Many gays do not have one-night stands frequently, though they struggle with the same issues of monogamy and fidelity as do the rest of the population. It has been suggested by some antihomosexual factions that AIDS is the plague sent by God to punish homosexuals for their sins. It might just as well be claimed that legionnaires disease was sent by God to punish legionnaires. Hypocrisy often requires such nonsensical comparisons to reveal its true nature.

A great number of homosexuals enter into heterosexual marriages, and many have children. A young woman attending a large California university loved a young man deeply, though she was troubled by their infrequent, unsatisfying sexual relations. When she began making remarks about marriage, her lover informed her of his predominantly homosexual orientation and said that he'd like to marry her anyway. She felt tremendously conflicted over her decision and ultimately chose not to marry him. They remained close friends, however, and several years later he attended this young woman's wedding to another man.

On the other hand, when Ann Landers printed a letter in her column from a woman married to a homosexual male, she received hundreds of letters from women married to homosexual men. The women's letters said, in effect, that they had better marriages than most of their friends who were married to heterosexuals. Of course, a large number of women are very distraught when such news is revealed.

Some homosexuals, in gay, lesbian, and heterosexual relationships, have adopted children or had their own biological children. There is no evidence to suggest that children raised in these homes are influenced in any way to become homosexual themselves, or that they develop problems in greater proportion than other children. Among some segments of society, some opposition to the adoption of children by homosexuals exists. Yet, all people who support the rights of homosexuals to adopt believe that they should meet the same criteria as heterosexual parents must: would they be good parents? Provide a good home, nutrition, loving support? Would they be stable emotionally, vocationally? There is a short supply of white infants for adoption, but tens of thousands of other children who are disabled, minorities, or over five years of age are candidates for adoption. Why eliminate homosexuals as prospective adoptive parents?

Most studies, as well as our personal experience, reveal that most homosexuals do form affectionate, enduring relationships. Some couples are married in homosexual churches and their vows have for them great meaning, though no legal contract is involved. This legal exclusion has many practical implications: joint income taxes cannot be filed; partners may not be able to be beneficiaries on life insurance policies, or to rent living quarters that prohibit occupancy by unrelated tenants; partners cannot be included on each other's health insurance policies and may be prohibited from visiting an ill lover in the hospital because they are not immediate family.

Homophobia, though alleged to be rampant in our contemporary society, seems to afflict men in far greater numbers than women. It's best defined as a fear of homosexuals, or a fear of being diagnosed as homosexual, or a fear of being seen as effeminate, nonmasculine. Homophobia is a metaphor for a fear of being different in any of countless ways. It interferes with friendships and the expression of affection among members of the same sex. Even more profoundly, it emerges as justification for the above-mentioned denial of civil rights and an alienation of segments of society from each other.

FOR PARENTS AND POTENTIAL PARENTS

It is understandable for parents to hope their children will not grow up to be homosexuals. Owing to the hostility emanating from society, and the antihomosexual messages individuals receive as part of their upbringing, strong wishes for heterosexual children are not surprising. People often misinterpret the meanings of their children's behavior, however, and conclude that the child is, or is becoming, homosexual.

A true story might provide an appropriate illustration. Two fourteen-year-old boys regularly went to the attic after selling newspapers. There they would masturbate each other while looking at "girlie" magazines belonging to one of the boys' father. On one occasion one of the boys picked up a male body-builder magazine and looked at it. The other boy immediately said, "What's the matter with you, are you a faggot?" The fear that the partner might be homosexual negated the pleasurable experience. This story, described to us by one of our students, illustrates how ludicrous thinking can be about the topic. Both boys grew up heterosexual. Neither has been known to have any further homosexual interests or experiences.

Out of a wish to prevent their children from becoming homosexual, parents often treat their children in strange ways. For instance, fathers may withhold affection from their sons or push them into rough contact sports. Mothers may discourage children of either sex from participating in cross-sex activities. Most research to date, however, reports that fathers reinforce sex-role stereotypes more than mothers do and are thus more influential in their children's sex-role development. *No evidence* exists that parental behaviors one way or another can either encourage or discourage the development of homosexuality in their offspring.

It is important to teach children that they are not at fault if propositioned by a homosexual, or a heterosexual, nor are they to be blamed if approached by a rapist or child molester. Rather, they must be taught to protect themselves. It must be emphasized here that 75 percent of the victims of child molesters are children who have been entrusted to their care. The molester is often a child's own parent. *All* child molesters, regardless of their sexual orientation, require professional counseling (see Chapter 13).

Let's return to our original position: It is perfectly all right not to want your child (or yourself) to be a homosexual, even if you are a liberal and strongly endorse gay rights. The real question is what to do if your teenager approaches you at age fifteen and says that he or she is gay or lesbian.

Parents need to be perfectly sympathetic: no jokes, no derisive comments such as, You must be kidding, or You'll get over it. Don't rush your child to a physician or psychiatrist to "get cured." The best first response is, I'm so glad you feel free to tell us (me) about this. Let's talk. How long have you felt this way? How do you feel about it? The point is to encourage a full and open discussion.

Parents may want to say to the child (or preferably, think it), I hope you aren't homosexual, but if you are, you remain my child. I will love you no less for it. I'm with you all the way. The part that must be verbalized is, I'm with you all the way.

Children should be encouraged to be openminded and to make no final decision about the matter until adulthood. Just as most parents do not favor heterosexual experiences for teenagers, they also oppose homosexual ones. Even if the youngster has had an experience (or a few), it is best for parents to discourage these experiences or relationships. Try not to give the message that homosexuality is evil or sinful: simply convey that the teenager is too young to decide. In any case, a few fantasies or even a pleasurable experience are not sufficient grounds for a lifetime decision.

It is true that this position is not evenhanded. For example, if a youngster suggested that he or she was heterosexual, parents wouldn't want to suggest waiting until adulthood before making this decision. This perspective can't be justified rationally, and yet not everything in life is fair and just. (But even so, our laws should be.)

Young people have declared themselves to be homosexual and have then been rejected by their families. The rejection has created enormous problems and has even resulted in many (especially males) becoming prostitutes. Some of these teenagers, however, have been successfully placed in foster homes that were headed by lesbian couples. This has proven both therapeutic and rewarding for all concerned. Although this involves only a small number of people, one needs to recognize that innovative approaches are being sought and have proved successful.

Teenagers, and even college-age students, who *come out* typically encounter severe ostracism. Very few schools or peer groups can tolerate this kind of acknowledgment. Yet some young people would be greatly relieved if their sexual orientation were revealed. In some of the larger cities in this country, gay and lesbian groups have provided clubs and recreational facilities for adolescents and young adults who want to identify themselves as homosexual. In general, these are few and far between and could serve only a small fraction of young people.

The following case study could be illuminating from a number of perspectives. A nineteen-year-old male student came to one of us and said, "I was one of your students. I need help. I have something terrible to confess. Can I trust you?" He received the following response: "No." He, in turn, responded, "What do you mean? You are supposed to be trusted." "I know, but I don't know you. I don't know if I can be helpful. You don't know me. Trust comes only at the end of a relationship. All meaningful exchanges between people involve risk." The student, getting the point, said, "Okay, I'll risk it. I'm homosexual." The conversation continued as follows:

Me: Do you want to be a homosexual?
Him: Of course not.
Me: Have you ever had a homosexual experience?
Him: Of course not, what do you take me for?
Me: I don't know yet. Have you ever had a heterosexual experience?
Him: Of course not, I'm a homosexual. You're making fun of me.
Me: So far the diagnosis is antisexual. Tell me your life history.

As the story unfolded, he recalled having had homosexual fantasies at age twelve or thirteen. He didn't know that they were normal. He felt overwhelmed with guilt and feared being "queer." The more guilt, the more compelling and more obsessive the thoughts; it became a self-fulfilling prophecy. On entering college, he searched for his identity in the index of a psychiatric textbook. It didn't help because he had never had a homosexual experience, so he consulted an advanced psychiatric textbook, where he found the concept of latent homosexuality. He was then fully self-diagnosed, without having had any sexual experience.

Although some professionals disagree, our view is that "latency" is a figment of the psychiatric imagination. You might as well say that all women are latently pregnant. A person who is afraid of being homosexual or afraid of homosexuals isn't necessarily homosexual. It just means that the person is afraid. The fear may be irrational, but no generalizations about its meaning can validly be made.

The above case history is important because there are many individuals who suffer from misinformation, teasing, or downright harassment. Peers often cruelly accuse people of being queer or gay because they don't conform to popular stereotypes. The so-called effeminate male or butch female—blatant types who flaunt their homosexuality, often to protest the hostility of the "straights"—constitute a small percentage of homosexuals in our society. It is terribly important to support people who are harassed or in any way threatened by a peer group.

What if all societal prohibitions and inhibitions relative to the free expression of our sexuality were eliminated, and it was acknowledged that all people were potentially bisexual? In all probability, about 90 percent of people would opt for a basic heterosexual orientation anyway. They might not, however, be so homophobic or attach so much significance to occasional homosexual thoughts or experiences. To pursue the speculation all the way, about 4 percent would opt for a basic homosexual orientation, 5 percent would be bisexual and 1 percent celibate.

Many families do not have to deal with a member's homosexuality because this information is not confided. Some parents prefer not to know. There are those who know and prefer to pretend they don't.

There also exist families who never got along well but who developed a new family solidarity when a son or daughter revealed a homosexual orientation. Being taken into confidence is a sign of trust, and despite the despair and anxiety, parents who accept their child's reality can be more helpful than the parents who are rejecting. It is always a mistake to break off communication with a child no matter what he or she has done. Excellent books in this area are Laura Hobson's sensitive novel based on her personal experiences *Consenting Adult* and *Now That You Know: What Every Parent Should Know About Homosexuality* by Fairchild and Haywood. Also, get in touch with the National Gay Task Force (80 Fifth Avenue, New York, New York 10011). This group can put you in touch with other families who are willing to serve in a supporting capacity. Some courageous parents have marched with their homosexual children in parades for gay rights carrying signs that read We are proud of our gay children.

Some readers may be confronted with a parent's acknowledgment of his or her homosexuality. At first, this may contradict one's very beliefs about human sexuality: people who reproduce are surely heterosexuals. It can also be very unsettling to learn that a parent, whom one has known all one's life, could harbor such a secret. Children of parents who come out sometimes feel rejected, and during a period of transition may have little contact with the gay parent. Generally, however, with time comes the realization that the parent loves the child no less, and that the homosexuality has little direct significance to the child. When friends and acquaintances hear the news, some may react with disapproval or even disgust, but others will offer the same friendship and support as they had previously. It is important for children of homosexuals to understand that they need not feel stigmatized (and that homosexuality in a parent does not mean the child now will develop in that direction). Only through this process will the child be able to eventually accept the parent.

What if your spouse reveals or is found out to be homosexual or bisexual? A similar situation was described once by a woman seeking help from "Dear Abby." Her letter prompted responses from a "surprising number of readers" who said they were happily married to bisexual mates. A typical letter revealed a woman who had been married to a bisexual man for thirty-three years. They had four wonderful children, all of whom grew up to be heterosexuals and didn't love their father less when told as adults about their father's sexual orientation. Another letter from a woman married to a "gay" suggested that their everyday relationship was more important than his occasional extramarital encounters.

It has been fashionable to assume that a marriage can't work when one of the partners is homosexual or bisexual. This is not true. Professionals are beginning to realize that a large number of such marriages are working out, while many fail. More often than not, one partner, as is true with heterosexual marriages, cannot tolerate the *extramarital* sexual relationship, regardless of its orientation.

For years we have been conducting a survey among Syracuse University students. One of the questions, along with possible responses, reads as follows:

You discover that your best friend is homosexual when he or she reveals that he or she would like to have a sexual experience with you. What is your response likely to be?

1. One of distress. I would want to terminate the relationship.
2. I would refuse the invitation and say that our friendship depended on the homosexuality being kept private so that I wouldn't be subject to embarrassment.
3. I would refuse the invitation, but say that his/her homosexuality would not affect our friendship.
4. I might consider experimenting once with such an invitation, even though I'm pretty sure I'm heterosexual.
5. I would be pleased.

Of the 420 students responding to the most recent survey (Fall, 1983), 17.1 percent gave number one as an answer; 11.3 percent responded with number two. 59.5 percent indicated number three. 6.9 percent responded with number four. 1.6 percent selected number five. 3.6 percent gave no response at all. Over the past ten years, of more than 9000 students, the percentage of individuals giving a number three response has increased slightly each year from a base response of 45 percent.

Society is making progress, though many myths prevail. People still think that homosexuality is hereditary. Not a shred of evidence suggests this. Others insist on hormonal imbalance. There exists some very slight, but not very convincing, evidence

Happy Anniversary Ray . . .
Love, Brian

by Brian McNaught

Some time in May, Ray and I will have been together six years. There won't be any cake or flowers or hurt feelings if the day is not remembered because we don't celebrate one day as our "anniversary" and we wouldn't know which day to pick.

From what I understand, six years is the current national average length for heterosexual marriages. I'm not sure what the national average is for gay couples but I would imagine it's probably about the same. We seem to share the same reasons for coming together and the same reasons for breaking apart. And why shouldn't we? What we do in bed doesn't alter the fact we all are human and seek security, approval and the satisfaction of our dreams. We also get bored, possessive and demanding.

Especially today, with many straight couples not wanting children and several gay couples now having them, with liberated men and women abandoning preconceived gender roles and with most couples deciding for themselves the meaning of relationships, gay and straight couples are very much the same. With that in mind, many of our straight friends are curious about the success of our relationship.

It is not the length of time which merits us their label of "success" but rather the openness, sensitivity and laughter which characterize our time together. Our love for one another is gentle and yet energizing; it is constant though not unquestioned. Our relationship is not the ideal because each relationship is unique, but it is near perfect for us. I rely upon it but try not to presume upon it. If I quit growing, the relationship will end. If the relationship quits growing, again, it will die.

When Ray and I came together, we did so as strangers and roommates. Each having recently left a disappointing relationship, we openly swore that we would never again bother to get involved. We felt especially safe around each other, for though we became fast friends, we weren't each other's "types." For us, there was no "magic," no long days when we couldn't concentrate because we were preoccupied with thoughts of the other, no "hot flashes" when the other appeared in front of the television in a bathrobe.

Because we were friends, we talked a lot, or perhaps, we became friends because we communicated honestly. We enjoyed each other's company and laughed at the same jokes, usually mine. Ray liked being with my family and we shared many other interests, like social justice issues, bridge and good food. As mature gay men, we felt comfortable expressing the affection of our friendship sexually. Though we didn't satisfy each other's fantasies of the perfect body, we found that, in bed, we composed symphonies.

"This is really nice, but remember," we would each warn the other, "I'm not interested in another relationship." Yet, we did prefer each other's company and

continued

neither of us ventured off on our own into the world where our fantasies might be realized; at least not when we had the choice of being with the other.

We never announced we were in a relationship, but we were aware that it had happened. Ray insists it took me over a year before I would let down my guard. I'm not sure how it occurred but I know it happened gently. That's why I encourage people to refrain from opening joint checking accounts or from buying any major item together until they have been together at least a year. If you are not ready for relationship, you don't need financial pressure to keep you in one.

We began our time together insisting upon sexual openness and then soon discovered that we both operated under double standards. "I know that I can have sex outside of the relationship and that it doesn't affect the way I feel about you, but I don't trust that you can do the same," we would say to each other. Because of our fears, we then opted to be genitally exclusive. Later we wanted to open things up and then, again, decided to be what is erroneously called "monogamous." Finally we decided not to decide.

"But you *must* decide!" a therapist demanded of us. "No we don't," we said at what was to be our last visit. If we label our relationship "monogamous," we know it causes unnecessary tension. There is nothing more exciting than forbidden fruit. And, if we call it "open," we seem to be insisting that something must happen. We would rather say we trust the love of the other and though we hope we are never confronted in an embarrassing way by the activities of the other, we won't fall apart if either of us has sex outside of the relationship.

We do other screwy things too. For instance, we each have our own bedroom. And I'm not saying this for you, Mom. I'm a thrasher and upon entering a bed, I immediately pull the covers out and wrap myself up in a variety of spontaneous folds. Ray sleeps perfectly still and can make his bed in less than 30 seconds. Besides, we like our space.

"But you *can't* have separate bedrooms," insist many of the people who tour the house. "Sleeping together is the best part of a relationship!" Not for us. Besides, whose business is it anyway? As with the understanding about the code of sexual conduct, everything is individual. What matters most is that you talk honestly about your needs and your feelings and that you listen intently when the other does the same. Then, the name of the game is compromise.

Our ability to communicate in an atmosphere of trust and support has enabled us to talk about issues such as the disparity of our incomes, the hostility of some relatives, the concern over social behavior, sexual needs, household tasks, materialism and spiritual hunger. We know we are pioneers. We know that we don't have any healthy straight or gay role models to whom we can turn, so we need to struggle with each issue as it comes up. Past mistakes, made by both our parents and ourselves in previous relationships, have helped steer us clear of destructive behavior. Our relationship works because it authentically reflects our individual uniqueness.

What's funny about our experience is that we have become each other's type. Today there is magic. Today we are often distracted during the day by thoughts of the other. Today, there are "hot flashes." Though we probably relate no more often than

continued

any other couple, gay or straight, who have been together six years, our sex is rarely, if ever, boring. Yet, sex is still low on our list of priorities.

Relationship for us is a wonderful way of growing to our full potential, of experiencing God in an unique way and of celebrating daily life at its best. It requires work, self-sacrifice, openness, risk, patience, attention and commitment.

I used to believe that everybody in a relationship envied those who were "on the prowl" and vice versa. I no longer envy people who are single but nor do I think everyone ought to be or needs to be in a committed relationship. A person has to want it, be ready for it and understand that love is not something that happens at the beginning, but later on, when you've worked hard and when you least suspect it. Whether you're gay or straight, the effect is the same.

Postscript: Three years have passed since our sixth anniversary and we continue to grow in love. Not much has really changed: We still refuse to define our relationship as "monogamous" or "open"; we still work hard at communicating in an atmosphere of trust and support and we still laugh a lot. What has changed is that we now share the same bed. I'm still a thrasher and Ray continues to sleep perfectly still. The entire bed is a mess by morning, but we share the burden of my ways. On weekdays I tuck in the king size sheets the folks sent for Christmas and on weekends, Ray makes the bed.

Brain McNaught is an award-winning freelance writer, lecturer, and certified sex counselor. He and Ray live in Gloucester, Massachusetts with their Irish Setter, Jeremy, and their canary, Bing Crosby.

in this direction. The strong mother, weak father theory keeps cropping up in various disguises such as the seductive mother and rejecting or passive father. Few homosexuals themselves endorse the neat categories developed even by some respectable researchers in the field. The best research we know about, however, supports the view that cause is still unknown (see C. A. Tripp, *The Homosexual Matrix*).

There are fathers who are reluctant to be affectionate with their sons after age five or six for fear that the child will become homosexual. This is unjustified and very distressing to the child. Some parents overreact to their children's play when it is not according to long-standing stereotypes. This occurs especially with boys who are fond of dressing in women's clothing or like to play with dolls, or girls who are tough and like sports. Certain parents are upset because their young sons like to read a lot. Though these may be signs that the child is growing up homosexual, the chances are that intervention will not alter the situation.

Some of the most creative people in our society have reported childhood experiences that included long periods of isolation, accusations of effeminate behavior, or an overtly affectionate relationship with the mother. Most grow up to be heterosexual, though some become homosexual. It is probably true that a disproportionate number (perhaps as high as 15 percent) of well-known writers, composers, artists, and dancers have been known to be homosexual. Professionals don't know why this is so, but it still remains true that 85 percent of people in these categories are heterosexual.

Homosexuals are more visible these days, yet no evidence exists to suggest that there are, in fact, more homosexuals. The real change lies in the fact that they are more open to discussion and generally more accepting of themselves.

People often speak about homosexuality in prison. It is well known that almost all violent incidents related to homosexual behavior in prison are perpetrated by *heterosexuals* who take advantage of weaker inmates. This point illustrates the need to distinguish between "transitional" homosexuality that takes place in situations where members of the opposite sex are not available (prisons, during warfare, and at same-sex boarding schools and colleges) and *constitutional* or *fixed* homosexuality. If people are not of this latter type, one can expect them to revert to their former sexual orientation when no longer forced to live only with members of their own sex.

Despite significant improvements in the last decade, popular polls and recent municipal elections suggest that a large number of Americans do not approve of gay rights. One need recall that our Constitution was designed to protect the basic rights of a minority, even if a majority does not approve. If our black population had to wait for a majority of people in the country to accept "equality of all before the law," we would still be where we were before the landmark Civil Rights Act of the recent past.

REFERENCES

American Psychiatric Association. Press release, 1973.

DeFrancis, V. *National Analysis of Official Child Neglect and Abuse Reporting*. Denver: American Humane Association, 1983.

Hobson, L. Z. *Consenting Adult*. New York: Warner Books, 1976.

Kinsey, A. C. et al. *Sexual Behavior in the Human Male*. Philadelphia: W. B. Saunders, 1948.

Kinsey, A. C. et al. *Sexual Behavior in the Human Female*. Philadelphia: W. B. Saunders, 1953.

Masters, W., & Johnson, V. *Homosexuality in Perspective*. Boston: Little, Brown, 1979.

McNaught, B. *A Disturbed Peace*. Washington, DC: Dignity, 1981.

McNeill, J. J. *The Church and the Homosexual*. New York: Pocket Books, 1976.

McWhirter, D. P., & Madison, A. M. *The Male Couple—How Relationships Develop.* Englewood Cliffs, NJ: Prentice-Hall, 1984.

Tripp, C. *The Homosexual Matrix.* New York: McGraw-Hill, 1975.

RECOMMENDED READING

Fairchild, B., & Hayward, W. *Now That You Know: What Every Parent Should Know about Homosexuality.* New York: Harcourt, Brace, Jovanovich, 1979.

CHAPTER 10

Sexual Experiences You Feel Guilty or Angry About

It's been written that in being born, males struggle violently to get out of the birth canal and then spend the rest of their lives trying to get back in. A corresponding piece of folklore, first proposed by Freud as "penis envy," postulates that women wish strongly to possess the organ that they were born without. The truth is that all people are born sexually inexperienced and along the way toward discovering sexuality have a range of experiences, some good, some bad, and some mediocre. In the process, nearly everybody has sexual encounters that they regret, feel angry about, or that produce an enduring sense of guilt.

These feelings may arise from a myriad of different situations. A college junior complained to his closest friend that he was feeling terribly guilty. He was engaged to a lovely young woman whom he'd been seeing for about two years, and yet recently had had a brief, intense sexual encounter with another woman. He didn't love this other woman, but he got carried away and felt overwhelmed with despair. In exploring the issue, it was discovered that his guilt derived from his fiancée's finding out, not from the fact that he had made a mistake. He acknowledged that he was vulnerable to outside temptations and couldn't be sure it wouldn't happen again. After all, he reasoned, he was young and didn't want to deprive himself of spontaneous experiences.

This is a good example to illustrate two varieties of guilt: *mature* and *immature*, or rational and irrational. Rational guilt occurs when individuals feel they have done something wrong, and they wish to avoid making the same mistake in the future. It will result in a sense of expiation and motivate people in the direction of asking forgiveness from themselves and/or from others. Mature guilt acts as a caution against making the same mistake again; it organizes you and stimulates you to do the right thing the next time around.

The young man in the example above, on the other hand, was experiencing immature, irrational guilt. The only thing "wrong" about which he felt guilt was his fiancée's discovering his behavior. This kind of irrational guilt disorganizes people and creates the atmosphere wherein the same experience can be repeated. This couple's relationship was in jeopardy, and it was clear that his guilt was going to serve no constructive purpose. In effect, this young man had at least two choices: he could either accept his need for sexual diversity or commit himself to a monogamous relationship with his fiancée.

For some people, guilt is a constant companion to sexuality, whether or not they are sexually experienced. A deep sense of pervasive guilt over sexual thoughts and feelings and fantasies often springs from early childhood, along with messages one perceives from parents and society. Such feelings, which are often disconnected from any actual experiences, are nearly always irrational (as detailed elsewhere in the book, all sexual fantasies and turn-ons are normal). Mature guilt seems to be time-limiting, whereas immature guilt often becomes obsessive and requires no real incident to trigger its emergence. It is often the case (though certainly not always) that such irrational guilt is more difficult to alleviate. The more disabling your guilt is (in the respect that it interferes significantly with your enjoyment of friends, school, family) the more strongly you may want to consider some professional help in understanding it.

A lasting sense of guilt can also grow from compulsively repeating the same mistakes over and over again. One woman in her early twenties who was being seen in therapy revealed that over the years she had engaged in a series of brief, unsatisfying sexual encounters, many of them one-night stands. She felt terribly guilty and hated herself for these experiences, yet felt unable to stop or to behave differently with men. She reported feeling desperate that she wouldn't ever get married or find a man to love her as deeply as she needed to be loved. She was vulnerable to a man's suggestion that they have sex; she was nearly unable to say no, and several times had contracted a sexually transmitted disease. For a time when she was involved with a man, she was unable to tell him that intercourse was painful for her; she wanted him to see only her happy, joyful side, not the angry, moody, jealous, "bad" side.

The situation came to a head when she became pregnant and had to choose among an out-of-wedlock childbirth, adoption, or abortion. After her abortion, she began to understand more fully her sexual masochism and guilt, which invariably were used to express hostility at herself. The things that she desired most in life—love and intimacy—had become the things that were most hurtful to her. She realized that her strongest guilt came from the feeling, both conscious and unconscious, that she was unworthy to have the love she needed. Once these things became more apparent, she gradually became able to exercise more control over her sexual behavior.

Why do people say yes to requests for sexual behaviors when they mean no? Carol

Cassell comments on the dilemma for women (*Swept Away*, 1984): "The central fact—and fault—of women's sexuality is that all too often we deny responsibility for it: we wrap our desire in a cloak of romance, need 'love' in order to have sex" (p. 24). In this way, women have sex because of a possibility of love, and men more often have sex because of the possibility of sex. Impulsive decisions made in this way are inevitably disappointing—the chances of forming a loving relationship based on first impressions are scant.

Cassell doesn't suggest that brief encounters are always inappropriate. She does emphasize that women need to be clear about the agenda. The agenda might mean that the woman desires an interesting interaction with a man that includes sexual involvement, and she's not hoping for any relationship beyond that. Trouble develops when the man and woman's agendas conflict with each other, usually with one person desiring more commitment than the other. When the agenda is not explicit between people, this generates guilt, anger, and hostility. Sometimes people worry that if they do verbalize their intentions (e.g., I'm interested in spending an exciting evening with you, no strings attached or I really care about you and hope that we'll be seeing more of each other, but I'm not ready for sex just yet), this leaves little room for romance and spontaneity. Usually this is an unjustified fear. Couples can have a lovely evening without sex. In most cases, it's not a good idea to have sex on the first date, or even in the first several weeks; sometimes sex is not desirable at all in some relationships.

People may say yes when they mean no out of fear of rejection. If you feel that your self-esteem is low (meaning you fear people don't like you, you have nothing to offer, nobody would be interested or attracted), and that all you have to offer another person is sexual gratification, then the will to protect and care for yourself by having sex only when *you* feel like it may be diminished.

Sometimes the answer is yes instead of no out of fear of being perceived as not hip, with it, modern, avante garde, radical, chic, daring, spontaneous, loving or giving enough. A friend of ours who was in college during the early seventies recalls being propositioned by a young man who was part of her college group of friends. She didn't really want to and said so, but his response was, "What's the matter? You uptight, unliberated?" This was in the days when peace and free love were flowing, and fewer stigmas were worse that being labeled as unliberated or uptight. She reluctantly agreed to have sex with him and felt disgusted by the whole thing afterward. In fact, the more she thought about it over the months and years that followed, the angrier she became. "That was exploitation in the guise of liberation," she said, "and I didn't have the nerve at the time to tell this guy he was full of it." Much is unchanged today, and pressure still exists to grow up, be open and liberated, express your feelings. This is not necessarily bad, except that people sometimes forsake their own values and feelings to appear "normal."

One young woman at a university in Ohio told us of her meeting an invitingly handsome man at a party one night. They spent the evening dancing and talking, and discovered that they had a broad range of shared interests, including hiking and gourmet foods. When the party was dwindling and he asked her back to his room, she hesitated. She didn't have a single compelling reason for not wanting to have sex with him. She just didn't feel like it and felt uneasy about what might be a one-night stand. And besides, she was feeling horny, which only added to her ambivalence. Her decision, after mulling it over, was not to go home with him. If the relationship couldn't survive that, she reasoned, it wasn't worth pursuing. Her wisdom in this area was summed up with these words: My simple feeling of "I don't want to" was reason enough not to. Why did I need a fancy reason to say no to sex?

Guilt over sexual behaviors is often due to wanting something sexual, but feeling that it is "dirty." One man in his early thirties, for example, desired oral sex with his wife very much. She reluctantly agreed to let him perform cunnilingus on her but would fellate him only while he was wearing a condom. The two of them felt enormously guilty over their desires yet occasionally acted on the forbidden impulses despite the guilt. It came as a surprise to them to learn that most couples have and enjoy oral sex. Their fear of discussing sex had prevented them from learning things that might have helped assuage their deeply felt shame. Sometimes education, as opposed to (or in addition to) more involved psychological insights, is what is needed to help people deal with their guilt feelings.

Anger and/or guilt in response to a sexual experience often are preceded by the thought, *It* won't happen to me. This is a delusion of immortality, a rationalization that people use to convince themselves of endless things that are potentially harmful to themselves. The "it" may be a sexually transmitted disease, pregnancy, heartbreak, abandonment by a lover, or shame and embarrassment. The negative consequences may seem all the more unfair because often they result from a single mistake or bad judgment. In fact, it would be hard to find a single person among any of your friends who, if telling the truth, would not confess that they had made not one, but several sexual mistakes.

If you find yourself feeling guilty, angry, or regretful about any sexual experiences you've had, consider the following. It is likely that the whole issue has grown out of perspective, and that you now feel guilty about feeling guilty. In creating a means to grow beyond the mistakes and tragedies in our lives, the most difficult realization for us can be that we're all human, we make mistakes, and it's the individual's responsibility to turn these mistakes into lessons. If you've done something wrong and feel (rationally) guilty, use the guilt to avoid a repetition of the incident. Forgive yourself. The greatest disability with which some people live is the conviction that they are terrible people (usually with little evidence to substantiate the belief). Some people's self-image is mortally wounded when they realize that they are imperfect. Then they relentlessly punish themselves for this "flaw."

You may, on the other hand, feel extremely angry because someone else has mistreated you. Many people nowadays have contracted herpes, and in some cases, they've gotten it from someone who knew of his or her condition, but who did not reveal that information before the two had sex together. It's bad enough that you've gotten the disease; don't punish yourself twice. Even people who are cautious, who use contraception, and who choose their sexual partners carefully, get hurt. Accidents occur to the "best" people. It's bad enough that you've been hurt or betrayed. Why compound the hurt with self-hatred?

Memories of past painful events are sometimes kept vividly alive because of an inability to forgive the person who originally exploited you. The other person may have long ceased to be a part of your life and may have long since forgotten you. The initial sense of outrage may be useful, in the sense that it leads people to become social activists, politically involved, or to work for the rights and healing of people who've been similarly hurt. As mentioned, it may also serve to help turn the bad experience into a lesson for oneself. A gnawing, relentless sense of anger that persists for months or years, however, usually has as its main effect the disruption of *your* life. The ability to trust people may be impaired so that intimate relationships may not be allowed to develop beyond a fairly superficial level. The counsel of most psychotherapists would be to work through the feelings of anger, understand their meaning for yourself, and then forgive the person and get on with your life. Otherwise, the risk is that people become "stuck" in a past period or episode of their lives.

There are people who chronically hurt others with callous disregard for others' feelings or needs. Sometimes such people (referred to in psychiatric literature as narcissistic or antisocial personality disorders) are aware of their patterns of hurtful behavior and don't care about it, but at other times they are mostly unaware of it. For instance, some men can be heard saying, "I can't live without women, and I'm going out tonight to get laid." Such a man goes down to a local tavern or disco, and his goal for the night is to pick up a woman who will be the object of his desire: she is an object to him in every sense of the word. It may matter little who the woman is, what her personality is like, how she looks. Men who are constantly on the make, and who often pronounce how much they love women and can't get enough, basically *hate* women.

Promiscuous sexual behaviors among either men or women, conversely, are usually an indication of self-hatred, as we mentioned above. The compulsive need for a new, exciting lover every month (or week) often masks an underlying fear of closeness and of rejection. The "victims" of such people may have expected a caring partner but instead felt exploited and used afterwards—and understandably feel angry. In another dimension, there is a distinction to be made between those who are promiscuous and who behave in an exploitative way toward others, and those who allow themselves to be used in a promiscuous way because they are lonely and feel desperate. This is reminiscent of what Tennessee Williams said—that promiscuity represents the possibility of love.

Whatever the circumstances of your anger, it's okay to feel angry, to want to take revenge. The real question concerns the effects that prolonging these feelings has on your own health and well-being. Forgiving another person may mean little to that other person, but it frees one's own energy and emotions for involvement elsewhere. Unresolved anger sometimes interferes with other areas of functioning in a person's life, so that relationships with friends and family, or pleasure in work and leisure pursuits are compromised.

Angry feelings about sexual relationships are sometimes unprovoked or arise because two people have different interpretations of the facts. A common experience occurs when a couple attends a social gathering, and one or the other seems to be attracted to or spends a lot of time with someone else. The perception of one partner is, You had eyes only for the other person, you seemed turned on, and you ignored me. The response of the accused often is, What are you talking about? I was just having a good time. That's what parties are for, to meet other people. Stop being so jealous. Many couples break up, and marriages are destroyed, because of such irrational anger. There may be a failure to understand that just because two people are in love with each other, sexual attractions and turn-ons do not cease, and the desire for friendships and caring relationships with others are not finished. If a person acts on the attraction in a sexual way, that's another matter entirely. Irrational anger develops when one partner cannot accept that his or her partner/lover/spouse will be interested in other people as well.

Infidelity (adultery) may lead to justified, rational anger in many if not most of the situations in which it occurs. Often it symbolizes a betrayal of trust and a shifting of priorities, wherein the new lover begins to receive more attention than one's primary relationship (spouse, lover). There are also times, however, that anger over infidelity, though perhaps justified, can become exaggerated and destructive. One example of this appeared in the column of a nationally known advice columnist, in which a woman wrote that she was devastated to learn that thirty years ago, when he was in the military, her husband had had an affair with another woman. This woman reported that she had five wonderful children and a fantastic husband but was unable to get over her husband's infidelity early in their marriage. As the result, she felt that her marriage was ruined, and she was contemplating divorce.

Where do your sympathies lie? It's hard, in our view, to say anything but that this woman is stupid. In a counseling situation, were we to be that direct, this woman would undoubtedly seek another counselor, yet it's difficult to reconcile her excellent marriage and family life with the havoc caused by this one mistake so long ago.

The husband's motives for telling his wife of this incident also need to be questioned. Why did he tell her? He may have wanted her to understand him better and relate to his wife in a more honest fashion. Telling the whole truth about one's sexual past, sexual feelings and fantasies, however, sometimes is done mainly to relieve one's own guilt feelings. As such, it can occur as an expression of hostility at one's partner. The partner, sensing the hostile message in the telling, may respond in a like manner, with hostility and anger. In telling the truth, one needs to evaluate first one's reasons for doing so. Clearly, not all aspects of one's life should be communicated, no matter how intimate partners are.

Anger is a healthy response to hurts and disappointments, in that it helps motivate the person to avoid similar hurts in the future. There exists some disagreement among therapists concerning how much of one's anger should be expressed, and how much kept to oneself. The popular psychology notion is that bottling all one's anger up inside is unhealthy and may lead to symptoms such as ulcers, stuttering, nightmares, etc. This is sometimes the case, though it's equally true that unharnessed expressions of anger, particularly those that are repeated often over time, have a way of developing into hostility and hatred, which may, as a primary consequence, be destructive to the individual.

Once you've expressed your anger over a felt grievance and communciated with the other person about it to the point that all that needs to be said has been said, anger has usually served its constructive purpose. If the reason for the anger reoccurs and you feel angry again, that is a different matter. Many women, for instance, are faced with the decision of how long to stay in a physically abusive relationship. Our feelings on this are: women are justified remaining with a man after a single abusive incident, provided she feels secure it won't happen again, loves the man, and is committed to the relationship. Any woman who remains in such a relationship after a second incident of abuse needs professional help (as does her lover or husband, of course).

Guilt, anger, and regrets in relation to sex are less likely when sex is an expression of loving and caring for another person. It is true, however, that sometimes sex becomes instead an expression of guilt, poor self-esteem, hostility, fear of rejection, personal insecurity, or strong dependency needs, rather than a wish for intimacy, pleasure, and love. Sex may be an expression of anxiety rather than an expression of caring.

Sexuality is one of the most vulnerable areas of many people's lives, and for this reason people suffer when they feel guilty about their sexual experiences. If you identify with significant elements in this chapter, perhaps you'll want to consider how to respond to your dilemma. One alternative is to declare a moratorium on sexual experiences, and concentrate on developing insight into these feelings. Usually (though there are exceptions) an inability to stop self-hurtful behaviors is a good indication that some outside help is called for. Most of the readers of this book are young enough that making changes now can help to alleviate feelings of guilt and/or anger that otherwise might persist for years.

CHAPTER 11

When and How to
Seek a Therapist

At various points throughout this book the possibility of personal therapy is discussed: if you have been raped, sexually abused as a child, find yourself sexually dysfunctional, fixated on pornography, or, perhaps, a sexual fetish. This chapter is intended as a guide to help readers answer such questions as:

- When should I get into therapy?
- What kind of therapist should I look for?
- How long should I stay in therapy?
- What happens in therapy?

Psychotherapy is only one of many opportunities available to people who are looking for ways to understand themselves better and improve their situation. People create changes in their lives in surprising ways—sometimes taking a vacation provides the motivation for change. Attending an important conference or going on a retreat are other paths to different perspectives. Although some individuals are not well suited to psychotherapy, they do benefit from yoga or meditation, or even a change in diet and exercise patterns.

Human growth and change occur in a myriad of ways. For reasons that are not always understood, some people do feel better simply through the passage of time. For instance, some victims of sexual abuse reach adulthood with a healthy sexual and psychological adaptation without ever undergoing therapy or any help-oriented program. Similarly, it is often unknown why some people who were raised in ghettos get an education and escape the cycle of poverty, and others from near-identical circumstances remain destitute for their entire lives.

People have their own unique sense of timing concerning how they respond to stresses and crises. How long after a death of a close relative (spouse, sibling, parent, offspring) do you think a person should recover and return to normal? A friend of ours whose teenage son was killed in an automobile accident remained unconsolable for over a year after the tragedy. Her husband had long since returned to work, and her other children had adjusted well, but she was unable to stop grieving. Friends became very concerned and encouraged her to get on with her life. Eventually, she did resume most of her usual activities, and her depression lifted somewhat. Her comment on the experience was that every death has a life of its own. She needed to follow her own process of mourning. Though other family members recovered more quickly, that could not shorten her own grief.

How long is too long; that is, how long should you wait for your problems to alleviate before seeking help? One way to answer is to assess how significantly your life is affected in areas other than the specific problem area. If you are troubled by an inability to reach orgasm, does it negatively influence your work, sleep, appetite, leisure activities? The more that the problem spreads into other areas of your life, the more you may want to consider getting some help. No real time-oriented guidelines exist, but for those who organize themselves chronologically, the further beyond one year that your problems last, the more indication there is that you might want to try consciously to make some changes.

Some common symptoms of mental distress such as depression and anxiety are relieved when people discover a sense of purpose in their lives. A surprising number of individuals have no compelling reason to get out of bed in the morning—no cause they support avidly. One of the best ways to feel better is to find a sense of purpose, perhaps in becoming helpful to others. Performing *mitzvahs* (good deeds without expectation of return) elevates the spirit and helps people to feel useful and needed. Often sexual or psychological problems cause people to feel isolated from others around them, and developing a sense of purpose may reconnect them to others and encourage their own good feelings to reemerge.

Many people spend years feeling themselves powerless to change problems that significantly interfere with their daily functioning. The interference might be an unhappy marriage, temper outbursts, isolation and withdrawal from others, depression, as well as those specifically sexual problems mentioned above. Yet, a number of psychological blocks prevent them from really considering getting psychotherapeutic assistance.

Perhaps the person feels too guilty or ashamed about his or her problems to let someone else know about them. For some, therapy still carries with it the stigma of being sick or mentally disturbed if you need it. You may fear friends or family will discover you are in therapy. What if they disapprove, or get angry, or feel that your therapy is implicitly accusing them of being bad parents or spouses? There may be stubborn determination to deal with one's problems alone; this is often accompanied by the sentiment that only dependent wimps who are too weak to handle their own problems turn to others for help. People have many other reasons for not seeking out therapy, and generally they are labeled by therapists as *resistance*.

There may be some validity to some of the reasons. Perhaps the family won't approve, and there may be uneasy moments when filling out job applications that ask, Have you ever been treated for a psychiatric disorder? (Generally, this is asking if you have ever been hospitalized for an extended period for a disorder.) It may also be true that therapy will stir up numerous painful feelings of rage and helplessness and despair. Understandably, some people wish to avoid confronting these issues in their lives.

Clearly, the choice of whether or not to enter therapy is up to the individual. The person needs, however, to consider the alternatives, which might include endlessly reliving the same troubling nightmares or self-destructive behaviors, enduring bitter marriages or love relationships, remaining friendless and lonely, etc. Both authors of this book have been therapists for a number of years, and it is usual for people to enter therapy with some of the above-mentioned fears and apprehensions. Some people are successful in conducting a kind of self-therapy, in which they work through their feelings and gain better insight into their problems, but other people find themselves stymied by this process or going in circles.

As a first step it might be necessary to accept that therapy *will* be painful at times, and to try it out anyway. If it turns out to be unsuccessful or more than you can bear, you can always stop. For some people, just reaching the decision to begin therapy is a great relief. Talking things over with a trusted member of the clergy may provide the additional ego strength needed to get started.

Psychotherapist is a generic term that refers to professionals with training in such fields as psychiatry, psychology, marriage and family therapy, and social work. Of this group, only psychiatrists may legally dispense prescription medications such as tranquilizers, antidepressants, etc. Otherwise, many similarities and differences may exist among the different professionals, depending on which school of psychology or "modality" they practice.

The term modality refers to such clinical orientations as psychoanalysis (Freudian), Rational Emotive Therapy (RET), gestalt, transactional analysis, behavioral, and systems (of which Bowenian, structural, and strategic are categories). A therapist's modality determines to a great extent how he or she responds to a client, how problems are conceived, what techniques of therapy are employed, and what the goals of therapy are.

Generally, a psychodynamically oriented therapist (psychoanalytic practitioners are included in this class) believes that therapy should consist of careful examination of patterns of behavior and feelings from as far back in the person's life as memory permits. The meanings of family interactions are explored, and feelings generated in these discussions are reality-tested to see how adaptive they are in one's present life situation. Psychodynamic therapists believe that there are many significant connections between a person's childhood and present emotional state, and that gaining insight into these connections helps to produce desired changes in lifestyle and behavior.

Another general group of therapists is less interested in insight and past experiences and more interested in the present problems. The crucial issue for them is not that your mother rejected you at age five; what counts is how an individual responds to it in the present. The key element here is change in behavior and interactional patterns with other people; if insight develops along the way, great, but if not, no great loss. Behavioral, structural, strategic, and RET therapists share some of this emphasis on behavior, though the above comments are greatly simplified and do not necessarily apply to each of these modalities.

Before getting into therapy, reading about these different approaches might help to familiarize readers with general principles and practices. In addition, once you have agreed to meet with a therapist, ask him or her in the first session to discuss with you what orientation he or she works within. Find out how therapy will be conducted, what your respective roles will be, and what you can expect to accomplish. If the first therapist with whom you meet is not to your liking, arrange an appointment with another person. Naturally, if you shop around and are continually dissatisfied with the therapists whom you meet, it is likely that the problem is yours, rather than their inability to meet your needs. As a consumer, however, it is your right not to "buy" the first therapist you meet.

Sex of the therapist is an important issue for some potential clients (some therapists also call people whom they see in therapy "patients"). This can be an especially sensitive consideration where sexual issues are most pronounced. If, for instance, you were sexually assaulted as a child by a male, you might feel apprehensive about sitting across from a male therapist and telling him your deepest feelings and fears. At other times, people prefer a therapist of a particular sex but are not sure of the reasons why. Therapists themselves generally concur that a competent practitioner of either sex should be able to handle clients of either sex, coming in with a variety of problems. But they also understand the need of some people to be seen by a therapist of a specific sex.

Where to start looking for a therapist may seem like an overwhelming task—the yellow pages of some phone books are filled with columns of names and credentials of therapists. Be wary in your selection, especially if you reside in a state without licensing standards for therapists. In some states, almost anyone can hang out a shingle that says "therapist," advertise, and begin doing counseling. Be sure that you are consulting a person who is properly educated in his or her field. This would involve an M.D. for a psychiatrist who had completed a residency in psychiatry, an M.S. or Ph.D. degree for a clincial or counseling psychologist, an M.S.W. degree for a social worker, and an M.A. or Ph.D. degree for a marriage and family therapist. In addition, there are certifying organizations for each profession. Marriage and family therapists are clinically certified by the American Association of Marriage and Family Therapy (AAMFT, 1717 K Street, NW, Rm. 407, Washington, DC 20006). Social workers are certified by the

National Association of Social Workers (NASW, 7891 Eastern Avenue, Silver Springs, Maryland 20910). Psychologists are certified by the American Psychological Association (APA, 1200 17th Street, NW, Washington, DC 20036). Sex therapists are certified by the American Association of Sex Educators, Counselors, and Therapists (AASECT, 11 Dupont Circle, NW, Suite 220, Washington, DC 20036). The American Psychiatric Association (1700 13th Street, NW, Washington, DC 20009) certifies psychiatrists.

These organizations are good sources of referrals to therapists in your area. If you cannot locate a local chapter, write to the national headquarters and ask for the name of a qualified person in your area. Another good source is pastoral counseling centers. Though many people believe that the word pastoral means these centers are religiously oriented, generally they are nondenominational (though if you wished to discuss religion as part of your therapy, that would be fine). Such centers are accredited by the American Association of Pastoral Counselors (AAPC), and their standards are high for the conduct of therapy. The Onondaga Pastoral Counseling Center in Syracuse, New York, for example, has about twelve full-time and thirty adjunct therapists on staff, working in twenty outreach centers in different locations around the metropolitan area. Fees at such centers are charged according to a sliding scale, determined by your income and number of dependents in the family; thus fees are generally lower in centers with sliding scales than with therapists in private practice.

The expense of therapy is a prime concern. Obtaining the services of a therapist in private practice, for example, might run from $40 to $80 per session, depending on the person and where you live. Many health insurance plans pay a proportion of each session's fee, which helps to lessen the expense for the client. Nevertheless, therapy could take up a major portion of an ordinary household's monthly budget. Some therapists are willing to negotiate fees and payment plans, perhaps stretching your payments out over the period beyond when you terminate therapy. Feel free to discuss your financial concerns with your therapist; he or she won't be surprised.

It surely comes as no surprise to readers that students usually are on shoe-string budgets and may have little money for therapy. Thus, it may develop that the only affordable therapist will be a graduate student-in-training, perhaps in a social work, marriage and family therapy, or psychology program. Most universities have counseling centers that are staffed by these clinical interns, and fees are nominal (ranging from $3 to $10 per session). These student-therapists are closely supervised, and the quality of treatment you'd receive is generally adequate.

Sexual issues within therapy sessions can become highly emotionally charged for clients (as well as for therapists). When discussing sexual details of their lives and histories, people sometimes become aroused, ashamed, or guilty. The arousal, combined with feelings of trusting and being cared for by the therapist, leads some people to feel that they are falling in love with their therapist. This is a fairly common experience; if you are able to, it is best if you can discuss the feelings with your therapist.

All the professional organizations mentioned earlier in this chapter have specific regulations against any kind of client/therapist sexual interactions. Though it is the therapist's responsibility to prevent therapeutic relationships from becoming sexual, some violate this responsibility and become sexually involved with a client(s). The great majority of clients eventually experience this as a betrayal of their trust in the therapist. Even though a few clients may benefit from the experience and perhaps even marry their therapist, this in no way compensates for the negative feelings of most other individuals.

Beware of any therapist who suggests that sex with him or her is the best way to overcome your sexual difficulties! It is perfectly all right for you to feel attracted to him or her, and exploring those feelings can be a vital part of therapy. Nevertheless, therapists who are proved to have had sexual interactions with clients are generally ejected from their professional organizations and barred from the practice of psychotherapy.

Therapy requires a strong commitment to growth and personal exploration. How long you remain in therapy will depend on factors too numerous to delve into here, and the decision of when to terminate is usually a part of the process of therapy itself. If you get into therapy expecting immediate results—as many people in this age of "instant gratification" do—you will be disappointed. There is no magic, no incantations, or formulas potent enough to resolve easily what are usually longstanding problems (though periods of rapid growth and change often occur). Some problems, to be sure, are more amenable to relatively swift improvement (such as premature ejaculation and some other sexual dysfunctions, which often require behaviorally oriented treatment).

Couples or families are sometimes seen in therapy together, to work on issues that directly involve more than one person. Even if you are a single person living alone, it might be beneficial to be seen together with your parents, or lover, or siblings. Bringing more than one person into the therapy room changes the chemistry and emotional feeling of what happens there and often leads to changes that would be difficult to accomplish if only one person were attending. Sometimes people are seen in therapy individually for a time, and then spouses and/or other people are then included; this process may be reversed, so that the conjoint (marital, family, etc.) therapy comes first.

As for what happens in therapy: The single most important guiding principle is that *it is a place where anything can be talked about.* Anger, hatred, and other feelings which people in other situations may mistakenly label as unacceptable or "bad" are open for discussion. This concept of openness, though at first intimidating for some people, usually comes to be felt as liberation from former fears. As people come to trust that they will not be rejected for their feelings or statements, they are able to learn more about themselves.

Many therapists themselves undergo therapy as part of their training. Therapy may not be ideal for everyone, though there is scarcely a person who would not benefit from learning more about him or herself, however self-actualized the person appears to be. Whether help is sought for sexual or other problems, it usually has a strong impact on the person's life.

People need to think through for themselves how they react to disappointments and difficulties that are part of everyday existence. For some people, their problems are relatively mild; their problem in fact may be more of an inability to tolerate the normal frustrations of daily living. In fact, some of the prophets of the "feel good" school of psychology have created the erroneous impression that feeling depressed once in a while is a disorder. We as a society might do better to legitimize a certain degree of depression and to help people understand that some disappointments are to be expected. Therapy may help people learn how better to accept these experiences but probably should not be entered into until other alternatives have been explored.

Psychotherapy has become chic—the thing to do—among some segments of the population (usually upper-middle class communities in larger cities). This is an elite group with the resources to easily afford therapy. Chances are that for most of them, therapy is not necessary but is rather an interesting part of their lives. Nevertheless, charges for psychiatric services have become the greatest expense for some of the nation's health insurance companies, outstripping even claims for surgery and other medical services. Americans take their mental health seriously—and psychotherapy is just one way of working toward it.

PART THREE
Social Issues

CHAPTER 12

Against Women's Will: Rape, Sexual Assault, and Harassment

RAPE AND SEXUAL ASSAULT

The statistics are grisly: In 1983 there were 78,918 reported rapes in this country (Uniform Crime Reports, 1984). These figures are up 42 percent from 1974 and up 3 percent from 1979. The overall rate with which rapes occur, however, seems to have fallen slightly in recent years: sixty-six of every 100,000 women were rape victims, down 3 percent from 1979. This amounts to *one rape every seven minutes,* one of the highest rates of rape in any industrialized nation in the western world. In addition, the FBI states that rape is one of the most underreported crimes in existence—only an estimated one in four women reveal what has happened to them. Also, in 1983 only about half of reported rapes led to an arrest and only 4 percent resulted in conviction.

Rapes occur more frequently in large metropolitan areas and are more numerous in the summer months. There really is no such thing as a *typical* rapist or victim, but some apparent trends have emerged. A man forcing a woman to have sexual relations with him is most likely between the ages of fifteen and twenty-five, as is his victim (though all age groups and races have been affected). Most rapes occur in the victim's home, and contrary to the smug attitude that they somehow "asked for it," no woman wants to be assaulted.

The subject of rape has captured national attention in recent years, notably through such crimes as occured in Big Dan's Tavern in New Bedford, Massachusetts, where a woman was gang-raped on a pool table while a crowd of onlookers cheered and shouted. Images such as this one, together with images of women being accosted and dragged into dark alleyways, comprise the popular notion of what rape amounts to. Yet, forced sex on a date or in other situations where the offender and victim know each other—known as "date rape" or "acquaintance rape"—is the most common form of rape and accounts for about 60 percent of all *reported* rapes (Newsweek, 1984). It is built on the age-old belief that a woman really means yes when she says no. Thus, since the woman was not supposed to desire sex, her only alternative was to feign resistance and then submit with growing passion. The pages of Gothic romance novels are filled with this scenario.

Many writers have documented widespread fantasies among women of being over-powered by a man and of being forced into various sexual acts. These fantasies have been used to make the distorted claim that women obviously wish to act them out. This is nothing more than a lamentable rationalization for men's violence against women. People typically experience a broad range of fantasies from the mundane to the perverse, through murder, revenge, and horror to heroics and personal glorification. Suggesting that women wish to act out their rape fantasies is as absurd as suggesting that men wish to enact their fantasies of dying on the battlefield as war heroes.

These issues are especially significant on college campuses. A study conducted at Kent State University reported that over 50 percent of the women had experienced verbal threats, physical coercion, or violence related to sex. Twenty-seven percent of the men at Kent State acknowledged that they used some level of emotional or physical force against women who resisted their sexual advances, and one in eight women reported having been raped (Barrett, 1982).

Writers in this field have almost unanimously embraced the notion that rape is not a crime of passion or sexual desire. Rather, it is viewed as an act of violence with associations of power, dominance, submission, and sadism. Although rape is an act of violence against another human being, it also results from exploitive sexual impulses. Certainly the victim experiences rape as a violent assault on him or herself. Labeling rape only as violence ignores the rapist's erection and sexual drive; there is an obvious difference between a man who assaults and beats a person violently, and one who rapes as a result of being refused the expected "finale" of a date.

The person who has been raped needs immediate support and comfort as well as medical attention. Many women, however, report being subjected to humiliating and condescending interviews at the police station. The doctors who later examine them for physical damage, evidence of penetration and venereal infection, women have complained, are brusque and uncaring in their procedure. Once in court, the woman has characteristically been ruthlessly cross-examined. The defense attorneys may imply that she is a whore, pry into her history of sexual relations with the defendant and other men, ask if she attempted to defend herself, and generally try to make her story sound implausible. Women who are prosecuting their attackers often feel as if *they* are the ones on trial, having to prove that they did not consent to the event.

In some locales, this situation is certainly changing. Owing in part to the work of feminist groups and rape crisis centers, the ways in which police, physicians, and the courts treat rape victims have become more humane. If you are raped, a female police officer may be assigned to question you. Consciousness-raising seminars have been held in many precincts, and in many instances these have helped to eliminate abusive treatment of rape victims. If you are raped, there are also excellent services available through many rape crisis centers. The center in Syracuse, New York, for example, offers

- 24-hour telephone hotline for information and crisis counseling;
- Support and counseling for victims, their families, and friends;
- Advocacy through medical and legal systems if the victim chooses to report the crime.

These centers may provide a companion to accompany you to the hospital and/or police station, and this person (usually a woman) will often keep you company all night, if you wish, to help you feel more secure.

Rape is always a traumatic experience, but the important idea to remember is that there is no reason for women to feel guilt or shame any more than if they had been robbed or mugged. They are innocent victims. Research at Boston City Hospital by Burgess and Holstrom (1978) has identified a *rape trauma syndrome* that many women experience following being raped. It takes many women six months, a year, or longer to recover, during which time they are plagued by fear and self-blame (What if I had done something differently? Couldn't I have avoided it?), anger, hostility, and other intense emotions. Often social ties and employment are disrupted, and love relationships may suffer. The woman may fear going out alone or be afraid to return home. Dark streets, crowded places, or nearly any situation may trigger the woman's fear. She has been violated and slowly must learn to trust again.

Rape victims, as is true of some victims of sexual abuse as children, sometimes recover relatively quickly. Not all people who are raped go through a lengthy or predictable struggle for readjustment. Some, for reasons that are not always understood, are able to mobilize themselves with the conviction that they will not allow the rapist to seriously disrupt their lives. In effect, for them the best revenge is living well and refusing to remain a victim for long. Nevertheless, all people adapt to crises at their own pace. There is no need to let the experiences of other people make you feel inferior for working things out in your own way.

A return to one's usual level of sexual functioning after rape may take months or even years. A woman teaching assistant who was raped by an intruder in an abandoned academic building late one night found herself fearful of any sexual contact with her husband afterwards. She felt reassured in his embrace, but when the contact became explicitly sexual, she recoiled with the memory of the other man's brutal touch. Her husband, who ordinarily considered himself to be an understanding and patient man, found his patience stretched to the limit after about eight months of celibacy. The couple eventually worked it out. This involved the husband resolving his anger at the rapist and at his wife for denying him. The woman gradually found herself able to trust her sexual feelings and to feel safe enough to respond sexually.

How would the male readers of this book respond to the rape of their loved one? An ideal response of caring support is sometimes sabotaged by an underlying reaction that blames the victim. Some men are unable to shake the feeling that the victim somehow asked for it or is now dirty and used. They agonize over feelings of jealousy and their impotence to take any kind of revenge against the rapist. One man who had just graduated from engineering school learned early one morning that his fiancée had been raped by a man who broke into her sorority house through a locked window. In the ensuing months, his anger and despair overwhelmed him, and he was unable to accept that his rejection of her was irrational. The woman herself suffered not only the trauma of being raped but also the rejection by the man she wished to marry.

Every woman, especially if she is alone, can be said to be vulnerable. That's why it's important to take reasonable precautions (which is very different from becoming paranoid). Keep a watchful eye in public, avoid dark places, and if common sense tells you that you may be in danger, don't shrug it off. In addition, do some reading or attend a seminar on what to do if you are attacked.

Tips on prevention focus on what to do while walking, driving, or sitting at home. If you are walking, for instance, the Rape Crisis Center in Syracuse advises you to walk at a steady pace, look confident, avoid carrying heavy packages, wear shoes that are suitable for running, and cross the street or change directions if you suspect you are being followed. While driving, lock the doors and roll up the windows, check the back seat before getting in, and have car keys ready when going to the car to avoid fumbling. If you break down on the road, open the hood of the car and get back in, locking the doors. If someone offers help, ask him/her to call the police or a tow truck—don't get out. At home keep locks secured on all doors and windows. Install a peephole, keep entrances well lit, and don't use your first name on a building directory or telephone listing. Be wary of hallways, elevators, laundry and garbage areas, especially at night. The Center emphasizes that women should incorporate these suggestions into their daily lives so that they become an automatic part of a woman's routine.

One approach to educating women about how to respond in rape situations is *How to Say No to a Rapist—and Survive* by Fred Storaska. Some women's groups oppose his approach because they feel it is too passive and implies that the victim is partially to blame. Though we do not agree with their interpretation of Storaska's approach, you may want to get several points of view and make your own decision. The main points Storaska makes are the following:

1. Control your own terror.
2. Establish communication with the man and treat him as a human being.

3. Gain the attacker's confidence.
4. Wait to act until you are sure you can do so safely.
5. Use both imagination and good judgment.

If you've been raped, there are a few steps to keep in mind. Don't bathe, wash your clothes, douche, or apply any medication; the examining doctor will need to see you before the evidence is washed away. Call the police and/or a rape hotline immediately and get a friend to accompany you to the police station and hospital. Request a female officer or doctor if it makes you more comfortable. Women who have been assaulted sometimes try to block the whole event out of their minds and so have difficulty recalling the rapist's description, clothes he was wearing, type of car he may have gotten into, etc. In their own best interests, women must try to remember every last detail, force themselves, if necessary, to aid the prosecution and purge themselves of the incident as well.

Though it occurs much less frequently than among women, men are occasionally raped; current estimates are that perhaps one in ten rape victims is a man. This happens outside prisons as well as in prisons, where it is not uncommon for one or more inmates to force themselves on a weaker one. In any case, it is overwhelmingly men raping other men—women rarely rape men. Men who are raped experience the same feelings of violation and outrage that women in similar circumstances do.

Society, especially the police, judges, juries, physicans, and other officials who deal directly with rape victims, needs to continue working to improve the way it treats assaulted women. Toward this end, some states have passed laws prohibiting the woman's sexual history as evidence at her rapist's trial. People often see the situation in a new light when asked to imagine that it is their own wife, mother, daughter, etc., who has been raped. Yet, the sexist attitude that some victims encounter persists, even among women: a large proportion of the crowd outside the courthouse in New Bedford that protested the conviction of the rapists in Big Dan's Tavern was women. We have a long way to go before all but a small group of women will feel free to come forward and report what they have experienced.

The personal dilemma that confronts a significant proportion of our population, however, is: How will I respond if I, or someone I love, is raped? Despite their best intentions, people sometimes react in hostile, blaming, ways toward the victim (even if it is themselves). If this happens, it's an understandable, albeit irrational, first impulse. Beyond this initial reaction (lasting perhaps several days or more), people need to organize themselves around doing what is optimally helpful to the victim and her family. Even it you cannot help feeling that the woman must somehow be to blame, act in a supportive and caring way. If after a while you don't begin to feel better, seek the help of a competent therapist. The most destructive pattern, and unfortunately, one that is enacted in some relationships, is for the tension and recrimination to stagnate, with no effort made to work things out. A negative undercurrent of animosity and fear is lethal to relationships, and people need to find ways of resolving *together* the pain that follows rape.

SEXUAL HARASSMENT

Though millions of individuals—usually women—endure various forms of sexual harassment, it occurs in so many different ways that is is difficult to define. One very general interpretation was created by the Equal Employment Opportunity Commission in 1980, which was based on guidelines established by Title VII of the Civil Rights Act of 1964. It states:

> Unwelcome sexual advances, requests for sexual favors, and other verbal or physical conduct of a sexual nature constitutes sexual harassment when:
> 1. submission to such conduct is made either explicitly or implicitly a term or condition of an individual's employment,
> 2. submission to or rejection of such conduct by an individual is used as the basis for employment decisions affecting such individual, or
> 3. such conduct has the purpose or effect of substantially interfering with an individual's work performance or creating an intimidating, hostile, or offensive working environment (Deane and Tillar, 1981).

Besides places of employment, college and university campuses are environments where harassment is equally likely to occur; thus, the above guidelines can be applied to professors and students as well, where grades, acceptance of theses, and/or recommendations may be tied to sexual behaviors. In fact, Title IX of the Education Amendments of 1972, which is designed to eliminate discrimination on the basis of sex in educational settings, has been held to apply to sexual harassment. Thus, harassment is defined as an act of discrimination. Some universities have adopted the above guidelines as their own policy on the topic; one of them, Syracuse University, added the following stipulations:

1. Every academic and administrative official of the university should make sure that the university's disapproval of sexual harassment is known to the faculty and supervisory staff and to those most likely to be victimized—students and employees.
2. If any person has a complaint, it should be taken to the individual's supervisor, department head, dean, or director. Complaints may also be taken to the personnel office or the affirmative action office, if that seems appropriate.
3. All complaints are to be investigated in a prompt and confidential manner.

Harassment crosses all racial and socioeconomic boundaries, and in a random sample of over 20,000 federal workers, 42 percent of the women and 15 percent of the men said they had experienced it. Studies on college campuses produce similar figures, though the nature of the harassment there is sometimes less overt, with fewer outright suggestions of blackmail and/or bribery.

Sexual harassment can be overt:

- A secretary's boss habitually sits very close to her while she's taking dictation, and places his hand on her upper thigh. He says, "You know, things could be a lot nicer for you around here if you'd come across once in a while."
- An assistant manager in a department store is cornered in the employee lounge frequently by the store manager, who places his hand over her breast and tells her how much she turns him on.
- While talking with her professor about a poor grade on a midterm exam, a student gets hints from him that perhaps they could find an alternative way to improve her performance.

Or covert:

- A woman is passed over for promotion three times and suspects that her rejection of a supervisor's advances is the cause.
- While talking with male coworkers, or walking through a room, a woman is aware of the inevitable leers and stares at her breasts and buttocks.

Sexual harassment almost always involves an imbalance of power. Between equals, unwelcome sexual proposals can be declined without fear of reprisal. Harassment can continue between peers, however, in situations where superiors (boss, college administrator) are not receptive to complaints. Feeling themselves powerless, victims often experience a loss of self-confidence or esteem. Guilt, disillusionment, and fear of consequences are common responses, which are sometimes fueled by the nagging suspicion that one is somehow to blame.

Unfortunately for themselves, many times the victim's response to harassment is to ignore it and hope it goes away. Women's upbringings have socialized them, to a large extent, not to pursue grievances or assert their wishes. Beyond this no one, male or female, wants to be perceived as the office or campus prude, troublemaker, or tattletale. One thing is certain: the experiences of people who have endured harassment indicates that the trouble won't go away if it is ignored. Often it gets worse, as silence is interpreted to mean cooperation. Some women succumb to the pressure because of their feeling that this is less painful than the severe consequences they face by refusing to engage in sexual activity.

In 1984 the University of Minnesota revised its policy and declared that even consenting relationships between faculty members and students were "very unwise" (Mitgang, 1984). The fact remains, however, that thousands of students and professors nationwide continue to develop relationships, and in some instances, get married. There is a vast difference between the teacher who says, "Come across or you get a C," and one who says, "I find myself attracted to you. Can we go out and have a drink?" In the latter situation, sexual harassment exists only if the student feels that she can't say no without repercussions. An expression of sexual interest in another person can be just that; it becomes criminal when the person in power can't handle the rejection magnanimously.

What can a person do if he or she is subjected to sexist comments, verbal abuse, fondling, leering, or threats? A first response might be to

- decline the sexual proposition politely and firmly.
- state that you prefer not to be ogled, touched, or spoken to in that manner, and perhaps suggest an alternative: Let's see if we can't work together in a friendly atmosphere.

Then, hope that the directness of your response was enough to clear the air. If this is not effective, a range of alternatives exists, though all involve confrontation. It's easy to be a hero in somebody else's situation (meaning that for authors to give advice is painless; *you* have to live it out), and even the most thoroughly justified and documented grievance procedure can backfire. Some colleges and places of employment have established committees to hear complaints about sexual misbehavior; others have no such committees but are receptive to taking action when needed to rectify bad situations, and still others ignore complaints or make the woman sorry that she didn't keep silent.

Women's (and in some instances, men's) silence on these issues has been as detrimental to their welfare as has men's aggression and exploitation. Passivity itself *is* a response. (A friend of ours suggests carrying a miniature tape recorder to record the threats or intimidation and then turn the tables; threaten to play the tape back to his wife or mother.) The Alliance Against Sexual Coercion has conducted surveys that demonstrate how in three-quarters of the cases, if the woman ignored the sexual overtures, they continued or got worse.

If one can gather the support of one's fellow students or workers, sometimes a more favorable outcome to complaints can be expected. In fact, once these problems become public, other women often step forward to state that they too were the victims of the accused male(s).

The gross failure of society to protect its women and to offer comfort represents the worst aspect of institutions that have remained insensitive to instances of sexual coercion. Some progress has been made, and yet successfully prosecuted cases are still novel enough in the public's eye to make headlines.

REFERENCES

Barrett, K. "Date Rape." *Ms.*, September 1982, pp. 48–51, 130.

Deane, N. H., & Tillar, D. L. *Sexual Harassment: An Employment Issue.* Washington, DC: College and University Personnel Association, 1981.

Holstrom, L. L., & Burgess, A. W. *The Victim of Rape.* New York: Wiley, 1978.

Mitgang, L. Sexual Harassment of Women Students Called Widespread. *Los Angeles Times,* May 27, 1984, Sec. I-A, p. 2.

Newsweek. The Date Who Rapes. April 9, 1984.

New York Times, UPI. "Sexual Harassment on Federal Jobs Called Costly." May 3, 1981, p. 63.

Storaska, F. *How to Say No to a Rapist—And Survive.* New York: Random House, 1975.

Uniform Crime Reports. *Crime in the United States.* U.S. Department of Justice, September 4, 1984.

CHAPTER 13

Sexual Abuse of Children

Chances are that many of the readers of this book have memories of sexual abuse or incest from their childhoods. A whole spectrum of behaviors and situations may be involved: perhaps it was an uncle who slipped his hand down your pants and fondled you for several seconds, or an older neighbor child who knocked you to the ground and forcibly examined your genitals. Or the memories might be of more explicit contact with a parent or sibling, or a nonfamily member.

Therapists and workers in this field generally agree that the following criteria are key in assessing the impact and meaning of child sexual abuse:

—Was the perpetrator more than four years older than the victim?

—Was the child under age twelve when the abuse began?

—Was the perpetrator in a position of power over the victim?

—Were force, coercion, bribery, threats used?

—For how long did the abuse last? Single event or lasted for years?

—What sexual behaviors were involved?

—Who else knew of the abuse?

—If/When the abuse became public knowledge, what happened?

Sexual abuse does not generally refer to voluntary sexual exploration between peers or siblings of the same age (although these events may be remembered later in life with great shame, anger and/or guilt). There is little rational justification for guilt over such childhood games as doctor, which is a nearly universal game among children. It is not uncommon among older children or teenagers to have an incident of mutual masturbation with friends or even a family member, and these too need not lead to prolonged guilty feelings. If, on the other hand, the person were several years older, physically larger and intimidating, then elements of coercion and abuse may indeed exist. There is a sensitive line here between exploration and exploitation, depending on how the incident was originally perceived. When learning about sexual abuse for the first time, some adults—perhaps including readers of this book—suddenly remember childhood sexuality events, which may result in some guilt. There is no good reason to start worrying in the present if the event wasn't painful when it first happened.

Sexual abuse invariably involves exploitation and harm to a child, as those who have experienced the abuse are painfully aware. There are scarcely a handful of documented cases in which a child enjoyed being molested and still feels positively about the experience as an adult. The overwhelming majority, *numbering in the millions*, felt hurt, enraged, betrayed, dirty, and terrified. Even though most recover (in the sense that they function adequately at jobs, maintain intimate relationships, raise healthy children), the experience may pose some recurring dilemmas for a lifetime.

The American Psychological Association estimates that between 12 and 15 million American women have been the victims of incest. About 25 percent of these cases are father-daughter, 25 percent stepfather-stepdaughter, and the rest are attributed to grandfathers, brothers, uncles, cousins, adoptive fathers, half-brothers, brothers-in-law (Brozan, 1984). Since many cases are never made public, only rough estimates can be made about annual occurrences: researchers estimate that between 100,000 and 500,000 children are molested each year. Finkelhor (1984) reported that 15 percent of the mothers and 5 percent of the fathers in his study said that they had been victimized as children, and he concluded from these findings that one boy is molested to every three girls. Diana Russell (1983) found even higher percentages: a random sample of 930 adult San Francisco women revealed that 28 percent had been sexually abused before age fourteen.

Until recently, very little attention was paid to the sexual abuse of boys, which is now known to be more widespread than was previously believed. Sexual abuse perpetrated by women, once thought to be extremely rare, is now thought to occur in perhaps 5 percent of the cases (Lindsey, 1984). Homosexual males, who have been banned from teaching in many public school systems because they have been feared as recruiters and abusers of children, are about as likely as women to abuse children sexually (Groth, 1979). The overwhelming majority of abuse is committed by heterosexual males. Louise Armstrong, in her powerful book *Kiss Daddy Goodnight*, has suggested that sexual molestation of children is so common it would seem not to be a taboo at all. Talking about it is, though this seems to be changing just in the past year or two.

Child molestation crosses all social, economic, and racial boundaries and affects a wide range of people and family situations. Stereotypes that portray the offenders as obviously neurotic, lecherous, dirty old men (or psychotic) are inaccurate. The phenomenon does usually seem to be accompanied by individual feelings of low self-esteem and self-destructive behavior in the molesters. Incest can continue only in secret, and the families involved are typically isolated from friends and the mainstream of life.

The Federal Child Abuse Prevention and Treatment Act of 1974 defined child abuse, including sexual abuse or exploitation, as injury or maltreatment of a child ". . . by a person who is responsible for the child's welfare." The National Center on Child Abuse and Neglect has adopted a broader definition:

> . . . contacts or interactions between a child and an adult when the child is being used for the sexual stimulation of the perpetrator or another person. Sexual abuse may also be committed by a person under the age of 18 when that person is either significantly older than the victim or when the perpetrator is in a position of power or control over another child.

The very nature of the power relationship between parents or other adults and children often inhibits the youngsters from revealing the event of sexual advances made against them. Subtle or overt threats are often made to discourage exposing the situation, and the child her- or himself may perceive some of the consequences: loss of family income, police or social service intervention and subsequent court trials, the possibility of psychiatric treatment or incarceration, the breakup of the family and public shame. Once in the open, the situation must be handled sensitively for the child's own sake; interviews, medical examinations, and court procedures must proceed with an awareness of the child's acute fears and anxieties. Though molestation may occur to children of ages from infants through the teenager years, the average age is from eleven to fourteen years old.

Not long ago, a close friend of ours from the midwest called one evening in a near-hysterical state; her twelve-year-old daughter had been approached sexually by her grandfather, the woman's father. The grandfather, as is sometimes the case, was a responsible member of the community, a proverbial pillar of family values. Her daughter's experience had triggered a memory the mother had long repressed; when she was the same age as her daughter, the same man (her father) had sexually molested her. She told her mother, who slapped her for lying, and asked her if she wanted to destroy the family. As a young teenager, she had dealt with the incidents fairly well, told no one else, and repressed the incident altogether. Though she had managed to overcome her feelings of fear and guilt, in retrospect she realized that it had inhibited her sexual responsiveness and healthy adult adjustment. When she confronted her father with the truth, he denied it absolutely and acted as if she had imagined the whole thing. Her mother accused her of hating her father. There the matter rested, except for the decision of our friend to break off all relations with her parents, and to alert her two siblings about what happened to protect their children.

These reactions are not atypical; only a fraction of child molestation incidents are brought to the attention of authorities, and even fewer are successfully prosecuted. In truth, no absolute guidelines can be set for the disposition of such cases. Not all cases should be dealt with outside the context of the family itself and certainly not all should come under legal jurisdiction.

Once upon a time, parents' main precaution was to tell children never to accept candy or rides from a stranger. Strangers, as statistics point out, represent about 25 percent of the offenders, though when it does occur, enticements are involved. Parents as well as child-care workers need to convey a somewhat different message to children. They should be told that no one—strangers, neighbors, relatives, or family members—has the right to touch or fondle their private parts. We need to be explicit that we are referring to the penis, vulva, vagina, breasts, and anus. The child should understand that even if it is someone he or she knows and loves, it is still not all right.

Generally speaking, the message to the child might say: "If someone ever touches you or asks or forces you to touch them, tell us right away. Say *no* to the person and get away from them if you can. Even if the person makes you promise not to tell anyone, that is a promise you should not keep. If you are threatened or forced to do things, you may have to go along with it, but even if you swear to God not to tell your mother, God doesn't expect you to keep promises that hurt you. Whenever someone says, Don't tell your mother, that's a good way of knowing whatever they are asking you to do is wrong." Children can be told these things without causing excessive alarm or scaring them unduly.

Relatives as well as the victims themselves often develop a keen desire for revenge and punishment for the molester. Jail and retribution may not be rehabilitative and helpful in the way that counseling and therapy might, however. Child-abuse hotlines and special counseling centers now exist in every state, and offer support, counseling, referrals, and legal assistance to victims as well as victimizers. With over 800 chapters nationwide, Parents Anonymous (PA) is a major resource (toll-free 800–421–0353; in California 800–352–0386). Nearly every major community also supports a rape crisis center.

Legally, in the past, a child's accusation of molestation against an adult required some corroborating testimony: the child's word alone was not sufficient for a conviction, or in many cases, even an indictment. This was a flagrant double standard: in robberies and other crimes, a child's testimony did not require corroboration. In 1984, New York became the forty-ninth state to pass a law eliminating the need for further evidence, and it is hoped that this will facilitate the court proceedings, help ensure greater justice, and offer further protection for children against repeat offenses.

During the past several years, incidents of child molestation and incest have captured headlines as never before, especially in day-care centers. This has been accompanied by a public outcry against the perpetrators (once referred to as "offenders"). This desire for revenge and punishment is understandable in light of the pain suffered by children.

What is too seldom publicized is the fact that the victimizers were themselves often victims as children. Studies conducted of both juvenile delinquents and older prison inmates reveal that as many as *50 percent* of them were beaten, abused, neglected, and/ or sexually molested in their own childhoods (see Spinetta and Rigler, 1980). Many parents and relatives who molest their own or others' children were sexually abused as children by *their* own parents or relatives (or both). These facts do not amount to license nor an abdication of responsibility or a release from blame for the perpetrators. But they do help to temper our response with an awareness that people who molest or abuse children are not simply "bad" or "evil" people.

This is a tremendously complex area that is often made more confusing by adults' reaction to it. When a child reveals that molestation has occurred, for instance, adults' first words often are, Why did you let him do it? This often leaves the child feeling 1) It's my fault, 2) I'm a bad person who deserves to be punished and unloved, and 3) I can't talk openly with mother/father, etc., about sexual or other sensitive things.

When major scandals involving sexual abuse in day care were publicized, a first reaction was to be surprised that none of the abused children had ever told parents of the incidents. Upon closer inspection, this turned out to be a mistaken impression. Children had indeed given their parents messages, perhaps by saying, I don't like it at day care, or, My teacher scares me, or even Sometimes I get hurt there. Rather than attending to the child's feelings and discovering the cause of the trouble, parents typically responded, Of course you like day care. You'll get used to it. You're supposed to like your teacher. What these responses betray is a bias, in which adults are always supposed to be listened to (if you're a child), and children are perceived as lying, to get out of school.

To a significant extent, a child's eventual adaptation to a crisis such as sexual abuse will depend on how parents respond to it. Tactics that serve to blame the victim reinforce feelings of hopelessness, self-hatred, and enduring difficulty in forming and maintaining intimate relationships with other people. Many women experience sexual dysfunctions with partners later in life, perhaps because of the feeling that letting oneself go sexually and trusting another person bring with it inevitable hurt and abandonment.

Long after the social workers, therapists, lawyers, and other helping persons have left the scene—perhaps years later—the family is still likely to be coping with the residual feelings stirred up by the abuse. Bystanders, such as aunts, uncles, friends, may state emphatically, I could only *hate* a person who did such a despicable thing. To be sure, hatred and rage are usually *some* of the feelings the victim has toward the perpetrator. But when the perpetrator is a family member, feelings are likely to be ambivalent; in addition to the hatred and anger are likely to be feelings of love, caring, and missing the person if they no longer see each other. These tender feelings do not necessarily represent a masochistic tendency or an acceptance of self-blame. They represent a human need for loving, for family unity, and belonging. In a sense, adjusting well to sexual abuse means accepting *all* one's feelings, both negative and positive.

If you were sexually abused by a father or older relative, there may well have been other children in the family—siblings most likely—who were not molested. Feelings of Why me? may emerge, as described by one woman: "How come my father picked on me, when there was my older sister in the house too? I was only five when it started, and I kept thinking there must be a reason why he chose me. What did I do wrong? Sometimes I think it's because I was the one who really worshipped him; saw him as the one who could do no wrong. Why didn't I stop him? I always had the feeling that if I said no firmly, he'd stop, but I couldn't say it. I was too afraid of what would happen to the family if this news got out. So I was the family's sacrifice to hold things together."

Family therapists discuss how such children become family scapegoats, both in sexual terms and by being blamed for most of the family's problems. As adults most people are able to realize intellectually that there was no rational reason for the scapegoating. As one woman put it, "I heard so often that I was to blame, that I was bad, and the incest just cemented that message. It's hard even today to overcome those feelings."

Sometimes, however, sexual abuse pervades the family system. An eleven-year-old boy who was seen in therapy by one of the authors had been sexually abused by both his mother and father, as had his older sister and younger brother and sister. These incidents had taken place during the course of some six years, and when they came to light, the department of social services removed all children from the home and placed them in foster care. Despite all the harm that had been done, this boy maintained that he wanted to go home and live with his parents again. This was very frustrating to the various case workers and court representatives who were involved in the case because the boy kept running away from his foster homes and resisted attempts to explain why he was prevented from seeing or living with his parents.

Clearly, sometimes a physical cut-off and separation of children from abusive parents is beneficial, either short or long term. But people who expend great amounts of energy trying to suppress their feelings for the alienated family members are creating a climate for poor emotional health. As young adults, some victims have profited from finally confronting their parents with the abusive behavior. For others, such situations breed catastrophe because the earlier patterns of rejection and blame continue even years later. Whether or not feelings are acted on, however, may be less important than how the individual works them through for him- or herself.

Although this chapter has been discussing sexual abuse and incest in similar contexts, there clearly are some important differences. Molestation committed by a parent or close family member may be even more traumatic to the child's adaptation. Nevertheless, as adults, the question remains for those who have been abused: How am I going to resolve this issue? Is it possible for me to understand what happened, accept the reality of it, perhaps forgive those involved or at least get on with my life satisfactorily?

Time is not always the great healer, and many people find that their daily functioning is impaired well into their twenties, thirties, forties, or fifties. There *are* things that individuals can do to work toward emotional health.

First, be glad that you can remember the incident at all. Some people find the abuse so painful that they manage to deny it ever happened, and the memories of it remain repressed in the unconscious. They are often, however, very troubled by other symptoms, which are signs of inner turmoil. These symptoms may include sexual dysfunctions, fear of intimacy with another person, an uncontrollable temper, a history of self-damaging sexual promiscuity, a string of bad relationships, or a host of physical symptoms, such as migraine headaches and gastrointestinal disorders. Although incidents similar to those mentioned earlier in this chapter may spring the memories from the unconscious, usually a trained, caring therapist can help the person remember and deal with the memories.

If you've been sexually abused, the best "revenge" is living well. Next best is being helpful to others who have faced similar situations. You triumph when you do not abuse your own children. Abuse is often repeated from generation to generation, but many people are able to organize themselves around the resolve, I'm not going to repeat my family's mistakes. I'm going to love and care for my children better now that it's my turn. This can be one of the best forms of therapy: to feel that one is succeeding as a parent (or as a loving, nonabusive spouse or partner).

Another key realization is that life is not over after sexual abuse or rape. Some victims overcome their pain through the conviction that just because I've been a victim doesn't mean that I have to be victimized for the rest of my life by the memory of it. I will not allow the rapist to control my life. What a triumph for the perpetrator if his violent act achieves its goal! For people who adopt this perspective, there remain scars and grief, but they successfully fight the belief that all people are bad and not to be trusted. In fact, the best way to begin feeling better about oneself *and* others is to be useful and helpful to other people, in the spirit of altruism.

We unequivocally encourage anyone who has a history of sexual abuse, and who feels he or she has not come to terms with it, to seek the help of a psychotherapist. This recommendation is not made lightly (see Chapter 11). Most probably, people who reach a stage in their adult lives where they continue to feel troubled have tried many solutions to their problems, most or all of which have failed. In fact, most people enter therapy for help in figuring out why their solutions have not worked and to discover one(s) that will succeed.

Outside therapy, the process of working through trauma related to sexual abuse and/or incest may be facilitated through a number of insights. First is the fundamental realization that the victim is not to blame for the behaviors. Even if you were a flirtatious, seductive little child, or one who was gullible and easily persuaded, you were not the cause of things. This is no simple matter: children typically feel, If I were a better child or more lovable, this would not have happened. Later in life, all the rational understanding you can muster might not alleviate this basic, perhaps unconscious, feeling.

For many victims of sexual abuse, the memory remains a closely guarded secret that is rarely, if ever, shared with friends, lovers, or even spouses. This secretiveness is often accompanied by the sentiment that other people would also feel the victim was dirty, shameful, and to blame. It can be extremely difficult to overcome this fear and to take the risk that others will not reject one as one has rejected oneself. In reality most people can be counted on to be compassionate, though a few might be accusatory and blaming. The process of unburdening oneself and talking over one's feelings can be a tremendous relief. Keeping secrets usually deprives people of the help and support they might otherwise receive from others and serves to perpetuate the problem. Surely the choice of with whom to share the information will be made carefully: the right person will be one who, from past experience, can be counted on to be empathic, supportive, and loving.

Opening the matter up for family discussion is another possibility, as already discussed. The author of *Father's Days*, Kathleen Brady, wrote of how she finally confronted her family with her father's incestuous behavior with her when she was a child. Each family member reacted differently: Her sister accused her of lying and refused to believe the stories, even after the father had acknowledged the truth; her mother reacted with horror and then admitted that she had suspected something wrong going on; her father at first denied the story, then soft-pedaled it, and finally gave his daughter what she sought—a full confession—along with a statement of his own responsibility. During this period, the family (minus the sister, who refused to participate) met with a family therapist for help in dealing with the emotional fallout. Though they hardly lived happily ever after and there remained much anger and bitterness, the author felt that she had made a good decision.

There is a growing awareness among professionals that some victims benefit the most from therapeutic support groups, in which victims have the opportunity to discuss their common experiences. It may be easier for some people to lower their defenses and open up more in a group setting where the possibility of being harshly judged is minimal. Both inpatient and outpatient therapy groups have also been established for the perpetrators, in which they confront each other's rationalizations and denials of responsibility and develop ways of resisting their infantile sexual impulses. These treatments have been reviewed by the Center for the Study of Anti-Social and Violent Behavior in the National Institute of Mental Health.

Controversy surrounding the treatment of perpetrators of both rape and child sexual abuse now focuses on the use of libido-suppressing drugs. The drug used, Depo-provera, has been successfully tested at the Rosenberg Clinic in Galveston, the Johns Hopkins University Hospital clinic by Berlin and Meinecke (1981), and in some Scandinavian countries. Depo-provera is also used as an oral contraceptive in some countries, though this use too is controversial. The drug therapy allegedly helps men control their aggressive sexual impulses; the conflict over its use concerns the fact that some perpetrators have gotten off with light sentences or probation as a result of volunteering for the drug program (it cannot be used against the person's will). Proponents of the drug claim that since some sex offenders have brain, chromosomal, or hormonal disorders, physiological interventions are the only reliable method of treatment. Those who question use of the drug argue that this may be true, but it does not absolve the person of responsibility for his actions, and thus he should be punished similarly to those who are not treated with Depo-provera.

The criticism most often heard in public debate, however, is that since rape and molestation are crimes of violence, not sex, reduction by chemical means of the sex drive would not affect the violence. This claim is not substantiated by follow-up studies at the above-mentioned clinics. Another debate is raging about possible health risks and side effects known to exist when the Depo-provera was tested with animals.

Most efforts in the area of child sexual abuse have been devoted to teaching children how to say no assertively, and teaching parents how to communicate effectively with their children. Preventative efforts that focus on children learning to say no are inadequate. Recent revelations now suggest even if a child says no many, if not most, will be molested anyway if the adult is determined to do so. Not nearly enough work has gone into preventative programs which seek to 1) reach molesters with crucial messages about their behavior and 2) provide all members of society with an adequate sexuality education. Most of what society conveys to offenders/perpetrators is a sense of horror, outrage, and condemnation. A more complete message, to readers of this book, and anyone who is tempted to become sexually involved with children, might be as follows:

> We know you are turned on by children, maybe even your own child. We know you get sexually aroused by thoughts of rape, being tortured, hurting someone, forcing or tricking a child into masturbating you, and imagining yourself watching people in the sex act. What you don't know is that people get sexually aroused by all kinds of things.
>
> What no one ever taught you was that, in and of itself, thoughts are not harmful. Almost everyone has weird sexual thoughts. If you feel guilty about these thoughts, you'll have them over and over again. These thoughts will become obsessive and create a lot of tension. To relieve this tension, most of you masturbate. But having been taught that masturbation is wrong, instead of decreasing tension, masturbation increases it, and the guiltier you feel the more preoccupied you become with your obsession. Then you feel you can't help it. You're addicted. You have these terrible urges to satisfy and, at times, you feel you must have sex with a child. After it's over, the tension is relieved and you feel better, but you know it's not for long. Sometimes you even say you feel guilty and promise yourself you'll never do it again.
>
> We know that you know it's wrong because you tell the child not to tell anyone what you have done and even threaten the child with harm. It doesn't matter what

excuses you give to the child or to yourself. It is *always* wrong and harmful to the child.

We know you, the molester, are not impressed when *Time* magazine (1984) suggests that "in an age of sexual freedom more people will act on forbidden urges." You know, and we know, that you do these terrible things not because you are sexually *free* but because you've become an addict—a sexual addict—because you have these overwhelming sexual urges that you feel you cannot control.

What we know, and what you may not like to think about, is that you've been taught the wrong things. Here is what we think you should do if you get these urges:

If you get an urge to have sex with a child, go off to a private place and masturbate. If you realize that masturbation is okay, it will decrease your tension temporarily. Even if the masturbating becomes compulsive, there's not much harm in it. It is far better than raping a child. Sex with a child is rape because no child can legitimately or legally consent to have sex with an adult. If you masturbate, it will give the child a chance to escape from your urges and it will give you a chance to think, I need to get some help. Admit to yourself that you are a sex addict. Call your local helpline, crisis center, or mental health center for an appropriate source. (The most helpful book for anyone with impulses toward sexual molestation is *The Sexual Addiction* by Patrick Carnes.)

We know you've probably gotten into this mess because you've been molested yourself as a child or for reasons no one understands, but there is never any healthy reason to take revenge on a child. Why spoil any child's life, or your life, because bad things have happened to you?

As a postscript to the above message, authorities who have worked with child molesters have found that many of them have been abusing children for years and that as many as *600* children may have been abused by one man.

The concept of *punishment* is both a political and philosophical snare: What is its purpose—to appease society's conscience? To help the victim feel that he or she did not suffer in vain? To rehabilitate the criminal? Our view is that the primary goal is to ensure the crime does not happen again. Rates of recidivism indicate that traditional methods, such as imprisonment, have not been very effective in protecting society from its violent members. It's interesting that those prisons both here and abroad that incorporate humanitarian counseling and rehabilitation techniques into their programs are those with the lowest rates of recidivism. The dilemma is that such institutions are accused of coddling criminals and not satisfying society's desire for revenge. A provocative question is: Can people who originally became criminals due to abusive treatment in childhood be rehabilitated through further abusive treatment? We think not. At the same time that we advocate humanitarian treatment, however, our paramount wish is to protect our own families and the lives of our neighbors.

Many individual paths exist for dealing with sexual abuse and incest, which anthropologists have found are near-universal taboos. It is perhaps most important for victims to realize that *they are not powerless* to improve their situation, to work toward feeling better, and to reach a stage of mental equilibrium and health.

The intense public outcry and accompanying coverage in all the media have created in some people's minds the fear of a backlash, in which adults become preoccupied about the meaning of their every contact with children. In this scenario, parents would be fearful of being accused of molestation in the everyday bathing and dressing of their children. Day-care workers would fear being accused of sexual abuse if they hugged and kissed the children in their care. In fact, the fear goes, nearly all physical and emotional contacts with children may be closely scrutinized to prevent people from crossing the line between affection and molestion.

In practice, this paranoia is largely unjustified. It is not difficult for adults in practically all cases to distinguish between healthy, loving affection, and contacts that are explicitly sexual in meaning and intent. Children themselves are remarkably sensitive to the difference, though they may not articulate it well.

In short, parents and those who work with children know that children thrive on normal expressions of love and affection, and so do adults.

REFERENCES

Armstrong, L. *Kiss Daddy Goodnight*. New York: Pocket Books, 1978.

Berlin, F., & Meinecke, C. F. "Treatment of Sex Offenders with Antiandrogenic Medication: Conceptualization, Review of Treatment Modalities, and Preliminary Findings." *American Journal of Psychiatry*, 1981, **138**, 601–607.

Besharov, D. J. "U.S. National Center on Child Abuse and Neglect: Three Years of Experience." *Child Abuse and Neglect* **1**, 1977, 173–177.

Brady, Kathleen. *Father's Days*. New York: Dell Books, 1979.

Brozan, N. Helping to Heal the Scars Left by Incest. *New York Times*, January 9, 1984.

Carnes, P. *The Sexual Addiction*. Minneapolis: CompCare Publications, 1983.

Child Abuse Prevention and Treatment Act, 1974. United States Code Annotated. Title 42, *The Public Health and Welfare*, pp. 199–205.

Finkelhor, D. *Child Sexual Abuse: Theory and Research*. New York: Free Press, 1984.

Groth, A. *Men Who Rape: The Psychology of the Offender*. New York: Plenum, 1979.

Lindsey, R. "Sexual Abuse of Children Draws Experts' Increasing Concern Nationwide." *New York Times*, April 4, 1984, A21.

Russell, D. E. H. "The Incidence and Prevalence of Intrafamilial and Extrafamilial Sexual Abuse of Children." *Child Abuse and Neglect*, 1983, **7**, 133–146.

Spinetta, J. J., & Rigler, D. "The Child-abusing Parent: A Psychological Review." In
J. Money & G. Williams (Eds.), *Traumatic Abuse and Neglect of Children at Home.*
Baltimore: The Johns Hopkins University Press, 1980.

Time. April 12, 1984, p. 73.

RECOMMENDED READING

Gordon, S., & Gordon, J. *A Better Safe Than Sorry Book—A Family Guide for Sexual
Assault Prevention.* Fayetteville, NY: Ed-U Press, 1984.

CHAPTER 14

Pornography, Erotica, and the First Amendment

Very few people are able to agree on a working definition of what actually constitutes pornography. One interesting approach would be to ask yourself, What specific aspects of my own sexual behavior, if filmed or explicitly described in print, would be pornographic? Getting dressed in the morning? Undressing and taking a bath or shower? Holding hands, kissing, hugging, petting? Masturbating? Having sexual intercourse, a homosexual encounter, group sex? Some people would answer all of the above, some, none of the above, and most people would fall somewhere between these two extremes.

Today, the most common definition of pornography derives from guidelines set down by the United States Supreme Court in the 1957 Roth case, modified by subsequent court rulings. This definition has three criteria. First, for the average person, the dominant theme of the material, on the whole, must appeal to a "prurient" interest in sex. Second, the material in question must be "patently" offensive because of an affront to "contemporary community standards" regarding presentation of sexual matters. Finally, the material must be "utterly lacking in redeeming social values." Rather than clarifying the issue, these criteria have created a great deal of uncertainty.

However much some people think that *Playboy, Playgirl,* and *Penthouse* are pornographic, that is not our view nor is it the view of the majority of Americans. *Hustler,* and even cruder, more explicit publications that degrade human sexuality through dehumanizing, violent portrayals, are more like pornography. Depictions of sadistic acts against women, children, and men also fall into this category (there is a tendency to think that sexual violence is directed against only women and children, but men are also treated violently in some of the material we've reviewed).

Who uses pornography? Available data suggest that about 85 percent of all men and 70 percent of all women in the United States have been exposed to one form of pornography or another. The great majority of this exposure is voluntary. Statistics show that highly educated people are more likely to have read or seen pornography than their less well-educated neighbors. In fact, the average patron of a pornographic movie house is white, male, between the ages of 26 and 45, a white-collar worker or professional with a college degree and an annual income in excess of the national average (Presidential Commission, 1970).

More recent studies, as well as a commonsense look at the various media, demonstrate that personal experience with pornography is widespread—most people have seen it at least once.

For a long time researchers contended that men and women respond differently to pornographic stimuli. Early studies done in the 1940s and 1950s by Kinsey and his associates suggested that men were more stimulated by pornography than women. Some research now suggests that men and women have similar reactions both in terms of arousal and response (Heiman, 1975).

Three basic theories exist to describe how pornography affects people (see McCormack, 1978). The first, or "modeling" theory, argues that people imitate the sexual behavior that they witness in pornography. A second, or "cathartic" theory, suggests that exposure to pornography *lessens* pent-up sexual drives, thus mitigating the possibility of antisocial or violent sexual behavior. The third, or "null" theory, states that pornography has neither a stimulative nor a depressive effect on human sexual behavior.

Most contemporary research indicates that pornography is not harmful and does not corrupt. In this respect, the Danish experience is instructive. During the 1960s, Denmark experienced a rapid increase in the availability of pornography following its legalization. Sociological studies demonstrated that the overall number of sex crimes in Denmark *declined* in proportion to the *rising* availability of pornography. At this point, it is premature to conclude that pornography lowered the number of sex crimes in Denmark. Other factors could be involved. Yet, we can note that wide availability *did not* lead to an *increase* in any category of sexual offenses during the period under study.

Another important study of pornography was conducted by P. H. Gebhard (1965) under the auspices of the Institute for Sex Research. Gebhard interviewed over 2700 men—convicted sex offenders as well as controls who were also prisoners. Exposure to pornography among this group was almost universal. The study concluded that, for the most part, pornography did not stimulate this cross-section of inmates. Instead, the sight or thought of a woman stimulated them. We might conclude that campaigns of censorship will not succeed in reducing the number of sex crimes.

The United States Commission on Obscenity and Pornography, established by Congress and appointed by two presidents, conducted the most extensive study of this subject to date. In its 1970 report, the Commission found no reliable evidence that exposure to pornography plays a significant role in promoting either delinquent or criminal sexual behavior among adults or children. The Commission recommended abolition of all antipornography laws as they apply to adults, but advocated certain restrictions on the availability of pornography to children without parental consent.

More research is needed to interpret the effects of massive saturation of pornography in society. Many citizens do not agree with the Commission's findings and recommendations. Some of the commissioners themselves filed strongly worded minority objections, and President Nixon rejected the final report of the Commission.

We do not think that pornography is educational, and there are at least two persuasive arguments against banning it. The first has to do with "forbidden fruit." The second involves the constitutional right of adults to look at or read anything they want to.

It is clear that if pornography were banned, criminal elements who already control most of its production and distribution would earn more money. Anything that's banned immediately becomes more expensive and often more readily available. The more governmental regulation and restriction, the more possibility of organized criminal activity and control. Society should have learned a lesson from Prohibition.

If pornography were banned, the trend might easily snowball to include artistic, yet controversial areas. Persons often fail to distinguish between pornography and perfectly good films and literature. We need to remember that the works of D. H. Lawrence and books such as James Joyce's *Ulysses* were considered obscene in their time.

Unfortunately, the book banners are still with us. Here is a list of books recently banned in some American schools and libraries. This list is provided to encourage you to read *these* books. These books do not remotely resemble pornography, but their banning demonstrates that opening the door to censorship even slightly threatens all literature.

John Steinbeck: *Of Mice and Men*
J. D. Salinger: *Catcher in the Rye*
Piri Thomas: *Down These Mean Streets*
Ernest Hemingway: *For Whom the Bell Tolls*
                    To Have and Have Not
                    A Farewell to Arms
Ken Kesey: *One Flew Over the Cuckoo's Nest*
Hermann Hesse: *Siddhartha*
Kurt Vonnegut: *Slaughterhouse Five*
Alexander Solzhenitzyn: *One Day in the Life of Ivan Denisovich*
Bernard Malamud: *The Fixer*
Lewis Carroll: *Alice in Wonderland*
Mark Twain: *Huckleberry Finn*

Germaine Greer: *The Female Eunuch*
Malcolm X: *The Autobiography of Malcolm X*
Anthony Burgess: *A Clockwork Orange*
Ralph Ellison: *The Invisible Man*
Norman Mailer: *The Armies of the Night*

The unending battle against pornography has been waged recently by two diverse camps: feminists (e.g., Women Against Pornography) and conservative fundamentalists (e.g., The Moral Majority). Traditional challenges to sexually explicit materials based on obscenity have not proved successful in recent years, and now the attacks focus on pornography as a violation of women's civil rights. In late 1983, the city council of Minneapolis passed an amendment to the city's civil rights ordinance that defined pornography as "a form of discrimination on the basis of sex." The mayor vetoed the amendment, but in mid-1984 a similar measure was signed into law by the mayor of Indianapolis (later ruled unconstitutional).

The American Civil Liberties Union, The Association of American Publishers, and the American Booksellers Association have vowed to fight the laws all the way up to the Supreme Court, based on free speech guarantees of the First Amendment, which states

> Congress shall make no law respecting an establishment of religion, or prohibiting the free exercise thereof; or abridging the freedom of speech, or of the press; or the right of the people peaceably to assemble, and to petition the Government for a redress of grievances.

For many political activists and commentators, it has been a strange sight to see the far right allied with the allegedly radical elements of the women's movement. A 1984 panel discussion in *Harper's* magazine added a further dimension to the antipornography effort. If censorship were to be permitted in any instance, might not those opposed to abortion argue for the suppression of *Ms.* magazine and other publications that support a pro-choice stance? Some critics believe that the women's movement in general is contributing to the destruction of the American family and might thus argue that feminist publications should be banned across the board to save the family. Perhaps a repression of public speech rights would follow: in World War I, 2000 people were imprisoned for speaking against the war effort. Have we progressed far enough beyond those days that history would not repeat itself? These are questions to which each side of the debate has answers. Where do you stand?

In particular, the new crusades against pornography center on the proliferation of materials that portray women being beaten, tortured, humiliated, and even killed. There is an equal revulsion to kiddie porn, which shows children as young as age three involved in sexual activities. It is, and should remain, a crime to produce child pornography, or to force men or women into any behaviors to which they do not consent.

Beyond this, the depiction of consensual sexual behaviors among adults violates no one's civil rights (though they may be revolting and violent), provided that they do not intrude into the public domain. In other words, pornography should be kept behind closed doors, out of eyesight of those who do not wish to see it.

Recent research has focused more on violent pornography and its effects. Edward Donnerstein, a psychologist at the University of Wisconsin, did a study of violent, X-rated films with male students and concluded that exposure to such films led the students to feel less sympathy for women who had been raped. Once the violent aspects had been removed from the films, however, there was no desensitization. This correlation between violence and attitudes leaves unanswered the fundamental question: Are such attitudes translated into subsequent violent behaviors and/or sex crimes? It is well known in sociological research that attitudes are not necessarily accompanied by actions that reflect them: college-educated men, for instance, support the egalitarian principles of shared domestic work and the ERA but are not likely to perform more domestic chores or child care than those who don't support the ERA. Donnerstein himself states, "We can show a causal link between exposure to porn and effects on *attitudes;* but no one can show a causal link between exposure to porn and effects on behavior" *Newsweek,* 1985).

Dr. Diana Russell, a professor of social science at Mills College and author of *The Politics of Rape,* believes that a large proportion of males have a propensity to rape and that violent pornography may lessen their inhibitions against acting out violent impulses. Others, such as Ernest van Den Haag, a professor at Fordham University Law School who also opposes pornography, nevertheless believe that no serious research exists that demonstrates pornography is a cause of crime.

Such studies are almost impossible to conduct for a number of reasons. How would a researcher document when in a person's life exposure to pornography began? How can it be said that pornography caused a particular antisocial or criminal behavior, as opposed to having endured an abusive childhood? Should victims of violent crimes be permitted to file civil suits against the perpetrator's abusive parents? Laboratory experiments can only suggest relationships between factors and cannot determine cause and effect. Thus, those who both oppose and support pornography are frustrated by a lack of real evidence to support their position.

Aryeh Neier, formerly national executive director of the ACLU, has found that in repressive countries in Central America, Africa, and Eastern Europe, hostility and sexual violence against women are widespread and are used as a main form of political repression. These very same countries have virtually no pornography, though rape, sexual torture, and abuse of women is part of the system. Neier thus concludes that pornography itself is not particularly important in light of actual violence against women worldwide.

Pornography is most likely a symptom of, rather than the cause of, some men's oppressive attitudes and behavior toward women. Banning pornography does not address the central issue, which is that many people—both men and women—are turned on by fantasies and depictions of violence and explicit sexual scenes. Many people who consider themselves politically liberated, and who have devoted much energy to raising their consciousness, are disturbed by a lingering fascination with pornography. Pornography is an estimated 7-billion-dollar-a-year industry, a figure that supports the established fact that even many respectable people occasionally attend an X-rated movie or buy some explicit magazines. Even if they find the materials somewhat disappointing, they may return for more sometime later. In this way, cycles of addiction to sexually stimulating materials may be built, similar to the process of addiction described in the chapter on child sexual abuse. In this cycle, tension and anxiety are relieved only temporarily, and the addictive object, material, or substance is periodically sought out to relieve the need.

In fact, the *Harper's* panel mentioned earlier suggested that pornography is so prevalent because it is inherently unsatisfying. That is, a person may feel compelled to experience it, but since it fails to be as exciting as the person's fantasy, more pornography is sought out in the hopes that it will meet the person's expectations.

Personal *fixation* on pornography is usually a symptom of neurosis. This does not refer to subscribers to such magazines as *Playboy* or *Playgirl*. We mean pornography in its hard-core connotation. Typically, men who are regular consumers of pornography have received little or no sexuality education and feel guilty about their sexual impulses. Although many such men are married, often their spouses have little awareness of the husband's pornographic pursuits. Whether or not the interest is acknowledged between partners, it often serves to alienate them from each other. Sexual and emotional energy that might otherwise go into the relationship are diverted into what is an impersonal experience.

There is an important distinction to be drawn between erotica and pornography. Erotica in literature and the arts has an ancient history dating back thousands of years (see the book *Erotic Art* by Drs. Phyllis and Eberhard Kronhausen). Erotica provides an aesthetic appeal and stimulation of the senses that many people find appealing. Most well-known modern artists at some point in their career express their libidinal energies with artistic flair. Although some people find such erotic depictions as objectionable as the most explicit pornography, this "lumping together" seems more representative of individual inhibitions.

Within today's movies and other media there also exist presentations that are most accurately labeled as erotic. Often, the sexual aspect occurs within the context of a loving, caring relationship, with some meaning attached to it, as opposed to the detached, cold performances and sadomasochism one finds in pornography. Whichever label is used, however, an obsessional fixation on sexually related materials probably represents an unresolved personal problem. If a reader of this book feels that is the case for him- or herself, it might be useful to attempt to discover the roots of the obsession, and to determine if for you the pornography tends to leave you feeling isolated, guilt ridden, fearful of discovery, and as if you can't help going back for more.

A college junior who was seen in therapy for a time explained that although he had a fair but increasingly troubled relationship with his girlfriend, he was obsessed with girl-watching and pornography. His routine included regular trips to an X-rated movie or adult bookstore. In the peepshow booths in the bookstores, he would feed quarters into the minimovies and masturbate. Although he was able to maintain his sexual relationship with his girlfriend, thoughts of sex, followed and accompanied by masturbation, consumed most of his waking hours.

A tremendous amount of guilt and anxiety always followed these experiences. Each time, he would promise himself never again, and yet within a day or two his thoughts would focus more and more on thoughts of sex and pornography, and he would be seized with desires he just couldn't help and couldn't control. In fact, the more guilty he felt, the stronger the compulsion to gratify his urges became. This young man was helped to understand that guilt was the energy for the repetition of his unacceptable (to him) behavior. If his powerful sexual urges had been accepted as normal, the compulsive element associated with them would have subsided. At the conclusion of his counseling, he still fantasized often about sex and occasionally masturbated while viewing pornography. The behavior was, however, less compulsive—he had gained some control over his actions and thus had more of a choice.

Even when people voluntarily purchase pornography and conduct loving relationships at the same time, problems can arise. One father kept a secret cache of magazines hidden in his attic, inside a box he was sure no one would disturb. His eleven-year-old daughter spent one rainy Saturday in the attic while her father was on a business trip and discovered the materials. The parents had never discussed sexuality with her, and she was terribly confused and upset by the pictures—she had no perspective with which to understand them and was probably affected more negatively than would another child whose parents had educated her. A shock wave went through the family after the discovery of the pornography, and the parents contemplated separating for a while because of the wife's feeling of having her trust betrayed. As the couple explored why the husband had hidden his magazines, it became clear that the root of the problem was an inability to discuss any sexual issues, preferences, and desires. Many other aspects of their lives had remained hidden from each other as well.

In both the above cases, pornography was one link in a circle of self-damaging behavior that, although it was not pleasurable, was repeated over and over again. It *is* possible to enjoy erotic materials occasionally in a healthy way. But given our society's relative immaturity in the sexual dimension, and the fact that most children have imparted to them very little knowledge, pornography most often exists within a framework of guilt, exploitation, snickering, and secretiveness.

American society, and mental health professionals in particular, have devoted much effort to cataloging the various sexual and psychological dysfunctions, deviancies, and pathologies. Little work has gone into developing a positive, healthy model of adult sexuality. We know how to define and describe an unhealthy sexual adjustment, but how would we describe a healthy sexual adaptation? It is interesting that an interest in erotic materials has been alternately viewed as a sign of deviation and as evidence of a zestful, exciting acceptance of one's sexuality.

The energy consumed in banning pornography would be better spent in establishing good sex education programs in our schools. Society needs to deal with the problems that cause the desire for pornography instead of focusing on the symptoms. Educated people who feel good about themselves find pornography uninteresting after a while. And if they do enjoy it, they are well able to control the degree of their experience with it.

Here is an excerpt from a report by Sweden's State Commission on Aspects of Sex and Personal Relationships in Teaching and Public Education:

> Teaching should systematically combat the picture of the relationship between man and woman promulgated by pornography and "sexism." The separation of sexuality and sexual life from the context of life at large, and, particularly, the presentation of woman purely as a sexual object, are incompatible with the objectives proposed for sexual education.

A later publication by the Swedish Institute (1984) added that ". . . we must vigorously reject the human degradation which normally permeates all pornography." Sweden is an example of a society in which pornography has been accepted as a legal and social reality yet is counteracted with an enlightened approach to sexuality education.

Pornography is a response to society's unwillingness to promote a responsible sex education at home and in the schools.

REFERENCES

Boethins, C. B. *Swedish Sex Education and Its Results*. Stockholm: Swedish Institute, 1984.

Gebhard, P. H. et al. *Sex Offenders: An Analysis of Types*. New York: Harper & Row, 1965.

Heiman, J. R. Women's Sexual Arousal—The Physiology of Erotica. *Psychology Today*, April 1975, 91–94.

Kinsey, A. C. et al. *Sexual Behavior in the Human Male*. Philadelphia: W. B. Saunders, 1948.

Kinsey, A. C. et al. *Sexual Behavior in the Human Female*. Philadelphia: W. B. Saunders, 1953.

Kronhausen, P., & Kronhausen, E. *Erotic Art*. New York: Grove Press, 1968.

Lapham, L. H. (moderator). The Place of Pornography. *Harper's*, 1984, 269 (1614), 31–45.

Newsweek. "The War against Pornography." March 18, 1985, pp. 58–67.

CHAPTER 15

The Disabled and Sexuality

At a Sexual Attitude Reassessment (SAR) experience held recently, a movie depicting sexual activity between a paraplegic man and his nondisabled wife was shown. The film was graphically explicit but what amazed the viewers was the diversity of erogenous areas on the man's body. While he lacked sensation in his genitals, he described how he can reach orgasm (not ejaculation) through having his neck stroked. Other viewers were astonished that a "normal" woman would want to marry a person with a disability. Yet in this movie the quality of love and caring between the two was unmistakable. Overall, people watching the movie were confronted with their own prejudices and fears concerning interaction with people who have handicaps.

There are so many myths and misunderstandings in this area that they are difficult to catalog:

- People tend to shout or talk loudly when conversing with a blind person.
- When talking even with handicapped adults, people often resort to baby talk and infantile expressions.
- People tend to stare at people with handicaps and yet avoid making eye contact.
- Some disabled and retarded people are suspected of being sexually dangerous and/or aggressive.

It is difficult to say where the story of the handicapped being sexual molesters or assaulters began. What is known is that in the overwhelming majority of instances, they themselves are the victims of sexual abuse or rape. This chapter will challenge many readers' conceptions of sexuality, the disabled, and personal attitudes. Perhaps most challenged will be some disabled individuals themselves, who have ingested a steady stream of negative messages about their sexuality, and who now must struggle to achieve a sense of self-esteem and acceptance of their sexual selves.

As a point of departure, read the following quote from Gloria and Barry Blum (1981):

> Many parents view their handicapped daughter or son as asexual or devoid of any sexual or sensual desires, much less as able to satisfy any of these desires in any way. No wonder disabled young people also view themselves as asexual. It serves no purpose to blame the parents, the disabled, or anyone. There is no blame. Instead, there is a situation that has great promise to be resolved—directly or indirectly. Parents need to become aware that there are people who are severely handicapped (loss of sensation, movement, movement control, and body parts) who still have very satisfactory sexual, sensual, and emotional interpersonal relationships, whether heterosexual, homosexual, autosexual, or any combination. These relationships are satisfying not only to themselves, but also to their partners.

A while ago one of the authors was addressing a meeting of several hundred severely disabled individuals, their parents, and related health professionals. After he had spoken enthusiastically for half an hour, the gathering remained sullen and unimpressed with the presentation. The speaker had spoken positively of the rights of all individuals to sexual expression and intimate relationships, and yet the audience did not respond. Finally, a nerve was struck that ignited a storm of protest and controversy. There was a particularly emotional outburst from one workshop leader. She shouted, "How can you say things like that when you see before you people who need only look at themselves in the mirror to know that what you say represents empty promises of a future that is not possible for any of them!"

The answer came from a woman confined to a wheelchair. She said, "You know, when I look only at myself, I feel depressed. When I take in the world I live in, I'm impressed. And when I allow God to touch me, I feel blessed."

Pandemonium broke out. The formerly unreceptive, frustrated crowd became a group of people wanting desperately to talk about their hidden aspirations, mainly in terms of their strong desires for love, companionship, and sexual expression.

Society has conspired to deny disabled individuals their inherent sexual nature. Parents, as well as institutions to which they may be confined, have responded to the rehabilitative and educational needs of the disabled in all major areas save that of sexuality. A victim of an automobile accident who is suddenly paraplegic, a child born cerebral-palsied, and others with a variety of disabling conditions are taught how to handle the orthopedic devices, wheelchairs, prostheses, and other special adaptations that are required. In many cases, extraordinary inventiveness has been displayed in overcoming tremendous difficulties. In the area of life that most yearn for regardless of their physical or mental incapacities, however, a desire for intimate human relationships, little effort has been made. If you have a disability, you may have found that it came to overshadow all other areas of your existence.

In this way, people come to be existentially defined by what they are not, and what they cannot do: *dis*-ability. The focus develops around a person's deficits, and corresponding areas of adequacy and *pro*-ability may not receive the same attention.

Most disabled individuals suffer from extremely low levels of self-esteem. If you look in the mirror and see deformed limbs, spastic and uncontrolled body movements, you may worry, How could anyone ever love me? Those with mentally handicapping conditions also fear that they are unattractive to other people. Perhaps they have already failed in school or been relegated to special classes, had to face the fact that they will never be able to hold a job as their peers will, and come to grips with a lifetime of needing other people to survive. Isolated from the rest of society by physical barriers and often spending the majority of their time at home or in an institution, they see little hope for their future.

This is not painting an unrealistically grim picture. Despite the enormous difficulties they face, it is time for people who have disabilities to think about themselves in these terms: Yes, I want to love and be loved. Yes, I want to express my sexuality in whatever ways are possible. Apart from the obvious difficulties your disabilities pose, the main problems you have are usually a lack of friends and companionship, things to do that are interesting to you, and frustration of your sexual needs. The disability itself can emerge as a minor problem compared to feelings of worthlessness and despair.

Physiologically, you may have catheters to be dealt with, braces to be removed, or transitory sensation in your genitals. You may have to struggle out of wheelchairs or cope with shaky hands and may slur the intimate words you speak to another. These are secondary considerations to the emotions that may exist between two people, disabled or not. A young woman quoted in *Coping* (1984), described herself as having a great capacity for compassion, passion, understanding, sensitivity, and love. She said, ". . . my heart often aches to share these qualities within myself with another human being . . . but I cannot walk, I use a wheelchair, I am handicapped. How do I get across the idea that I'm a person with a sexual identity? That I have a warm, tender, caring side of me that I want to share with another human being? It angers me that I must prove that this special part of me exists. The anger and frustration builds and builds to the point of utter discouragement and painfully felt sadness."

A birthright to full sexual expression, however, is accompanied by the same responsibilities that apply to any other person. Disabled individuals who experience sexual intercourse must be as careful to guard against pregnancy and sexually transmitted disease as their nondisabled counterparts. They must be as sensitive to other people's feelings as "normal" people and must be taught not to exploit or hurt partners for their own selfish desires. These values apply whether the person is retarded, learning disabled, or has a colostomy.

Evidence suggests that parents of youth with disabilities spend more time than other parents in discouraging their children's sexuality, and masturbation in particular. This can be especially devastating for the young person with a disability who often does not have the same opportunities for socialization and dating available to others. Many institutions spend inordinate amounts of energy in guaranteeing that patients do not even have enough privacy to masturbate. *Any* person who is prohibited from exploring his or her sexuality in this way and is made to feel guilty about it may suffer a variety of emotional consequences. As we stated unequivocally in the chapter on masturbation, it is a normal sexual expression for people of any age, provided it is voluntary and enjoyable. Some disabled people seem to masturbate a great deal, which is often a response to boredom or lack of outside interests. This is not a sexual problem per se. The solution, if the behavior really is excessive, is to become stimulated in other ways and to create social experiences and interactions that satisfy the need for human relationships.

Institutions for the disabled are perhaps most unresponsive and repressive toward the sexuality of their patients. In a Florida home, those boys caught masturbating were forced to do it in public to shame them from repeating it in private. One Pennsylvania institution cut down all the bushes on the grounds so their handicapped residents would not have any hiding places for time alone.

In another institution for the developmentally disabled where one of the authors recently addressed the staff on the basics of sex education, aides and nurses were invited to submit questions in advance of the presentation. The majority of the questions could be summarized as follows: How can we stop masturbation? A considerable amount of staff energy was devoted to catching or curbing the masturbators.

In addition, great emphasis was put on discouraging any other form of sexual behavior. While this institution was composed of only male residents, much effort was spent in punishing or curbing homosexual behavior, but now with females added as residents, the main thrust was against any expression of heterosexuality. It was suggested that the staff examine their attitudes toward their own sexuality. In that way they might become more sensitive toward themselves and to look upon the people in their charge with more compassion.

For people who simply do not have sufficient motor control to masturbate themselves, vibrators can be used with satisfying results. The disabled need not feel squeamish or wrong for buying a vibrator any more than they should feel awkward asking for a date. People with disabilities sometimes need others' assistance in arranging dates or being deliberately placed in situations where they have opportunities to meet other people. If they cannot walk down the street to meet their friends or get to dances under their own steam, they may need help.

Some college campuses have organizations for the disabled that offer a combination of educational events and opportunities for involvement with other students. For instance, the Organization for Disabled Students at Syracuse University has approximately 150 members. In addition to twice-monthly meetings, they sponsor an annual

Awareness Week, which includes films, campus lectures and presentations, and other public events. In essence, the organization provides the opportunity for disabled students to get acquainted with each other, to ask questions, and to gather information. Otherwise, there is nowhere else to turn.

One of the difficulties that such organizations face is the reluctance of some students to identify themselves as disabled by joining a group. This is often accompanied by a refusal to befriend any other disabled people. The wish to appear "normal" and to have only "normal" friends is understandable. If this is your sentiment, give some thought to whether it represents a very negative opinion of yourself. Chances are that if you find other similarly handicapped individuals unfit companions, you also question your own desirability as a friend. It is equally limiting to associate only with either disabled or nondisabled people.

Sometimes disabled people become so immersed in self-pity that they decide in advance that nobody will ever love them or want to marry them. The alternative to making grim prophecies and waiting for time to bear them out is to find or create new reasons to love and respect oneself. Positive self-regard is what counts: If I look like I am mightily enjoying my own company, chances are somebody else will soon be along wishing to share it.

As people mature in their social relationships, they may begin to think seriously about marriage. Popular mythology notwithstanding, many disabled persons do marry and adjust quite successfully. Others prefer to remain single; the problem is with those who would like to marry but who fear their impairment makes them ineligible, or their parents would never approve. The parents might simply not want to be saddled with yet another financial burden. (This is of no concern to those who are self-supporting.) Parents who have already accepted permanent financial responsibility for one disabled child may find that with the help of a second set of parents their share of supporting two is less expensive. There will be others to share shopping, laundry and chauffering, rent, utilities, and phone bills. Moreover, with new feelings of independence, and with the energy generated by the loving relationship, the disabled partners may become less emotionally dependent on their respective parents. It would be a mistake to dismiss matters of cooking and cleaning as trivial, and if the partners are unable to handle these chores between them, perhaps the two sets of parents could share the duties with each other.

Disabled people who want to have children may be confronted with objections from doctors and families. In this situation, one cannot talk blithely of the right to bear offspring, or the joys of nurturance and comfort a child might bring the couple. Romantic fantasies about parenthood abound: cuddling sweet sleeping infants while they gurgle delightedly and loving them to pieces with never a scream in the middle of the night, rashes, emergencies, indigestion, or two weeks of diarrhea. The best approach is to evaluate realistically whether you are able to care for a child. There are added expenses, and the child's need and right to be raised in a stimulating environment. Those who think they would like to have a child but aren't sure of their ability to manage might volunteer to work in a nursery or day-care center for a while to get an idea of what is involved. It's not foolproof, but it can be instructive. (Some adults, disabled or not, are simply unsuited emotionally or physically to raise a family.)

Marriage for the disabled is often more successful without children, without the inevitable disruption and strain involved in child-rearing. Other drawbacks include the possibility that a normal child born of developmentally disabled parents may subsequently become retarded as a consequence of inferior care and insufficient stimulation during the formative years. It can be difficult for even a mildly retarded or learning disabled couple to understand the future implications of having a child and providing years of care; more commonly an emotionally disabled husband and wife will tend to focus on the present, the pleasures and satisfactions of the moment, at the expense of hard thinking about tomorrow's consequences and responsibilities.

In some cases voluntary sterilization (vasectomy for the male; tubal ligation for the female) may be the best answer for seriously disabled couples, for those who couldn't possibly expect to cope with parenthood or for those who are certain that they do not, and never will, wish to have children. Sterilization should be considered as permanent and therefore inappropriate for anyone who is uncertain about choosing a childless lifestyle.

An unplanned or unwanted pregnancy can mean exceptional hardship for the disabled, from coping with the rigors of pregnancy to caring for the child after it is born. In such cases abortion may be a solution; adoption might also be considered.

A great deal of protest has arisen over the involuntary sterilization, or forced abortion, sometimes inflicted on those with severe disabilities. Though far more prevalent in the past, such incidents occasionally occur even today. Some few disabled individuals are not intellectually capable of giving informed consent to any such procedure, and those decisions must be made for them by legal guardians, parents, and in some cases, custodial institutions. Certainly, there have been abuses in these areas, which lobbyists and advocates for the disabled have successfully addressed (in most cases) through the courts. Only the most vulnerable of citizens would ever be affected by these issues, and no easy remedies can be applied to all cases. What if a severely retarded woman were to become pregnant? If legal or parental authorities were not able to arrange for abortion, then the child would be taken away immediately at birth. If sterilization were not allowed, the possibility of future pregnancies may cause great anxiety, as some severely disabled individuals do not manage well the mechanics of contraception.

The basic principles that apply to a well-structured sex education program for "normal" individuals apply also to the disabled. The goals are the same. The disabled are equally curious about "where they came from," differences between the sexes, changes at puberty, mate selection, dating, premarital sex, marriage, homosexual relations, masturbation, and contraception.

There are special considerations for the disabled, commensurate with their particular disability. Sex education for the retarded is best presented in simple terms with considerable repetition. For the blind, more emphasis is placed on tactility: The use of dolls with genitals is preferable to neutered dolls, and rubber models are available similar to those used by medical schools. For the deaf, a visual emphasis is most beneficial. Materials with detailed drawings of male and female anatomies, prenatal development, birth, and contraceptive information is necessary. Young adults with catheters, ostomies, braces or, other special devices should get instructed on how to adapt themselves sexually. The overprotection that is commonly experienced by this group has blocked an exchange of information with peers, making them feel isolated and misinformed; most of all it has exaggerated feelings of being different. Film presentations portraying disabled people and their need to give and receive affection are available.

MAINSTREAMING

In an era that is becoming more complex with each passing year, the difficulties experienced by the disabled have grown more traumatic. Frequently they find themselves neglected, isolated from the mainstream of events, and inappropriately educated in useless skills. Mainstreaming means integrating persons with disabilities into the world of the nondisabled to the fullest extent of their abilities.

To make the social aspects of mainstreaming work, all students, administrators, professors, employers, and other involved people need to know that it is not unusual for them to sometimes feel uncomfortable with a disabled person. If people can acknowledge their discomfort, they can deal, cope, or relate in a mature way to people who are disabled—not by pity or rejection, which often accompanies feelings of guilt in response to being uncomfortable. Even if we are uncomfortable, we can still go out of our way to be helpful. There's nothing wrong with being empathic, useful, and doing something for another human being.

It must be understood that mainstreaming requires considerable preparation, readiness, and a transitionary period leading from segregation to integration. Also, to be realistic, we are not suggesting that some facilities not remain homogenous, but rather that the disabled be given every opportunity to function in the most normal fashion. The implementation of such needed programs must come from the schools, habilitation services, and public assistance agencies in all communities.

It should be acknowledged that for a small minority of disabled individuals, segregated activities might be considered an acceptable lifestyle. However, it is almost incomprehensible that if you are disabled you could not normalize at least *some* components of your life. It is our experience that feelings of being involved, included, and just being a part of what's happening is necessary for optimum mental health for all individuals.

It is just as incomprehensible that a disabled person is incapable of *some* variety of intimate physical expression. The sexuality of a disabled person might not conform to a parent's or society's view of sex as genital contact leading to orgasm. Special people need special, creative ideas and attitudes, and it is cruel to compound their difficulties because some might not be comfortable with the notion that they are indeed able and anxious to express sensual, sexual feelings. A great many families must grapple daily with these concepts; it is estimated that one in ten individuals is disabled. Many more people experience temporary handicaps due to accidents, strokes, etc., and it is the rare family that has not been touched by these occurrences in some fashion. We are all of us sexual and have needs to give and receive love—every last one of us.

Here are a few messages for people who have disabilities, especially those who are feeling sorry for themselves. In our society, you score no points for being disabled. Every person who is disabled has to struggle to make it.

1. Nobody can make you feel inferior without your consent.
2. If you have an interest (hobbies, work, talents, passions) someone will be interested in you.
3. If you are bored, you are boring to be with.
4. If you do not have a sense of humor, develop one.
5. Join an advocacy group for the disabled.
6. Do not dwell on the meaning of life. Life is not a meaning. Life is an opportunity for any number of meaningful experiences.
7. Read. Discover as much as you can about yourself and the world. For heaven's sake, do not watch more than a couple of hours of television each day. Haven't you noticed that the more television you watch, the more exhausted you are?
8. Operate on the assumption that the so-called general public is uncomfortable with you. Most people are uncomfortable in the presence of people who have disabilities. And, if you announce that they do not have to feel guilty about being uncomfortable, then they will not have to respond by withdrawing from you or having pity. Take the initiative and tell people what you would like them to do. And somehow convey to them that it is okay to feel uncomfortable.

These "rules" are the basic steps toward realizing your own goals, though the process of achieving them is not easy. In fact, all really meaningful experiences in life involve risk, hard work, and the ability to postpone momentary gratification for long-range satisfaction.

If you have not gotten the message, let us say it another way. Socialization skills and opportunities are more important than anything else. If you feel good about yourself, someone will feel good about you. If you feel friendly, someone will be friendly to you. If you are open to sexual expression, someone will want to be sexual with you.

REFERENCES

Blum, G., & Blum, B. *Feeling Good About Yourself,* 1981. Available from Feeling Good Associates, 507 Palma Way, Mill Valley, CA, 94941

Maine Association of Handicapped Persons. *Coping,* May 1984.

CHAPTER 16

Aging and the Elderly

What is a chapter on sexuality and aging doing in a book primarily geared for college students? One theme of this book is that sexuality encompasses the entire lifespan from birth to death. Readers of this book will be called on to deal with sexual issues among the aging in their careers and/or in their families. Barring premature death, each will someday be old him- or herself and will be subject to the taboos and discrimination that today's elderly endure. Becoming sensitized to these issues may help you to appreciate that sexuality is as much a matter of how people feel as it is what they do, and that there is a range of behavior that is considered sexual.

Citizens over sixty-five years of age represent the fastest growing group in the population of the United States. There are currently 29 million Americans over the age of sixty-five (about 12 percent of the population). In ten years, according to recent Census Bureau estimates, this number will increase by approximately 10 percent. It is no surprise that many types of businesses—travel agencies, hotels, restaurants, grocery stores, banks, apartment complexes—are taking a new look at this segment of the consumer population and directing products and services their way. The elderly themselves are organizing into advocacy groups such as the American Association of Retired Persons, an important force to be reckoned with.

Young people have always had difficulty imagining their parents as sexual beings. Even people in their fifties often have great difficulty imagining their own parents being sexual. You're too old for that, they often wisecrack. Our society appears to hold the notion that sexuality stops, severely declines, and/or is not as exciting as it used to be after a person reaches retirement. This attitude produces bad jokes—do old people do it or don't they?—and stems from a potpourri of societal myths and biases.

One myth holds that sexual intercourse accelerates the aging process. Thus, to live longer, one should abstain from sexual activity after a certain age. Actually, physicians encourage their elderly patients to maintain physical and sexual activity at levels appropriate to their ability: both help them stay in shape. It has been reported that sexual activity triggers the release of steroids into the bloodstream and temporary relief of pain stemming from, for example, arthritis, is often experienced. But myths about the sexuality of older individuals remain more pervasive and disheartening. People often think of sexual intercourse as the *only* form of sexual activity. It is often forgotten that touching, holding, genital play, oral sex, and other intimate expressions all constitute human sexuality. Perhaps some older persons place less emphasis on erection, lubrication, or orgasm in favor of other sexual expressions. Does that make them less sexual?

In one instance, a cardiologist was discussing some impending heart surgery with his patient, a seventy-eight-year-old woman. He asked her how often she and her eighty-year-old husband made love, and she replied, "Oh, we make love every day." The doctor was astonished!

"Do you mean you and your husband have sex every day?" he asked.

"I think you misunderstand," she answered. "We have sex about once a week, but we make love every day."

Plastic surgery, the cosmetic and clothing industries and pushers of the "beautiful people," movies, and television glorify our youth-oriented culture. Romantic love is characterized by superheated sex. These absurd stereotypes pay little homage to the real family of humankind, or the weathered look of wisdom and beauty that comes with age. Physical changes take place over the years. If we make room for honest evaluations, not many young people measure up to these unrealistic standards either!

Single-minded notions concerning sexuality and aging suggest that to be old is to be sexless. Unlike tribal or rural societies, our modern urban society gives lip service to the values of maturity, while placing the strongest possible emphasis on the joys of youth. Many older people accept the sexless bed that society has laid for them. Not wanting to be ridiculed or feel society's disapproval, many suppress their sexual desires for fear that they might be tagged as "abnormal," "inappropriate," or even "dirty" by their friends, neighbors, and children. And so they conform.

An old man with buoyant sexual drives is often referred to as a dirty old man—or a lecher. Perhaps some are, but they hardly approach the proportion of lechers found among younger people. One theory of aging held by some scholars maintains that people who age successfully discover ways of gradually withdrawing from prior social roles and their former involvement in the wholeness of life. In a sense, this involves a preparation for death. Such a disengagement from life might naturally include decreased sexual activity, leading ultimately to total abstinence. Years ago, Kinsey discovered that many older people do remain sexually active, though this fact appears to be one of society's best-kept secrets.

A theory that reflects the reality of more older Americans was first proposed by Carl Jung. Jung believed that as people went through their middle years and aged, their repressed natures became more prominent. For women, this meant that their *animus,* or male side, became a stronger force, and for men, their *anima,* or female side, came to exert greater influence. Research conducted in the last decade by Guttman (1977) and others confirms this theory. As men near retirement, they often express interests in such traditionally feminine pursuits as cooking or gardening. Women of the same age may wish to return to the "male" world of work or may assume other traditionally masculine roles. Successful aging has been found among people who are able to allow these repressed sides to emerge without needing to hold rigidly to more sex-stereotyped patterns of behavior.

For a great many people, reaching old age means being an elderly woman (usually a widow), living alone. Statistics show 80 percent of aging men, but only 50 percent of aging women, still have a spouse. Women outlive men by a full seven years, and although in 1900 over one-third of the elderly lived with an adult child, today only about 7 percent do so (Population Reference Bureau, 1983). Thus, the trend has been toward more independent living for America's aging population, particularly among women (this trend is compounded by the fact that husbands are typically several years older than their wives).

A major concern for these aging adults, who often desire companionship and intimacy, is the loss of social security benefits and pensions should they remarry. To avoid this crucial loss of income, a sizable minority of older citizens have elected to cohabit without getting married. (Does this make their sexual involvement "premarital sex"?) In some instances, this presents a tremendous moral conflict for the people involved. They may have counseled their children not to have sex outside marriage, and yet are now faced with poverty if they hold to their own moral principles. Adult children sometimes rebel at the apparent hypocrisy of aging parents who live with another person, when this same parent criticized the child for living with a lover.

Younger readers of this book may be confronted with an older parent who becomes attached to a companion or lover. One of our students told us, "I hated the thought of my father marrying another woman after my mother died. It felt disloyal; a betrayal. And I felt betrayed too, like 'how dare you bring this stranger into our family!' I feel guilty admitting that I worried about the will and whether this woman would get some of the money that would have been inherited by myself." Eventually, this student and her father reached a balanced understanding, based on his need for companionship and love, and her need to be reassured of her position in the family.

Several physical changes inevitably accompany the aging process in both men and women. These changes are not as dramatic as was once assumed and do not necessarily have an effect on an individual's desire for sexual activity or potential for sexual satisfaction. Nor do they imply the onset of impotence. Also, these changes may affect some people more than others. They may occur at different ages in different individuals.

Men often notice the following changes:

- It may take longer to achieve an erection.
- The erection may be less hard.
- The ability to delay ejaculation increases.
- Release of semen may be less forceful.
- A second erection may be possible only after a longer period of time.

Some changes occur in women as well:

- Thinning of the vaginal walls can cause irritation during intercourse.
- Less vaginal lubrication can make intercourse uncomfortable.
- A longer time may be required to become excited.
- Orgasm may be shorter or less intense than previously.

Both men and women cope with these changes. For instance, if a man finds it hard to achieve a complete erection he and his partner can take the penis and place it in the vagina manually. Once there, it will often become hard enough for intercourse. A woman might combat discomfort caused by thin vaginal walls and/or lack of vaginal lubrication by using an over-the-counter vaginal cream or jelly. Physicians have demonstrated that continuing sexual activity through the lifespan is the best way to preserve sexual capacity. Well-known people such as Picasso and Pablo Cassals were said to be sexually active well into their nineties.

An eighty-two-year-old man commented on his changing sexual abilities: "I come maybe once in every three sexual encounters these days with my wife. My erection comes and goes, and it's not a big concern to us. I get as much pleasure from touching and thrusting as I do from an ejaculation. When I was younger it was inconceivable to me that I might enjoy sex without an orgasm, but I can see now that in those days I missed out on some pleasure by making orgasm such a focus."

Corresponding psychological factors can affect men and women in the later years of their sexual lives.

An older man might experience monotony or overfamiliarity with his partner. Monotony may develop from a sexual relationship that has lost its meaning or from feelings of idleness at the end of his career. Thus, coitus becomes a dutiful act or something engaged in solely for the relief of sexual tension. The issue often relates more to having nothing to do (but sit on the park bench). All areas of older persons' lives, including the sexual, might be infused with energy if they enter constructive purposeful activities. Despite the apparent injustices in forced retirement policies, many businesses are eager to secure the services of a person with years of useful experience. Understaffed volunteer organizations welcome all the help they can get.

On the other side, a man might remain a workaholic all his life. Increasing responsibility and reward deriving from his career may leave little time for his wife and family.

Communication as well as sexual rapport might be seriously disrupted, but the answer is not necessarily to retire to Florida or Arizona. The few men who maintain this vigorous level of work sometimes deteriorate very rapidly when forced to retire. Counseling might be sought—a few lines of advice here will not likely assuage such a long-standing situation.

For many women, the time of psychological reckoning arrives when the last child leaves home. If the woman maintains at least a part-time career interest or has hobbies she enjoys while the children are growing, the trauma of loss might be softened. Many other women suddenly find themselves adrift, wondering what to do with all the time on their hands since the household tasks no longer keep them busy. Sex, if she thinks of it at all, may emerge as an afterthought—or she may turn to her husband in fierce emotional dependence. Women in similar circumstances usually go back to work, which infuses other areas of their lives with energy. For people of all ages, staying active and productive is a good aphrodisiac.

Psychological changes in a woman may also relate to changes in her hormone levels. Menopause for many women provides a strong reminder of advancing age: the loss of childbearing capacity that may have defined her self-concept of femininity. Women react to this in different ways. Some react with sexual inhibition. Others may develop a desire for frequent intercourse, thus in a sense trying to recapture their womanliness. For others, though, with the fear of pregnancy gone, sex itself is enhanced.

Recent medical research has suggested that many women's experience of menopause is not caused by physiological factors alone. Radical changes in mood, hot flashes, and other physical symptoms, rather, may be equally caused by the culturally induced expectation that the woman *will* experience the phenomena.

Another concern for women may be the reduced sexual performance of older men. This situation can be aggravated by the fact that often husbands are several years older than their wives. An age discrepancy that made little difference in younger years may become more pronounced as time passes. Often the deepening qualities of love and companionship more than compensate for declining sexual appetites. Yet, as Alex Comfort advises in his book *The Joy of Sex: A Gourmet Guide to Love Making* (1972), "Over 50, the important thing is never to drop sex for any long period—keep yourself going solo if you don't for the time being have a partner: if you let it drop you have trouble restarting." (p. 224).

Again, the double standard rears its head. Growing old presents less of a problem for men than for women. Society treats a divorced or widowed older man as a desirable target for matchmakers. He is seen as graceful, charming; his gray hair appears refined. Yet, we feel that an older woman, in the same position, has become ineligible: Her gray hair and wrinkles signal an end to her greatest possession: her looks. Movies confirm the acceptability of pairing an older man with a younger woman: Cary Grant and Audrey Hepburn. As an exception, the marvelous film "Harold and Maude" portrays an older woman with a young man. Even in public life and in the public eye, older men—ex-Supreme Court Justice William Douglas, Senator Strom Thurmond, and the late Aristotle Onassis—take much younger brides. People may remark at such pairings, but accept them with equanimity. We are now witnessing a reversal of this trend among older women who are increasingly taking on younger mates.

Few of the health problems associated with old age need cause people to give up their sexual activity. Hysterectomy, colostomy, mastectomy, prostate surgery, and many types of heart conditions do not necessarily mean ending one's satisfying sexual life. Physicians or counselors can offer advice or answer questions. Some illnesses and operations affect one's sexuality only temporarily. For example, medication for a particular problem may affect potency or desire. In other cases, such as diabetes, the effect may be permanent. Even when an illness or operation make sexual functioning per se impossible or impractical, it does not rule out the possibility of other sensual, sexual closeness.

Perhaps the greatest single distortion of the sexuality of elder citizens occurs in nursing and old-age homes. Patients are often confined in single-sex environments. Staff members at nursing homes often consider their patients to be devoid of any sexual needs. They are horrified if they discover any sexual activity taking place, and the policies of many such institutions actively discourage it. Single older persons who have lost a spouse certainly do not abandon sexual desire or capacity. No officials, nor the person's own children, have the right to say that "premarital" sex for these individuals is wrong. Self-stimulation may be an acceptable, healthy, and pleasurable alternative both for the single older people as well as for individuals confined to single-sex nursing home facilities.

It's essential for everyone, parents, children and older persons themselves, to accept the proposition that human beings remain sexual throughout their entire lives. Even after age seventy-five, when we notice significant decreases in sexual activity, intimacy and sexual involvement are desired. Closeness to another human being becomes an important link to life. The policies and attitudes that young people establish today toward their older citizens will affect themselves tomorrow.

We agree with Woody Allen's comment when asked about his views on sex. He replied, "I think sex should be confined to one's lifetime."

REFERENCES

Comfort, A. *The Joy of Sex: A Gourmet Guide to Love Making*. New York: Simon & Schuster, 1972.

Gutmann, D. "The Cross-cultural Perspective. Notes toward a Comparative Psychology of Aging." In Birren & Schaie (Eds.), *Handbook of the Psychology of Aging*. New York: Van Nostrand Reinhold, 1977.

Thornton, A., & Freedman, D. *The Changing American Family*. Washington, DC: The Population Reference Bureau, 1983.

CHAPTER 17

Prostitution

Prostitution is of concern to people from two different angles: the one in which they may be customers, and the one in which they provide the services. Sex-for-sale, the "oldest profession," is not restricted to seamy red-light districts in poorer sections of large cities or to lower-class segments of society. Though it is illegal in all fifty states (with the exception of a few counties in Nevada), it exists in all states in a variety of forms.

Prostitutes refers to themselves as being "in the life," and to their customers as "tricks" or "Johns." It is discussed here because some of you and your husbands, fathers, sons, and brothers will visit prostitutes; some of you and your sisters, mothers, wives, and daughters may at some time provide sex for pay. In addition, it is a pressing societal dilemma, insofar as much police and court energy is devoted to suppressing prostitution, and expensive prison space houses those who are convicted.

Perhaps more than any other area, prostitution highlights the flagrant double standard that exists in American society. Arrest records around the country reveal that as many as ten prostitutes are arrested to every customer. It is just as illegal to pay for sex as it is to accept the money, but the prostitute herself is the one arrested. The hypocrisy also extends into attitudes that people hold: a man who visits a prostitute is "sowing his wild oats," and the woman who accommodates him is a whore, an outcast. The woman is utterly devalued, but the man, perhaps among his male friends, may even gain in stature. Ask yourself: would you be more upset to discover that your sister was a prostitute, or that your brother often paid for a prostitute's services?

Occasionally in police crackdowns, however, men who solicit prostitutes are arrested. The daily newspaper in Syracuse, New York, regularly publishes the names of men arrested for soliciting. The *Chicago Tribune* (1984) reported that in Nashville, Tennessee, scores of men were arrested, including " . . . a local college basketball coach, a pharmacist, a truck driver, an engineer, a minister, a milkman, a musician, a construction worker, a retired banker, the president of a printing company, students and several government employees." The basketball coach stated that he had received an anonymous tip that one of his players was at a local motel: "I was investigating," he said.

Prostitution is a worldwide phenomenon, one that apparently fulfills an unmet need in many men. Libby, Nass, and Fisher (1984) discuss the many different types of prostitutes: call girls, prostitutes who work in brothels, streetwalkers, massage-parlor attendants, bar girls and strippers, and male homosexual prostitutes, all of whom cater to male customers. Although some lesbian prostitutes and male heterosexual prostitutes offer services to women, the overwhelming majority of customers are men. Call girls and those who work in massage parlors tend to be surprisingly well educated (many with college degrees); others, such as streetwalkers, tend to be less well educated. With the exception of some call girls, who cater to a wealthier clientele, most prostitutes are frequented by men who are middle-aged, middle-class, and married.

In a compelling sense, prostitution represents society's failure to provide protection, love, and nurturance to its members. Among streetwalkers, for instance, as many as 65 percent were runaways from chaotic, unhappy childhoods. Some studies indicate that as many as 80 percent of prostitutes were the victims of incest, rape, and/or physical or sexual abuse as children. Once women enter the life, though it may appear to be a voluntary decision, many are viciously exploited by pimps, beaten and abused by their tricks, arrested, and prosecuted through a judicial system that is ill-equipped to resolve the complex problems involved in prostitution.

Men who visit prostitutes often state that they are seeking escape from loneliness or from cold, loveless marriages. Some want sex without the possibility of romantic entanglements or want help with some sexual dysfunction, such as secondary impotence. Others report that in requesting such sexual acts as fellatio, they are seeking to bolster their own masculinity, impress their peer group, or simply get something that they can't get at home.

It would seem that there has been a failure for these men to fulfill their needs for love in an intimate relationship with one other person. If one examines the classified pages of underground newspapers that advertise sexual services, an astounding number offer sadomasochistic, infantile, fetishistic behaviors. They include: enemas, bondage and discipline (most often with the man submitting to a dominant "mistress"), golden showers (a woman urinating on a man), dressing the man in diapers, and spanking. Prostitutes who advertise these services often have apartments fully equipped with "dungeons" sporting a wide assortment of whips, chains, paddles, handcuffs, ropes, and other accessories. In their ads, the women appear as "dominant bitch goddesses" who offer to "force you to your knees, humiliate and torture you beyond your wildest fantasies."

Although it is beyond the limits of this chapter to analyze the meaning of such behaviors (see the section on sexual fetishes and aberrations), a few comments can be made. The need to be hurt, abused, humiliated, or treated like a little child often represents a wish to relive such incidents from one's own childhood. The pain associated with mistreatment as a child may be unacceptable to the individual, and so the memory is eroticized and turned into something pleasurable. This may be especially true in the case of spanking or whippings received as a child. The rituals of enemas or diapering may become eroticized, as these contain elements of nurturance, and attention to erogenous parts of the body. In any event, the fixation on the infantile activities invariably interferes with the ability to relate to another adult in a mature, exciting way.

In a sense, prostitutes have been keenly perceptive by detecting these needs and arranging to meet them. In a significant way, prostitutes also become the keepers of shameful secrets that cannot be shared with wives, lovers, or friends. When and if one's wife or lover discovered the secret, it would probably trigger a crisis in the relationship. This is the fear in which some men live and a great deal of energy is expended in hiding that part of themselves. This "double" life or identity can require many white lies in accounting for one's whereabouts and activities.

Similar disguises are required for some prostitutes, who exist both as prostitutes and as girlfriends, wives, etc. to unsuspecting other people. Once they "retire," there is sometimes a strong desire to hide the facts of the past occupation and so elaborate stories may be constructed of their work history.

Some prostitutes make the claim that they are simply formalizing an arrangement that exists in most marriages: the husband provides the paycheck, and the wife dutifully submits sexually—both are upholding their end of the bargain. The argument continues that if the wife wants something, such as a fur coat, she may use her sexual wiles, or withhold sex, as a way of making her husband comply. Prostitution eliminates this hypocrisy, some believe, and makes the transaction more overt.

Any relationship in which sex becomes a lever or a bargaining chip risks deterioration. Those who turn to prostitutes to fulfill their needs should be aware that they may be ripped off or abused while with her. Anytime that people act out sexually and consistently take their grievances or needs outside the relationship rather than dealing with them directly with a partner, it is a clear sign that the relationship is on the rocks. It would be preferable for these issues to be dealt with between the partners themselves: in this way, the issue can be resolved, or the relationship terminated.

Those who visit prostitutes, and who are not involved with anyone, have a different set of concerns. For some very lonely men, an occasional visit to a prostitute can feel like a positive experience. Some men report that they were initiated sexually by a prostitute, and that this helped them to overcome the "performance anxiety" that might have been present with a girlfriend. In any event, the possibility remains that prostitutes may come to be a substitute in a person's life for ongoing interactions with friends or with the desire to develop intimacy with no fees attached.

For many people, however, the moral dimension concerning prostitution is the most vital. To them, there are no circumstances in which it could be considered a positive experience or even marginally acceptable. That's the reality and probably not subject to change, regardless of what is written here. Nevertheless, there needs to be a perspective on what others blithely term immoral and condemn. In the New Testament, Christ is asked by the Pharisees whether they should stone a woman caught in the act of adultery. He replies, "He that is without sin among you, let him first cast a stone at her" (John 8:7).

It is all right to have one's own moral framework, but prostitutes have become the scapegoats for some people who are unable to come to grips with their own particular vulnerabilities. Persecution of any group, such as prostitutes or homosexuals, invariably is an expression of people's fears about themselves, which are projected onto others. In this way, instead of confronting the problems in oneself, one can attack another person and thus feel safe from persecution oneself. Some of the most vociferous moralists among political and religious leaders have been revealed subsequently to have had illicit sexual involvements with those of the the the same and/or opposite sex.

Scapegoating prostitutes also represents an attempt to dehumanize them and thus absolve society of any responsibility for their well-being. In this way, people turn a deaf ear to their suffering and exploitation, and feel self-righteous in doing so. In a sense, this is the root of human affliction: those who are designated "untouchable" are abandoned to fend for themselves.

You'll need to work out your own values and attitudes in this area. Males especially will want to determine whether seeking a prostitute is compatible with their own values. Some women, particularly within the women's movement, believe strongly that prostitution symbolizes women's sexual slavery to men, and the exploitation of their bodies at the expense of their personhood. Though we share this notion to a great extent, there remains the fact that some prostitutes ply their trade voluntarily and resent efforts that pressure them to give it up.

Legislatures have decided that engaging in prostitution is a criminal activity and have established penalties of fines and imprisonment for those who break the law. The result of this is that society has produced a class of criminals—prostitution itself has not diminished. The laws have also made prostitutes vulnerable to extortion from corrupt police organizations, lawyers, and judges, as well as those involved in organized crime. An interesting, loosely woven coalition of groups has emerged to lobby for decriminalization of prostitution, which to some represents freeing women to control their own sexuality. This coalition includes the American Civil Liberties Union, the National Organization for Women, and the National Task Force on Prostitution.

Decriminalization would involve removing antiprostitution laws from the books and instating a system in which the health of prostitutes (particularly with regard to sexually transmitted diseases) would be regularly monitored. Just like any working person, the prostitute would be required to report her income to the IRS and to pay taxes. This would admittedly be a major deviation from the American tradition, in which anything considered immoral is declared illegal. Yet, as our experience with outlawing drugs, alcohol, prostitution, and even some sexual behaviors between spouses has shown, making something illegal does not decrease people's appetite for it, and society pays a high price for policing private, consensual acts.

Over a decade ago, the news was splashed in headlines nationwide that some sex therapists were using sex surrogates to help people (both men and women) with sexual dysfunctions. The surrogate was a paid sexual partner, who was trained by the therapist to work with men on such problems as premature ejaculation and impotence, and with women on preorgasmia and vaginismus. Some people claimed that using surrogates was thinly veiled prostitution, and as such the topic evoked the same moral dilemmas as did prostitution itself. The authors of this book believe that the two are not equivalent, and that in some instances surrogates have been useful to both therapists and patients. Indeed, therapists and surrogates themselves are outraged by the comparison (just as many prostitutes view themselves as simply earning a living and resent the suggestion that they should feel sinful or ashamed).

There is an inherent hypocrisy in the United States' laws concerning prostitution, which discriminate against the woman, overlook the patron, and exile millions of people to the fringes of society. In some major European cities, such as Hamburg and Amsterdam, there is a designated red-light district where prostitution is licensed and regulated by the state. This model may not be appropriate for our country, but it highlights an unwillingness here to address basic realities. Prostitution very likely will always exist, and a more benign legislative response might be to protect those who engage in it and to offer them the fellowship of broader society. Those with religious beliefs against prostitution might accept this as a challenge to "Love thy neighbor as thyself."

REFERENCES

Chicago Tribune. "Men Seized Trying to Hook a Hooker." November 26, 1984.

Nass, G. D., Libby, R. W., & Fisher, M. P. *Sexual Choices: An Introduction to Human Sexuality.* Monterey, CA: Wadsworth, 1984.

CHAPTER 18

Population, Please

We want to touch briefly on population issues. Even though it is not a main subject of the book, it is of great concern to peoples of all nations. We are using the fact that sex and population are intimately connected as our rationale to sound an alarm.

It took from the beginning of history until the year 1850 for the number of inhabitants on earth to reach a billion. By 1930 the population had doubled, and another billion was added by 1960. Then, after only sixteen years, the population of the world reached 4 billion. In the year 2000, at the present *decreasing* rate of growth, there will be well over 6 billion people, with about 70 percent living in underdeveloped and poverty-stricken countries. (If the growth rate remains at the 1984 level, the numbers could rise to 10 billion by the year 2000, according to United Nations estimates.)

The United States population is growing at a rate of 2 million a year; we will have 268,000,000 citizens by the year 2000 (the age sixty-five and over group will increase by 20 percent).

Of the larger nations in the world, the United States is by far the richest; yet 25 million of our own people live in abject poverty. The United States represents about 6 percent of the world's population, yet we possess more than half the cars, telephones, and refrigerators, and consume more than 40 percent of the world's oil production. The list goes on and on. The crucial question may soon be how will we respond to the threat of millions of starving people in India, Ethiopia, Bangladesh, Egypt, and Pakistan? Assume that we find a way of providing adequate food and shelter for our own citizens. What about Mexico and our South American neighbors? Mexico already "sends" (illegally) some 500,000 people across our borders that it cannot feed *each year*. According to Population Reference Bureau estimates, Mexico will increase its present population of 78 million to 115.2 million by the year 2000 and will probably reach 162 million by 2020.

Furthermore, 90 percent of the additional 2 billion people projected to live in the world by the year 2000 will live in countries where 20 percent of the inhabitants are already severely malnourished; 30 percent lack safe water or adequate health care; 50 percent over fifteen years of age are illiterate. In the year 1984, 30 million children under the age of five died from causes related to malnutrition.

There is some reason for cautious optimism: The International Conference on Population in 1984, and the Population Reference Bureau in 1985, reported that the global growth rate had fallen to 1.67 percent a year, down from 2.03 percent a decade earlier. A modern success story exists in Thailand, where in the last thirty years the birth rate declined by nearly 40 percent from 44.6 per 1000 people to 28.6. The progress can be largely credited to a government effort that provides health care and family planning in rural areas. The unfinished job: the World Bank estimates that almost 8 billion dollars must be spent by the end of this century, if substantial declines in fertility are to be achieved around the world.

We agree with Paul Ehrlich, "Whatever your cause, it's a lost cause without population control." Readers who want to learn more about this subject can write to:

Zero Population Growth
1346 Connecticut Ave., NW
Washington, DC 20036

Population Reference Bureau
2213 M Street, NW
Washington, DC 20037

PART FOUR
Parents as Sexuality Educators

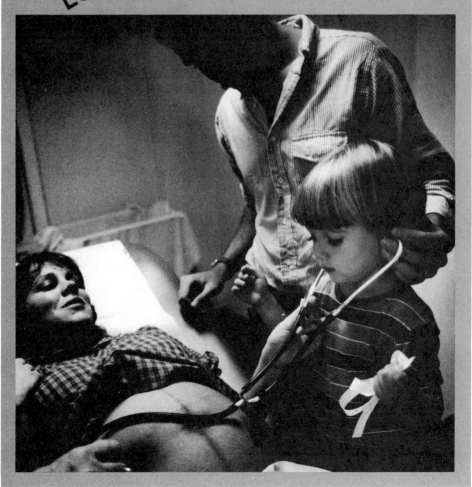

CHAPTER 19

Sexuality Education—Do It Right Your Time Around

About 90 percent of students in college today will marry, many in the next several years. On the average, they'll eventually give birth to (or father) 1.8 children. Yet in survey after survey, we are finding that these parents, even college-educated ones, are not educating their children in sexuality. In studies we have conducted at Syracuse University over a span of fifteen years and involving some 10,000 students, our current estimate (of the not-yet-completed studies) are that only about 15 percent of our students felt satisfied with the information and values imparted to them by their parents about sexuality. Typical responses were:

My parents? You must be kidding!

I learned a little from my friends, only to find out after I left home that most of what I thought I knew was not true.

I wish my parents had canned the stork story and fairy tale explanations and told me the truth.

I wish my parents sat me down and told me about sex instead of just saying, Don't let anyone in your pants.

I wish that my parents had talked to me about sex—going beyond menstruation, pubic hair, etc. I wish they had explained birth control, orgasms, and other important things.

I wish they had told me how easy it was to get pregnant, not how easy it is *not* to get pregnant and what they would have wanted me to do about it.

I wish my parents had been more open about sex and not treated it as a big dark secret to be discovered and experienced after marriage.

I wish they had told me not to feel so inhibited about my body. I wish they had told me that there was nothing wrong with making love with someone if it is right and special. It is now hard to erase the guilt. It is leaving slowly.

I wish my parents spoke to me more about birth control and let me know that in trouble I could turn to them.

I wish mom had told me that first sexual encounters, meaning intercourse, per se, would probably be fairly disappointing in most ways!

I had hoped that my parents were more open about sex. We rarely discussed it. And now, I wish that I could still talk to them about my relationships because I love them and will share the rest of my life with them.

Apart from questionnaires, we asked the students in our human sexuality class (numbering 450 students each semester) to take home during the spring or fall breaks a children's sex education book geared for four- to seven-year-olds, entitled *Did the Sun Shine Before You Were Born?* by Sol and Judith Gordon. Students were to ask their parents to read it, and then interview them, asking questions like, Would you have read this book to me when I was five years old? Why, or why not?

The students were, for the most part, astonished by their parents' responses, and, regardless of whether or not the critique of the book was positive or negative, about 85 percent of the students reported that it was the best sexuality discussion they'd ever had with one or both parents. Here are some typical responses from the students' reports:

Student #1:
Mother: "Alright, so what if we don't use the book. You still can't wait too long to tell him. For all we know, he knows already. Look at the television shows today—they're so suggestive. It would be a lot better if John (her son, six years of age) didn't have to guess at the meanings of things."
Father: "John isn't old enough to understand any of that yet. There's no sense teaching him yet. We'll wait until he asks or until we think he's ready."
Student: "Maybe he's scared to ask. I think that it is your job as parents to initiate a talk on sex. The longer you wait, the harder it's going to be."
    "Well, I'll tell you one thing. When I have kids, they're going to know about sex when they're John's age. Sex is a part of life and everyone has a right to know about it. By informing John of the basic aspects of sex, you won't be giving him a full understanding of sex and love—that will come with time—but at least it's a start."

Student #2:

My father's criticisms were that the book didn't stress that you shouldn't have sex (or children) until you were married. He also thought that age four to seven was much too young to read this kind of book. He felt that at the start of your teen years, or when you felt the desire for sex, would be the right time to have a child read this book. But all in all, he thought it was a good book and that he would feel comfortable reading this to his children when we were younger.

My mother liked the book also. But she felt that age four was much too young of an age to read the book to a child, but she also felt that age seven was too young. Then she changed her mind, realizing that she was thinking in terms of sixteen years ago. She now thought that at age four they wouldn't understand but may be able to get something from the pictures and that age seven would be a good age to read it to a child.

She also thought that the book should have placed some emphasis on not wanting to have sex or children until you were married. She was a little bothered by the pictures of the families, or in her eyes, the lack of family. She didn't like the idea of making children think that one-parent families were all right. She thought the book should have tried to influence the younger generation to start and keep "real" families. All in all, she thought it was a good book.

The student, herself, then commented:

I think age four is a good age to read them the book. I feel, like my parents, that they might not understand it, but they have been exposed to it, and the information is stored for future reference somewhere. Then at a later age, you might want to refresh their memory with it and go into a little more of a discussion session with it.

Once a child has been exposed to the book, then they realize what they don't know and if mom read me the book before, then she shouldn't mind if I ask her a little more. I feel the book is a good first step to becoming an "askable parent."

I felt this assignment was very beneficial. Personally, it brought my parents and I together a little more with a subject that was always hush-hush. That was probably the most important thing I got out of the assignment. It gave me a book to use in the future, and also a little background information and feedback from my parents on how important it is to be an "askable parent."

Student #3:

My parents are very down-to-earth traditional people. They were brought up strictly Roman Catholic and made sure all six of us were too! They never talked about sex or sexuality openly but did instruct us individually in as short a time as possible. In many ways they are a bit liberal, but I had no way of knowing just how they would react to *Did the Sun Shine*. At first they said things like, Oh, that's nice, and, What a cute idea, but when they got to the section on how babies are made, their expressions changed and they seemed a bit flustered. After they had finished, they still seemed puzzled and unsure about how to react. We talked about the text and the illustrations in the book and I found that they were not as upset about the text as they were the pictures. The pictures of the naked woman, and babies in particular, had put them off. When I questioned them about this, they said that it just seemed too far to go to prove the point. I tried to convince them it was necessary to the point of the book to prove it was real, but they seemed unable to accept it. We talked more about the text and I explained that it was meant as a guide to be read aloud with the child, and to my great surprise, they thought that it seemed like a pretty good idea (except for the pictures!). When I told them I was surprised at their almost casual reaction, they accused me of being old-fashioned and went on to say that if they had had a book like that when I was young, they would have considered reading it to me, but not the pictures!

From the beginning I knew this would be an interesting, if not enlightening, project. It proved to be this, and more. Talking about sex and sexuality with parents is something that both parties dread for the most part, but for me, at least on this occasion, it provided me with the opportunity to have a meaningful and mature exchange with my parents. I was also very happy to learn that my mother loaned the book to a friend with a five-year-old boy. This type of honest communication with one's children, I feel, is a basic parental obligation, and it is one I won't overlook when I become a parent.

Student #4:

Initially I had many misgivings about this assignment, considering my mother's background. She has spent most of her life in an environment that was very conservative, very southern, and very Christian, all of which adds up to her not being very open about sexuality. While my father was alive, he was much the more liberal of the two in all respects. He was fairly open about sex, but whenever he mentioned anything with sexual connotations, he'd be sure to get an "Oh, Tom!" from my mother.

As it turned out, my expectations were only partially realized. She did seem somewhat taken aback when I first brought up the subject, but she became more and more relaxed as the discussion progressed. Furthermore, her reaction to the book was far more positive than I expected. I thought she would feel that the book would, in Dr. Gordon's words, "overstimulate a child with knowledge." Instead, though, she felt that the book was a good vehicle to initiate a sex talk with a child.

One of the first things I found out was why my mother had always seemed so reluctant to talk about sex. She said that she never knew how to bring up the subject for serious discussion but thought it was too heavy a subject to just talk about casually. Since she always seemed embarrassed when my father would make a casual reference to sexuality, I always felt that it was a subject to be avoided around the house.

Overall, I agree with my mother's reactions. I believe that if I had talked with my parents about sex even a little when I was young, I wouldn't have thought of sexuality as such a taboo subject when I got older. It took two or three years of college to "deprogram" myself from that kind of thought. Much of this probably could have been avoided if I had viewed my parents as "askable" when I was growing up. Had the book been available then, a major step towards them becoming askable could have been their reading it with me, thus making sexuality seem a more natural topic for discussion.

Student #5:

My mother reacted better than I thought she would. I assumed that she was still living slightly in the old days when things like this were taboo. I found I was wrong. She has changed with the times and I am glad to see that. Our discussion of the book even prompted us to discuss other things that we would usually feel funny talking about. This was encouraging and I am glad that I had her read the book. My father, at first, did not have any interest in reading the book. He told me, "Let your mother handle it." This was typical of him and I think it was this type of thing that discredited him as being an askable parent when I was a child. We finally got him to read it, and I was quite startled by his reaction. He said that he would have been comfortable reading the book to me. When I asked him why he did not, he told me that he was too busy trying to make money to feed us. This was true back then and I can sympathize with that. When I asked him if he would recommend the book, there was a hesitation in his answer. He said he would in the right situation, although he really didn't know what the right situation was. This indicated that he is not as open-minded as mother, which is what I expected. Yet, he was much more open-minded that I had perceived him to be.

Student #6:

As far as my using this book with my children (some day, but not right away, thank you), I'd be crazy to say that I wouldn't. Hell, I want to pass this course! In all seriousness, I do think that I'd be comfortable reading this with my kids. This book, as well as the class itself, have given me a good insight into how parents should help their children by being their educators, even in difficult areas such as sex. There's nothing wrong with discussing the proverbial "birds and bees" with children, and I'd certainly rather have them learn about it from me than from an unknowledgeable friend. I will, at least, attempt to be an askable parent.

Regarding this assignment, I am now very glad that it was given. I think that this could very well have been the first time that I talked about a lot of things with *both* of my parents. It was a good opportunity for all of us and really a nice, refreshing change. I only wish that I had taken this course a long, long time ago!

Student #7:

I thought the assignment itself was good because it provided my parents and I an opportunity to talk about issues that we would not normally discuss, in great detail. The project induced discussions about birth control, religion, the role of sex educators, the legal implications of the sexual education process, and of living-together arrangements. They agreed with my point that it is important to explain sex to a child at an earlier age in order to establish a child-parent relationship which reduces tensions and makes the parents askable. In conclusion, all of us enjoyed the project and would feel comfortable using the book with a child with personal modifications.

My father thought that the primer was well written and illustrated in good taste. However, since it is written to be read aloud by parents to their child or children, he thought that the authors ignored the fact that our laws sanction monogamy as the only form of legal cohabitation between the sexes and that (heretofore) the primary purpose of sex is procreation, not recreation (in reference to the page with the man and woman in bed). He feels that parents must be afforded an opportunity to convey this concept to their progeny by sex educators in their own way, according to the dictates of their own religions or ethical beliefs. Therefore, he would say that if the author changed the sentence which reads, "When a woman and a man who love each other go to bed they like to hug and kiss . . .", to "When a woman and a man who love each other get married in our church, according to our laws, go to bed . . .", it would afford the parents an opportunity to wait for the child to ask, what church (if any) and what laws or rules. This could be easily accomplished: "When a woman and a man who love each other get married (in our church, if preferred) according to our laws . . .", no parent could object.

Student #8:

I don't ever remember my parents explaining to me how two people fall in love, the making of babies, or the process of menstruation in women. What I do remember is fourth grade "sex education" when all the little girls were hauled off to the gym to be subjected to the use and function of a training bra, a belt and pads, or tampons. We were all just a bunch of giggling girls, always asking, "Why aren't the boys here?" I still wasn't very clear on most of the facts about my body, or for that fact, others around me. Did we all function the same? Do boys have to go through *this* once a month? Why hasn't mom told me?

ON BECOMING AN ASKABLE PARENT

The clearest message to emerge from our work in this field is that children do appreciate openness and candor at an early age. Parents who rarely communicated with their children when young have the most difficulty talking with teenagers, whom they finally perceive as being old enough. Often the credibility of parents is diminished when they give the impression that any area *except* human sexuality is open for discussion.

It might be instructive to know a little about how one of us (Sol Gordon) got into this field. In some ways it is a funny story. I was working in a child-guidance clinic at a time when sexuality was not much discussed. This was no accident because almost no medical school or professional school of psychology, social work, or nursing included courses in sexuality. Thus, professionals who were supposed to know the most often didn't know any more than the people who were asking the questions. What this amounted to was a conspiracy of silence, even in the heyday of psychoanalysis when sex was assumed to be the root of all neurosis.

Under the circumstances, such discussion was so abstract to the average person that it didn't seem to help them understand their own sexuality, their children's sexuality, or some of the conflicts they had over this topic. People freely discussed Oedipal fantasies and penis envy, but very few seemed to be able to deal with practical questions regarding penis or vagina size, the clitoris, the role of communication in sexual functioning, as well as a host of others.

Once, as part of a study, we asked 100 teenagers (50 boys and 50 girls) if their parents had talked to them about sex. Each one said no. Then we asked the parents if they had spoken to their children about this subject. All said that they had in fact done so. These results were fascinating because one seldom gets such widely divergent findings. We pursued the matter eagerly, asking the teenagers if they really couldn't remember and whether they perhaps weren't telling the truth. When pushed, nearly all the girls remembered that their mothers had talked to them about menstruation. The rest of the communication could be summed up in one word: don't. The boys were less impressed by our efforts to jog their memories. Once we spoke of the possibility of "going out for a walk," about half the boys remembered this ritual taking place when they were about eleven years old. Together, we decided they remembered the walk because they hadn't been asked to do anything like this before nor were they ever asked to go for a walk again. They also remembered an awkward discussion about the birds and the bees. Both father and son were so embarrassed that very little real communication took place. Some did recall the father ending the conversation with the remark that if worse came to worst, the son could always find some condoms in the father's drawer.

This research is twenty years old now, but it still seems to contain elements of truth. Whenever large mixed adult audiences are confronted with it, there is nervous laughter suggesting that perhaps this had been part of their own experience. This reaction reinforces our strong belief that sex is not something one limits to a single talk or even an occasional talk coupled to significant developmental stages in a child's life. It should be an *ongoing process*. Becoming an askable parent starts long before the child goes to school. The parent who has discussed sexuality openly with the young child can expect the teenager to share confidences later.

Most parents, after all, want to educate their children about sex. They realize that schools, churches, community organizations, and the mass media can offer only supplementary sex education at best and in any case, cannot be expected to mirror their personal values. Many parents also fear that too much information too soon will overstimulate their children. This attitude is the first of many roadblocks to effective sex education in the home.

Contrary to a *few* experts in this field, we've never been able to discover a documented case of a child's having been overstimulated by facts alone. Should parents err in the direction of too much information, children will simply get bored, turn them off, or cut it short with an irrelevant question. Overstimulation *is* a problem when it derives from fears, unresolved curiosity, and ignorance. Our campaign against ignorance has led opponents of sex education to tell jokes. An example is the child who asks where she came from and whose mother responds with an elaborate explanation of the seed and the egg. At the end, the child explains that she only wanted to know if she came from Philadelphia. To this, our response is very simple: So what? Now the child knows not only where she was born, but how she got there. The moral of this and similar stories: most children would learn very little if education were restricted to what they themselves chose to learn.

Quite understandably, many parents who did not receive sex education in their homes feel uncomfortable talking about sex with their children. There is no instant remedy for such feelings, but it may be helpful to reemphasize that no one is really comfortable about anything these days. When was the last time someone told you not to worry and you stopped? It simply is not necessary to feel totally comfortable about your own, or anybody else's, sexuality to communicate effectively about this subject with your children.

As the primary force in your child's life, you are providing sex education in one form or another no matter what you do. The question is not *whether* you will teach your children about sex, but how well. Silence teaches no less eloquently than speech. If you convey to a young child, or a teenager, the impression that you feel a bit awkward discussing love and sex, chances are good that *you'll score*. Your child might well respond to your honesty with affection and appreciation, with a hug and a kiss and verbal assurances that your discomfort is perfectly understood. Many a parent has been happily surprised to hear a child say "Don't worry, Mom (Dad)! It's all right."

Parents who worry that they don't know enough about the subject to be effective teachers ought to pause and consider these questions. How much is it really necessary to know? To a particularly technical or baffling question, a parent can always respond with the truth: I don't know, but I'll look it up for you and tell you tomorrow. Let's look it up together, would be an even better response. A small child's questions can usually be answered with a few words of elementary explanation. Older children are more likely to ask questions about values than anatomy. Even so, with excellent books no more distant than your local library, what excuse do you really have?

Some parents are concerned about making honest mistakes or giving wrong answers. Parents should realize that they can make mistakes without harming their children. A few examples may be illustrative.

A child wanders into the bedroom while his or her parents are having sexual intercourse. What should you do? Tell the child: Leave. In the morning you can apologize for not having said, *Please* leave. Then you can explain what you were doing. If your child asks to watch the next time, tell him or her that he or she cannot. Kindly but firmly explain that sex is private. A child may not understand the prohibition, but later in life he or she will grow to appreciate the concept of privacy. In fact, fifteen years later when you walk in on your child having sexual intercourse and he or she says, Get out, it's private, perhaps you will remember how well you prepared this person for that response! Most important, learn to laugh at the outrageous proposition that a child who has witnessed sexual intercourse will need years of analysis to get over it. The person who, as a child, never once saw his or her parents being naturally and openly affectionate is a more likely candidate for analysis.

Let's not worry about the neighbors. Suppose your child tells the truth about sex to some little friends. Their parents hear about it and inform you, in no uncertain terms, of their horror and indignation. Let's take it from the opposite point of view. What about parents who tell their children that babies grow in cabbage patches? Do you suppose they care about your feelings when your children come home with such news? Your responsibility is to tell your children the truth and without instructions to keep it confidential. If your neighbors don't like it, that's their problem. Get new neighbors! It's about time that the well-educated children become an important neighborhood resource with respect to sex education. No matter what parents do, children will share whatever information they have about sex. Your first loyalty is to your children and not to your neighbors. Though your child may be deprived of a playmate, in the long run dealing with this kind of sensitive experience could make for a more creative, happier, and better-adjusted child.

Does sex education belong exclusively in the home? It is grossly unrealistic to try to protect children from all external influences. Parents can't have total control over the sex education of their children unless they are prepared to rear them in isolation. It seems extraordinary that some parents are willing to risk their children being educated by peers, pornography, and television, rather than being taught in schools and churches.

Here are some concepts that are important for parents to understand about sexuality. Parents need to understand what experiences affect children in their early years, especially if they are to help them develop positive attitudes toward themselves and others.

Sexual pleasure is not confined to stimulation of the genitals nor is *all* pleasant physical contact related to sex. This is true even of the youngest of babies who learn about the pleasures of physical contact through constant loving fondling. Parents stroke, kiss, and cuddle them and they respond with affection. Babies find great satisfaction in using their mouths when eating and when sucking on their toes or other objects.

An infant is learning even though he or she does not yet talk. The infant will use this early learning later in life. What infants learn about love, affection, and physical contact will affect their sexual attitudes and behaviors when biologically ready to have children. Many of a person's sexual feelings and attitudes are determined before the age of five.

For instance, toilet training before children are ready might create feelings of self-doubt, guilt, and shame. These feelings could trouble the youngsters for the rest of their lives, though they probably won't even be aware of them. In other words, what if a child has an "accident" and is punished and told that he or she is "bad" or "dirty"? If the child is not capable or old enough to control elimination, he or she may become seriously (and honestly) confused and develop feelings of anxiety, guilt, and inferiority.

Children must be handled with patience and understanding. This means that parents must stop and think before punishing too quickly, deciding as honestly as possible whether their first purpose in so doing is really for the child's good or is merely a reaction to their own, possibly unjustified, fears.

This is also true when infants begin to discover and explore their bodies. If parents slap a child's fingers or pull the hand away from playing with the genitals but coo and smile and comment on how cute the child looks when playing with its toes, he or she will be confused and may associate the genitals with feelings of guilt and shame.

No one expects babies who are barely old enough to walk, talk, or know where the bathroom is to be anything but innocent and carefree. When children are old enough to go to the bathroom on their own, parents can teach them not to touch the sex organs in public, just as they have been taught not to suck their thumb.

In a very real sense, sexuality is something we *are*, rather than something we do. When a baby is born the first question often is, What is it? Is it a boy or a girl? This first response seems to be related to the child's sex. The child is then programmed according to its sex as he or she gets older. It may be less popular these days for children to be identified in terms of dress—blue for boys and pink for girls—but this stereotyping remains a factor in the lives of many people as they grow up. A more important factor is behavior identified as appropriate only for girls or for boys. There are still families where remarks like, That's not for a boy, are common. Boys and girls get the impression that nothing is more terrible than acting like a member of the opposite sex.

Parents do worry about sexual confusion and sexual identity. Even liberated parents become concerned when their little boys appear to enjoy dressing up in women's clothing. There is somewhat less concern for girls who take on tomboyish traits.

Most often, but not necessarily, it is a transitional stage and nothing more. Our advice is to test it out and see if by not fussing, other interests become predominant. When these traits maintain themselves over a long period of time, they may indicate gender confusion. Yet, one should be concerned only if it seems to reflect a basic neurotic trend in the development of a child and symptomatic of other areas of maladjustment. A child who makes friends, enjoys life, and is relatively free of symptoms—stuttering, failure to thrive, bedwetting beyond the fourth or fifth year, or extreme introversion—and who, at the same time takes on the so-called sensitivity of the opposite sex (in terms of our own stereotypes), may be evidencing the background for creativity and a good emotional development. Our feeling is to be concerned only if it seems to reflect a general disorganization of the personality.

Why do students need to think about these things now? Such thoughts provide a certain rehearsal behavior. Even the most sophisticated and alert parents get confused when confronted with questions asked by their children at unexpected moments. Parents should think beforehand of their responses to such questions as, Where did I come from? and How did I get into you?

You may feel that a child's question is inappropriate, which it may be from your adult perspective. The child should not be given the impression that he or she asked the wrong question, that the timing is wrong, or that there is something wrong with the child for asking the question in the first place. Parents often prefer for everything to be done according to their expectations, in line with certain developmental stages, or at points when they personally feel ready. But children are full of surprises. That's part of the excitement of raising children, and they need to have the experience of your response.

There are sexually related questions about which parents are concerned. For example, how should you react to a child who wants to climb in bed with you? We feel that this activity is okay. Some children report that some of their most pleasant experiences took place early in childhood when they could have a lot of fun with their parents in bed. Some parents worry about sexual stimulation, but most are quite comfortable with the idea. Parents often have the experience of becoming stimulated by this contact and are able to acknowledge the sensual delight of loving their children so closely. There is a natural warmth between parents and children, and sharing this affection provides children with a sound basis for loving themselves and others later on. The activity usually becomes a playful, "roughhouse" experience, rather than one that is specifically erotic.

On the other hand, we, along with many child development experts, don't think it is a good policy to allow children to sleep with parents. If children have traumatic dreams or nightmares and want the comfort of sleeping with parents, it might be a good idea to say, I'll stay with you for a while until you fall asleep. Or allow the child to come to your bed for a while until comforted and then carry the youngster back to bed. It is quite common for children to have upsetting nightmares, but it's not a good idea to tell them not to worry about it. Parents could tell children that they know nightmares are frightening but that everyone has them at one time or another. The important thing is to reassure children that all they have to do is open their eyes and the nightmare will disappear.

Parental concern over television is certainly legitimate, not because of the exposure to sexual information, but because of the violence. It is wise for parents to exert some control over television-watching habits, especially if used as a substitute for activity, learning, and achieving. It's a retreat from an active involvement in the pursuit of experiences and learning.

The school age is a time for a tremendous amount of learning and experiencing. The old notion that this constitutes a "latency" period when children are not particularly interested in anything sexual is just another myth perpetuated by adherents of a Freudian point of view. Perhaps children appeared to be this way in Freud's day. We've rarely met children of school age who were not aware and excited, interested in, and affected by the sexual aspects of their lives. They'll ask questions and be curious. They'll certainly observe what's happening on television. They'll observe pregnancies, and wonder where the puppies next door came from.

There are two areas for which no parent should avoid responsibility: preparing girls for the onset of menstruation and preparing boys for nocturnal emissions. They should know well in advance, so the events do not come as traumatic surprises. Girls should be told about nocturnal emissions and boys should be told about menstruation. Both sexes should be informed fully of these and other developments affecting their own as well as the opposite sex. No later than the age of ten, a mother or female relative should specifically demonstrate the proper method of using a belt and sanitary napkin (few girls start out with tampons). The demonstration should be explained in very positive terms as being a normal and healthy stage of development that all girls experience between the ages of eleven and fifteen or so. It is very important that the young girl looks on her growth into womanhood as a positive step in her development.

Also around the age of ten, boys should be told by either the mother or father that wet dreams happen to almost all boys and are a normal stage of development. Explain that between the ages of 11 and 15 or so, most boys experience nocturnal emissions. The boy should be told that you understand his bedclothes and linens may be wet, and that he can put them privately into the hamper.

NINETEEN QUESTIONS . . . AND ANSWERS

Of the thousands of questions we get from parents, the following are the most common. The answers are stated as if readers are already parents and are concerned about their own children. The responses reflect our personal values, but if any of them conflict with yours, stick to your own. Perhaps we might have some minor differences, but agree on a more fundamental level.

The key question for all should be, Do I intend to be an askable parent? Put somewhat differently, the question reads, When should I tell? The answer is simple: It is time to tell whenever the child asks. If you are an askable parent, your child may come to you with questions about sex from the time he or she is two years old. Young children's questions are sometimes nonverbal. For example, a child may constantly follow you into the bathroom. Some shy children might ask no questions at all, even of the most askable parents. If your child hasn't raised sexual questions by the age of five, you should start the conversation. Read a book with your child. Tell him or her about a neighbor or a relative who is going to have a baby. While it's fine on occasion to make analogies to animals, do not concentrate on them in your explanations. People and animals have very different habits.

People who foresee becoming askable parents will find some of their values and attitudes reflected in the series of questions and answers that follow. Others may find themselves feeling somewhat provoked and perhaps indignant. In either case, readers are encouraged to examine critically their own values and attitudes as they proceed.

How much should I tell? You should tell your child a *bit* more than you feel he or she can understand.

How explicit should I be? Make it a point to use the correct terminology. Avoid such childish expressions as "pee pee" or "wee wee." Say directly that when a man and a woman love each other and want to have a baby, the man's penis is placed into the woman's vagina. If the sperm from the man's body joins with the egg inside the woman's body at the right time, a baby gets started. Depending on the child's age and other factors, you might say more: Sometimes it takes a year or more before a child is conceived. Or, Your father (or mother) and I enjoy loving each other in this way. Right now we are using birth control because our family isn't ready for a new baby just yet (or at all).

The main idea is that parents can be explicit without overstating the case or feeling compelled to describe sexual relations to a child who hasn't yet grasped much more basic ideas. It is also wise to say at the start that a baby has its beginning in the mother's uterus, not the stomach.

Is there such a thing as giving too much sex education too soon? Parents worry a great deal about whether they can "harm" their children with "too much" information or tell their children things that they won't understand. Let us state again emphatically that despite the protests of a few professionals, knowledge is not harmful. It does not matter if the child does not understand everything you say. What counts is that you are an askable parent. If the child can trust you not to be rigid or hostile in your response, he or she will ask you questions and use you as a source of wisdom and guidance.

What about nudity in the home? Many parents are relaxed about undressing in front of young children or about bathing with them. These are good opportunities for children to ask important questions. How come you have one and I don't? How come yours is bigger than mine? How come you have two and I don't have any? Parents should respond directly to these and similar questions.

A question also arises when a child wants to touch a parent's genitals or breasts. There are several acceptable responses, one of which is simply that you don't want him or her to do this. Even if children protest against that familiar double standard—but you touch me—you can explain that this is because you have to bathe them and keep them clean. For parents who do not object to their children's requests to touch, it is important to remain casual about it. A child's own growing sense of modesty will tell you when to start undressing in private. When a child wants to go to the bathroom alone or to undress without an audience, parents need to respect that developing sense of privacy.

Is too much masturbation harmful? Masturbation is a healthy, normal expression of sexuality at any age. The only thing wrong with it is the guilt people are made to feel. It is this guilt that creates the energy for impulsive and involuntary masturbation. All children old enough to understand the concept of privacy can be taught that masturbation should be done in private. They will realize that as long as it is pleasurable, it cannot be overdone.

What about the use of obscenities? Children invariably use vulgar language to find out what it means, to get a rise out of their parents, or to test a new and powerful weapon. If a child uses an obscenity, the parent should quickly and calmly explain its meaning, perhaps using the word itself in the explanation. Even the most common four-letter word can be handled in this way, provided the parent explains its gross intent as well as the fact that it's a crude synonym for sexual intercourse. The advantage for the parent using obscenity itself is that it defuses the word as a "weapon." Furthermore, it reinforces your role as an askable parent.

What about the child who likes to look at his father's "girlie" magazines? There is no harm in this. In fact, it may provide for teachable moments. You might point out that ordinary people don't look like that. Men sometimes like to look at nude photographs of women, and women sometimes enjoy looking at photographs of nude men. It's not a big deal. Generally speaking, frontal nudity is becoming more common in established magazines.

Pornography, however, is something else again. True, it has not been proved harmful but it is clearly not educational, and parents would understandably prefer to keep their children away from it. Although it may not always be possible to shield a child from pornographic material, parents can take some comfort in the fact that people who have received enlightened sexuality education tend to grow bored with pornography.

What about embarrassing questions in public? Children have a great knack for asking the most delicate questions in the supermarket or when special guests have come to dinner. The best approach, no matter how embarrassed you are, is to tell the child that he has asked a very good question; if you still have your wits about you, proceed to answer it then and there. In most cases, your guests will silently applaud. If you feel you can't answer the question right away, it is very important to praise the child for asking and to state specifically when you will discuss it. In general, it is better to risk shocking a few grown-ups than to scold or put off your own child.

What should I do if my husband thinks it's my job? Sex education is properly the responsibility of both parents. It is reflected in their behavior with each other and in communication with children. If your husband stubbornly refuses to have any part of it, you must take it upon yourself to explain sex and love to all the children in your family. Incidentally, it has never been established that girls are better educated by their mothers or boys by their fathers. Single parents, relax.

What can I do to prevent my child from becoming a homosexual? Some parents have rather strange notions of what constitutes "prevention." Contrary to the opinion of some professionals, our view is that there's nothing parents can do to prevent their children from becoming homosexual. No specific attitudes or behaviors have been found to discourage the development of a homosexual orientation. Similarly, there is no convincing evidence that parents can *cause* homosexuality in their children. Although it is perfectly all right not to want your children to become homosexual, it is important to understand that good mental health is not necessarily a function of sexual orientation. Just as homosexual adults can be happy and creative individuals, heterosexual adults can turn to drugs, crime, and generally lead unhappy lives.

Parents should convey an attitude of acceptance for people who have different orientations. At the same time they should make it abundantly clear that their children are to reject any sexual overtures made by adults. They must emphasize that such overtures do not in any way suggest that a child was to blame or must be homosexual simply because of having been approached.

What if my children think I'm old-fashioned? They will probably be right! Most parents are old-fashioned. Acknowledge it and continue expressing your views without worrying which label your child might attach to them.

How can I talk to my teenage daughter about birth control without giving her the message that it's all right for her to have sexual intercourse? Some parents erroneously believe that teenagers equate information with consent. Your teenage children know very well what your values are. It's one thing to tell a daughter that you will disown her if she becomes pregnant. It's quite another to explain your feelings something like this: We really think you're too young to have sex, but if you're not going to listen to us we urge you to practice birth control. We don't ever want you to feel that there's anything you can't talk to us about.

I worry about my children being molested. How can I talk about this without frightening them? A little-known fact is that as many as 75 percent of all child molestation cases involve someone the child knows, such as a father, stepparent, or babysitter. As part of a family's general discussions about sexuality, children should be taught not to go off with strangers and not to allow anyone to touch their genitals. Some individuals force children to submit to sexual activities and make them promise never to tell anyone what happened. Should you suspect that your child has been abused in this way, it is essential to make him or her understand that such promises should not be kept. The fact that most people are decent and kind must be balanced with the reality that some people take advantage of children. The critical point is to discourage a child who has been molested from feeling any guilt or blame whatsoever. Some parents unthinkingly ask, Why did you let him do it? Such crimes are *always* and *entirely* the responsibility of the adult who committed them. (See Chapter 13.)

We've never talked about sex. Now I want to, but my teenage son absolutely refuses.

What should I do? This is a common situation and it is appropriate for the parent to begin the conversation something like this: I really made a mistake by waiting this long and I wished we had talked when you were younger. I can understand why you might feel embarrassed to talk with me. Plan ahead for such discussions; have a book ready. Tell your son that you think he might be interested in it. Explain that some of the material might embarrass him, but that you're going to leave the book around just the same. The main thing is for him to understand that you are available to talk anytime he is ready. Another technique is to "hide" a book. Most teenagers are very adept at finding such "hidden" material.

Here are some of the most frequently worrisome questions teenagers have that they are *not likely* to ask their parents.

Am I masturbating too much?

Do I have homosexual tendencies?

Am I abnormal if I have thoughts about sex with people I know, even family members?

Are my breasts too small?

Is my penis too small?

How can I tell if I have VD?

Is there something wrong with me if I remain a virgin?

How can I say no?

How can I tell if I'm pregnant?

How come I have all these unexplained erections?

Think back to when you were growing up and the kinds of questions you had about sexuality. Then you'll be able to better appreciate your child's concerns.

What if I find my child undressed and playing doctor with a neighbor's child? This is a fairly universal game children play. It must be considered a normal developmental episode for many preschool children. The most important thing is for parents not to lose their cool. Convey the message that you understand why they want to play with each other; tell them you'd rather they wouldn't. Indicate that you feel their genitals should be private at this time. Then ask them to get dressed and play other games. It is not appropriate to send the other child home or to make a "big deal" of it in any way.

What is your opinion of premarital sex? We're opposed to teenagers having sexual intercourse. Teenagers are too young, too vulnerable. They do not have ready access to contraception. They tend to be impulsive. The double standard is still, alas, very much with us. In addition, teenage pregnancy is definitely unsound from medical, moral, and psychological points of view.

Although we are opposed to sex for teenagers (teenagers are defined as anyone under age eighteen who's still in high school), in thirty years of clinical experience, no teenager has ever asked for our consent. It is unrealistic for parents to assume that their teenagers will not have sexual relationships in the absence of parental permission. Parents still can exert a *positive* influence. Without anger and without recriminations, they can explain reasons for waiting. Even young adults who are working or who are in college could receive similar parental messages. The decision is up to them, but if they should choose to have sexual relationships, it is their duty, to themselves and to their partners, to act responsibly.

What should be the role of public schools in sex education? Sex education should be part of the regular curriculum. It is currently excluded because of censorship and extremist pressures against school boards and administrators.

What if my child doesn't ask? If a child does not ask a question by the time he or she is five or six years of age, the parent should take the initiative in talking to them about sex. The parent could point to a pregnant neighbor or relative. Other strategies might include utilizing the opportunity of another child coming into the family or reading a children's book together.

The most important information is conveyed by love for the child and an affectionate relationship between the parents. Even askable parents are not always approached with questions by their shy children. It is also possible that they simply aren't interested in knowing; this doesn't mean that they shouldn't be taught anyway.

How can I bring up my children to respect the values of other people? This depends largely on the parents' lifestyle and the kinds of values they translate into behavior with others. As models for children (which, of course, does not imply perfection), parents have the best opportunity to foster a true respect for individual differences.

For a final comment, let's return to our initial proposition: sex education is a family affair. It is related to how you feel about yourself and your ability to communicate with your husband or wife. Askable parents talk to each other. They also have a sense of humor: not everything is a trauma. Children with askable parents tend to talk to them, and they respect that their parents have a lot of common sense. If you feel you've made mistakes, you can smile and say, "I've made some mistakes. My child will understand when I explain that I don't know everything." And then you'll feel more askable than ever.

THE SINGLE PARENT

One of the most striking consequences of the high rates of separation and divorce in the United States has been the emergence of the single parent family (SPF). In the year 1970, only 11 percent of all children under eighteen years of age were living in single parent families; by 1982, that figure had risen to 19 percent. Presently, close to 12 million children live in such family units, and about half of all children born in the 1980s will live in a SPF at some time during their childhood. Overall, there are

Will You Be an Askable Parent?

Parents are the sex educators of their own children, whether they do it well or badly. Silence and evasiveness are just as powerful teachers as are the facts.

Everybody says that parents should be the primary sex educators, but who is preparing the parents for this role? Indeed, in terms of the values and spiritual life of the child, no outside group or agency could replace the family. Thus, we see education for sexuality taking place within the context of the family's value system, which strives, it is hoped, toward a family life free of racism, sexism, and prejudices against people with other values. Most churches and educators officially support this position, but few are doing anything about it.

Studies consistently have revealed that children do not acquire the information they need from parents. It is time for parents to assume this responsibility. Parents, of course, cannot be the sole educators; if they wanted to be, they would have to prevent their children from reading books, newspapers, and magazines, keep them away from television, movies, and public bathrooms, and certainly prohibit them from having any friends at all. Parents are the *main* educators, with schools, religious, and community groups as partners in a lifelong process.

Society consistently underestimates the capabilities of parents and their children. You can't tell a child too much: Knowledge doesn't stimulate inappropriate behavior; ignorance does. If you tell children more than they can understand, they will ask another question or turn you off. Parents must work toward being *askable*. We know most parents want to educate their children, but they are often uncomfortable and don't know how. Obviously, parents who find it difficult to talk to their children about any important issue will not be ready to talk about sex. However, it seems that most parents are ready but want some support.

It is essential for parents to be alert to extremist propaganda and political maneuvering, especially by those groups claiming to have a monopoly on the Judeo-Christian ethic. Censorship in the schools and media is one method used by extremist groups who want to impose their views on everybody. Parents should not be intimidated by scare tactics used as subterfuges for acquiring power on school boards or in churches. In support of these principles, PTA's, foundations, church- and synagogue-related groups and community organizations can develop ongoing institutes, workshops, seminars, and media presentations and put together bibliographies and library and bookstore displays to get the public involved (continuing education is more effective than one-shot lectures). It is expected that religious groups in particular will develop programs based on their own moral beliefs. Community-minded groups should discover opportunities for getting their message heard via public service options on TV and radio, as well as in newspapers and magazines. We must counter the propaganda that information is harmful or constitutes license for irresponsible behavior. It's time that the "silent" majority expressed itself vigorously, visibly, and vocally.

nearly 8 million single parent families; thus, they represent the fastest-growing type of family unit.

Since many readers of this book will themselves be single parents, the questions surrounding sexuality education and parenting are very pertinent. Women especially may be affected, as they outnumber men as single parents by a ratio of about five to one.

The ordinary problems encountered in two-parent households may become magnified when there is only one person to face them. An abundance of literature exists advising single parents of the unique difficulties involved, the trials of day care or financial woes. The problems are not nearly as insurmountable as was once assumed, however, and in many instances a special bond develops between children and their single mother or father. One or two parents is not the issue: rather the quality of love and care the child receives in the home will determine his or her overall adjustment and well-being.

Single parents often worry that their children will grow up psychologically impaired; yet, there is no evidence that single parent families produce traumatized children any more than the conventional two-parent family guarantees emotional stability. Children are amazingly resilient and resourceful. They will be understandably hurt by divorce, or the death of a parent, which is essentially a healthy response to grief. It is most important to reassure the children that they are still loved, and that they were in no way responsible for the absence of the other parent. Children are apt to say, It's my fault that daddy left, or, If mommy had really loved me she wouldn't have left. The children in these instances will not respond to vague consolation and should be encouraged to explain *why* they feel that way.

The single parent must tell the child, in the case of divorce, that the parents did not get along. If it's appropriate, the reasons can be explained, but in general it's not a good idea to reveal details of sexual incompatibility or other highly personal motives. On the other hand, it is probably unwise to attempt to conceal the "other" man or woman, if there is one. These states of affairs have a way of becoming obvious over time, and it may injure the child's sense of trust if he or she finds out inadvertently. If the absent parent abandoned the family, children will not usually believe or welcome suggestions that the parent still loves them. If the abandoner has lost interest or found another home, the child might be encouraged to accept the reality of it, instead of pretending for years that the parent may be coming back or "thinks of you all the time." Assurances of enduring love are called for only if there is some credibility for them. In general, it is best to be honest about the circumstances of single parenthood and encourage the children to accept them realistically.

In many instances, a single parent is more desirable than two parents. When the home has been plagued by battles and bitter feelings, children often fare better when the war is finally ended. The child's sexual identity will not necessarily suffer without the appropriate male or female role model: There's an abundance of role models among relatives, school teachers, and parents of friends.

The ongoing responsibility of sex-educating the child can be assumed by the single parent for children of both sexes. Children appreciate their own parent's candor and openness, but if the parent is too uncomfortable discussing sexual issues, perhaps a relative or close friend might be willing to fill in. Since a father cannot very well demonstrate how to manage a belt and sanitary napkin for the onset of a daughter's menstruation, it might be better in this case to seek female assistance. All other matters pertaining to sexuality, however, can be sensitively and competently handled by single parents.

Single parents are correct in assuming that their child's sexuality and needs are no different than those in two-parent homes. The children require the same anatomical, contraceptive, behavioral, and attitudinal information imparted to all youngsters. Discipline and guidance are just as crucial, and no special allowances need be made because the child has only one parent.

Single parents themselves are sexual beings. Most do not live with their lovers, but the majority do have ongoing relationships and/or sexual encounters. According to researcher Morton Hunt (1974), within the first year of separation five out of six individuals become sexually active again. How can the single parent live a sexual existence and still appear responsible and stable to the children?

In the early stages of their sexual relationships, most single parents confine their sexual activities to times when the children aren't home or are asleep, or to the other person's house or apartment. Children may at first feel somewhat threatened or jealous of the parent's interest in another partner. There may be feelings of loyalty to the parent no longer at home or the desire to protect the parent from getting emotionally hurt in the new affair. These feelings are apt to be stronger if the child isn't included in any of the activities you and your lover share, and it's sometimes a good idea to involve the child in whatever card games, conversation, or recreation that goes on. At the point that the child begins to suspect your feelings for this new person are important, he or she may likely ask if you have plans to remarry, or if your feelings for each other are serious. Children need and deserve honesty at this stage: parents can acknowledge their feelings without feeling compelled to cover up or make excuses.

Our view is that unless there is a sense of continuation to the relationship, it is best not to spend the night together in the house while the children are there. It can be very difficult for the child to adapt to a new lover every so often if that is the single parent's lifestyle. A time may come in more ongoing relationships, however, when it becomes very inconvenient and enervating to arrange constantly for sexual relations outside the home: the parent can weigh the child's needs and likely reaction against their own desires for intimacy.

The decision is likely to be easier if the child has accepted the boyfriend or girlfriend and seems to like him or her. It is often the case, in fact, that children develop deep emotional ties to these other partners and consequently suffer a sense of loss if the relationship ends. The children may welcome the camaraderie of having another person in the house and appreciate the positive effect on the parent. Sex itself thus becomes a secondary issue and yields in significance to other intricate considerations that come with living under the same roof. It is not uncommon for children to press the parent to marry, which of course should not influence the parent's decision—although if marriage is desired, it's good to know the children approve. If there has been a dispute over child custody in divorce or separation, the single parent might want to get the advice of a lawyer on the probable effects of a new sexual relationship. Even after divorce, one parent's sexual life and morality may be dragged back into court as the basis for new custody rulings. Even if the absent parent is involved intimately with another person, the parent with custody has sometimes been declared unfit on the basis of exerting an indesirable influence on the children.

In the early stages of any new relationship, it's best if the role of parent and disciplinarian remains solely with the parent. Children often resent the interference of a lover and may retort with, Leave me alone, you're not my parent. As the relationship progresses, children may come to welcome the advice and guidance of another adult, which they see as prevalent in the friends' two-parent households. Some people who have no children of their own, however, do not feel comfortable with children and have no idea how to relate to them. They may treat the children as little adults or else simply not understand their perspective. The parent may be confronted with a child's ultimatum: Either he goes or I do. It's very important to be sensitive to the child's feelings and not automatically assume he or she is just spoiled or selfish. The parent might respond, I love you both differently, but I can't let you make my decisions. You'll always be my child no matter what happens, and I'm not sure what the future holds for my lover and me. But you and I will always love each other, and that's the difference.

Regardless of the circumstances of single parenthood, people in this position often meet with discrimination. Many couples see singles as a threat and exclude them from their circle of friends. The labels *divorcée, separated,* and *illegitimate* carry negative stigmas for some segments of the population, and people may be judged on the basis of these alone. Although it may be limiting, some single parents find that it is best to seek companionship with people who are not prejudicial. The late anthropologist, Margaret Mead, had this to say: ". . . I do think that family living will become increasingly narrow, cramped and frustrating unless married couples open the doors of their homes and bring some singles into their lives. And I also think that singles cut off from friends with families will seldom gain a sense of wholeness in their lives."

Deprived of a second parent, children will usually find another adult to relate closely with. It may be a teacher, coach, relative, or boy- or girl-scout leader. A volunteer from the Big Brother or Big Sister program can be very helpful. The person may adapt the role of "significant other" or may simply provide the child with a measure of closeness and friendship. It is a good idea for the single parent to encourage and support these liaisons. One-parent households sometimes have a tendency to turn inward and become cut off from important interaction from the outside world in the dramatic sense of you and me against the world. It is, after all, only natural that an extraordinary bond of love and closeness should develop between children and parents in such circumstances. The important consideration is to love the children, but as separate entities. Single parents want to help them grow physically, intellectually, and emotionally and to have the courage to watch them grow up and develop their own sense of independence. This may be painful for many parents, particularly the single parent who has invested a great deal.

A number of theories have been advanced concerning the relative effects on the child of being placed in day care or nursery school while the single parent works. It may be that a babysitter or grandparent cares for the child during the day. Whatever the case, child psychologists and other professionals have been studying how children react to being away from either parent during the day in the care of another person. To date, there is no convincing argument that these situations interfere with the child's growth or lead to feelings of abandonment. If the quality of care is competent and takes place in an atmosphere of creativity and acceptance, the child is likely to be positively influenced. There remains plenty of time in the evening for togetherness and nurturance between parent and child. The child's own sense of personal capabilities often flourish with the stimulation of playmates his or her own age. In addition, the parent's own independence is enhanced, and he or she is free to pursue a life and career apart from the family unit. For both parents and children there are opportunities to meet other people. Without such supplementary child-care facilities, the only alternative is often to apply for welfare, as few companies or places of business now offer their own day-care services. The following statistics highlight the dilemma: The median family income of American families with children under age eighteen was $26,200 in 1981. Among all women who were head of their own households, median income in the same year was only $9200. The Census Bureau further states that families headed by women are six times more likely to be below the poverty threshold than are families headed by two parents (1983).

It is to be hoped that agreeable arrangements can be worked out concerning child care and visitation rights and the payment of alimony and child support. Often this is not the case, and even when alimony is awarded, it is often never paid: Only half of such payments are ever made in full (U.S. Census Bureau, 1981). A high level of conflict typically surrounds divorce proceedings, and the children themselves often become enmeshed. Often parents will use their children as pawns in the power struggle, playing loyalties against each other and demanding that the child states which parent he or she prefers to live with. This is upsetting to the child, who usually wishes to continue loving and being loved by both parents.

In the child's better interests, parents with custody should not disparage the absent parent or try to convince the child not to continue with the visitation procedures. Often divorced parents will ply the children with questions to obtain gossip or news of the other. Or one parent may demand financial concessions as a prerequisite for seeing the child. The increasing practice of joint child custody avoids some of these situations; the parents take turns living with the children at six-month intervals or other time schedules. Most children have adapted to this situation positively and do not resent being shuttled back and forth. Joint custody is most likely to be successful if the child is able to continue attending the same school and is not made to feel guilty for leaving one parent for the other.

If the single parent has a reasonably open and mature relationship with the children, they will grow up making choices instead of succumbing to some predetermined "fate" that befalls all children of single parents. The point is that nothing is inevitable, even if it is easier for a couple to raise their children than it is for a lone parent.

REFERENCES

Hunt, M. *Sexual Behavior in the 1970s*. Chicago: Playboy Press, 1974.

U.S. Bureau of the Census. "Characteristics of the Population below the Poverty Level: 1981." *Current Population Reports*, Series P-60, No. 138, 183, and "Money Income of Households, Families and Persons in the United States: 1981." *Current Population Reports*, Series P-60, No. 137, 1983.

U.S. Bureau of the Census. "Child Support and Alimony: 1981." Table 1.

PART FIVE
Prevention and Wellness

CHAPTER 20

Sexually Transmitted Diseases

If you are between the ages of fifteen and fifty-five, chances are *one in four* that you will contract some variety of *sexually transmitted disease* (STD) in your lifetime. This amounts to 27 thousand new cases every day for a total of at least 10 million infections each year in the United States alone. Physicians now are familiar with about twenty-five different diseases that are transmitted through sexual contact, which together cost the public over 2 billion dollars annually in health care (Newsweek, 1985).

The emotional trauma suffered by individuals, combined with the stresses that STDs place on relationships, are not so easily measured. STDs now constitute the

---

Health Alert

Due to the AIDS crisis, oral and anal sex are not considered to be safe, especially for homosexuals, bisexuals, and their partners. Heterosexuals should avoid any sexual contact with partners whose behavior they are not sure about. The use of condoms is thought to help prevent transmission of the AIDS virus but should not be considered to be absolute protection.

---

number one reportable communicable disease in the United States, meaning that tens of millions of individuals are afflicted not only with physical difficulties, but with the emotional fallout as well. The tragedy, in hindsight, is that in the majority of instances, STDs are preventable.

VENEREAL DISEASE PREVENTION FOR EVERYONE*

The venereal diseases were previously thought of as a limited few such as syphilis, gonorrhea, and several other less common infections; a later concept expanded the field to include a more extensive group now identified as "sexually transmitted diseases" (STD).

Today, for a better understanding of disease prevention the sexually transmitted diseases (STD) should not be categorized solely by their mode of transmission, but must be viewed within the broader spectrum of communicable diseases.

The feelings of shame and guilt traditionally associated with these diseases must be eliminated. After all, such communicable diseases as polio, typhoid, or tuberculosis, not usually thought of as sexually transmitted, may be as easily spread during sexual contact as syphilis or gonorrhea.

PERSONAL HYGIENE AND DISEASE PREVENTION

Washing

It is vital to individual and collective health that everyone learn the importance of personal hygiene in the prevention of sexually transmitted and other communicable diseases.

Every male and female should be taught the responsibility to wash genitals and rectal area before and after sexual contact, reducing the germs and secretions exchanged, in protection of one's own health and that of one's sex partner.

---

*The authors are grateful to the American Foundation for the Prevention of Venereal Disease, Inc., whose pamphlet entitled "Venereal Disease Prevention for Everyone" (11th revised edition) is reprinted in this chapter. Copies of the pamphlet may be obtained by sending $1.00 or more as a tax-deductible donation to: 799 Broadway, Suite 638, New York, NY 10003.

For Male and Female

Infectious germs which are always found in the lower digestive tract may be transmitted from the rectum during sexual activities. Among the many dangerous germs present in feces may be the virus which causes hepatitis, and parasites which cause intestinal disorders if they enter the mouth (fecal-oral route). To reduce the risk of transmitting such intestinal and urinary tract germs, restaurant owners and kitchen supervisors must take the responsibility to teach their cooks, waiters, and any other food handlers to wash their hands before beginning work and particularly after each use of the toilet. This applies also to those preparing food in households.

The male and female mucous membranes, especially those of the genito-urinary (GU) system, are highly susceptible to infection by some of these germs from the rectum, which may cause urethritis (inflammation of the urinary canal) in the male and vaginitis (inflammation of the vulvo-vaginal area) in the female. For example: As a result of wiping from rectum toward vagina by the female after toilet, germs are easily spread to the vagina where they may cause infections, and from which they may be transmitted during vaginal, as if during rectal, intercourse. Therefore, females must wipe from front to back, and not in the direction of rectum to vagina.

Today it is considered that excessive douching may disturb the normal bacterial balance of the vagina; frequency and content should be discussed with a physician.

Personal hygiene before and after sexual contact can be greatly aided by the bidet, a low bathroom fixture designed to facilitate washing for disease prevention and proper cleansing after toilet. Not everyone, unfortunately, has been informed on the advantages of the bidet. It is rarely found, for instance, in homes or hotels in the United States, whereas in many parts of the world it is widely used and significant to personal hygiene.

Good hygiene requires washing of genitals and rectal area before and after sexual activities.

The infectious agents of certain sexually transmitted diseases (STD) prefer to infect mucous membranes, while other STD germs attack membranes and/or skin surfaces particularly in the presence of abrasion or break in the skin.

The germs that cause syphilis and gonorrhea, as well as some other STD, are sensitive to soap and water. Wash before sexual contact for hygienic purposes. Wash after sexual contact to reduce the possibility of catching STD.

It is suggested that the following procedure for the male immediately after intercourse may furnish prophylactic value against urethritis: Work a bit of soft, mushy soap into urinary opening; then urinate.

Extended exposure or delay before washing diminishes the effectiveness of this preventive measure. Washing is doubly important since even in the absence of syphilis or gonorrhea, other sexually transmitted germs can cause infections such as NGU (nongonococcal urethritis) or NSU (nonspecific urethritis).

The foreskin covering the head of the penis may trap germs that can cause infections. Therefore, special attention should be given to washing the uncircumcised penis.

If lubricants are involved in the sexual act, water-soluble preparations that will wash away should be used. Those with oil base that can leave a film to trap germs should not be used.

Note—It is possible that vaccines against certain STD will be developed; in that event, good personal hygiene will remain necessary to help prevent other STD.

For example: A gonorrhea vaccine will not prevent approximately half of the reported cases of male urethritis which are not gonorrhea.

THE CONDOM

STD Preventative and Contraceptive for Male and Female

The condom, which is beneficial to both male and female, plays a major role in the prevention of sexually transmitted diseases (STD), and serves simultaneously as an effective contraceptive (pregnancy preventative, birth control device), involving no health risk or side effects.

The condom acts as a physical barrier, preventing the spread of germs from one sex partner to the other; at the same time it traps the male sperm, preventing possible pregnancy.

Condoms, sometimes called "prophylactics," "rubbers," or "French letters," are made of thin rubber or processed animal membrane, perfected to insure high sensitivity. The condom is of cylindrical shape, serving as a sheath to cover the penis during sexual activities. It should be put on before foreplay or penetration.

In using the condom that does not have a reservoir end, a half-inch space should be left at the tip end to collect the semen. It is pulled down over the entire length of the erect penis, where it must remain throughout the sexual act. On completion of intercourse, the male should hold on to the open end of the condom to keep it from slipping off on withdrawal, and to prevent the semen from spilling into the area.

The animal membrane condom is packaged prelubricated. The rubber condom is offered dry or prelubricated, straight-sided or shaped, smooth or textured, colored or natural, with or without reservoir end. A brand of condom is now available with lubricant containing the spermicide nonoxynol-9 which may also provide germicidal action against certain STD.

For maximum protection, the condom should be kept away from heat and should not be used a second time. Old, dried-out condoms should never be used. Oil base products may damage the rubber condom; a water-soluble lubricant should be used if lubrication is wanted.

Traditionally, the use of the condom has been considered the obligation of the male sex partner; today, with the wide availability of condoms, the female can share the responsibility of using this easy method of disease prevention and contraception.

The male should use the condom especially with a new sex partner, or if he has multiple sex partners. Anyone, regardless of age, can obtain condoms from pharmacies and other outlets.

Whether or not the condom is used, both males and females should wash genitals and rectal area before and after sexual contact.

GERMICIDAL PREPARATIONS

For the Male—The "Pro-kit"*

(To be used after intercourse by the sexually active male only.)

Already in successful use in America and Europe, during World War II the U.S. Armed Forces ordered to be manufactured and then made available the "pro-kit" to servicemen who found it effective as an STD preventative; men have used it effectively in civilian as well as military life.

This germicidal preparation to prevent gonorrhea and syphilis, sometimes called "Pro-kit," is a single-application, post-exposure preventative for self-use by the sexually active male. It comes in ointment form and must be used immediately after intercourse.

After washing the genitals and then urinating, the user squeezes the ointment from its small tube into the urinary opening, and for more extensive protection, applies it externally to the penile shaft where it should remain at least an hour. Instructions included with each tube, may vary slightly from product to product.

Delay in using the ointment, or extended intercourse of more than possibly one hour after initial sexual contact, may diminish the effectiveness of this preventative measure.

As always, genitals and rectal area should be washed before and after sexual contact.

In the United States, the "pro-kit" is available from certain pharmacies, or

Doughboy Prophylactic®
Reese Chemical Co.
10617 Frank Ave.
Cleveland, Ohio 44106

---

*Authors' note: The use of these germicidal preparations is a somewhat controversial area among the medical establishment. Some physicians believe that their use will encourage a careless attitude toward STD and may prevent some people from obtaining proper medical treatment once infected despite the use of these preparations. Individuals need to decide for themselves whether these substances will play a role in their sexual behaviors, in consultation with their physicians.

The Sanitube®
Sanitube Co.
19 Concord St.
South Norwalk, Conn. 06854

In Europe, from certain pharmacies, or

Veto Prophylactique®
Dr. Kurt Egloff's Erben
Victoria-Apotheke
71 Bahnhofstrasse
Zurich 8021, Switzerland

Any mention of brand names herein is for public information and does not imply endorsement by the foundation.

For Male and Female

All commercially available vaginal spermicidal contraceptive foams, creams, suppositories, and jellies intended for use by the female before intercourse may benefit both male and female sex partners since these preparations have germicidal properties which may prevent certain sexually transmitted diseases (STD). A scientific study on the possible STD preventative benefits of these spermicides, limited to gonorrhea only, found that one of the products (Delfen®, Conceptrol®) containing nonoxynol-9 "offered a fairly high degree of protection against gonorrhea."

Additional studies indicated that the female users of vaginal spermicidal contraceptives containing nonoxynol-9 had a lower incidence of certain STD. Laboratory experiments showed that these contraceptives also have viricidal properties which may provide some protection against herpes.

It has been frequently suggested (though not necessarily provable) that immediately after sex activities, a mouth wash-gargle with products such as hydrogen peroxide 3% (1 part to 3 parts water) or "Listerine Antiseptic"® (26.9% alcohol) may furnish some prophylactic value against oral-pharyngeal STD infection.

Further scientific studies in germicidal preparations are needed.

POINTS ON STD PREVENTION

The American Foundation For The Prevention Of Venereal Disease, Inc., realizes that abstinence may be considered, but presents preventive measures, recognizing that needs vary according to the individual. A physician may advise on personal requirements.

The birth control pill and the intra-uterine device (IUD) serve only as contraceptives and do not prevent sexually transmitted diseases (STD).

STD prevention makes preferable a sexual relationship with one person. Having multiple sex partners places one in a high risk group with increased exposure to STD; having fewer sex partners reduces the risk of acquiring STD.

STD prevention advises that one avoid having multiple sex partners and avoid sexual contact with those who do.

It is preferable that sex partners know each other and as much as possible about each other's sexual activities. Knowing each other enables infected persons to later notify their partners in the event of necessity for an STD exam.

Important to every effective STD prevention program is epidemiology which, through case finding, locates the source of disease and breaks the chain of infection by prompt treatment of contacts.

Successful STD control requires the patient's complete cooperation in identifying sexual contacts; all information is confidential.

More than one STD may be transmitted on the occasion of one sexual contact. Having had an STD does not provide immunity; reinfection is possible on exposure to that disease.

The male should use a condom with a new sex partner, or if he has multiple sex partners.

Under discussion is the possibility of acquiring STD from moist seating surfaces successively occupied by unclothed persons, some of whom may be infected.

The use of preventive methods such as the condom, washing, and germicidal preparations, can significantly reduce the STD rate.

SYPHILIS

Syphilis ("bad blood," "siff," "pox," "lues")—

The syphilis germ (a spirochete, Treponema pallidum) requires warmth and moisture for survival. It dies quickly outside the human body; it would seem, therefore, unlikely to be acquired, as rumored, from toilet seats, towels, or drinking cups.

May be transmitted by infected blood, or through intimate bodily or sexual contact with a syphilitic lesion (chancre, sore) or its exudate (containing large numbers of spirochetes); may also be transmitted if the exudate has been secreted into and is present in such bodily fluids as saliva, semen, or vaginal discharge of an infected person during an infectious period.

The germ enters the body through a mucous membrane or break in the skin and invades the bloodstream. Unsterilized acupuncture, tattoo or (especially among intravenous drug abusers) hypodermic needles contaminated by blood during previous use on an infected person may transmit syphilis.

The diagnosis of syphilis is based on symptoms and/or blood testing. It may take 2–12 weeks or more after being exposed to and acquiring syphilis for the disease to show up in the blood and to be accurately reflected by a positive blood test. Therefore, even in the presence of syphilis, a blood test taken too soon after exposure may result negative. The taking of antibiotics for other purposes, not powerful enough to cure syphilis, may mask its symptoms.

Having had syphilis does not provide immunity; reinfection is possible on exposure to the disease.

At any stage, the visible symptoms may go away without treatment, but the infection will progress, sometimes causing irreversible damage. During pregnancy, untreated syphilis can cause severe birth defects. Due to the seriousness of untreated syphilis, the patient should follow carefully the attending physician's instructions as to further treatment or testing.

Syphilis may be highly infectious in the primary and secondary stages.

Primary Stage—The incubation period is 10–90 days (average 21 days). The first symptom is a chancre (red swelling or bump), which becomes a usually painless, open, then encrusted, lesion (sore). More than one may develop, usually smaller than a quarter inch in size.

Unless treated, this lesion may remain, before disappearing, 1–5 weeks at the site of infection on the genital or anal parts, or on that part of the body at which the germ entered through a mucous membrane or break in the skin. There may be no initial symptom, or the sore may be internal and go unnoticed. There sometimes follows a firm, painless bubo (swelling) in the nearby lymph gland. If untreated, the disease progresses to the—

Secondary Stage—In a period varying from several weeks to 6 months or more after exposure, a rash or pimple-like sores may appear on the palms, soles or anywhere on the body; moist papules (large flat bumps, condylomata lata) may occur on the moist parts of the body such as the genital and anal areas. Mucous patches may be found in the mouth, throat, or cervix. If untreated, in 2–6 weeks or more after their appearance, symptoms of secondary syphilis may disappear, sometimes recurring during 1 year after exposure.

Other possible symptoms include generalized lymphadenopathy (lymph gland enlargement), sore throat or flu-like syndrome, alopecia (temporary, patchy hair loss), headaches, weight loss, bone pain, fever, malaise.

Early Latent Stage (within 1 year of exposure)—Indicates untreated syphilis without visible symptoms, occurring between primary and secondary stages, or after symptoms of secondary syphilis have disappeared.

Late Latent Stage—Indicates untreated asymptomatic syphilitic infection present more than 1 year after exposure.

Tertiary Stage (Late Syphilis)—The course of untreated syphilis is variable; it may remain latent for as long as 20–40 years or it may attack the body with the following possible consequences: Heart Disease—Blindness—Nerve and Brain Damage—Paralysis—Insanity—Death.

The use of the condom, germicidal preparations, and washing after sexual contact help prevent syphilis.

GONORRHEA

Gonorrhea ("drip," "clap," "dose," "strain")—

The gonorrhea germ (a bacterium, the gonococcus Neisseria gonorrhoeae) requires warmth and moisture for survival. It dies quickly outside the human body; it would seem, therefore, unlikely to be acquired, as rumored, from a toilet seat.

Transmitted usually by sexual contact, possibly intimate bodily contact, with the surface of, or secretion (containing large numbers of gonococci) from an infected mucous membrane or gonococcal sore.

The germ attacks and infects the mucous membranes, but can possibly cause a gonococcal lesion (sore) on contact with a break in the skin.

Incubation period is 2–9 days or more. The diagnosis of gonorrhea is based on symptoms and/or specimens taken from those areas involved in sexual activities such as the penis, rectum, throat and female genitals including the cervix and urethra, and examined through smear and culture tests.

Having had gonorrhea does not provide immunity; reinfection is possible on exposure to the disease.

Direct contact of the gonorrhea germ with the eyes can produce blindness. Newborn infants receive silver nitrate eye drops as prophylaxis against possible gonococcal infection. The following parts of the body are also highly vulnerable to infection:

The Penis: Pain or burning may be present on urination, accompanied by a white or yellow discharge from the urethra (urinary opening). The infection may also be asymptomatic (without symptoms).

The Female Genitals: There may or may not be inflammation, pain or tenderness in lower abdomen, or genital discharge. Usually the infection progresses without noticeable symptoms.

The Rectum: There may be irritation, itching, pain on bowel movement, pus in the stool. Or, the infection may go unnoticed.

The Throat: Gonorrhea germs do not seem to survive as long in the throat as in the penis, female genitals, and rectum. There may be a sore throat, nearby swollen lymph glands, or no symptoms. It would appear relatively rare that gonorrhea is transmitted from the throat.

Gonococcal infection is systemic when it enters the bloodstream becoming disseminated gonorrhea, with such possible results as skin lesions, arthritis, endocarditis, meningitis.

Penicillinase-producing Neisseria gonorrhoeae (PPNG) is a strain of gonorrhea resistant to penicillin; its presence is determined by special test. It can be treated with other antibiotics.

Due to the possibility of serious complications, patients should return to the attending physician for test of cure several days after completion of treatment, or as directed.

The possible consequences of untreated gonorrhea are: Infertility—Blindness—Arthritis—Heart Disease—Meningitis—Prostatitis—Epididymitis—Pelvic Inflammatory Disease (PID).

The use of the condom, germicidal preparations, and washing after sexual contact help prevent gonorrhea.

OTHER SEXUALLY TRANSMITTED DISEASES (STD)

Male
Nongonococcal Urethritis (NGU)
Nonspecific Urethritis (NSU)
Postgonococcal Urethritis (PGU)—

NGU and NSU are terms sometimes used interchangeably. NGU refers to urethritis (infection of the urinary canal) not caused by the gonococcus; NSU refers to urethritis the cause of which is not determined. Certain studies have indicated that as many as half of the cases of male urethritis were NGU or NSU.

Postgonococcal urethritis (PGU) is urethral infection remaining present after gonococcal urethritis has been cured, in which instance PGU is caused by germs not sensitive to the drug which was prescribed to treat the gonorrhea.

Urethritis in the male (incubation period variable, 1–5 weeks) may be caused by such micro-organisms as Chlamydia trachomatis, Ureaplasma urealyticum, E. coli, Trichomonas vaginalis, Candida albicans, or undetermined factors. Symptoms include burning or pain on urination, and slight discharge from the urethra (urinary opening); urethral residue especially noticeable in the morning.

NGU, NSU, and PGU, may be the result of germs not common to the male urethra, but which may be acquired from the vagina or rectum. These infections sometimes disappear without treatment, then reappear.

Female

Vaginitis Inflammation of the vulvo-vaginal area. Can be caused by micro-organisms present in the individual's own genito-urinary (GU) system which become infectious, or by germs transmitted from the rectum, or by germs carried by the male sex partner and transmitted to the female through sexual contact. [It] may result from the effects of antibiotics, low resistance, or excessive douching which can influence the normal bacterial balance of the vagina. The attending physician may indicate other causes.

Cotton underpants should be worn because they allow air circulation; underpants made of synthetic material should not be worn since they retain moisture, encouraging vaginitis.

Vaginal infections may be transmitted by sexual contact, appearing in the male with or without symptoms. Therefore simultaneous treatment of both partners is necessary to avoid reinfection. Two prevalent types of vaginitis are:

Candidiasis (candidosis, monilia, moniliasis, yeast) A fungus, Candida albicans, may cause infection with thick, white, curdy, vaginal discharge, discomfort with intense itching and swelling.

May be transmitted from one female to another by a damp washcloth previously used on the genitals of an infected female. Also transmitted to the male by sexual contact, appearing as NGU; as genital thrush with itching, burning, redness on the penis (balanitis); as oral thrush with rash or pimples.

Trichomoniasis ("trich") A protozoan, Trichomonas vaginalis (incubation period 4–20 days, average 7 days), may cause infection with foamy, yellowish, vaginal discharge, unpleasant odor, itching, and discomfort. May be transmitted by sexual contact, appearing in the male as NGU or prostatitis. This organism may survive on moist surfaces for several hours at room temperature, making it possible to be acquired from toilet seats or damp washcloths previously used by an infected female.

Pelvic Inflammatory Disease (PID) PID is an extremely serious female condition involving infection of possibly the uterus, fallopian tubes (salpingitis), ovaries, and abdominal cavity (peritonitis), due to the spread of a vaginal or cervical infection caused by gonococcal or nongonococcal organisms. PID is often the result of untreated gonorrhea or Chlamydia trachomatis infection. The attending physician may indicate other causes.

Symptoms may include lower abdominal pain or cramps, fever, nausea, vomiting, vaginal discharge, painful intercourse, irregular menstrual periods. Immediate treatment is vital.

Possible consequences of PID are infertility and ectopic (extra-uterine or tubal) pregnancy.

Various factors may be considered in preventing pelvic inflammatory disease (PID); the condom provides protection against genital transmission of certain germs and infections.

Since germs always present in the lower intestinal tract can cause infections in the genito-urinary (GU) system, the female, after bowel movement, should wipe from front to back to avoid spreading infectious germs from rectum to vagina.

Females with numerous sex partners are at high risk in contracting pelvic inflammatory disease (PID) and sexually transmitted diseases (STD); it is advised that they have an STD exam three times a year.

MALE AND FEMALE

Acquired Immune Deficiency Syndrome (AIDS)

AIDS is a condition of dangerously lowered resistance in which the body cannot properly defend itself from disease, and is highly susceptible to Kaposi's sarcoma (KS) and such opportunistic infections as Pneumocystis carinii pneumonia (PCP), cryptosporidosis, oral candidiasis (thrush).

The infectious agent of AIDS and AIDS Related Complex (ARC), thought to have originated in Equatorial Africa, is a retrovirus designated by the Americans as HTLV-III, human T-lymphotropic virus type III, known to the French as LAV, lymphadenopathy-associated virus.

Although this devastating disease (incubation period one month to eight years) is not completely understood in 1985, it is documented that most of its victims are from the following high-risk categories: (1) Sexually active homosexual and bisexual males, some of whom have had numerous sexual contacts and history of repeated STD. (2) Those who received blood transfusion (including hemophiliacs). (3) Intravenous drug abusers who shared hypodermic needles. (4) Sex partners of the above.

Associated symptoms are lymphadenopathy (swollen lymph glands, usually in the neck, armpit, or groin); unexplained bleeding or weight loss; night sweats; low-grade fever; persistent fatigue and diarrhea; dry cough; sore throat; recurring infections; painless, purplish bumps or spots on any part of the body including mucous membranes. Those with such symptoms, especially those from high-risk groups listed above, should be blood-tested; a seropositive result indicates the presence of antibodies reflecting previous exposure to HTLV-III.

Seropositive persons, those from high-risk groups, or their sex partners, who are likely to have HTLV-III infection, should be instructed that—
(1) They can, whether or not they have symptoms, transmit the virus to others. Continuing medical evaluation is advised, particularly for those with symptoms suggesting AIDS.
(2) They must not donate blood, plasma, sperm, body organs, or other tissue. Blood donations will be tested for HTLV-III antibody and the donors' names placed on a deferral list, as in the case of other infectious diseases.
(3) They must, if found to be seropositive, so inform their previous sexual contacts; they must inform those providing medical or dental services of their seropositive status or high-risk category so that precautions can be taken to prevent possible transmission.

Males and females, heterosexual, bisexual, or homosexual, may acquire or transmit AIDS. Females who are seropositve or whose sex partner is seropositive are at risk of acquiring the disease, and those pregnant are at risk of giving birth to an infant with AIDS.

HTLV-III has been isolated from blood, semen, urine, tears, breast milk, and saliva. There is risk of transmission through sexual intercourse whether heterosexual or homosexual, or possibly by exposure to saliva on intimate kissing. The condom may provide some protection against genital transmission.

The exchange of, and exposure to, body fluids or discharges are highly significant to AIDS transmission. It appears that the disease is not transmitted casually through such common exposures as sneezing, coughing, or sharing meals, but that the virus must enter the bloodstream or body by direct, or intimate sexual, contact.

Personal implements such as razors and toothbrushes that could become contaminated with blood should not be shared. Hypodermic, acupuncture, tattoo needles, or other such devices that puncture the skin should be adequately sterilized by steam (autoclave), boiling, or appropriate chemicals before reuse, or safely discarded. Disposable needles and equipment should be used whenever possible.

In response to countless inquiries concerning decontamination:

Floor surfaces or objects contaminated, for example, by an accident resulting in bleeding may be washed with a freshly diluted solution of 9 parts water to 1 part household bleach (5.25% sodium hypocholrite).

Hydrogen peroxide 3% may be used on broken skin surfaces; ethyl (grain) or isopropyl (rubbing) alcohol (70% or higher) on objects or intact skin surfaces, always avoiding mouth, eyes, mucous membranes, and never taken internally.

Inadequate rest and diet leading to low resistance, antibiotic misuse, and the abuse of certain drugs such as nitrite inhalants called "poppers," are factors suspected by some (though not necessarily proved) to be involved in immune system breakdown or AIDS-associated conditions.

Whatever the lifestyle or behavioral pattern, practicing disease prevention remains essential to good health.

Chlamydia Trachomatis Infection

Chlamydia trachomatis, a bacterium (incubation period 7–21 days), is transmitted by intimate bodily or sexual contact with an infected mucous membrane or its secretion, causing in the male nongonococcal urethritis (NGU), and in the female vaginal or cervical infection which may lead to the serious complication of pelvic inflammatory disease (PID). Sex partners must be treated simultaneously to prevent reinfection.

[Chlamydia may be the fastest-growing STD in the United States; about 3 to 4 million Americans contract it annually, and this results in sterility for 11,000 women each year, who may display no symptoms until it is too late. Chlamydia poses a serious threat to the fetus and newborn infant, in whom it can cause lung and eye infections.]

Gastro-Intestinal Diseases

Amebiasis, caused by a protozoan, Entamoeba histolytica (incubation period variable, few days to several months; usually 14–28 days).

Giardiasis, caused by a protozoan, Giardia lamblia (incubation period variable, 1–8 weeks).

Shigellosis, caused by a bacterium, Shigella (incubation period 1–7 days, usually less than 4 days).

These are among the parasitic intestinal diseases occurring without symptoms or with possible symptoms of diarrhea sometimes with blood or mucous, bloating, gas, fever, chills, hives, weight loss, nausea, malaise, abdominal cramps.

Accurate diagnosis is by immediate examination of a fresh stool specimen by a specialized laboratory.

The lower digestive tract may be a repository for these germs which are transmitted if traces of infected feces from a sex partner are transferred from the genital-rectal area by oral contact or by hand or other means, to the mouth of the other partner during sexual activities (fecal-oral route).

Also spread through food and water contaminated by sewage, or traces of infected feces transferred by food handlers or flies. Those who prepare food must wash their hands thoroughly before beginning work and after each use of the toilet.

Meticulous personal hygiene, to include brushing fingernails, is essential for those infected persons who must not expose others to their infected feces.

These parasites, which inhabit the intestinal tract of infected persons, may cause life-threatening complications if they enter the bloodstream and then form abscesses in the liver, lungs, or brain.

Every individual should wash genitals and rectal area before and after sexual contact, and must wash hands before eating and after each use of the toilet.

HEPATITIS

A serious and complex communicable, sometimes sexually transmitted, viral disease that attacks the liver. Symptoms may be mild or severe including nausea, fatigue, fever, abdominal discomfort, darkening of the urine, loss of appetite, jaundice (yellowing of the eyes and skin). The infectious agents of the forms of hepatitis may be found, variously, in body fluids and discharges such as blood, feces, saliva, semen, urine, vaginal secretions of an infected person.

Hepatitis may enter the body through direct or sexual contact, by way of mucous membranes, the bloodstream, or a break in the skin. May be spread by ingestion of contaminated food and water, blood transfusion, by unsterilized hypodermic, acupuncture, tattoo needles previously used on an infected person. Blood testing will indicate the presence of hepatitis.

Hepatitis A virus (HAV) (incubation period 2–6 weeks, average 30 days), causes what is traditionally known as "infectious" hepatitis. The intestinal tract may be a repository for hepatitis A virus (HAV), which is transmitted if traces of infected feces from a sex partner are transferred from the genital-rectal area by oral contact or by hand or other means, to the mouth of the other partner during sexual activities (fecal-oral route). Males and females should wash genitals and rectal area before and after sex contact.

Immune globulin (IG) by injection before or immediately after exposure to HAV may offer protection against, or lessen the severity of, the infection.

Of great concern to community health are the outbreaks of hepatitis A (HAV) caused by public food handlers who are infected and carry the virus in their intestinal and urinary tracts, contaminating the food they serve and spreading the disease as they work. Restaurant owners and kitchen supervisors have the obligation to teach their cooks, waiters, and any other food handlers to wash their hands before beginning work and especially after each use of the toilet. This applies also to those preparing food in households.

Hepatitis B virus (HBV) (incubation period 45–180 days, average 60–90 days), causes what is traditionally known as "serum" hepatitis. Primarily associated with transmission by way of infected blood transfusion, or among intravenous drug abusers, shared hypodermic needles.

Hepatitis B is preventable. Those at risk should be tested for HBV immunity, receiving HB vaccine if not immune. Hepatitis B immune globulin (HBIG) possibly along with HB vaccine by injection after exposure to HBV, may protect against, or lessen the severity of, the infection.

The Delta hepatitis virus is activated only in the presence of HBV, causing an extremely dangerous infection which is also preventable by way of the HB vaccine. NON-A, NON-B (NA, NB) hepatitis is an additional form of this disease.

HERPES SIMPLEX

[Together with AIDS, herpes has probably created more public fear than any other diseases in recent memory. About a half a million people contract herpes each year, and it is estimated that between 15 to 20 million Americans now have some form of herpes.]

Herpes 1 and 2 are caused by Herpesvirus hominis (incubation period 1–5 days, possibly 2 weeks), type 1 traditionally associated with face and lips, type 2 traditionally associated with genital region. Both types can be transmitted to either area from one person to another.

The virus invades the body and establishes itself permanently in the nervous system; when inactive, without symptoms; when active, appearing eventually as small, painful, fluid-filled bumps or blisters.

The first outbreak may be accompanied by flu-like symptoms such as fever, aches, malaise. These symptoms are usually less severe on subsequent outbreaks; attacks may come and go indefinitely, without pattern to their recurrence. They begin typically with itching, burning, or tingling sensation, followed by appearance of the blisters which usually break, releasing fluid containing the infectious virus.

Transmission of the disease is possible on the occasion of an attack when the virus is being shed before, during, or without, the eventual appearance of the blisters. May be transmitted by sexual contact or intimate bodily contact (such as kissing) with an infected person. One sex partner may be infected and the other not, a matter of individual resistance.

Both types 1 and 2 may be transferred to other parts of the body; for example, persons with genital herpes may transmit the infection to their eyes unless they wash their hands after touching their genitals.

It is traditionally recommended that the infected area be kept clean and dry to promote healing, with cotton underwear worn to allow air circulation. However, the attending physician might advise other procedures, prescribing the drug acyclovir in ointment or oral form.

Due to the association with cervical cancer, females with genital herpes should have a yearly Pap smear. The pregnant female with a history of genital herpes should so inform her physician since Caesarian delivery may be necessary; in the presence of genital herpes, normal delivery could be fatal to the newborn.

Attention should be given to maintaining good physical and emotional health since it is thought that such factors as stress, poor diet, and insufficient rest may trigger recurrences of herpes.

Sexual contact must be avoided when herpes symptoms are present. Those with herpes have the responsibility to so inform their prospective sex partners. The use of the condom may offer some protection against genital transmission.

Venereal Warts (Condyloma acuminatum) Caused by the human papilloma virus (HPV) (incubation period estimated 6 weeks–8 months). Transmitted by intimate bodily or sexual contact, appearing as soft, irregularly surfaced growths, possibly multiplying and enlarging on genital or anal areas. When small, they may be removed by chemical application; if enlarged, surgery is necessary. In the female, venereal warts may grow to cause obstruction of the vagina. Recurring venereal warts in the female may be associated with cervical cancer; therefore periodic Pap smears are advised.

OTHER (LESS COMMON) STD

Chancroid ("soft sore," "soft chancre")

Caused by a bacterium, Haemophilus ducreyi (incubation period 3–7 days; if site of infection is a fissure or abrasion, as short as 24 hours), which enters the body through skin or mucous membrane. Transmitted by intimate bodily or sexual contact with a lesion or its exudate, appearing in the genital-anal area as painful, red papules (bumps) which usually become open sores, possibly spreading to adjacent areas, accompanied by a bubo (swelling) in a nearby lymph gland. May be asymptomatic in the female. Traditionally occurring in tropical zones; now found also in temperate climates.

Granuloma Inguinale (Donovanosis)

Caused by Calymmatobacterium granulomatis (incubation period possibly 1–12 weeks). Transmitted by intimate bodily or sexual contact with a lesion or its exudate, appearing on skin or mucous membrane of the genital-anal area as painless, red papules (bumps) which ulcerate, spreading to form granular or fibrous masses. If untreated, symptoms may include fever, malaise, leading to pain and itching, odorous ulcerations, possible fistulas (holes) in rectum and bladder, elephantiasis, destruction of underlying tissue and organs involved. Granuloma inguinale occurs in tropical zones more often than in temperate climates.

Lymphogranuloma Venereum (LGV)

Caused by a bacterium, Chlamydia trachomatis types 1, 2, 3 (incubation period 3–30 days). Transmitted by intimate bodily or sexual contact of skin or mucous membrane with an infected person. This systemic infectious disease of lymph channels and lymph nodes may begin with a small, painless papule (bump) or lesion (sore or blister) in the genital-anal area, often going unnoticed. This is followed about 1–21 days later by an inguinal (groin) bubo. The nearby lymph glands become tender, enlarged, abscessed, and drain. If untreated, complications may include growths, fistulas (holes), anorectal ulceration, elephantiasis of the genitals and legs. Lymphogranuloma venereum occurs in tropical zones more often than in temperate climates.

Molluscum Contagiosum

Caused by pox (DNA) virus (incubation period 2–7 weeks). May be transmitted to skin surfaces by intimate bodily or sexual contact, appearing as small pink papules (bumps) each with central core. In temperate climates, the head, eyelids, trunk and genitals, are affected most often. In the tropics, lesions usually occur on the extremities.

Pediculosis (Infestation with lice)

May be treated with various non-prescription preparations available from a pharmacist. Since eggs hatch in about 7 days, re-treatment may be necessary. Both sex partners must be treated at the same time to avoid reinfestation.

Head Lice (Pediculosis capitis) agent Pediculus humanus capitis, are transmitted by direct contact with an infested person, bedding, combs, hats, etc., attaching to the hairs of the scalp, causing itching.

Body Lice (Pediculosis corporis) agent Pediculus humanus corporis are transmitted by intimate bodily or sexual contact with an infested person, bedding, clothing, toilet seats, etc., attaching to the hairs of the body, causing itching.

Genital Lice (Pediculosis pubis) agent Phthirus pubis, called "crabs," are transmitted by intimate bodily or sexual contact with an infested person, bedding, clothing, toilet seats, etc., attaching to the hairs of the genital area where they cause itching.

Scabies

Caused by a mite, (Sarcoptes scabiei), which penetrates and produces line-like burrows under the skin, with intense itching and discomfort, and possible lesions (sores). Transmitted through intimate bodily or sexual contact with an infected person, bedding, clothing. May be treated with lindane 1% (Kwell®, Quellada®, Kwellada®) available on prescription. Both sex partners must be treated at the same time to avoid reinfestation.

EXAMINATION AND TREATMENT

Anyone with a genital discharge, sore, warts, or pimples on genitals or in rectal area, pain or burning on urination or bowel movement, reddish or darkened urine, a persistent sore throat, or enlarged lymph glands in neck, armpit, groin, must go without delay for a sexually transmitted disease (STD) exam which is confidential and easily available from a physician or a free public health clinic.

Infected persons must assume the responsibility to notify their previous and present sex partners of the necessity for an STD exam.

It is suggested that those with multiple sex partners get an STD exam at least twice a year. Most state laws permit the examination and treatment of minors without parental consent.

For complete STD exam, the physician should be told (1) About any previous STD infections, along with past and present symptoms; (2) Whether the patient is currently taking medication or antibiotics since this is vital to accurate diagnosis; (3) If sexual activities involved the throat or rectum, requiring discussion of the need for an exam of these areas.

STD treatment is simple and consists of antibiotics that can be given orally or by injection. Instructions regarding medication should be carefully followed.

People must not try to treat themselves with antibiotics since these may cause serious side effects and interfere with STD diagnosis. For example: Symptoms of syphilis may be suppressed and the accuracy of the blood test affected while the disease progresses.

Both syphilis and gonorrhea are frequently acquired during a single sex contact. The antibiotic treatment given to cure gonorrhea may not cure incubating syphilis, but might suppress its symptoms, necessitating a later syphilis test to determine its presence.

In the case of a male infected with urethral gonorrhea, his discharge may disappear soon after receiving medication; this does not mean he is cured. Although there is no noticeable secretion, he may still be infected and capable of transmitting the disease.

For males and females, a follow up visit to the physician, as directed, may be necessary to determine whether the initial medication has been effective, or another form of treatment is required.

For everyone, until completely cured, no sex contact which may spread the disease; no alcohol during treatment, and especially during treatment for urinary tract infections, no alcohol which may irritate the genito-urinary (GU) system and retard healing.

Those being treated with tetracycline should remember that this drug is a skin photosensitizer, increasing susceptibility to sunburn.

Sexually transmitted diseases (STD) may be passed back and forth (ping-pong'ed) from one sex partner to another; steady partners must be treated simultaneously to avoid reinfection.

Self-treatment or home remedies should not be attempted. Only a physician can properly diagnose and treat STD.

REFERENCES

Newsweek. "A Nasty New Epidemic." February 4, 1985, p. 72–73.

CHAPTER 21

Sexual Communication and Pleasuring

One of the most oft-heard complaints in the offices of marriage and family therapists is, We don't communicate with each other. As the story unfolds it becomes apparent that the lack of communication spans many spheres: sexual, emotional, spiritual. It is difficult in most instances to determine when the communication began breaking down, but it is equally clear that little deliberate effort was made to reorient the relationship.

The push for people to *communicate* with each other has become endemic, a societal phenomenon, a cliché. The paradox is that enhanced intimacy has not necessarily resulted, which in turn has given rise to the charge that communicating was a pop California fad that swept the country and then deflated. It remains true, however, that the more people are in touch, the greater their possible sexual satisfaction and happiness with each other (see for example the work of Tavris & Sadd, 1977).

Part of the difficulty in discussing sex is discomfort with the language of sexuality. People may have a hard time saying *vulva,* but are at ease in saying the slang term *cunt.* The former seems to them clinical and strange, the latter vulgar. It is difficult to overcome the feelings of shame that may accompany sexual conversations—the unspoken fear may be, What would my parents think if they heard me? No matter the age of the adult, childhood socialization exerts a powerful effect.

Sexual communication is a way people have of educating their partners and of learning from them. This goes beyond what is said in verbal exchanges, and incorporates the myriad things that people do for each other. In the book *Do I Have to Give*

Up Me To Be Loved By You? Jordan and Margaret Paul (1985) describe how people occasionally make love when they're not in the mood, say I love you when they don't feel it, and give of themselves when their spirit isn't really into it. The authors counsel: "When you do what you do because you care—even when that means doing what the other person wants you to do—you do not give yourself up. *You give yourself up when whatever you do comes from fear, obligation or guilt*" (p. 3). Thus, if your motivation is based on loving another person, being selfless may help to carry the relationship through rough times. If, on the other hand, your intentions are hostile, that is how the message will be received, regardless of whether or not you accommodate the other person.

Communication about sexual feelings per se often flounders on the rocks of, I don't want to hurt his/her feelings, or even she/he would be angry if I voiced my feelings. With one couple, the woman was preorgasmic but had been pretending to have orgasms for many months. She confided to her best friend that she was afraid she'd damage his ego if she revealed this to her lover. Finally, in the midst of an argument, she blurted out that she'd never experienced orgasm. Her lover was enraged at her months of deception, and it was several weeks before they saw each other again. His ego was indeed damaged but more by her pretense than by his own supposed failure to satisfy her.

Talking about sexual preferences sometimes creates more conflicts than it resolves, at least initially. One partner might desire something that the other finds undesirable. There might be a question of, Where did he/she learn about *that?* For some people, a positive suggestion of, I like to be touched in this way, has hidden implications of, I don't like the way you've been touching me all along. Feelings of jealousy may develop, along with a conviction that one's partner is self-centered and a poor lover. These are not unusual and in some form are part of most loving relationships. If a basic commitment to each other exists, there is a good chance that these feelings can be worked through. What eventually might emerge will be a more satisfying relationship in many dimensions.

The pragmatic side of communication is that it is *preventative:* of misunderstandings, alienation, long-standing resentments, and sexual maladjustment to one's partner. Although communication stands to draw people closer together, there is also the risk that once people open up to each other, they will not like what they see, and the relationship will come apart. Though this will be painful, it is infinitely preferable to a gradual disintegration of love over the years.

There is more than a pragmatic side to communication. It allows us to be playful as well as serious, joyous as well as sad. In relationships in which feelings of anger, sexuality, pain, and other "sensitive" areas cannot be expressed, there is also little room for the expression of exuberance or intimacy.

The enrichment of a couple's sexual relationship begins with communication. Awareness and understanding of sexual behavior itself is a part of this communication, but it also involves the quality of time spent together outside sex in seeming nonsexual interaction. Conversations and the interplay of emotions and ideas and acceptance of each other's personalities and idiosyncrasies help determine the tone of their sex life itself.

A characteristic of people who have the greatest difficulty in sexual relations in the broadest sense is a view of sexuality in the narrowest sense, as a separate entity of life. A second characteristic is that they don't discuss their sexual relations much or at all. Couples who have the most expressive and buoyant sex together are consciously, seductively, and playfully sexual with each other mainly outside coital sex. Hugging, kissing, and cuddling are seen as intimately sexual, affecting their bodies and emotions. They have a sense of imagination and acceptance of a wide range of desires, and a pervasive sense of humor to enjoy times when sex is fantastic and to accept occasionally mediocre experiences. Their fantasy life is active and varied. This does not imply that unless couples experiment with new ideas, they are necessarily repressed or unfulfilled.

In mature sex lives there is very little jealousy; openness and friendship with other people are not viewed as inherent threats to the relationship. Problems associated with sex often arise from a rigid approach, an overbearing concern for who does what to whom. There is a preoccupation with routine, with each sex *act* being a compulsive repetition of the last. Over time a feeling of monotony may set in for a couple, and though they may not talk about it, each is simply going through the motions for lack of any better ideas. Couples who have managed to preserve the original excitement of their relationship, however, appreciate spontaneity in each other and the freedom to experiment. They are able to communicate their desires and turn-ons. Too often people are simply afraid to say what pleases them and expect their partner to guess how to proceed.

Marriage manuals and how-to books galore have appeared to help people develop a wider repertoire of sexual behaviors and responses. Many people are turned off by step-by-step approaches; this chapter presents some creative ideas that will enable people to discover what they might find enjoyable. Couples who have rarely or never verbalized their sexual feelings before may be discomforted at first and tempted to give up the enterprise. More likely, though, they will find that periods of silence have provided them with endless room for growth. Those presently not involved in a relationship won't be bored with the following ideas either.

Sexual communication *does* have a lot to do with expressing individual desires within sex itself. A good place to start is revealing what each partner wants to experience in their sexual encounters. It is best to be direct and to provide information to your partner. A series of "I" messages works best: I'd like you to be gentler in our lovemaking. I want to spend more time kissing and holding each other. Communication in this way leaves little room for doubt; it is plain what each person means. Later on, when you understand each other more fully, you may want to talk over *why* you've communicated poorly in the past. Initially, though, *what* you each feel and desire is the main issue.

Share some ideas on how to make it easier to accept each other's feelings and needs. You will find that communication involves elements that are nonverbal: The undertones and implications of what is said, the things typically *not* said, language of the eyes and body, tone of voice, all play a role in understanding each other. Men especially may feel that revealing their feelings makes them vulnerable and open to rejection. These are socially ingrained attitudes that may betray a basic lack of trust in the relationship itself. If there is an essential bond of love in the relationship, the man may come to see how increasing his choices and taking more active responsibility for the quality of sexual relations are signs of strength.

Sexually speaking, many men tend to be sensually impoverished. For them, sex is goal-oriented (intercourse and orgasm), with only minimal interest in other physical intimacies: cuddling, bathing and showering together, massage, holding hands. Many men's sexual feelings may have become centralized in their genitals and thus inhibit their ability to enjoy their entire bodies. In glorifying intercourse, pleasurable activities such as massage and stimulation of the nipples and other erogenous areas have come for these men to seem immature, or just a prelude to intercourse. Such men seldom masturbate (or refuse to admit it) and are likely to believe that if they don't *perform* well in every sexual encounter, there is something wrong with them. Certainly not all men display all these attitudes and inhibitions, but many do to varying degrees. Men have traditionally complained that their wives were too romantic, slow to respond, and too passive, which severely reduced the men's enjoyment of intercourse. Ironically, these very same noncoital responses are invariably related to factors that could help keep a couple's intimacies from sinking into boredom.

The concept of *pleasuring* has gradually come to replace the notion of foreplay, which implied that such physical contacts were merely the snack before the main course. Pleasuring involves an awareness that nongenital caresses as well as genital ones are rewarding in themselves, regardless of what does or doesn't follow. A good way to start developing sensory awareness is to deliberately choose a time when both partners are in the mood. Often sexual relations occur only at bedtime, sometimes on predetermined nights of the week. Take a little time to create an intimate atmosphere; dim the lights, put on fresh sheets, play some music, light a candle, whatever pleases the senses. Decide (even if it is in a somewhat self-conscious way) not to have intercourse for a while, or until both partners want to.

Begin with one partner active, one passive. If you have not already done so, the passive partner can verbally communicate what touches and caresses are most pleasurable, which motions and pressures are best. Guide your partner's hand with your own. If you don't like a particular feeling, instead of saying in a negative way, I don't like that, put the feeling in a more positive, helpful way: I really like it better this way, or Why don't you try this instead? Use oil or powder if you like. By exploring every part of your partner's body you will both discover your own preferred style. The object is pleasure and intimate time spent together. Switch roles. Afterwards, you might like to lie together and fondle each other, slowly fall asleep, or proceed to intercourse, if that is what you both want. As already mentioned, however, it is a mistake to feel that intimate physical contact *must* lead to intercourse. In fact, the feeling that intercourse will inevitably result makes some people leery of reaching out to their spouses or initiating any sort of sexual interaction.

On the other hand, intercourse need not always be proceeded by lengthy pleasuring. Sometimes a fast and vigorous encounter can be immensely satisfying for both partners. In the long run, experimenting with new and varied intimacies will seem more like work than fun if it is perceived as just standing in the way of "real" sex. The individuals involved can give themselves permission to accept and enjoy their bodies and sexuality—no one "gives" another person pleasure or an orgasm.

The single most common complaint that women have of their lover's approach to intercourse is that it doesn't last long enough. We don't want to reduce sexual intercourse to a mechanical matter of time involved, but generally speaking if the man ejaculates within the first half minute or so, most women are left unsatisfied and frustrated (ejaculatory control is discussed in Chapter 22). Sex therapists have found that it is more difficult for men to hold off in the male-on-top (missionary) position, which also happens to be the most common position for intercourse among couples. Many men are resistant to alternate positions, especially the female-on-top position, because they feel it places themselves in an inferior, submissive posture. Yet, in this position, with the woman controlling at least half the thrusting, her enjoyment is often greatly increased; and it adds some novelty and variety to the couple's sex life as well as making it easier for the man to control when he ejaculates.

Within intercourse itself, there is a wide range of response. Some couples engage in coitus once per encounter, some more. The woman's vagina may become tender and raw when exposed to lengthy thrusting. After ejaculation, some men's erections return in fifteen minutes, others in an hour or more. Owing to such factors as the timing of her menstrual cycle, a woman may not produce sufficient lubrication for intercourse, even if she's highly aroused. A water-based lubricant (such as K-Y jelly) can be used (petroleum-based gels and creams are not readily washed out by the woman's body).

Some women experience multiple orgasms in intercourse, others a single orgasm, and some women rarely or not at all, though they may enjoy it immensely. Stimulation of the clitoris during intercourse, either by herself or her partner, provides the extra sensation some women need for coital orgasm. Whether a woman experiences orgasm in intercourse or not, however, is no barometer of her psychological health or maturity.

For people raised and imbued with a sense of guilt, shame, and furtiveness toward sexuality, actively and joyfully pursuing sexual pleasure may at first seem wrong or undignified. This probably can't be helped, at least initially, and it may take quite some time before such individuals overcome significant aspects of their upbringing. Since it is mainly a matter of social conditioning, most if not all people are capable of relearning.

The script for traditional lovemaking after intercourse or other forms of sexual expression is usually that the man rolls over and falls asleep, leaving his partner unsatisfied and/or desiring to savor the closeness and relaxation that sex provides. Sex therapists today describe the sensations following sex as *afterglow*. It is that dreamy pleasant state between sleep and waking that follows orgasm—stay awake and relish it. Hold each other, speak in soft tones and whispers. Sometimes the best communication occurs at this point, when defenses are at low tide and the outside world seems distant. For many people, this is the time when they feel most in touch with the spiritual elements they associate with sexuality.

Ultimately, the give and take in sexual relations themselves are greatly influenced by the overall rapport and texture of the relationship outside sex. Couples cannot be out of touch with each other or quarreling all day and suddenly expect to warm up in bed, despite the fact that some couples report using sex to make up after a "good" fight. In the special language that exists between partners that only they understand, there are often signals or trigger incidents that can cause instantaneous tension. These patterns in communication often draw their energy from past hurts and events that are waiting to break through the veneer of civility into arguments and discord.

Sexual relations will not always be fantastic, and each couple has their own particular history of coming to terms with this fact. Some couples start out with tremendous satisfaction, enjoying the excitement and newness that comes from being together at first. Perhaps after a few years, sex for them loses its original, spontaneous rhythm and drive. For other couples, sex has never been that great at any time. Whatever the particular circumstances, virtually all couples find that at some time or other, they experience some kind of sexual dysfunction. Perhaps the woman begins to have trouble in achieving orgasm, or the man finds himself impotent on occasion. These are common occurrences. Generally speaking, if the individuals do not become obsessed with the situation and focus undue negative attention on it, they will be able to weather it and possibly emerge with a greater understanding of themselves and their sexual responsiveness. If, however, they dwell endlessly on the difficulty, it is likely to get worse. Such factors as fatigue, tension, the addition of a child to the family, or excessive alcohol consumption can cause episodic sexual dysfunctions. At other times, unspoken hostility and resentments towards one's partner can be the cause.

For other couples, however, the sexual difficulties are more pronounced and may have a longer history. Perhaps the man chronically ejaculates prematurely, or the woman has never achieved orgasm. For such individuals, we recommend following the exercises and instructions in Chapter 22. If these are tried without success, have already been attempted unsuccessfully, or you suspect that some medical problem may be the cause, the services of a sex therapist and/or physician should be obtained.

Part of the difficulty that people experience in communicating sexually derives from a societal notion that males and females are radically different in their emotional and intellectual make-up. Despite the obvious physical differences and certain more subtle psychological differences, too much emphasis has been placed on them. They have tended to separate the sexes in many ways, and as a result men and women often tend to view each other as members of different species. The literature is rife with descriptions such as "mysterious" or "unable to be known or understood" when referring to relations between the sexes. Some of the mystique is good—it fuels curiosity, stirs passions, and helps keep life exciting, but it also makes for monumental misunderstandings. Certain sex roles and stereotypes serve a purpose, though perhaps less today than they once did when divisions of labor were more distinct. There has not been a deep enough appreciation of the similar roles that love, friendship, eroticism, and spirituality play in the lives of both men and women. There is great common ground for mutual communion and sharing of this heritage.

Much of what is said of sexuality and human relations is generalization. There are couples who basically dislike each other and yet who have a satisfying sex life together. There are other couples who share the spontaneity, sense of acceptance and excitement that we have been describing, who love each other deeply, and yet have a relatively unsatisfying or dysfunctional sex life together.

Statistics detailing sexual behaviors recorded by researchers are deliberately not mentioned in this chapter. Unfortunately, the scientific study of sex has fostered the all-American spirit of competitiveness and caused people to compare their preferred rates and styles with everyone else's, or else struggle to attain what they mistakenly perceive as the norm in sexual relations. Nothing could be more self-defeating or more of a discouragement to cherishing and enhancing individual preferences.

On the other hand, sex researchers, writers, and therapists have made profound contributions to society and individuals: they have made known the range of *choices* available and enhanced the sense of freedom to explore and experiment. Behaviors such as oral-genital relations, anal eroticism, and other styles of sexual expression have been legitimized. Decisions not to have children, or to have them only when the couple feels ready, are not the overwhelming social stigmas they once were. Improved (though still imperfect) methods of contraception have been devised; alternate lifestyles have been examined and have become more acceptable. If feelings of dissatisfaction or alienation from one's sexuality persist, competent therapists and treatments can be sought. *However*, the study of human sexuality was never intended to replace the old mythology with a new set of standards and myths to live up to. Nor should the new knowledge be used to make people who endorse traditional styles feel guilty or inadequate for not changing with the times.

Couples who have been together for years often evolve a deep appreciation of the comfort and beauty of each other's bodies and psyches. The familiarity of a partner's skin and the textures and feel of response become dependable, satisfying experiences. Once couples are truly comfortable with each other's bodies, they can move on and reach deeper levels of understanding. They can care for each other if one becomes ill or distressed. The binding and healing properties of the relationship add further dimensions to the qualities of sensuality and communication between them.

FIDELITY AND MONOGAMY

In the final section of this chapter, we'd like to include a discussion of infidelity. In the following anecdote I (Sol Gordon) was traveling and became friendly with an interesting couple I met at a seminar. In the course of our group getting together I became aware of spending time with the wife and being animated and excited by our intimate conversations. Suddenly, I felt insecure and wondered what the husband was feeling. On impulse I decided to approach him and ask whether he was threatened or jealous. He smiled and replied, "If I felt you were taking my wife away or it interfered with our marriage, I would resent it. But since you are my friend I am delighted you get along so well." The insecurity was entirely mine.

The issue of infidelity, either in marriage or other relationships, is integrally related to honesty. Though we cannot provide scientific documentation, it is our clinical view that total honesty is not necessarily a positive aspect of a good relationship. There are many reasons—chief among them is that few couples have the same background or perspective for accepting such revelations. The best time to reveal one's past is certainly before getting married; after that, it is wise not to dwell on the complete details of past sexual encounters. Often, what appears on the surface to be honesty is actually hostility and a desire for revenge. In addition, people are entitled to their private thoughts; it is not at all uncommon for individuals to fantasize having sex with someone other than their partner. Some people enjoy sharing these images, but others are threatened and hurt by them.

The critical issue, though, is sexual relations outside the relationship or marriage that are unacceptable to one or both partners. Let us first skirt the issue and demonstrate that it is not entirely cut and dried. Imagine a couple who spend little time together and have few pleasures with each other. The male enjoys drinking, hunting, and card games with his buddies, and the female enjoys socializing with her women friends (we realize these are sexist stereotypes). They are monogamous and have what they consider to be adequate sexual relations every Saturday evening. Imagine a second couple who love each other and enjoy being together. The marriage is top priority for both of them. Two or three times a year one of the spouses has a brief encounter but doesn't tell the other, as there is no commitment to the outsider. The experience is seen as essentially new and refreshing.

Where are your sympathies?

These are not extreme, rare situations. In our society monogamy is the most viable arrangement, at least in the public eye. If one or both partners can't handle a lifetime of sex with just one person, automatically terminating the marriage is not the only, let alone best, recourse, though in some circumstances divorce is an appropriate response to a basic violation of trust.

It is another matter entirely if a genuine affair is involved: meaning that priorities have shifted from the spouse to another person. Even emotionally mature marriages usually cannot sustain the bitterness and hurt feelings that arise. Sometimes the erring partner acknowledges his or her mistake and wishes to be forgiven. We think that it is not possible to be *in love* with two people at the same time. Being in love in a mature way generates tremendous energy and allows for outside friends. Yet, there is a critical difference between being *in love* with one person and having the capacity to love many people.

There is also a distinction between fidelity and monogamy. Monogamy implies sexual relations of any variety only with one person. Fidelity has far broader connotations and includes the mutual respect and spiritual commitment that partners share. Fidelity means that one does not speak poorly of one's spouse to others and does not make deliberate attempts to hurt or undermine the other's well-being, confidence, or emotional state. Writing in his book *Embodiment,* James B. Nelson further clarifies the issue:

> . . . the usual definition of marital fidelity is now being challenged. To summarize, it is argued that possessiveness of an emotional and possibly a genital sort is a major detriment to the marital relationship. Thus, a distinction must be made between "infidelity" and "adulterer." Adultery has a straight-forward meaning: sexual intercourse with someone other than one's spouse. Infidelity on the other hand, is the rupture of the bonds of faithfulness, honesty, trust, and commitment between spouses. On the positive side, the argument goes, fidelity is the enduring commitment to the spouse's well-being and growth. It is commitment to the primacy of the marital relationship over any other. Compatible with marital fidelity and supportive of it can be certain secondary relationships of some emotional and sensual depth, possibly including genital intercourse.

To be sure, millions of couples treasure the trust and confidence of their monogamous relationships. For some, it is a deeply religious covenant between themselves, their spouse, and God. But many others feel trapped by vows of exclusivity; they nonetheless love their spouses and have no wish to end the relationships. It is not really heresy to suggest that relationships should be able to accommodate experiments, imperfections, mistakes, indiscretions, remorse, and misgivings as part of the human experience. The real tragedy is not to learn and profit from experience.

Even Love

Really meaningful experiences in life
have peaks
    of brief duration
which are repeatable
    Even love
    is
    imperfect,
leaves us open
    to be
    hurt,
    vulnerable,
    misunderstood

yet
leaves room for
    growth,
    excitement,
    joy,
becoming more ourselves
    by offering more to the other,
but that doesn't mean
    that our timing is always right
even when we love each other.

S.G.

REFERENCES

Nelson, J. B. *Embodiment: An Approach to Sexuality and Christian Theology.* Minneapolis: Augsburg Publishing House, 1978.

Paul, Jordan & Margaret. *Do I Have to Give Up Me to Be Loved by You?.* Minneapolis: CompCare, 1985.

Tavris, C., & Sadd, S. *The Redbook Report on Female Sexuality.* New York: Dell, 1977.

CHAPTER 22

Sexual Dysfunctions: What to Consider Before Seeking Therapy

An area of significant vulnerability for some people is the possibility of sexual dysfunction. Many men and women reading this book have developed or will develop at some point one of the sexual problems discussed in this chapter. And though for most the difficulty will be transient, the prospect of sexual dysfunction arouses great anxiety. In one case, an elementary school teacher married to an accountant reported to us that when she ceased having orgasms with her husband for a period of some six months, their marriage was nearly destroyed in the process. She became able to think of little else, and her husband interpreted the problem as either she didn't love him anymore or was having an affair. The dysfunction became the focal point of their lives together, as it does with some couples and thus grew wildly out of perspective.

Though the discussion in this chapter reads as if it's geared mainly for heterosexuals, this is not meant to imply that homosexuals don't experience dysfunctions. Most of the difficulties described herein may occur among homosexuals, and much of what we write may be useful to them as well. Preorgasmic lesbians or impotent gay men may benefit from the self-help techniques and share them with a partner just as a heterosexual with the same problem might.

One's capacity to have and enjoy sexual relations *is* intimately connected to one's overall sense of well-being and self-esteem. People may fail to appreciate, however, that even when this capacity suffers, other areas of their lives continue to be enriching and satisfying. The woman in the example above received excellent job evaluations during her sexual malaise and never faltered in her love of cultural events that were presented in the nearby civic center and museum. In this most personal area of people's lives, there needs to be an understanding that, If I have a sexual problem, I'd dearly like to get over it (not, I'd give anything to get over it), and I'll do what I can to return to health. But I'll also try to keep the experience in perspective and not let it dominate all other areas of my life.

Major characters in the movie *The Big Chill* and the book *The Sun Also Rises* were permanently impotent due to war injuries; each was portrayed as a tragic figure who had withdrawn from intimate relationships with women. For some, this is the key dilemma of having a sexual dysfunction: They remove themselves from *all* intimacy with their lover, or even their friends, when it is only sexual ability that is impaired.

In addition to the many emotional and interactional difficulties that can lead to sexual dysfunctions (see Chapter 21), a number of myths about sexual functioning also interfere. A few you might be familiar with are

Men always want sex, and if they don't, or they can't get it up, there's something wrong with them.

The partner of a man who isn't always ready for sex may think, What's wrong with *me* that he doesn't want me all the time?

Women should always be available for sex to keep harmony and not lose the man to another woman.

Partners of someone who is occasionally not in the mood may worry, If you're not giving it to me, who are you giving it to?

Every time people feel sensual or aroused, they have to go all the way.

Each partner has to climax in every sexual encounter.

Sexual technique is equal to or greater in importance than loving and intimacy.

A self-perpetuating performance anxiety often develops in relationships wherein one or more of these myths is operating. People may become spectators in their own sexual behaviors, constantly worrying while they're having sex, Is he/she enjoying this? Am I doing the right thing? Did he/she just come? Do I look or sound funny when I moan? These thoughts are just one step away from a sort of detachment, in which the participant's thoughts wander to grocery lists and the worries of the day. Sexual arousal and functioning is understandably impaired in such situations.

Sexual functioning is more often a matter of personality development and communication than sexual techniques alone. Yet, many people experience genuine sexual dysfunctions at times. This does not refer to episodic difficulties caused by such factors as guilt, anxiety, fatigue, alcohol, or occasional emotional problems. It is not always clear why some people are dysfunctional, though experiences in childhood and religious training sometimes play a part. Some schools of thought assert that the reasons don't really matter and that behavior modification can effect the necessary improvements.

More traditional schools of psychotherapy hold that without exploring the underlying causes of the problems, changes made during behavior modification will be temporary at best. Still other therapists advocate a combination of behavior modification and counseling.

When a lot of tension and anxiety have been focused around a sexual dysfunction, it is usually advisable for the couple to give up sexual intercourse for a while—perhaps declare a month-long moratorium from it. Once this pressure has alleviated, couples can explore other nondemanding ways to pleasure each other, such as those described in Chapter 21. Some people experience success with this method of learning to be sensual without the performance anxiety that accompanies the urgent wish to be sexual. Giving up intercourse, incidentally, is often a primary intervention on the part of sex therapists when they are treating a couple.

The following ideas and exercises could also be implemented by couples and/or individuals with sexual dysfunctions before seeking professional help if abstaining from intercourse is not successful by itself. Especially if the problem is long-standing, a month or two of self-therapy is not likely to undermine professional help if these attempts are not successful. Perhaps half the couples suffering some variety of sexual dysfunction could profit from experimenting themselves with a few established therapeutic practices. Some of the ideas are not original and derive from the basic works of prominent sex therapists. Our version of "what to do" does not conform precisely with anyone else's view.

There is a wide range of sexual dysfunctions, and this chapter discusses those most common among the majority of people. Among women, these relate to a partial or complete inability to achieve orgasm (women who are preorgasmic), and the condition known as vaginismus or tightening of the vaginal muscles making entry by the penis painful or extremely difficult. Among men, we will discuss premature ejaculation (involuntary ejaculation before, or being perceived as too soon after, penetration), secondary impotence (frequent difficulty in achieving or maintaining an erection), and retarded ejaculation (inability to ejaculate even after prolonged sexual stimulation). Primary impotence in the male, or complete inability to achieve erection, even through masturbation, can be caused by a variety of medical conditions (diabetes, birth defect, prostate problems). Men with severe dysfunctions such as primary impotence or retrograde ejaculation (ejaculation into the urinary bladder instead of through the penis) are advised to consult their physicians without delay.

THE PREORGASMIC WOMAN (SOMETIMES REFERRED TO AS ANORGASMIC)

Inability to achieve orgasm is by far the most common sexual dysfunction among women. Sometimes the problem is caused by societal and/or parental conditioning, fear of pregnancy, guilt, or religious prohibitions. Whatever the cause, many, if not most, women are able to become orgasmic through masturbation. Those women who remain preorgasmic should not interpret it as some symbol of personal failure; the goal, if there must be one at all, is to learn pleasure and enjoyment of one's own body, with or without orgasm.

The woman should choose a time when she is alone and certain not to be interrupted—disconnect the phone. Select the most comfortable location in the house. It is a good idea to obtain a vibrator before proceeding, preferably the plug-in type because it produces more satisfying, consistent vibrations than the battery-operated models do. Most large pharmacies keep them in stock. While you are at it, stock up on oils and powders.

Lie back and relax for a few moments, then begin caressing different parts of your body, your breasts, belly, thighs. Don't begin caressing your genitals until you feel ready and feel comfortable with the whole idea of pleasuring yourself. Experiment with different degrees of pressure and rhythm and appreciate the sensuousness of arousal as your body begins to respond. If at any stage you begin to feel anxious, simply back off a little and relax and begin again when you feel ready. It may take you a few sessions to feel comfortable, especially if you have never masturbated before.

When you feel ready, begin caressing your vulva, perhaps beginning with the labia (lips), again exploring the touches you prefer. If you have never seen your genitals, you may want to get a mirror and examine them. Find the vaginal lips and opening; locate the clitoris which contains most of the nerve endings responsible for producing sexual pleasure in women. Some women find direct stimulation of the clitoris itself uncomfortable or even painful, so you might want to begin by stroking the clitoral shaft. Don't feel pressured to continue if you feel relatively little sensation or find the whole undertaking ridiculous. If, however, you find yourself becoming sexually aroused, you might want to continue the caresses or apply the vibrator on or around the clitoris to see how that feels. (Most vibrators are intended for application to external body parts, though some are specifically designed or come with special attachments for vaginal insertion).

Even if you have never done so before, try imagining some sexual thoughts or fantasies that are appealing to you. They might involve sexual contacts with your husband, a friend or old lover, or a particularly pleasurable sensation from your childhood. As we stated earlier, there is absolutely no reason to feel ashamed or guilty because of your sexual fantasies: for most people they are an integral aspect of sexual enjoyment.

If you continue exploring your sensuality over a period of a couple of weeks or even a month or two, you may find that you reach orgasm and develop a much deeper understanding of your own sexual responses. Don't be discouraged if it seems to take more time than you think it should. If you have lived for years feeling little or no sexual pleasure (in any case, less than you would like), it may take some time to change your feelings.

Many women have been helped by women's sexuality workshops. Sharing sexual frustrations and desires with other women and receiving their support often provides the impetus for overcoming old taboos and set patterns of inhibition. Women generally report that these groups are spiritually uplifting and help put them in touch with their repressed sexuality.

If the woman is involved in a sexual relationship, the goal would be for her to share her knowledge of her body with her sexual partner. He (or she) can be shown what caresses feel best in a gentle, nondemanding atmosphere. Both partners may need to appreciate that this is difficult for each other. Men may feel threatened or inadequate for not instinctively knowing how to please a woman. Women may feel embarrassed or fearful of the man's response; either partner may feel angry if the other's response seems to be critical or rejecting. It is best if together couples acknowledge that the process of learning how to have satisfying sex may take a while and that some patience and understanding of occasional "failures" will be helpful. Two highly recommended books for both men and women by Lonnie Barbach are *For Yourself: The Fulfillment of Female Sexuality* and *For Each Other: Sharing Sexual Intimacy*. Both are rich in ideas and will help to build bridges in communication and sharing between partners.

VAGINISMUS

Vaginismus is a much rarer but by no means uncommon condition. Here again, the woman should at first proceed by herself. Begin as in masturbation to caress your body in a nondemanding way, and when you feel ready, move on to your genitals. When you feel your muscles relaxing, gently begin to insert one finger into your vagina. If you feel your muscles begin to tighten, don't force the issue—relax and proceed again when you feel ready. This process may or may not be accompanied by sexual fantasies; the object of it is gradually to introduce yourself to the sensation of nonthreatening penetration. As you become more comfortable, you can progress to a larger finger, two fingers, or perhaps a smooth phallic substitute. Don't hesitate to use a lubricant like K-Y jelly.

The exercises for vaginismus can gradually be taught to your partner. As with masturbation and pleasuring, begin by sharing with your partner what you have learned about your body and guide him in the caresses that you have found most stimulating. This, too, will probably take some time before he understands your responses and you are able to feel comfortable in receiving them. In vaginismus exercises, your lover can begin by gently introducing his own finger, giving you time to accustom yourself to the feeling of being penetrated by another person. Partners should not proceed to intercourse until the woman feels ready. It is her decision.

Another way for women to get in touch with their sexual responses and to become more aware of the active versus passive role their vagina plays in sexual pleasure, is through an exercise called the Kegel technique. It involves a series of rhythmical contractions of the sphincter muscle that controls the flow of urine and the "gripping" capacity of the vagina itself. To learn where this muscle is located, try stopping the flow of urine in midstream. That muscle is your sphincter muscle. To help women develop some control and awareness of it, therapists recommend that they practice contracting it each day (but not while urinating). Generally, it is suggested that a dozen repetitions be done three times a day. Contract the muscle, count to three, and relax it. Contract, count to three, relax, etc. Gradually, toning this muscle helps women enjoy intercourse more and usually helps in the process of becoming orgasmic.

PREMATURE EJACULATION

By far the most common sexual dysfunction among men is premature ejaculation. Traditionally, men who wanted to last longer in intercourse tried biting their lips, grinding their teeth, or concentrating on some nonsexual, perhaps unpleasant thoughts such as their income taxes. This tends to distract the man from his pleasure and removes him psychically from the situation. Even if it prolongs the sexual experience, it may leave the man feeling alienated from his own basic response.

Before involving themselves in the more structured techniques for attaining eja-culatory control listed below, men may want to experiment with one relatively simple idea. Many men report that masturbating before intercourse, or being brought to orgasm manually or orally by a partner, helps them last longer when intercourse does occur. Even if this is successful, men may still wish to use the techniques that follow. Initially, however, it may help build confidence.

Therapists currently use two techniques to help men develop ejaculatory control, and they operate on the same basic principle. The first is the Semans method, also called stop-start masturbation. The man is instructed to stimulate his penis to erection and to continue masturbating until he senses the point of ejaculatory inevitability—that point when, even if he were to stop masturbating, he would ejaculate anyway. Just before he reaches that point, he should stop masturbating and wait a couple of minutes for the sensation to subside. He then repeats the procedure, bringing himself to just before the point of ejaculatory inevitability and then stopping before ejaculating. It is recommended that the exercise last at least fifteen minutes, and that the man approach orgasm at least four times before finally allowing himself to ejaculate. By gaining knowledge of this point when he is just about to ejaculate and learning his body's responses, men are gradually able to transfer the ability to prolong orgasm to sex with their partners. Rather than ignoring his pleasure, the man concentrates on it and thus learns more about how to control his responses. The Semans technique can be done, using the same procedure, by a partner. The same results can be expected as if done alone.

During the course of these exercises, which optimally should last at least several weeks, it is suggested that the man abstain from intercourse. Other forms of sexual relations can be indulged in. When the man and his partner begin having intercourse, the woman should be on top and thrusting by the male should be minimal; let the woman control the pace and rhythm. Men often have more control when lying on their backs, and this position should increase their feelings of confidence. Eventually, the male-on-top position can be attempted, but again, thrusting should be nondemanding. If at any point the male finds himself reaching orgasm before he wants to, he can stop moving or withdraw his penis until the sensation eases.

The second technique for developing ejaculatory control is called the squeeze technique and is very similar to the Semans. In it the man, alone or with a partner, stimulates himself until just before he reaches the point of ejaculatory inevitability. At that point, he or his partner gives his penis a firm squeeze, by placing the thumb just behind the glans on one side of the penis and two fingers near the coronal ridge on the other side. The squeeze should be firm enough to cause the man to lose his erection partially (don't worry if it goes down completely), and should last from fifteen to twenty seconds. This causes the male to lose the urge to ejaculate. After a minute or so, begin stimulating the penis until once again the male feels the need to ejaculate and then reapply the squeeze. During the exercise, the man should focus his attention on his pleasurable feelings but *not* concentrate on getting an erection. If a partner is applying the squeeze, the male should signal her when he feels he is approaching the point of ejaculating; this will allow her to apply the squeeze at the right time. Repeat the squeeze at least four times in each session. If the man goes past this point and ejaculates anyway, relax and enjoy it. There will be some trial and error before the man learns to recognize his own responses. As with the Semans procedure, when the man feels ready, intercourse should be attempted with the woman on top. When he reaches the point of inevitability, the woman disengages herself and applies the squeeze, again four or so times per session. In this way, the man learns to control his ejaculation while actually in the vagina.

The Kegel exercises previously described for women can also be employed by men wishing to learn ejaculatory control. The man, too, can discover his own sphincter by stopping the flow of urine in midstream and practicing the sets of contractions three times daily (but again, not while urinating). The exercises will tend to enhance his enjoyment of sexual pleasure and give him greater control over when to ejaculate. Many men report that when they ejaculate it "just seems to happen," with little or no control or awareness of it. At times, they might not want to control the event, but at other times, for both his own and the woman's enjoyment, many men state that learning control has improved their sex lives.

IMPOTENCE

There are two basic kinds of impotence. The first is primary impotence, when the man never obtains an erection. The other is called secondary impotence, which is characterized by the man having difficulty more often then he wants to. Of course, nearly every man has an occasional problem getting an erection due to such factors as too much alcohol, anxiety, or fatigue, and it should be no cause for alarm. Generally, sex therapists have stated that having difficulty more than twenty-five percent of the time means the man has a problem that needs attention.

In some instances, the man's ability to function is not necessarily related to anxiety or any psychological blocks. He may not be receiving the kind of stimulation or approach that excites him most. If the man finds himself impotent, his partner might lubricate the penis with some water-based jelly and stimulate him to erection. Sometimes having the female insert the penis in intercourse is very arousing. Try these, or other ideas of your own invention first. If they don't work, try the established methods detailed below.

There is a great variety of exercises that therapists suggest for helping men with erection difficulties. They are all similar in that they involve the use of masturbation and self-pleasuring with no initial concern for whether or not the penis gets hard or orgasm is reached. Later on in the exercises, the man can begin to work on them with his partner, but it is generally a better idea if the man explores his responses alone first.

The man should begin by making himself comfortable and choosing a time when he is not preoccupied with the pressures of his job, family, etc. With or without a lubricant, he stimulates his penis until he obtains an erection. Then he removes his hand and allows his erection to subside. Letting his erection go down by choice helps to reinforce the idea that it is not terrible if he loses it with a partner. When his penis is soft, he can begin again, stimulating himself to erection and again allowing it to subside. If he finds that his erection won't return, or he doesn't erect in the first place, it should not worry him. It is also a good idea to end the first few experiences not having reached orgasm (contrary to popular myth, there is no physical harm in becoming aroused without ejaculating).

As he moves through these exercises, the man should focus on the pleasure he is feeling without trying to have an erection. No one can will himself to become erect. If there are certain situations that cause anxiety when with a partner, fantasize about them while masturbating. If, for instance, you typically become tense when she plays with your penis, or when you try to enter her vagina, fantasize these situations and try to imagine yourself enjoying the encounters. It may take some time.

Another important element in regaining potency is choosing times for sex when you are aroused. Too many men make demands on themselves that they be in the mood for sex at all times and perform well each time. Yet, you should practice these exercises and have sexual relations with your partner only at times when you really feel like it. Otherwise, you may be forcing yourself to *perform*, while at the same time your limp penis is betraying the fact that you aren't ready.

When you feel ready, introduce your partner to the exercises you've been practicing. As before, stop at a certain point and allow your erection to subside. The first several times, don't ejaculate: instead, allow yourself to experience the acceptable feeling of losing an erection without worrying about it. Later on, when you feel more relaxed and comfortable, go ahead and ejaculate, and let yourself enjoy the experience.

During the course of these exercises with a partner, the woman herself may become aroused and desire to feel that your experience together is a mutual sharing. If both partners wish, the man can provide the woman with whatever stimulation is most satisfying to her. Don't be overly concerned if your own preferred style and rhythm of performing these exercises does not conform exactly to the general guidelines we've stated, or that you might read in another book. The object is simply to gain a greater understanding of your own sexual response and those factors and situations that tend to frustrate or inhibit your sexual expression. For both sexes, masturbation remains the most useful way to discover these feelings and transfer them to sexual contacts with a partner.

Throughout these exercises for both sexes, an understanding and cooperative partner is a great help. It may be necessary to rethink many set, rigid ways of approaching sex and thinking of each other sexually.

RETARDED EJACULATION

We have defined retarded ejaculation as an inability to ejaculate though the man has obtained an erection and experienced prolonged stimulation. This is less common than impotence but can be overcome using a similar set of exercises involving masturbation alone and with a partner. The critical idea is to take a step back and realize the set patterns and anxieties that have interfered. Some men report developing retarded ejaculation after having made a woman pregnant unintenionally, being subjected to shame and embarrassment when discovered masturbating by a parent, or from a pervasive sense of guilt over the whole area of having sexual feelings. Symbolically, the man may be withholding his ejaculation under the mistaken belief that it is therefore less "wrong." None of these instances may apply to your own situation. For men who are comfortable responding to exercises such as described above and who want more details, we recommend Gary F. Kelly's book, *Good Sex: The Healthy Man's Guide to Sexual Fulfillment.*

INHIBITED SEXUAL DESIRE (ISD)

Most of the sexual difficulties discussed in this chapter involve some problem with sexual functioning itself. But for some individuals and couples the sexual activity doesn't progress that far because of lack of interest. Some of the best work in this area has been done by Helen Singer Kaplan, and those who are interested are referred to the bibliography section. We'll outline the basic concepts in this area and how to respond if personally affected.

Kaplan (1979) describes people experiencing inhibited sexual desire (ISD) as asexual and hypoactive in their sexual behaviors. She writes that such a person: ". . . behaves as though his sexual circuits have been 'shut down.' He loses interest in sexual matters, will not pursue sexual gratification, and if a sexual situation presents itself, is not moved to avail himself of the opportunity."

The physical sexual capabilities of people with ISD are not impaired—they simply aren't interested. Of all the sexual dysfunctions discussed in this chapter, ISD is probably the most prevalent. There is a broad range of sexual appetites that can be considered "normal;" some people desire sexual activity very infrequently, have low sex drives, and are content with this state of affairs. Others have strong desires for frequent sex. Both ends of the continuum might be considered "normal." It is also not considered dysfunctional for people to experience ISD in situations where they are endangered or not emotionally secure. When force or pressure is involved, when the partner is not perceived as attractive either physically or in terms of personality, or when the anticipated behavior is felt to be self-damaging, it is not unusual for people to feel little or no desire for sex. Finally, when a conscious decision to remain celibate has been reached, ISD is not necessarily a concern.

It is not unusual for people with little sexual desire to be untroubled by their asexuality, although many individuals come to feel deeply disturbed about it. ISD is a problem mainly when the person feels it is a problem, or when a spouse or partner is upset by the lack of interest. The condition may, in fact, be a symptom of a dissatisfying relationship or a way of expressing discontent to one's sexual partner. Whatever the cause, ISD is usually very disruptive to relationships and may lead to feelings of rejection on the part of the still-interested partner.

Lack of interest in one respect can be seen as a learned behavior. From the time of birth females especially are taught that sex and sexuality are bad and to be feared. This powerful message often has a way of evoking guilt feelings in people who experience healthy desires and the guilt itself can act to suppress interest in sex. The conflict develops between strivings for sexual intimacy on one hand and needs to maintain the chaste, asexual image demanded by parents and society on the other.

A number of emotions can interfere with sexual desire. Anger and depression are foremost among them. It can be virtually impossible to feel turned on when experiencing these emotions. The feelings need not be related to sex itself: perhaps one is angry about an incident at work. *Anxiety* probably inhibits sexual desire more than any other feeling: it can appear as a sense of apprehension or self-consciousness that leaves sexual feelings out of the picture. In effect, nearly any strong affective state can interfere with a person's usual sexual desires.

Though there ordinarily is cause for concern when one's sexual interest wanes, a need exists to appreciate that these feelings ebb and flow across time. The intense arousals from early stages of courtship or marriage usually do not sustain themselves indefinitely, and over the years it may be "normal" for a person to experience various levels of desire. As with other sexual dysfunctions, the more negative concern and anxiety that gets focused on the problem, the worse it is likely to become. An understanding of one's own natural rhythms and an acceptance of the low tides might help keep the situation in perspective.

Changes that occur across the lifespan are also known to interfere with sexual desires. After the birth of a baby, for instance, mothers especially may find that their appetites decrease, though fathers, too, may undergo this change. For some new parents, the label of *mother* or *father* is incongruent with sexual intercourse (related perhaps to the difficulty of imagining one's own parents as sexual). Part of this problem may be the tendency for new parents to focus all their love and attention on the infant and to neglect crucial aspects of their marriage. It helps when people can feel that the arrival of a baby adds new love to the family system, rather than requiring that the love already there has to be spread around even more thinly. The resentments can build when one spouse feels that the partner has little time or energy for them.

Finally, as we discussed with other sexual dysfunctions, overwork, little sleep, poor eating habits, drug and/or alcohol use, a dramatic change in residence, occupation, or lifestyle can all affect sexual desire. If and when people find themselves with little interest, perhaps the best initial advice is not to become overly worried. If you are involved with a lover or are married, it will be helpful to communicate your feelings and to give the other person an opportunity to discuss his or hers. Although this may not have an immediate effect on your sex life, it will probably help to keep feelings of anger, rejection, jealousy, and betrayal at a minimum.

If, after a reasonable period of time, say two or three months, couples or individuals find that they aren't having success at overcoming their difficulties through self-efforts, professional help should be sought. Some people respond better to treatment directed by a therapist and find that structured routines and assignments give them greater motivation. In addition, a medical examination may be called for. Among some women, for example, a lack of sexual interest is sometimes related to the balance of progesterone and estrogen hormones in their bodies. There is certainly no "type" of either males or females who are prone to experiencing sexual difficulties, and no stigma need be attached to seeking outside assistance. Couples can gain a wider appreciation of the broad range of individual experience by examining (male and female) case histories such as those contained in Shere Hite's books *The Hite Report* and *The Hite Report on Male Sexuality.* If nothing else, it will provide the perspective that sexual dysfunctions and dissatisfactions are a part of the human experience.

REFERENCES

Barbach, L. *For Yourself—The Fulfillment of Female Sexuality.* Garden City, NY: Doubleday, 1975.

_____. *For Each Other: Sharing Sexual Intimacy.* Garden City, NY: Doubleday Anchor, 1982.

Hite, S. *The Hite Report: A Nationwide Study of Female Sexuality.* New York: Macmillan, 1976.

Hite, S. *The Hite Report on Male Sexuality.* New York: Ballantine, 1981.

Kaplan, H. S. *Disorders of Sexual Desire.* New York: Simon & Schuster, 1979.

Kelly, G. *Good Sex: The Healthy Man's Guide to Sexual Fulfillment.* New York: Harcourt Brace Jovanovich, 1979.

McCarthy, B., & McCarthy, E. *Sexual Awareness: Enhancing Sexual Pleasure.* New York: Carroll & Graf, 1984.

CHAPTER 23

Sexual Problems: Fetishes and Paraphilias

Before discussing the list of fetishes and paraphilias, a distinction needs to be drawn between these behaviors and some unconventional acts that occur in some couple's lovemaking. Some couples, for instance, enjoy including various sex toys and gadgets in their sexual lives, such as vibrators, dildos, lotions and oils, erotic movies, mirrors. Some like to be playfully adventurous, perhaps by having sex outdoors or in public places where there is little risk of discovery. Some like to dress up in each other's clothes or enact sexual fantasies as part of their lovemaking. A good discussion of these and other aspects of lovemaking can be found in Barry and Emily McCarthy's book, *Sexual Awareness: Enhancing Sexual Pleasure.* When these behaviors are voluntary and nonexploitative, they fall within what is considered the normal range of sexual expression. If, however, a couple's or individual's *main source* of sexual arousal and satisfaction comes from compulsions, even if the behaviors do not affect anyone involuntarily, professional help may be called for. The behaviors discussed below most often indicate the presence of a dysfunction; this is *always* the case when others are involved as unwilling victims or accomplices.

For reasons that are not entirely understood, most of the behaviors discussed in this section are far more common among males than females. *Paraphilia* (which means beyond love), is a psychiatric term for what are known elsewhere as perversions. The latter term is often a weapon that may assume global proportions: although a man may be an electrician, a father, a tennis player, and a husband, these may be overshadowed by the single identity attributed to him by others: pervert. Paraphilia, then, refers to a person's behaviors and is intended to neutralize some of the moralistic implications that accompany the term *perversion*.

The behaviors referred to in this chapter include exhibitionism, voyeurism, fetishism, transvestism, sadomasochism, bondage and discipline, obscene phone calls, pedophilia, necrophilia, zoophilia, coprophilia, golden showers, and infantalism (including enemas and diapers). This list illustrates how broad the spectrum of atypical human sexual behavior is, and how people are aroused by a seemingly endless variety of objects and situations. Whereas some may be familiar to you, others may seem bizarre or even frightening. Some of the behaviors occur furtively, in solitude, though others may well be inflicted on unwilling victims.

Exhibitionism and *voyeurism* are both extreme forms of behaviors that, in lesser forms, are part of most people's lives. Exhibitionism usually refers to a male who "flashes" his penis in front of unsuspecting females of any age. It might also include a person of either sex who habitually dresses and undresses in front of open windows. Finally, both men and women who dress provocatively are sometimes called exhibitionists; it can be seen that the range is from the disturbed flasher to the woman who wears no bra and leaves her top buttons undone. Voyeurism (peeping Tom behavior) might involve someone who looks in people's windows at night or who uses binoculars or a telescope in attempts to view people naked or perhaps having sex. Voyeurism in its lesser forms exists among men who ogle women (or vise versa), and in those who enjoy explicit erotica and its milder forms in the media (*Playboy, Playgirl*, etc.).

Any of the above that involves other people as unwilling participants is pathological behavior. Wearing revealing clothing and/or reading a provocative magazine do not tend to frighten or disgust other people. Though exhibitionists and voyeurs do not tend to be dangerous, victims do not know this and may fear for their safety. The horror, fear, and other strong reactions evoked in their victims is arousing for the flashers and thus reinforces their obsession.

A *fetish* is an obsession with some inanimate object, from which the person derives sexual excitement and pleasure. Well-known examples of fetishes are shoes, underwear, rubber and leather garments, and stockings and garter belts. Virtually any object can become sexually charged for an individual, however, depending on the person's experience. Fetishism tends to be a solitary pursuit and is supported somewhat by commercial enterprises: you'll see advertisements in some sex weeklies for "previously worn ladies' panties" and a variety of other things.

In one sense, a fetish is a harmless activity and gives people pleasure. Though it is often guilt-ridden and hidden from others, it is for some men their only sexual outlet. Fetishists might also attach great sexual eroticism to parts of the body, such as the buttocks, large breasts, or genitals. Though for some people the fetish exists alongside relatively normal social and sexual functioning, for others it represents a fragmentation of sex that separates them from others. A part of the body or an object are incapable of engaging in relationships with the person who has the fetish: How can you relate to an ass or a shoe? You might judge how harmless a fetish is by determining how much time and energy it occupies in your life, and whether you are equally capable of developing intimate contacts with other people as well. As we've stated elsewhere, guilt is often the energy for the repetition of thoughts and behaviors that are unacceptable to you. If you simply enjoy an occasional dalliance with your fetish and can walk away from it at will, very likely there is no problem.

Transvestites are people (predominantly men) who dress in the clothing of the opposite sex, sometimes appearing in public. Cross-dressers, contrary to myth, are usually heterosexual married men who, to all appearances in the rest of their lives, are well adjusted. Transvestites may be especially ingenious in concealing their practices from wives and family. A difficulty encountered in most locales is: how and where to shop for women's clothes when dressed as a man? A man cannot very well go into a woman's dressing room to try on a dress and will typically maneuver to avoid arousing the suspicions of salespeople. A few years back the movie "Tootsie" captured the nation's fantasy, though in truth most transvestites cross-dress in private and would be mortified if they were ever seen in drag.

As with some of the other paraphilias discussed in this chapter, it is somewhat difficult to assess the impact of transvestism. Since it is solitary, there is little or no exploitation of other persons. The origins often lie in childhood, where viewing a mother or older sister dressing may have evoked powerful sexual stimulation; for others, the origin is not clear. What can be said is: if you or your partner feel that transvestism is a problem, then it needs to be dealt with in some fashion. Some partners simply cannot accept the behavior, and ending it may become a condition of the relationship continuing. Others may be unconcerned, intrigued, or freed to divulge their own sexual idiosyncrasies, which had previously been secret.

Of all the atypical sexual behaviors mentioned in this chapter, the one most likely to affect most reader's lives is *obscene phone calls*. These cannot be considered harmless or pranks and are a serious violation of others' privacy. If you are an obscene phone caller, it is no laughing matter, as you are aware: you can't stop the practice despite the self-loathing and sense of inadequacy you feel when you call. Pretending that it's really not hurting anybody is a major form of denial and the best indication that professional help is needed.

If you are the recipient of an obscene phone call, perhaps the most important thing initially is to suppress whatever revulsion or anger you feel and gently hang up the phone immediately. Don't tell the person what a "sicko" he is, that he is disgusting, or slam the phone down; these are positive reinforcement, for they are exactly what the caller desired. After you hang up, you can feel proud of yourself, call a friend, the phone company, or the police, but in any case control it while on the phone. Men sometimes answer the phone while at home, only to discover that the person on the other end hangs up right away. This is sometimes an indication that an obscene caller was hoping for a female to answer. Some couples arrange for the male partner to answer the phone at night after a certain hour, as this is a more likely time for the calls to come through.

Though some people advise women to keep a whistle by the phone with which to rupture the caller's eardrum, this is only opening the door to further harassment and the possibility that the caller will get his own whistle and pay you back in kind. Should the calls continue, the phone company is often agreeable to providing you with an unlisted number free of charge. If the calls are threatening, police departments often cooperate in attempting to trace the calls.

Sadomasochism and *bondage and discipline* derive from the connection in some people's minds between pleasure and pain, or in clinical terms, between sexual and aggressive impulses. A sadist gets pleasure from inflicting pain, and a masochist receives pleasure from having pain inflicted on him or her. Among a sizable minority of people, some degree of mild pain is an occasional part of their lovemaking, in such forms as biting, scratching, or slapping. A person with real sadomasochistic inclinations, however, devotes a significant amount of energy to these desires and may require the presence of some sadomasochistic ritual or behavior to become sexually aroused.

Bondage and discipline refers to tying up or restraining one's partner and administering some form of discipline, perhaps in the form of a whipping, spanking, or verbal humiliation. Some people who engage in these behaviors do not thrive on the pain so much as on the tension that develops in the enactment of their sexual fantasy. Little pain may be inflicted or experienced; the anticipation and role playing may be the most exciting parts.

People who enjoy these behaviors are often thought to be reenacting some scene from their childhood, in which pain somehow became associated with pleasure and comfort. As with many behaviors described in this book, the question of whether sadomasochism is a disorder *for you* hinges on its prominence in your life. Is it the only way you can become aroused and satisfied? Does it tend to exploit your partner and leave you feeling guilty afterward? Or is it an occasional variation in your sexual repertoire that is neither compulsive nor mandatory for arousal? These issues are key in determining the meaning of these behaviors.

Pedophilia refers to an adult's (almost always a male) sexual interest in children. The man may desire contacts with either male or female children, and in all cases, these behaviors are considered to be criminal. Regardless of the sex of the child being sought, these men are most often heterosexual in their adult relationships, though many such men are unable to engage in mature sexual relationships or are in dysfunctional marriages. This is an area of some disagreement among professionals: some believe that many of these men are reasonably well adjusted in their marriages, but others, including ourselves, are skeptical of these findings and believe that self-reports of pedophiles cannot be trusted.

This section on pedophiles is intentionally brief, as the subject is discussed in depth in Chapter 13. Some people have become extremely upset by the existence of organizations that promote sexual contacts between men and children. These organizations admittedly are reprehensible, but it must be remembered that the few men who belong are deeply disturbed members of a fringe group, in the same way as those who belong to the Ku Klux Klan or who worship Nazism also suffer from severe disorders. Although many "normal" men and women are stimulated by the sight of naked children, or by the physical contact that comes from being playful with children or bathing them, the great majority do not translate this arousal into behavior. When the desires for overt sexual experiences with children become overwhelming or are actually translated into behaviors, professional help is *always* called for.

The following seven paraphilias are mentioned briefly, as they occur only relatively rarely. *Necrophilia* involves sexual contact between a living person and a corpse and occurs in almost all cases in mortuaries or funeral homes. *Zoophilia* (also referred to as *bestiality*) is sexual contact between a person and an animal. This is far more common among farm youth and includes rubbing against animals, intercourse, or having the animal orally stimulate the genitals of the person. Females have been found to participate in these activities to a lesser extent than males (though in some pornographic presentations, it is a woman shown sexually engaged with an animal). Besides a concern for the mental well-being of the person, there also exists a concern that these behaviors are sometimes cruel to the animal. *Coprophilia* means a sexual fascination with feces and may involve *coprolangnia* or defecating upon someone. *Urolangnia* (also referred to as *golden showers*) involves being urinated upon. *Infantilism* occurs among men who are aroused by being placed in diapers and babied. *Klismaphilia* refers to pleasure through the giving or receiving of enemas. *Frottage* (more common than the previous six) occurs when a man seeks to obtain pleasure by rubbing against women, usually in public places, such as subways or crowded places.

Many of the men who exhibit one or more of the behaviors described in this section are adjudicated through the court system and may come to a professional's attention because the person is mandated to receive some form of therapy. It is apparent that some of the behaviors are most likely to occur in solitary ways or between just two consenting people, whereas others are criminal and hurtful. This section illustrates the tremendous variety of sexual adaptations among people, even though some will seem bizarre or perverse to some readers of this book. This list is necessarily limited because in reality people find an endless variety of stimuli to be sexually arousing. Some are dysfunctional by definition, and others exist in a more gray area where the connotation and circumstances help to determine their meaning. Some people, for moral and/or religious reasons, do not share the belief that sexual behaviors other than marital, coital encounters can be considered to be anything but wrong.

Many people have a tendency to believe that individuals such as those described in this chapter are the only ones who ever experience these "perverse" feelings. A dichotomy thus develops between "us healthy ones" and "those perverts." In reality, virtually all people experience feelings, thoughts, and impulses similar to those disorders examined herein. What separates the two groups is that the former rarely, if ever, act on the impulses, and the latter group often acts on their impulses. Though some people with paraphilias are occasionally dangerous (and they *should* be dealt with appropriately by the law), some of people's fear and hatred of them is fueled by their denial that such feelings exist in themselves in any shape or form. And so society makes scapegoats of those who translate their "normal" impulses into unacceptable and hurtful behavior. In fact, this denial of sexual feelings in ourselves, we believe, fuels some of the moralistic crusades that occasionally persecute select groups such as homosexuals.

CHAPTER 24

Understanding Your Male Body

Dennis J. Krauss, M.D.

Our body, its structure and its function, tends to be a mystery to most of us. We are so complex that to those of us who know many of the finer points of physiology, etc., it becomes downright miraculous! So, how do some of us respond when something out of the ordinary occurs? Of course! Assume the worst and then panic! On the other hand, maybe we're "laid back," and we do the *natural* alternative: assume that whatever is going on, no matter how painful or extraordinary, must be trivial and, therefore, completely ignore it! In either case, we risk an expenditure of emotional energy that is draining and serves no useful purpose. Information and the confidence to see a physician promptly help to avoid such emotional torment and unnecessary delays in treatment. Remember, DPP (Don't Panic Prematurely). It is easy to say, and actually not too difficult to do. It reminds me of the time a patient said: "Doc, when was the last time someone told you 'Relax!' and you actually could?"

The human body is a fantastic machine with many parts, each of which operates according to basic mechanical, chemical, and electrical laws. A great many of these mechanisms we understand, some we know nothing about, and many we are in the process of learning. For example, the explanation of higher emotional functions of the brain is not known. You, as a nonphysician, can learn enough to understand what may be causing a particular symptom, what the recommended treatment should accomplish, and what your role is in achieving a successful outcome. Knowing enough to be able to ask questions of your physician is very important. This is the end of the twentieth century and the myth of the "M. Deity" is dying nicely. Most physicians are pleased to be able to have a patient and family who ask questions and who are anxious to understand fully the situation at hand. The following chapter is a description of the basics of sexual functioning, followed by discussions of various questions and situations.

PENIS

The human penis, unlike its female counterpart, the clitoris, is multipurpose. Its functions include reproduction, urination, and recreation. Anatomically, the penis is quite simple. It is composed of three cylinders (Fig. 1), all of which become erect (engorged with blood) during sexual arousal. The erectile tissue of the two corpora cavernosa is surrounded by a very tough covering, the tunica albuginea. The tunica

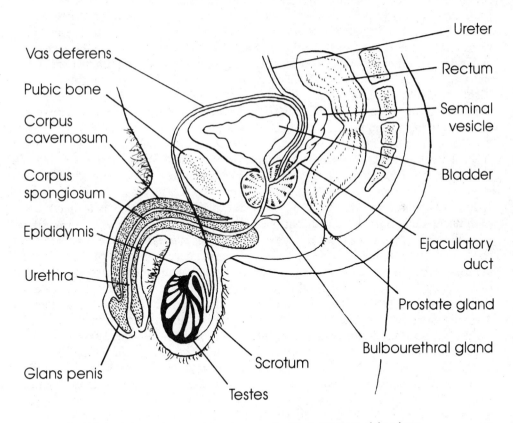

Figure 1. Male internal sexual and reproductive organs, side view.

provides resistance to expansion during erection and thus is a major factor contributing to the hardness of the erection. The third erectile cylinder, the corpus spongiosum, surrounds the urethra (urine and ejaculation tube). It also engorges with blood, but because it lacks the firm covering does not get hard. The glans (head of the penis) is part of the spongiosum, and during erection it also gets engorged, causing it to have a bluish hue, but remains relatively soft. The blood vessels, nerves, etc., which are vital to the penile tissue, are located along the top of the penile shaft under the tissue that is beneath the skin. The skin of the penis is thin and is vulnerable to any of the usual skin conditions.

ERECTION

The process of erection is complicated. It involves a delicate balance among the nervous, endocrine (hormone), and vascular (blood vessels) systems. The nerves to the penis that are concerned with erection and sexual arousal include those that control feeling (sensory) and those involved in the involuntary control of blood (autonomic) vessels (sympathetic and parasympathetic). Spinal cord nerves connect the above nerves with various parts of the brain so that sexuality and sexual behavior have both conscious and unconscious components. We all know how such complex factors as the senses (sight, smell, touch, hearing, taste), memory, fantasy, and emotions (happiness, depression, anxiety, etc.) greatly control sexual desire, arousal, and behavior. You can see that the brain is the most important sex organ we have.

Adequate blood supply to the erectile bodies is also essential for normal erections. The corpora cavernosa are essentially complex blood vessels. When the rate of blood flowing into the corpora increases to a critical speed compared to the speed of the blood flowing out, the penis becomes erect. After the erection is achieved, a different balance is attained to maintain the erection. Thus, the process of erection is a blood-flow phenomenon that is triggered and controlled by nerves.

What part do the male sex hormones play in this process? Believe it or not, we really don't know completely. We do know that during development of the baby in the uterus, every fetus would develop into a female if the male hormones were not genetically triggered to appear at a critical time to "turn off" female development. Likewise, the differentiation between the male and female brain occurs during fetal development. The next important time for male hormone influence is puberty. At this time, the male hormones, especially testosterone, stimulate growth of the male secondary sex characteristics (enlargement of the penis, testicles, scrotum; growth of hair on the genitals, underarms, chest; the characteristic male bone and muscle growth; deepening of the voice). In addition to these visible changes, the testicles enlarge and begin to produce sperm. The accessory sex glands (prostate, seminal vesicles, bulbourethral glands) enlarge and begin to function also under the influence of the male hormones.

Do the male hormones affect erections and sexual behavior? They do, but we are not so sure how. We know that testosterone influences many organs including the brain. Interestingly enough, it has been shown that the estrogen (female hormone) that the brain cells make from testosterone is an important stimulator of male sexual behavior. Without the influence of the male hormones a man can lose his sexual desire and activity; it can lead to loss of erections but doesn't always! For example, some men who have both testicles removed for medical reasons may continue to have erections and not lose them until many months later, despite the fact that their testosterone is almost gone.

Another hormone, prolactin, also is significant. We really don't know yet what its function is in the normally functioning male, but it probably involves sex gland growth and function. In some men with erectile dysfunction, there is an excess of prolactin in the blood. Treating this with medication, or sometimes surgery, will bring the prolactin back to its normal amount and restore erections.

Various other hormones and chemicals within the body also can affect erections. Details are available in more technical texts.

Thus, it is clear that we do not yet fully understand the complex physiology of erections and sexual behavior. Researchers around the world are working on the many aspects of these questions.

TESTIS

The testicles are egg-shaped structures, which in adults are approximately two inches high, one inch wide and one inch thick (Fig. 2). The measurements are only average and there is much individual variation. They lie vertically in the scrotum (sack). The testicles' positions normally are uneven, one higher in the scrotum than the other. They are composed of several types of cells with different functions: some produce the male hormone testosterone; some produce other substances; and some form the long, coiled, seminiferous tubes that produce sperm. The tubules have a composite length of almost one mile! They connect to the epididymis that can be felt behind each testicle. The epididymis is another coiled tube that connects the testicle to the vas deferens. The vas in turn propels the sperm up to the urethra at the appropriate time before ejaculation.

Before puberty, the testicles are small. With advanced age the testicles may also shrink a bit. I will discuss other changes of aging later. Shrinkage also occurs with some medical conditions such as diabetes mellitus, liver disease, and others.

PAINFUL TESTICLE

There are many conditions that may cause pain in the testicles or "scrotal pain." The pain may be mild or severe and can be felt not only in the testicle but also in the

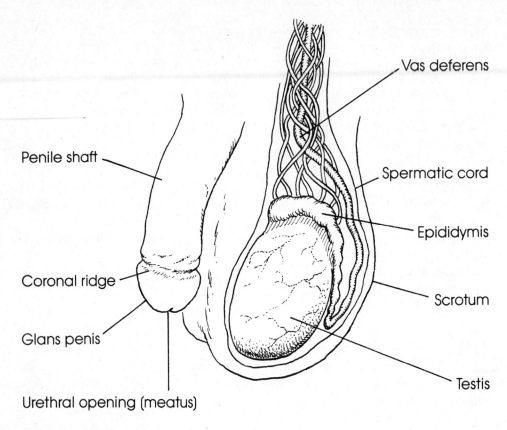

Penile shaft

Vas deferens

Spermatic cord

Epididymis

Coronal ridge

Scrotum

Glans penis

Testis

Urethral opening (meatus)

Figure 2. Male genitalia.

groin, sides, and back. Actually, pain coming from any other scrotal structure will be interpreted as "testicle pain." The most important causes are injury, infection or inflammation, and torsion (twisting of the testicle). We do not know the cause of torsion, but it is very painful and can stop the blood supply to the testicle long enough to cause it to die. Most commonly, torsion occurs in the twelve to twenty-five year-old age group. The pain comes on very suddenly and may even awaken you from sleep. Consult a doctor immediately if you have sudden, severe, persisting pain.

Infection or inflammation of the epididymis or testicle (epididymitis or orchitis) also can be severe. It is characterized by a gradual onset, problems with urination, fever, and sometimes swelling of the scrotum. Since it is sometimes difficult to tell the difference between epididymitis and torsion, do not delay in consulting your doctor.

TESTES—LUMPS, BUMPS, AND SWELLINGS

The words tumor or growth technically refer to any mass that may develop in the body. It may be malignant (cancer) or benign (not cancer). There are many kinds of tumors of the testicle and other scrotal contents. The most common benign tumor is the *hydrocoele*, a collection of fluid within the tissues surrounding the testicle. Except for certain particular circumstances, they require no treatment unless they are bothersome or become unsightly. When needed, the treatment is surgery. If your doctor simply uses a needle and syringe to draw off the fluid, the fluid will certainly reaccumulate. If the testicle is severely injured, the same tissues may get filled with blood and create a large mass called a *hematocoele* (not to mention one heck of a pain!). This requires a urologist's attention because surgery may be necessary.

A spermatocoele is a cyst of the tubes that join the testicle and epididymis. It is benign and always appears at the upper part of the testicle. It can grow large and sometimes may feel almost like there is a third testicle. Treatment is not always needed and should never consist of simply removing the fluid with a needle.

Another benign tumor in the scrotal sac may be composed of intestine because of an *inguinal hernia* (a "rupture"). This is not uncommon and is seen mostly in the middle middle and later years of life. There are various other types of benign tumors but they are not common and are beyond the scope of this work.

Treatment of cancer of the testicle, as hard as it may be to believe, has been one of the great success stories in modern medicine! From almost a death sentence fifteen to twenty years ago, testicular cancer now is one of the most treatable, with a remarkable cure rate. Naturally, the earlier it is detected and treated, the better the outlook (prognosis). The treatment is not always easy and may involve surgery and possibly drugs (chemotherapy) or radiation (x-ray) therapy, but the effort and some discomfort involved are *well worth it*. I stress this because fear and ignorance many times cause men to hide or deny the fact that they have a mass in the testicle. Such long delays in treatment (if the growth is malignant) make the therapy more complicated and the results less successful. Cancer may develop at any age, but the most common group to get testicular cancer is fifteen to thirty-five year-olds. The most common type of cancer of the testicle is called *seminoma* and is treated, after surgical removal of the malignant testicle, by radiation therapy. The types that are not *seminoma* (*embryonal*, *teratoma*, and *choriocarcinoma*) are treated differently and are a bit more complicated. The extent and success of treatment depends on many factors, so I repeat, do not delay. More good news is that the pure *choriocarcinoma*, which is the most difficult to cure, occurs in fewer than 1 percent of the cases.

Cancers of the other structures within the scrotum do exist, but they are quite rare and not worth mentioning any further. It bears repeating, however, that cancer of the testicle is curable in *most* cases. So see a physician as soon as any question arises. Now, how do we detect cancer early? We look for it routinely. Many lives were saved once the campaign was started to alert women about self-examination of their breasts. The same can be done with men examining their testicles. It is also not unusual for a sexual partner to suddenly feel something unusual and bring it to the person's attention.

SELF-EXAMINATION OF THE GENITALIA

No! You don't have to go to medical school to be able to examine your genitals, especially the testicles. It certainly helps to know the genital anatomy fully, but even that is not essential. As long as you examine yourself regularly, once or twice a month, and learn what is "normal" for you, you will be able to detect most any new growth. When you first start doing self-examination, make sure that a doctor "checks you out" so that the two of you can discuss what you are feeling and agree that all is "normal."

How do you accomplish this task? Easy! It can be done standing up or lying down in a warm room. Some doctors recommend doing it during a warm shower. It think that is unnecessary, especially in view of the cost of heating the water; you certainly don't want to examine yourself with the water running; take your time. With practice you will become confident and the examination will be quick and easy.

The first step is to look at the skin of the scrotal sac and penis. Are there any lumps, bumps, blisters, scratches, or anything other than healthy normal wrinkly skin? Next, feel each testicle by supporting it with one hand and ever so gently squeezing it between the thumb and forefinger of your other hand. Do this over the entire surface. Look for any lumps, bumps, or spots that are painful to touch. How gentle do you have to be? It may help to imagine yourself wearing a blindfold and trying to find a soft spot on a peach, without creating any new ones yourself.

Next, feel for the epididymis, the vertical tube that extends the whole length of the back of each testicle. It, too, should not have any painful spots and should feel softer than the testicle. The epididymis connects to the vas deferens, which is a small, hard tube hidden in a bunch of tubular structures called the spermatic cord. This cord should not be painful to touch and should also have no lumps. The spermatic cord is composed of the nerves, blood vessels, vas, supporting tissues, etc., that connect to the testicle from various points in the body. I guess you could call it the testicle's "life line." The cord also has muscles in it. When pain, cold, sexual, or other stimuli are applied, the muscles contract and the testicle is pulled up. As you gently squeeze the cord structures higher and higher toward the top of the scrotum, the cord will enter deeper into your body and you will no longer be able to feel anything.

Remember, each condition that you may detect by self-examination of the genitalia has a name and a treatment. You should not delay in learning the technique, and you should do it regularly.

EJACULATION AND ORGASM

Ejaculation, the propulsion of semen out of the penis via the urethra, is intimately associated with erection. They are not "cause and effect," however. Either one can exist without the other.

The nerves controlling ejaculation are "autonomic," with a predominance of the "sympathetic" system. Blood vessel problems are less significant in the ejaculation process, unless the blood supply is so bad that it damages the nerves by inadequate nourishment. Male hormones and prolactin also play some part in the ejaculation process.

The accessory sex glands produce the seminal fluid that makes up almost all the volume of the ejaculate, and the testes supply the sperm. The body mixes the components of the ejaculate in the urethra (emission) and then propels them out (ejaculation). This is a very complex process. Different medical or emotional conditions may contribute to dysfunction in any one or a combination of the steps and thus result in a number of different problems.

Orgasm is the combination of all the various muscle contractions, in the genitals as well as the muscle contractions in much of the rest of the body, plus the pressure changes that occur in the seminal tubes and urethra. Sufficient sexual arousal must precede the orgasm, but erection is not necessary. Subjectively, the pleasure of orgasm comes from the buildup of the various pressures and muscle tensions all over the body, accompanied by the sudden release and total body relaxation. The orgasm can be produced by any kind of sex play, but the emotional pleasure comes from the closeness to the loved partner. That, as Dr. Domeena Renshaw says, differentiates "making sex" from "making love."

FERTILITY

Fifteen to 20 percent of couples in the United States are unable to have a baby, despite many months and years of trying. Another 10 percent have fewer children than they desire. In about half these couples, the male is the infertile partner. For these couples, there is frequently emotional torment. They have heard all the intellectual arguments about adoption, etc., but emotions are strong. The numerous examinations and fertility tests also can be quite an ordeal.

For a man to be considered fertile, his testicles must produce sperm in adequate numbers; he must be able to store the sperm and then transport them up to the urethra at the precise time; and he must be able to propel them out of the urethra. For pregnancy to occur, the couple must coordinate that process in order to deposit sperm in the woman's vagina at the time of ovulation so that the sperm can swim up into the fallopian tubes to meet the ovum (egg). For something so complex, it is amazing that it *ever* works (let alone by accident in the back seat of a car).

The first source of difficulty in sperm production may arise from a condition that the man inherited in his genes or a defect in the fetal development of his testicle or surrounding tissues. In either case, the testicles may be incapable of producing any, or normal, sperm. Conditions causing abnormal hormone production will also affect normal sperm production.

Because of the testicles' position in the scrotum, their temperature is four to five degrees cooler than the core body temperature of 98.6 degrees F. This is required for normal sperm production. Anything which causes the testicles' temperature to be at or above body temperature will cause at least a temporary halt in sperm production. Such factors include illnesses associated with high fever and frequent hot baths. Some men who wear *tight* athletic supporters for prolonged periods, where their testicles are actually pushed up deeper into their body, may find they have a lower than normal number of sperm. Jockey-type undershorts are not tight enough to cause this problem.

Emotional stress has been shown to interfere with sperm production. I don't know how, but I guess that is a hormonal mechanism. Diabetes will interfere with fertility in several ways. Its effect on the blood supply to the testicle causes shrinkage of the testicles and loss of sperm and hormone production. The diabetes can also affect erectile ability and thus interfere with the deposit of sperm in the vagina.

Other factors that may cause loss of sperm production are ionizing radiation (x-rays, etc.), ultrasound, malnutrition, vitamin deficiencies, various medications and chemicals, allergic and immune reactions. Infections such as mumps, tuberculosis, chronic prostatitis, and others can also be significant in interfering with fertility if both of the man's testicles have been affected. Aging has a small effect also.

If the testicles are producing sperm, then the next steps for fertility to be complete are delivery and nourishment. If the delivery system is blocked, either surgically, by infection and scar tissue, or by some birth defect, the sperm cannot get to where they must be. Likewise, if the nerves controlling the process of emission and ejaculation are not functioning properly then the sperm will not be propelled as they should be (failure of emission) or will be deposited in the bladder (retrograde ejaculation). If the accessory sex glands are blocked, defective, or not getting the proper nerve signals, the sperm will not get the proper chemicals that are necessary for nourishment and survival.

Voluntary infertility is a very common practice worldwide. Researchers are working on developing a "male pill," but no safe, dependable one is available yet. One of the most popular sterilization methods is vasectomy. It is extremely successful, although it is surgery and does have its (rare) complications. We do the operation under local anesthesia (numbing the area) in less than one-half hour. There is some pain after surgery and there is a small risk of bleeding or infection. A very small risk is recanalization or spontaneous reopening of the channel. Because of the techniques we use now, recanalization is rarely ever seen and it should not be a worry to you. After a vasectomy, viable sperm remain in the vas for two to three months; thus, an additional birth control method should be used during this time to guard against pregnancy.

Almost all men who have a vasectomy develop "antisperm" antibodies because the sperm and their components get into the blood stream. Because that is not their natural location, the body forms antibodies. Are these harmful? We don't know for sure, but many studies of hundreds of thousands of men, many years after vasectomy, so far do not show that there is any significant increase in the incidence of any known condition because of the surgery. The one study that alarmed the world by saying there was an increase in blocked heart blood vessels (coronary artery disease) was based on observations in a few laboratory monkeys.

Vasovasostomy, or rehooking of the cut ends of the vas, is a much more difficult and demanding operation. It takes us several hours; it requires a major anesthetic, and we must use a surgical microscope. Not all urologists are experienced in the procedure, so you may have to see a few before you find one that can do it. More frequently, university-affiliated doctors have had the training and experience. The operation is also quite expensive and requires hospitalization for a few days. We can get the ends sewn back together in almost all cases. Reports of successful return of sperm to the ejaculate range from 70 to 95 percent. The success rate measured by resulting pregnancy is much less; not too much better than 50 percent. Here is where the antibodies may be taking their toll.

Thus, the choice to have a vasectomy must be made with permanent infertility in mind and has to be a decision arrived at by both partners. The most common reasons for wanting a vasovasostomy are: death of children, remarriage, and a desire to have more children.

A seemingly important and fairly common condition that we believe contributes to many fertility problems is called a varicocoele. It is an enlargement and proliferation of the veins that are near the testicle. The vast majority occur on the left side. There is much speculation that it causes infertility by increasing the testicles' temperature. Approximately one-half the time, surgery successfully reverses the problem.

The primary method of studying a man's fertility is a careful sexual and medical history, physical examination, and semen analysis. Since the semen specimen must be fresh, the man must catch his ejaculate in a cup and bring it promptly to the laboratory. Most doctors prefer that the specimen be obtained via masturbation in a private room right in the lab so that analysis can be started immediately. There are some religious objections to collecting semen for this test, and I urge anyone with a troubled conscience or any questions to consult a member of the clergy who is knowledgeable about the modern interpretations of the situation. There may be some proscription against "wasting seeds," but there is also the command to be "fruitful." Decisions concerning fertility are thus based on intensely personal religious and moral feelings.

In analyzing the semen, we want to know if all the sperm are of normal size, structure, and number (the average ejaculation contains 360 million sperm); if they can swim effectively in a forward direction; and if there are many dead sperm in the ejaculate. We test the seminal fluid also to see if it is of normal amount; if it has the proper constituents; and if it has the right amount of alkalinity (not acid). We also can test for various antibodies in the fluid; these can prevent the otherwise normal-appearing sperm from functioning properly.

A male fertility evaluation is always done in conjunction with a gynecologist who is investigating the female partner's fertility status. The doctor orders tests that are progressively more complicated and invasive (more hassle, more discomfort) depending on the results of each previous test; and only if the tests are absolutely necessary, and, of course, only if the partners both agree that it is worth it for them to persist.

One final thought about the emotional aspects of fertility. The long process of trying to conceive, then the possible long investigation process, all can contribute to frustration and depression, to questioning one's "manhood" or "womanhood," to marital relationship problems, even to sexual dysfunction. It is hoped the physician involved will be sensitive to these issues. If your doctor does not seem to be sensitive or for some other reason you are dissatisfied with him or her, speak up! You are the consumer, and you have every right to switch to someone else whom you prefer.

AGING

Our bodies are constantly aging. After forty or fifty years of age they begin to undergo noticeable changes that also influence aspects of sexual functioning. I mention this separately because I want to emphasize that these do not constitute sexual dysfunctions. They are natural and quite expected. Dysfunction occurs when either medical illness and its treatments complicate the situation, or emotional issues cause the man or his partner to lose patience and to lose the appreciation for whatever function he has.

The first change is that it takes longer to achieve an erection. It requires more concentration, more stimulation, and more patience. Some of my patients appreciate this because it "cures" their premature ejaculation. Maintaining an erection for long periods of time is less common. The man may lose the erection on occasion after less or only minor distraction compared to when he was much younger. Rather than suffer despair and frustration, he should relax for a few minutes, continue foreplay, and more often than not, he will get the erection back. It is not uncommon at all for some men to have hard erections for just a small part of their sex play. If and when the erection is lost, men can continue the pleasuring. There is always another day to regain the erection, and no reason to prevent his partner from reaching orgasm.

Another change is in the firmness of the erection. It may be softer than before but will still be usable, especially if a man and his partner understand why this is happening and what to do about it.

Aging also causes a decrease in the force of ejaculation; sperm will still be in the seminal fluid if no problem has occurred with the sperm production or delivery systems.

The refractory period, the time after ejaculation during which physiologically you cannot have another ejaculation, also is longer as the body ages. The reason for this is not known.

The testicles undergo changes with age. The most notable is a slight decrease in both size and testosterone production. Researchers have observed that there are gradual decreases in the percentage of normal-shaped sperm and in the sperm's progressive motility. There is no real change in the number of sperm or volume of ejaculate. It is not unusual for a man who is of advanced age and in good health to impregnate a partner.

The aging process may bring with it a decrease in the frequency and intensity of desire for intercourse. This does not mean that there is less desire for love, intimacy, or touch. On the contrary, there may be more desire for those. The reason for decreased desire is not totally clear, but such factors as illness, less physical energy, loss of a partner's interest in sex, death of partners, certainly are important. With age usually comes experience and maturity. More people realize that sexual intercourse is not nearly as important as it used to seem. I like to say that the pleasuring and caring are the cake and the icing; vaginal penetration by the penis is just the writing on top of the icing.

The section below presents the most commonly asked questions concerning male sexual physiology and offers brief answers to each.

SOME QUESTIONS AND ANSWERS

Am I the only one who comes too soon? Premature (rapid) ejaculation (PE) is extremely common. Some define it by a time limit after penetration, or number of penile thrusts, or time after achieving the erection. For practical purposes, I think of it as ejaculation too soon to satisfy yourself or your partner. Every man has experienced this on occasion, especially after long periods of abstinence, times of high excitement, or at awkward or unfamiliar times. It is a problem only if you do it on a regular basis, when it is the rule rather than the exception.

When you have a premature ejaculation, it is simple to compound the frustration, if you wish. All you have to do is stop lovemaking and either leave the room or go to sleep. Even better, say a few nasty words and then be silent. You will quite effectively have further frustrated and irritated your partner and yourself. It probably also will ensure your partner's not having an orgasm that time. Hey, what's wrong with a little anger and self-pity once in awhile? Then if you play your cards right, the next time you two make love, you may be so fearful and nervous that your thinking about the PE may make it happen again (performance anxiety, or fear of failure). Enough repetitions of this scenario and you may find yourself losing your desire for sex and/or losing your ability to obtain an erection altogether. And to think, you were able to engineer this pretty much all by yourself!

If the rapid ejaculation is only an occasional event, then you may want to make a second attempt the same night to take advantage of the refractory period or at another, more relaxed time. If it is indeed a chronic, frequent problem, then you must pay more careful attention to identifying the cause and curing the problem.

Can we choose the sex of our baby? On a purely scientific basis the answer is yes. Depending on which method you use, there will be a variable success rate. The least expensive and least accurate method involves self-help hints. Reportedly, a male baby will be more likely if intercourse (preceded by the woman taking a baking-soda douche) is performed at the time of ovulation; a female baby is supposed to be more likely if intercourse (preceded by the woman taking a vinegar douche) is performed during the fertile time, except for the two days just before ovulation. The "female sperm" are supposed to swim slower and last longer. Therefore, after two days of abstinence, the theory states that "female" sperm are available in the fallopian tube to fertilize the egg (ovum).

The most accurate method, which you should consider only in cases of possible serious genetic diseases, involves amniocentesis (sampling the fluid inside the baby's fluid sack with a needle) to determine gender and possible abortion. Since this must be done in the second trimester, it is risky to the mother and can be a very unpleasant physical and emotional experience. Consider it carefully because you will have to live the rest of your life with your decision.

A third method involves separating "male" sperm from "female" sperm artificially and then using artificial insemination. Presently, the most successful methods can recover only the "male" sperm and cannot detect any genetic diseases. Other tests for recovering "female" sperm are under investigation.

Other experimental methods involve the immune system or attempts at dietary manipulation in the female. The latter is concerned mostly with mineral intake, especially relationships between potassium, calcium, and magnesium.

The whole question of sex preselection is not to be taken lightly. It is a fascinating scientific and biologic topic, but it also has tremendous moral and ethical implications. My describing them in no way states or implies any agreement with their everyday use. My opinion? I'm against it unless you are trying to detect a serious genetic disease in the baby.

Is masturbation normal? "Normal" is a poor choice of words. Masturbation is completely natural. By the age of two years, most babies know the pleasure of touching their genitals. I don't call that masturbation because I think there is a difference between pleasant, tactile sensations and deliberate erotic stimulation. In their "preintercourse" years, children use masturbation as a sexual outlet. For the rest of adult life, masturbation can always add an additional dimension to your sexual life and take away nothing from your primary relationship.

Is masturbation dangerous? No! No one has ever shown that masturbation causes any physical defect, disease, or disability.

Why do I sometimes have erections "at the wrong time"? To be perfectly honest, we don't know. Most often the trigger for such an event is a sight, or smell, or memory, or touch. It can even be a casual thing like a daydream that sets off a chain of thoughts or memories that are especially pleasant or erotic. You may not even remember or recognize what started the events. It conceivably can be a manifestation of the brain activity that triggers sleep erections, at a moment when your inhibitions are down.

In any case, they are perfectly natural and will go away by themselves. If it is convenient, and the erection won't subside promptly, go off to a private place and masturbate. If you cannot do that, then divert your attention and the erection will eventually go away.

Can I use up all my sperm? Barring any injury, surgery, or illness, you cannot "use up" the sperm by ejaculating too many times. Sperm are constantly being produced and the ones swimming in the semen are approximately ninety days old.

What is "Blue Balls"? We really don't know. It consists of a heavy, aching feeling in the testicle and sometimes is relieved by ejaculation. It can appear after long periods without ejaculation, or prolonged excitement without ejaculation. What the exact mechanism is and why a certain few men get it and most others do not are two good questions.

What happens if I lose one testicle? If through injury, surgery, or infection, you lose a testicle, the remaining normal testicle can take over all the needed hormone and sperm production functions. I like to draw the analogy of installing a gas tank in your car that is half-size—you can still drive the car just as well. Problems can occur when there is no other testicle or if the remaining testicle is not a normal one to begin with.

Why do I sometimes wake up at night and have an erection? This is completely natural and is called "sleep tumescence." It is a physiologic function triggered by some area of the brain and is not necessarily associated with erotic dreams. It is a phenomenon that is associated with, but not caused by, rapid eye movement (REM) sleep. Many physical problems can cause a loss of these erections. I believe that some emotional problems also can interfere with sleep erections. This is speculation and yet to be proved.

How does a full bladder cause erection? The erection and full bladder that you awaken with are only coincidental; one does not cause the other. It is your final sleep erection of the night. The bladder is full because you have not voided all night. In men with spinal cord injury, it is a real phenomenon and is called "interoceptive, reflex erection." Such a reflex can also be stimulated by rectal pressure in these people.

How do penis rings increase the pleasure of sexual activity? They do not, and they are *dangerous.* Constricting bands can cut off circulation and if left on too long will cause permanent damage to, and disfigurement of, the penis. The swelling they cause also may make it almost impossible to remove the band without anesthesia. Any advantage they may serve is purely psychological. I mention this practice only to condemn it.

Why do condoms interfere with sex? Condoms interfere with *pregnancy.* They interfere with sex only when you allow them to do so. The price for protection against pregnancy is some decrease in sensation of the skin of the penis. If a man is not mature enough to understand this or cannot pause for the few seconds it takes to put on a condom before ejaculating, then he must find a different method of birth control. The alternative is an unwanted baby.

At times when I am able to have more than one ejaculation, why does it take a while before I can have the second? This is a phenomenon called the refractory period. We really don't know the exact physiologic reason, but within limits of variability among different men of different ages, we know that this is completely natural. It is an integral part of the fourth or resolution phase of the human sexual response, described by Masters and Johnson. As we mention elsewhere in this chapter, aging lengthens the refractory period.

Should I take vitamin E? As my mother used to say, "It don't hurt." Unfortunately, it is expensive and has not been proved effective in either improving erectile ability or improving semen quality in humans. Rats with vitamin E deficiency have severely damaged testicles. Any improvement in your erections may purely be due to placebo effect. If there is really some physiologic mechanism, it has not been described yet.

What is the placebo effect? The placebo effect occurs when a person's expectations from, and emotional reactions to, a particular drug or other substance cause the person to experience an effect from that substance that is otherwise unexplainable. I mention this without value judgment. There are many situations in medicine in which the placebo effect has succeeded when more conventional therapy has failed.

The value judgment comes with how the placebo is administered. If it is given as a sincere effort to achieve a response when all other acceptable attempts have been made and done on a personal basis when other emotional support can be given, then it may be quite acceptable. If the placebo is given as a scheme for some vulture to profit from an unfortunate person's problem, then it is quite unacceptable. The prime example is packaging inexpensive multiple vitamins, charging three times the retail price, then marketing them as some magic potion!

What if my erection won't go away? There is a fairly uncommon condition called *priapism*, named after a Greek fertility god, Priapus. It is associated with a painful erection that lasts for many hours and sometimes days. The key to realizing that there is something wrong is that the erection persists despite the fact that there is *no erotic stimulation or pleasure and usually the penis hurts.* You should see your doctor promptly and not let such a condition go on for twelve or twenty-four hours. The risk is injury to the erectile tissue and loss of all future erections. Usually we do not know the cause; if treating it with cold compresses, or heating pads, or any other "conservative" measures is unsuccessful, surgery may be necessary. Such an operation is considered minor and is usually successful. The fear is that if the priapism has gone on too long, it can damage your ability to have erections in the future. This is, fortunately, the least common result. Some important conditions like sickle-cell anemia and leukemia can cause the problem, so for many reasons you should seek medical help if you suspect that you may have priapism.

Can I be fertile again if I have retrograde ejaculation? There is hope. If the sperms are ejaculated into the urinary bladder because of a nerve problem, then some medications will reverse the situation and restore normal ejaculation.

Medications such as the antihistamines (phenylpropanolamine) and the proper autonomic acting drugs (ephedrine or "alpha stimulators") are sometimes successful. If your doctor cannot restore your normal ejaculation, then there are methods of collecting the semen from the bladder and trying for a pregnancy by AIH (artificial insemination: homolagous or husband).

What is the importance of zinc? The highest concentration of zinc in the male body is in the prostate gland. There may be a correlation between lack of zinc and fertility problems. *Some* men have had improvement of their semen analysis after zinc treatment. Discuss this with your doctor if he or she recommends it to you.

Whether zinc plays a role in sexual dysfunction is controversial. Articles have been published both for and against this hypothesis. So far the medical literature says no and nutrition literature says yes. Unless you take too much (and I'm not sure we know how much is too much), you won't really harm yourself, but it will cost a lot of money for only questionable chance of success.

What are the benefits of circumcision? No real benefits exist when you examine the question very carefully. There are opinions, but no one has proved whether the foreskin plays any part in sexual performance. The question of hygiene is important, but that is a personal matter. A man who cleans his penis and foreskin carefully should not have any problems. Someone with poor hygiene habits will be dirty regardless of the state of his foreskin. If you have a condition that predisposes to infection like diabetes, then you may need circumcision if problems with your foreskin occur.

The most common foreskin problems are: (1) *phimosis*, or inability to retract the skin to expose the penis; (2) infection of the foreskin, called *balanitis*; and (3) *paraphimosis*, the inability to replace the foreskin in its normal position after it has been retracted over the glans penis. These all need medical attention quickly.

Some people claim that the foreskin causes cancer of the penis. I don't agree. Poor hygiene is more likely a causative factor. Cancer of the penis is rare; it occurs usually in men over seventy or eighty years old and is *almost* unheard of in circumcised men. In some populations where genital hygiene is almost a ritual, the incidence of cancer of the penis equals that of circumcised men. The same is true for cancer of the uterine cervix in their female sex partners.

Should I have my baby boy circumcised? Not for medical reasons and not as a routine thing. It is an operation and should be discussed with your doctor. If emotionally you still feel that you want it, you still have free choice. Ritual circumcision is also an emotional issue and cannot be debated on medical grounds. If your religion dictates it, and you are not harming your child, that is your choice. If you are still in doubt *talk to your clergy person.* There may be some aspects of the ritual that fulfill the "requirement" without having to submit your baby to a complete circumcision.

Is circumcision harmful? Not really. It is a small operation, more complicated when done later than in infancy. Because it is surgery, there are complications and risks (including severe injury to the penis) that you must discuss with your doctor before you can give a proper informed consent. The issue of whether newborn circumcisions should be done with or without anesthesia is beyond the scope of this work; however, they are topics under discussion.

Why can't we have simultaneous orgasms? The vast majority of couples do not have simultaneous orgasms, and those who do are not able to achieve them every time they try. It requires excellent control of ejaculation and prolonging erection until your partner is sufficiently aroused. It is definitely fun to have. The real goal, however, should be enjoyment and each partner helping the other to have his or her orgasm without giving up in frustration. So remember, if we all were meant to have simultaneous orgasms every time we tried, we all would have been born with on/off switches!

Is my penis smaller than normal? There is an entity called *micropenis*, which is a congenital anomalie (birth defect). It is very rare. Giving so-called normal measurements of the flaccid penis is of little value because of the tremendous variation among individuals. There is also variation in how much size change there will be from the relaxed to the erect state. Also, the depth of the vagina is variable. The woman's most sensitive areas around and in the vagina are close to the surface, and not very far into the vagina: the clitoris, the labia, and the roof of the vagina with the outer urethra above it (the G Spot area).

The most common cause of "too small" penis is obesity. The more fat that you accumulate on your lower abdomen, the more your penis will seem to retract into your body. The penis does not get fat. If you push in on the fat or feel the shaft of the penis deep into the fat, you will realize that your penis is normal size, just hidden while flaccid. Thus the solution to "lengthening" the flaccid penis (easy to say, tough to do) is to *lose some weight*.

Why do two men with the same condition function differently? The emotional component can work for and against successful sexual functioning. You may have some physical factor that impairs your sexual functioning. The emotional or social factor may overcome that and you may continue to enjoy sexual activity. On the other hand, if the emotional component is negative, it can turn the impairment into a complete disability. In addition to that, I emphasize that no two men or conditions are the same. What appears to be similar in two men may really be completely different. It is dangerous to try to measure up to someone else, especially via the "magic" of assumptions.

Isn't alcohol great for sex? Alcohol is a central nervous system depressant. In small amounts, it may relieve inhibitions and thereby alter your sexual performance. Alcohol is also one of the leading causes of sexual (erection and ejaculation), emotional, family, and medical problems. Physiologically it depresses brain function and sexual desire, impairs reflexes, and decreases testosterone. The long-term ill effects of alcohol overuse on mental, physical, sexual, etc. functions are many and well known.

Is my doctor crazy? He wants us to use sperm from a stranger? Well, your doctor may indeed be crazy, but the statement above does not make him so. AID (artificial insemination: donor) is widely available. It does not involve sex with a (proper or improper) stranger. It does not involve any chance of fertilization by some life form other than human. It does not involve pain. It does involve some expense and time. It is done in the gynecologist's office. Sperm banks screen and categorize the donor's sperm precisely. They keep detailed health, intelligence, occupational, genetic, physical feature, and religious information about each donor. When your doctor orders the frozen sperm for you, they make every effort to be sure that the match is very close, and more often than not the baby has some "family resemblance" to the non-blood-related father.

This is a viable and rational alternative. Consider it if your doctor makes the recommendation.

What is the preejaculate? The drops of watery fluid that seep out of the urethra during arousal and plateau stages of sexual excitement are from Cowper's glands (bulbourethral). Unless there were sperm in the urethra already, there are no sperm in this fluid. Whether you can get a woman pregnant with this fluid really depends on whether you have had a very recent previous ejaculation and how skillfully you can use the withdrawal method. I would not recommend withdrawal as a dependable form of contraception because there is not much room for error.

When is it "normal" to be unable to achieve or maintain an erection? At times there are obvious stresses and distractions. Upcoming examinations in school, deadlines or problems at work, fatigue, anger, etc., are all common conditions that interfere with sexual desire or performance. It is called situational erectile dysfunction and essentially cures itself when the stressful situation abates. The danger, as with so many other problems, comes from having too great an emotional reaction and not keeping things in perspective. If you don't stop to think and realize why you are not up to par, you may be on the way to trouble.

What percent of sexual performance problems are associated with emotional problems? I must say first that 100 percent of sexual performance problems are associated with some emotional component, whether it be cause or effect. In our experience with 300 patients, approximately one-third have predominantly or exclusively emotional difficulties, one-third have predominantly physiologic problems, and one-third have a significant combination of the two. Our patient population is mostly between fifty and seventy years old. In general, the younger the population, the less common is the incidence of medical problems causing sexual difficulties.

Are there such things as aphrodisiacs? Aphrodisiac is the name given to any substance that supposedly stimulates the libido (sexual desire). Improvement in sexual performance, if any, is secondary. There are many drugs that affect the male hormone system or autonomic nervous system. Classically, administration of testosterone, especially to men who are deficient in it, increases sexual desire. Other substances that counteract the sexual ill effects of medical conditions or of medications may also improve desire. Libido is extremely sensitive to the emotional state and, therefore, your brain can stimulate or suppress it according to your feelings, etc., at any particular time. This makes libido very vulnerable to placebo effect.

Is it normal to have sex more than once during a lovemaking session? There is no "normal" answer here, either. Some men do; some don't. It is harmful to try to hold yourself up to some imagined ideal.

What are the accessory sex glands? The accessory sex glands are the prostate, seminal vesicles, and Cowper's (bulbourethral) glands. Their function is to provide the fluid delivery system, storage, and nourishment of the sperm. The sperm are incapable of swimming or impregnating an ovum if they have not been mixed with the seminal fluid.

What is the normal number of times per month to have sex? There is no such number. Whatever you desire and whatever influences are affecting you at a particular time will determine what is right for you.

Can my penis be injured during intercourse? Yes, but it is extremely rare and hardly worth the energy spent in worrying about it. Be gentle.

Is it possible that my sex problems are coming from the medicine my doctor prescribed? Certainly, but to a variable degree. The important factors to consider are the amount and frequency of the medicine and the severity of your condition. There are very few medicines that universally eliminate the ability to perform sexually. The above factors, combined with any emotional and/or relationship problems will determine how much or how little a particular drug affects a particular individual. Never be afraid to ask your doctor about the side effects of any medications he or she has prescribed. The *Physician's Desk Reference* is a complete source from which you can get a great deal of information about medications. Just remember, however, that this book is an exhaustive list of side effects and can be alarming if you don't discuss your findings with someone like your physician who can help you interpret what you have read.

Which street drugs help sex the most? None! Amphetamines may energize, but they also directly affect the autonomic nervous system and thereby can interfere with erection, ejaculation, and orgasm. Heroin causes ejaculation problems in the vast majority of users. It also causes loss of erection, and especially, loss of sexual desire. Methadone's action is similar to heroin's. Marijuana can lower the blood level of testosterone when used over long periods of time. It does not enhance erection or ejaculation and does alter the user's subjective perceptions of his sexual performance. Cocaine inhibits ejaculation. For cocaine and other addictive substances, chronic use becomes a way of life. It ceases to be a "leisure time sport" and instead becomes a substitute for many everyday activities. There are too many other drugs to mention. Be assured that with all the scientists, as well as entrepreneurs, in medicine, if any of the street drugs were useful, we would have found a way to refine it or in some way make it available.

CHAPTER 25

Understanding Your Female Body

Sharon Phelan, M.D.

In the following chapter, the uniqueness and complexities of the female reproductive systems will be explored in both their physical and emotional dimensions. The emotional and physical upheaval of puberty, through sexual activity, pregnancy prevention, pregnancy, and the medical issues related to these topics will be addressed. The focus will be on information that women will find useful in understanding themselves and in leading healthy sexual lives.

ANATOMY

Although the breasts serve only the function of producing milk for offspring (this is a trait that makes us mammals), they have acquired a great deal of sexual connotation. As part of their place as a "sexual organ" they have many names: tits, boobs, peaches, etc. Many young women and men get wrapped up in the mysticism of breasts and their size. Thus a woman's breasts, much like her weight, may be perceived as either too large or too small—whatever that means. The size of a woman's breasts has little to do with their ability to function in breastfeeding. One needs to remember that the majority of the breast tissue is *fat*.

Nonetheless, many women feel less about themselves because of their breast size. One solution chosen by some women is breast augmentation (enlargement), which now is a common procedure. It used to be done by injecting silicon into the breast. This method had many problems, including sagging and lumps as the silicon shifted. Now physicians use a plastic envelope that is slipped between the chest wall and the breast tissue and then filled with fluid (often water). This does require surgery. This method allows a woman to breastfeed, do breast self-exams, etc. A woman with particularly large breasts may have problems with posture or have chronic back pain due to the strain created by her EE bra. These women may elect to have breast-reduction surgery.

The other real concern is that of breast cancer. It is estimated that one in seven women will experience breast cancer. These risks are compounded if a person's mother or sister has had breast cancer. The breast self-exam (BSE) as described by the American Cancer Association should be learned and performed monthly by all women after the age of 18. (See pamphlet on pages 258 and 259.)

The external genitalia, or sexual structures, of a woman consist of the mons, the labia majorum, the labia minorum, and the clitoris. These areas rarely have any major

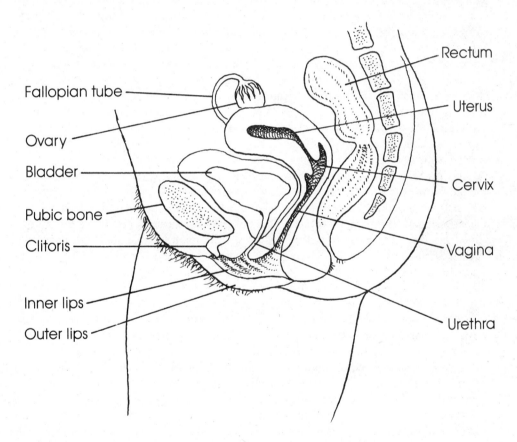

Figure 1. Female internal sexual and reproductive organs, side view.

problems during the reproductive years. The primary problems revolve around infections, especially sexually transmitted infections such as venereal warts, syphilis, or herpes, or common skin problems such as acne (pimples), eczema, etc.

The internal reproductive organs consist of the vagina, uterus (with cervix), fallopian tubes, and ovaries. The vagina is a potential space or tube. In other words, it is collapsed closed (like a glove without a hand in it) unless something is in it—tampon, speculum, penis, or infant. It has the ability to expand greatly, especially for childbirth. In short, no one has a vagina that is truly too small. If there appears to be difficulty inserting items (i.e., a tampon) into the vagina, it is most commonly due to tight muscles at the opening of the vagina. Occasionally it may be due to a hymen that is more developed than the average. (See the section on "Vaginismus" in Chapter 22.)

The main problems a woman may experience with her vagina are infections. These generally are yeast (candida), trichmoniasis, or gardnerella. Since these are common problems, it is worth devoting some time to review the most common forms of vaginitis.

Candida (yeast, monilia) is probably the most frequent type of infection. Women can get it from many different things. It is truly not a sexually transmitted disease, so it rarely helps much to treat the partner. The main thing that will cause a woman to be more likely to get yeast infections is a change in the normal, healthy bacteria in the vagina. Such things as using antibiotics, douching frequently, diabetes, or alteration in the normal hormonal levels may promote a yeast infection. The common symptoms are severe itching, a vaginal discharge that looks like cottage cheese, and a red area around the vagina. Yeast infections are usually treated with a cream or suppositories in the vagina. Sometimes if a person keeps getting them over and over again other tests or treatments may be necessary.

Gardnerella (hemophilus, nonspecific) vaginitis is also a common infection. Although it can be acquired other ways than sexually, once one person has it the partner may also catch it. For this reason it is becoming more common for a physician to treat the woman and her partner, especially if she is having repeated episodes of infections. The symptoms are milder than the yeast, with the main complaints being a creamy vaginal discharge and an odor (often fishy). Men rarely have any symptoms. Treatment varies from uses of creams in the vagina for mild cases to pills of ampicillen or metronidazole for more severe or recurrent cases.

The last type of vaginitis to be discussed is trichmoniasis (trich). This is not truly a bacteria. Although this also can be acquired from ways other than sexual intercourse, the most common means of acquiring it is having intercourse with someone who has it. The symptoms will range from nothing (just found on a routine pap smear) to severe itching, discharge, bleeding between periods, and pain with urination. Men, again, commonly will not have symptoms. Since this organism can also be in the bladder, the best treatment is metronidazole pills taken orally.

The cervix (mouth of the uterus) and the uterus (womb) take an active role in reproduction. Since the uterus is where the fertilized ovum implants and develops, it must have the ability to develop a lining that will nourish the developing embryo until

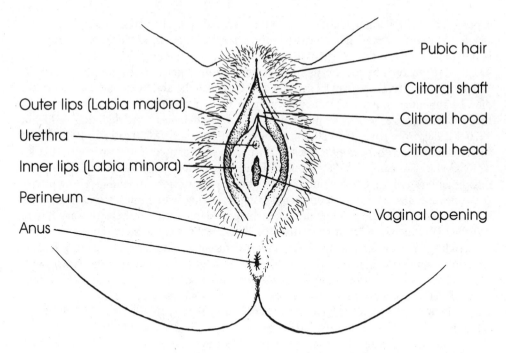

Outer lips (Labia majora)

Urethra

Inner lips (Labia minora)

Perineum

Anus

Pubic hair

Clitoral shaft

Clitoral hood

Clitoral head

Vaginal opening

Figure 2. External female genitalia.

the actual placenta forms, enlarge to hold the infant(s), and yet be able to push the infant out during labor. If a pregnancy does not occur, the uterus must sense this and shed the old lining and prepare a new one that will be appropriately timed to the development of the egg (ovum). The cervix in turn must be favorable to sperm transport during the fertile time in a woman's cycle and nonconducive to transport at other times. It must be able to remain closed during pregnancy until labor, when it needs to open from a channel that is approximately one-quarter-inch wide or less to four inches across, and then revert to the original state. The uterus and cervix's ability to do this comes from the special muscle cells that make them up as well as their response to other hormones within the body.

The fallopian tubes in the past were thought to be basically a pipe or tube to guide the ovum from the ovary to the uterus. We now know that not only do the tubes serve as a path for transportation, but they also actively move the egg along; they nourish the egg, and the fimbriated (fingerlike) end of the tube sweeps the egg off the ovary and down the tube. The two common diseases of the fallopian tubes that are especially important to women in the reproductive age are ectopic pregnancies and salpingitis.

Ectopic pregnancy is the occurrence of a pregnancy somewhere other than the uterus. The most common site is the tube. Were this to occur, the woman would experience pain in her lower abdomen that is severe during early pregnancy (first twelve weeks). On pelvic exam, her uterus would be smaller than expected for her length of pregnancy, implying that perhaps the pregnancy is elsewhere. Since the tube is not prepared to enlarge like the uterus, it will often rupture like an overfilled water balloon. When this happens there may be massive bleeding into the abdomen and a woman may die. Treatment involves emergency surgery to remove the pregnancy and sometimes the fallopian tubes as well. The number of ectopic pregnancies more than doubled from 1970 to 1980, from fewer than 20,000 cases in 1970, to over 50,000 cases in 1980. Black woman and women between the ages of thirty-five and forty-four are especially at risk.

Salpingitis means an inflammation of the tube (*salping-* means tubes, *-itis* means inflammation) with the most common cause being an infection. Infections of the uterus and tubes are most commonly contracted (caught) during sexual intercourse with some-one who has the infection. If the infection spreads to involve the tube and ovary it may be called PID (pelvic inflammatory disease). This means that the pus from the infection is spreading into the abdomen. The two most common causes for this type of infection are gonorrhea and chlamydia. Both of these are caught from having intercourse with someone with the infection. Gonorrhea usually causes severe pain early in the development of PID, so sometimes it can be treated before much damage is done.

Chlamydia, on the other hand, may smolder quietly with few or no symptoms to warn the woman that severe damage is being done. Thus a woman may not discover she has the infection until too late to prevent damage. Salpingitis may cause scarring on or around the tubes. This scarring may in turn increase the risk of recurrent infections and more scarring, ectopic pregnancies, or the inability to get pregnant at all (infertility). The treatment for PID is antibiotics. These may be given by shot or pills, but often in bad cases are given for many days through the vein in the hospital. Sometimes even surgery is necessary with removal of the organs involved (possibly the uterus, tubes, and both ovaries.) When we discuss contraceptives you will see that some methods increase this risk and others seem to protect against it.

The final reproductive organs to be discussed are the ovaries. These are the female gonad. The ovaries are the structures that produce the ova (eggs). Unlike the testicles of the males that are constantly producing sperm from puberty until death (although the number may decrease with age), the ovaries mature only one or two a month for approximately thirty-five to forty years (puberty to menopause). This monthly cycle is based on a very complex interaction of the two hormones from the ovary (estrogen and progesterone) and the pituitary and its hormones.

A woman is born with all the eggs she will ever have, and in fact, a large number of these die before puberty. She still will have, however, many hundreds of thousands left at puberty. Yet, after only thirty-five years ovulating, or 420 cycles (35 times 12 months/year) she appears to run out and enter menopause (the change). Humans are the only animal to experience this change. No one truly knows what causes or controls or dictates this phase of a woman's life.

MENSTRUAL CYCLE

Again, the uniqueness of the female system relies on the cycling of the hormones. At the beginning of each menstrual cycle (just as the menstrual flow is ending) the pituitary (gland at the base of the brain) sends a signal to the ovary via hormones to start maturing an egg (ovum). Initially, a number of eggs start maturing, but in a classic example of the survival of the fittest there emerges only one. As it is maturing, it in turn signals the pituitary of its progress via a hormone called estrogen. Once it is developed, the pituitary clicks on its "cycling" center that will send a burst of a hormone called Lh. This causes the follicle (cyst) where the egg is developing to rupture and release the egg to be picked up by the fimbra of the tube (ovulation). Now while the system is waiting to find out if fertilization took place (it will happen within twenty-four hours of the release of the ovum), the ovary starts producing two hormones: estrogen and progesterone.

These hormones change the lining of the uterus that has been built up by the estrogen in the first half of the cycle to a lining that can nourish the embryo. If pregnancy does not occur, the ovary stops making the hormones about ten to twelve days after ovulation (egg release) and the lining of the uterus is shed (a period). If a pregnancy occurs, then the embryo implants about seven days after the egg was released (about seven days before the woman expects her period). The developing embryo is also developing the placenta. The placental cells quickly start making a hormone (HcG) that signals the ovary and the pituitary that there is a pregnancy and to keep making the progesterone and estrogen that will maintain the uterine lining. In fact, pregnancy tests test for this HcG hormone. A blood test can easily detect it as soon as a woman realizes her period is late.

LIFE CYCLES: PUBERTY AND THE REPRODUCTIVE YEARS

When a female infant is born, she has all her sexual organs and all the cells destined to become ova (eggs). Yet, as we know, the reproductive system is not working yet: It slowly turns on during puberty. The sequence of puberty is fairly constant for most young girls.

In the early stages of puberty, the adrenal glands (just above each kidney) start making androgens (malelike hormones), which initiate the growth of pubic and axillary hair. This starts at approximately age ten. At about the same time, the breasts start to bud (enlarge). This is followed by a growth spurt about one year later. Remember how in fifth and sixth grade class pictures the back rows were all girls? This spurt in turn is followed a year later by menarche (starting periods) and eventually, by full development of breasts and pubic hair and by a widening of the hips.

Breast Self-Examination
BSE: Not For Women Only

Step 1: **Inspection**

A. **In Front of a Mirror**
Look for any change in the size or shape of the breast, puckering or dimpling of the skin or changes in the nipple.

B. **Inspect in Three Positions**
- With arms relaxed at sides.
- With arms held overhead.
- With hands on hips pressing in to contract the chest muscles. Turn from side to side to view all areas.

C. **Nipple Examination**
Gently squeeze the nipple of each breast between your thumb and index finger, looking for any nipple discharge.

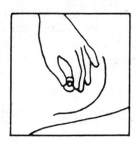

Step 2: **Palpation or Feeling**
A. **In Shower or Bath**
Fingers will glide over wet soapy skin, making it easier to feel any changes in the breasts. Check the breast for a lump, knot, tenderness or for any change in the normal consistency of breast tissue.

To examine your right breast, put your right hand behind your head, with the pads of your finger of your left hand held flat and together, gently press on the breast tissue using small circular motions. Imagine the breast as the face of a clock. Begin at the top, 12 o'clock and so on, making a circle around the outer area of the breast. Move in one finger width, continue in smaller and smaller circles until you have reached the nipple. Cover all areas including the breast tissue leading to the arm pit. Reverse the procedure for the left breast.

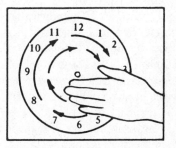

At the lower border of each breast, a ridge of firm tissue may be felt. This is normal.

B. Underarm Examination
Examine the left underarm area with your arm held loosely at your side. Cup the fingers of the opposite hand and insert them high into the underarm area. Draw fingers down slowly, pressing in a circular pattern, covering all areas. Reverse the procedure for the right underarm.

C. Lying Down
While lying flat, place a small pillow or folded towel under the right shoulder. Examine the right breast using the same circular motion as was used in the shower. Cover all areas. Repeat this procedue for the left breast.

Press firmly but gently while examining your breast, rolling the tissue between your fingers and the chest wall.

*The authors wish to thank the American Cancer Society for their permission to reprint this pamphlet entitled "BSE: Not for Women Only."

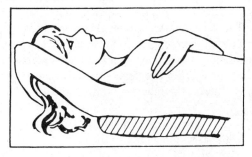

This sequence of events represents a gradual awakening of the hormone centers in the brain. What turns them on is uncertain. It may be a crucial weight or variation of weight to height. It is known that strenuous physical activity (olympic-level gymnast) or severe starvation (anorexia nervosa) will disturb this development and may even temporarily stop it. Although most young women start menstruation by ages twelve and thirteen, it is not uncommon for it to be later, especially if the whole series of changes starts later. However, a young woman who has not started undergoing the changes of puberty by age sixteen or who has experienced more than a two-year delay in the sequence of steps should see a physician to evalute for possible problems. Menstruation before the age of eight is known as precocious puberty. Although 90 percent of the time there is nothing wrong, sometimes this can represent a serious problem and needs to be evaluated.

The female reproductive system is an incredibly complex and delicately balanced system. Unlike most other human hormonal systems including the male reproductive system, the female reproductive hormones *cycle*. This system, on the surface, may not appear unique, but all other systems are geared to maintain a relatively constant flow or functioning. This need to cycle, in the functioning of the pituitary, the ovary, and the uterus, makes the female reproductive cycle very susceptible to outside forces.

These outside forces can include physical stress (surgery, losing weight), emotional stress (death in the family, wedding), and medications including oral contraceptives (the pill). What a woman may experience includes missing periods (amenorrhea: *a-* absence of, *-meno-* periods, *-rrhea* flow) or irregular menses where there is no ovulation. When this happens, it often means that her hormones are not going through their normal cycling—but instead are stuck at one point—just like the male hormone system. Without the cycling, an egg is not developed or released; thus the uterus gets mixed signals or no signal concerning when to shed its lining, and amenorrhea or irregular menses (sometimes called DUB for dysfunctional uterine bleeding) may result. Generally very little needs to be done for the younger woman in these cases. The main issue is to rule out pregnancy (still one of the most common causes of a missed period) or a tumor (abnormal growth not necessarily cancer) on the uterus, ovaries, or brain. If everything seems normal, then a physician can often give a woman a medication that may give her system a shove to start it cycling again.

The other major issue at this age (early teens through mid-forties) is pregnancy. Considering the complexity of things that need to happen for a pregnancy to occur, it is surprising that anyone ever does get pregnant. But we do. In fact, 15 to 20 percent of teenage girls get pregnant the first month they become sexually active. For a pregnancy to occur, the following must happen:

1. The sperm (in sufficiently large numbers) must be deposited close enough to the cervix (opening to the uterus) so that they can swim up through the cervical canal.

2. The cervical canal (passageway into the uterus) must be filled with a mucus that will allow the sperm to move up into the uterus (this occurs for only 3 to 4 days each month).

3. They (the sperm) then need to find the way to the tubal openings. Chance again plays a role since there are usually two tubes but only one leads to the ovary that is ovulating. This is because usually a woman releases only one egg per cycle. (Nonidentical twins occur when a woman gets pregnant during a cycle when she released two eggs.)

4. The hardiest of the sperm then make it to the ampulla, or far end of the tube, and hunt for the egg. They can hang around for about two or three days before they die.

5. If an ovum does appear, then one sperm will penetrate the outer coat of the egg and fertilize it. If the egg is not fertilized, it will die within twenty-four hours and dissolve. Also, it is the sperm that determines if the fertilized egg will develop into a boy or a girl.

6. The fertilized egg then starts dividing into many cells as it undergoes its five to seven day journey down the tube.

7. When it arrives in the uterus, the egg is now a small ball of many cells. It quickly attaches itself to the endometrium (the lining of the uterus) and starts developing into the placenta, fetus, and "bag of water," or amniotic sac.

8. As this development occurs, these cells secrete a hormone called HcG. This signals the ovary that a pregnancy has occurred and not to allow the uterine lining to be shed. Pregnancy tests (both urine and blood) test for HcG.

Any disruption of this sequence either planned, deliberate, or accidental may prevent pregnancy. All forms of birth control (contraception) are based on interference with this sequence. More on contraception will follow later. Also, couples experiencing infertility (inability to get pregnant) may have problems in one or more of these areas. An increasingly common cause of infertility is tubal damage or scarring. This is usually due to infection. These infections (including gonorrhea and chlamydia) are usually sexually transmitted (acquired from sexual contact with someone who has the disease). The more people a woman has sex with, the greater the chance that she may contract one of these infections. It may take only one infection to totally destroy a woman's ability to get pregnant or even to kill her. Lesser damage may allow the tiny sperm to get up to the egg but not allow the larger egg to get to the uterus; the result may be an ectopic (tubal) pregnancy. This is a very serious problem: when the pregnancy gets too large, the tube ruptures and the woman starts bleeding into her abdomen (belly). Women can bleed to death from this rupture if they don't receive immediate medical attention.

Two other serious infections are viral, herpes and condyloma. Neither one of these, especially herpes, is truly curable. The herpes virus will hide in the nerves and periodically express itself by the symptoms of pain and a sore. If a baby is born through a vagina with an active infection, it may catch it and then has a 50 percent chance of dying from it. Condyloma (wart) virus doesn't seem to have the serious consequences for an infant but can be serious for the woman. It now appears that certain groups of this virus may cause, or at least increase, the risk, of cancer of the cervix (see Chapter 20).

This stage in a woman's life (the onset of sexual activity, or age 18, whichever comes first) marks the time when she should start getting routine health checks. This should include a pap smear (checks for cervical cancer), pelvic exam, blood pressure, and breast exam. Also gonorrhea cultures, blood counts (checking for anemia), and urinalysis may be done in some cases. This routine is an important habit to establish since it will allow many illnesses, diseases, and problems to be detected early when they are more easily treated. Deaths from cervical cancer are becoming increasingly uncommon because of the practice of performing annual pap smears. Annual breast exams and, better yet, breast self-exams are allowing precancer and early breast cancers to be detected and treated at a stage when they may be curable.

Many women have heard terrible things about pelvic exams—how embarrassing they are, how much they hurt, how you can have them only if you have had sexual intercourse. Most of these stories are just that—stories. A pelvic exam is a simple procedure that doesn't need to hurt. It involves two parts: 1) looking at the vagina and cervix using an instrument called a speculum and 2) feeling the uterus and ovaries and sometimes the rectum.

To allow the examiner (this may be a physician or a nurse practitioner) to see and feel better, the woman lies on her back on the exam table with her legs supported by footrests (called stirrups) and her buttocks next to the end of the table. The examiner will then carefully look on the outside, checking to see that the hair pattern is normal and that there are no lumps, bumps, or discharge. In order to see inside the vagina to check for a discharge, to see the cervix, and to do a pap, it is necessary to use a speculum. A speculum is a small plastic or metal instrument that is slipped into the vagina like a tampon. It comes in different sizes depending on the woman. The examiner can then gently open the speculum, spread the vagina walls apart, and see inside. The main reason that this may be uncomfortable is that sometimes a woman may tighten her muscles. This makes the opening to the vagina smaller and thus makes it harder to get the speculum in. Once the speculum is in place, most woman feel no discomfort.

A pap smear involves using a wooden spatula (looks like a funny-shaped popsicle stick) to rub off some of the surface cells on the cervix. Many women cannot feel this, and others feel only a firm rubbing. After getting the pap smear, the speculum is slipped out of the vagina. Then the examiner slips one or two fingers into the vagina and places the other hand on the belly. Now with the use of both hands it is usually possible for the examiner to feel the cervix, uterus, and ovaries. This involves firm pressure but again, especially if the woman can keep her abdominal wall muscles relaxed, it doesn't need to hurt.

Some women are embarrassed by this type of exam. A woman should be no more embarrassed than if her heart or lungs or throat were being examined. Nonetheless, some women find it easier, especially for their first examinations, to see a woman physician or nurse practitioner.

CONTRACEPTION

Health maintenance for many women also includes the use of contraception, which allows a woman to space her pregnancies in a way that best promotes her mental and physical well-being. All women who are sexually active should exercise this right and responsibility to take control of this aspect of their lives. Nowadays there are many methods of contraception. The key issue is that each method is only as good as one makes it. If the method isn't used consistently and correctly, it won't work.

Women and couples give many reasons for not using birth control. Listed below are a few of them. The crucial question is: Do they want a child at this time? If the answer is no, a method should be used. The following are reasons and excuses for the misuse or nonuse of birth control.

- Denial. One denies having sex. People may deny this to themselves, but their anatomy won't be fooled and pregnancy may occur.
- Love. "I love you so much I am willing to have your baby." Fine if one is really prepared for a child.
- Guilt. If individuals are ashamed that they are having sex, they may have difficulty letting anyone else know, and to get contraception, someone will know even if it is only the clerk at the drug store.
- Shame. Some people are ashamed of not knowing everything, especially about sex and birth control, or of having sex at all.
- Gamesmanship. The one who uses or doesn't use birth control may feel that he or she has some control of the relationship.
- Hostility. Getting pregnant may be a way that an immature woman may use to get even with her lover, husband, parents, society, or herself.
- Masochism. An unwanted pregnancy may be a woman's attempt to punish herself for having sex.
- Eroticism. The risk of pregnancy is exciting to some couples—sort of like Russian roulette.
- Nihilism. Some women feel that they have no control over any part of their life.

- Fear and Anxiety. A woman may be frightened of the risks or dangers of the methods of contraception (these are usually exaggerated in the media) or that someone may find out she is using contraception and hence must be having sex.
- Abortion Available. Fortunately, very few women use abortion as their method of birth control.
- Opportunism. The opportunity to be intimate presents itself when the couple is not prepared.
- Iatrogenic. Occasionally a woman will be using a method (like birth control pills to clear up acne) and the physician will stop it for medical reasons (her acne is better) and forget to see if she needs it for birth control and/or prescribe another method.

It is hoped that couples will act responsibly and use a reliable method of contraception. Of the many current methods available, some are worthless, and others are excellent. Some will work best for some women: individual preferences differ enormously. Each couple needs to decide what is best for them at that particular time in their lives.

Unreliable methods include hope, withdrawal (pulling out before coming), douching (washing the vagina out right after intercourse), and the calendar rhythm method (trying to figure out when one is going to release an egg). It is best if a couple adopts another form of pregnancy prevention.

Spermicidal agents (chemicals that kill sperm) are among the reliable methods available. They are sold as wax suppositories that are placed in the vagina to melt and as foam or cream that is inserted in the vagina. The chemicals in the products kill the sperm before they can get into the cervical canal. They must be placed in the vagina just before the couple has sex, however, or they will not work. The theoretical effectiveness (if it is used every time and correctly) is 95 percent. This means only 5 women out of 100 will get pregnant if they use this method. The problem is that people do not use it correctly, and so the effectiveness in actual use is 75 percent. It is a good form of contraception since it does not require a prescription to get, and it helps to protect from sexually transmitted diseases.

A new variation of the spermicides is the contraceptive sponge. It is a small specially shaped sponge that is placed in the vagina next to the cervix and comes saturated with a spermicide as well. Thus, when a couple have sex, the spermicide kills the sperm and the sponge soaks up the ejaculant. Because the sponge holds the spermicide, it can be inserted up to twenty-four hours before having sex. Otherwise the advantages, disadvantages, and effectiveness are the same as the other spermicides.

Condoms are one of the only forms of reversible contraception that a male can use. They consist of a thin latex or animal membrane device that slips over the erect penis. A small space needs to be left at the top of the condom, if one is not built into it, to collect the ejaculant. After the man comes, he needs to withdraw his penis from his partner while holding on to the condom before he becomes soft (loses his erection). Since more men are wanting to participate in using birth control, condoms are becoming increasingly popular. They now come in colors, with ribs, lubrication or none, and other variations; they come in only one size.

Condoms are beneficial in that they allow the man to participate in preventing a pregnancy and thus show he cares. They also protect from many of the sexually transmitted infections. Finally, they do not require a prescription. However, some men refuse to use them because they supposedly decrease the sensations. Other man say they like this effect because they don't come as quickly. Yet other men feel that a *real man* doesn't use condoms. What is a real man? Is he a man who cares about and takes care of the people he is with? The theoretical effectiveness of condoms is 98 percent, but since many couples don't or won't use them every time, the use effectiveness is only 80 to 90 percent. Their effectiveness is increased when they are used in combination with one of the spermicides mentioned earlier.

These are the only reliable nonprescription methods. The remaining methods that will be discussed require a prescription, and thus a visit to a clinic or doctor.

The diaphragm is analogous to the condom in that it is a thin latex dome that is inserted into the vagina, over the cervix. It provides a barrier to prevent the sperm from passing through the cervical canal. It doesn't have as tight a fit as a condom, however, so the woman also needs to use a cream or jelly spermicide with the diaphragm. Diaphragms come in different sizes and so must be fitted by a physician. It is inserted no more than two hours before sex and is not removed for at least six hours after sex. It is inserted and removed much like a tampon. The diaphragm also partially protects from sexually transmitted diseases. The problems with the diaphragm include: 1) may cause allergies; 2) the woman must insert and remove it; 3) the spermicide tastes bad; and the diaphragm may cause some women to get bladder infections. The theoretical effectiveness is 98 percent, but again the use effectiveness is lower (85 to 95 percent). It won't work if it is left in the dresser drawer.

The IUD (intrauterine device) is a small plastic shape that is placed in the endometrial cavity (inside the uterus). There it is thought to help prevent the sperm from getting up to the tubes and the egg, if fertilized, from implanting in the uterus. This ability is due to the IUD irritating the uterine lining. Some IUDs contain copper or hormones along with the plastic as an attempt to make them work better. Since the IUD comes in different shapes and sizes and must be inserted, a woman must go to a clinic or physican to get one. The good thing is, once it is in, the woman has to do very little else to prevent pregnancy. It is recommended that she check to see if the IUD is in place by feeling for the thin string attached to the IUD that hangs out of the cervical opening. Although the IUD is an excellent method of contraception with a theoretical effectiveness of 95 to 98 percent and a use effectiveness of 90 to 94 percent, there are some important disadvantages and complications in its use.

Because it is in the uterus, it mainly protects from pregnancies in the uterus and not in the fallopian tubes. Thus, if women with IUDs get pregnant they are more likely to have it in a tube. Also, if they get pregnant in the uterus with an IUD in place, there is an increased risk of miscarriage or serious infection. For this reason the IUD should be removed at once if the woman is pregnant and if the string is still visible.

The other major complications with the IUD are infections of the uterus and tubes. Since the IUD works like a foreign body (think of a splinter in a finger), once there is an infection the body cannot fight it well unless the IUD is removed. Also, there seems to be a greater chance of bacteria moving up into the uterus to cause infections. Since even one infection may prevent a woman from ever having a baby, most physicians would prefer not to use an IUD in a woman who has not had children, especially if she has more than one sex partner (this is a major risk for infections). In fact, two studies reported in 1985 that the IUD doubles a woman's risk of infertility.

Finally, minor problems with the IUD include heavier menses with more cramping. Sometimes the uterus pushes the IUD out, thus eliminating any protection it can give. Therefore, although the IUD has some major advantages, the risks and complications make it not the best method of contraception for many women.

The final reversible form of contraception is the pill. In medical circles it is called the oral contraceptive pill (OCP). It is a combination of the two hormones that the body normally makes—estrogen and progesterone. By taking these two hormones, a woman fools her body into thinking she is already pregnant. When the body senses this, it will not release another egg, and if the woman doesn't ovulate, she cannot get pregnant. This protection relies on taking the medication as instructed. Missing even one pill may allow the body to realize it is not pregnant, ovulate, and thus allow the woman to get pregnant for real. This is one of the most reliable forms of birth control since the use effectiveness is 95 to 99 percent and the theoretical effectiveness is 99.8 percent. There are, however, major disadvantages as well as advantages that make it necessary for this to be a prescription medication (requires seeing a physician). It is important for a woman to be aware of the risks and benefits of the method before she decides whether or not to use it.

The disadvantages associated with the pill are commonly known owing to articles in various magazines and numerous news reports. Most of these are minor and are the same (although usually less severe) as the problems with pregnancy—nausea, vomiting, tender breasts, fluid retention, temporary weight gain, increase in blood pressure, and gall bladder problems. Most women do not experience these, and for those that do, the problem can often be eliminated by changing the strength of the pill or waiting a few months for the problems to go away.

Since the hormones in the pills can make certain problems and illnesses worse, it is important for the woman to be screened for these diseases. If she has them, or a tendency for them, she should consider another form of contraception. A partial list is as follows:

Blood clots associated with pregnancy or using the pill
Severe high blood pressure

Badly damaged liver

Cancer of the breast or uterus

History of a stroke

Diabetes

Heart disease

Severe depression

Over thirty-five and a heavy smoker

It is important to remember, as well, all the good things about the pill, and there are many:

Excellent method of contraception.

Decreases amount of menses; thus decreases risk of anemia.

Decreases menstrual cramps.

Improves acne.

Prevents many of the sexually transmitted diseases from getting up into the uterus and tubes; thus helps protect future fertility.

Protects from breast and uterine cancer.

Eliminates ovulation pain and prevents the formation of many ovarian cysts.

Protects from endometriosis, which is a disease that makes many women infertile.

The pill prevents more illness and disease than it causes. It is much safer to take the pill than it is to get pregnant.

There are also permanent ways to prevent pregnancy. These include vasectomy (for men: removing a small section of the tube leading from the testes to the penis) and a tubal ligation (for women: removing a section of the fallopian tube to prevent the sperm from reaching the egg). Sterilization is becoming one of the most popular forms of contraception. This is partly due to the relative safety of the procedures, as well as couples having fewer children and having them earlier in their lives.

In women, since the tube is inside the abdomen, a tubal sterilization does require surgery and thus has more risks than a vasectomy. The two most common ways of doing a tubal sterilization are either by laparoscopy or a mini-laparotomy. A laparoscopy involves filling the abdomen with gas and then inserting two tubes into the belly. One tube has fiber optics that allows the physician to see in the abdomen: the other holds whatever is going to be used to destroy a portion of the tube. That can include a clip, a rubber band, or most commonly, a clamp that passes electricity to cauterize (burn) the tube. The second method involves cutting a larger incision in the belly (about the size commonly used for an appendectomy). Each tube is grabbed, tied in two places and a portion cut out.

Tubal sterilization should be considered permanent, although about 1 in 500 women who have had their tubes "tied" will get pregnant. There is surgery that can attempt to reconnect the tubes after a tubal ligation. This surgery is very expensive, very meticulous, and may not work. Thus, a woman should not have her tubes tied unless she truly never wants any further pregnancies.

The following section answers questions that are often asked about a variety of issues.

Are legal abortions safe? First, a brief editorial comment. Any time a woman finds herself in a position where she is considering an abortion, it means there has been a failure: a failure to use a reliable form of contraception consistently; failure of society to educate people adequately in the area of sexuality and contraception; or perhaps a failure of a method of contraception itself.

Now back to the question. Yes, legal abortions are medically safe. In fact, it is safer to have an abortion than it is to carry a pregnancy to term and deliver. The earlier an abortion is done, the safer it is. The main medical risks are those of infection, bleeding, and injury to the uterus or cervix. The first two risks can usually be handled easily by antibiotics, iron supplement, or occasionally by a blood transfusion. The last risk (injury) is more subtle and often not as obvious. There is a concern that the more procedures a woman undergoes, especially abortions after twelve to thirteen weeks, the more chance that the cervix or uterus may be damaged, thus making it more difficult to get pregnant or possibly hold on to the pregnancy.

The final issue is: What does having an abortion mean to the woman emotionally? This is an issue only she can decide. In fact, this probably is a more important consideration than the medical concerns mentioned above.

Just before her periods my girlfriend gets cranky and irritable. Also she has bad cramps with her periods. Are these related: Should she be checked? Many women get moody a few days before their menses. It is unclear what causes this, but it seems to have something to do with progesterone since it mainly happens with ovulatory cycles (egg-release cycles). The progesterone also increases the presence of another hormone called prostaglandin. This hormone causes a woman to have menstrual cramps. Thus, if a woman is having dysmenorrhea (painful periods) and gets moody before her periods, she probably is ovulating. The best things to do for the pain is to keep active, if possible. If medication is needed it should be antiprostaglandins (destroys the prostaglandin), such as aspirin (not tylenol or acetominephen) or some prescription drugs like ibuprofen or mefenamic acid. Narcotic pain medications should be avoided since they can be potentially addicting. If medication that strong is needed, the woman should have a full exam since there are other medical problems that may be causing the problem.

I get moody just before my periods. Do I have PMS? Premenstrual syndrome (PMS) is a term used to describe a group of complaints women may have before their periods.

Although these symptoms have been around for many years, the term PMS is just recently getting a lot of mention in the media. The woman may notice certain changes before her period, which then go away when her period starts. The complaints may include bloating, weight gain, breast soreness, headaches, irritability, moodiness, depression, tension, and problems concentrating. Although many women may notice some of these symptoms in a mild fashion, a few women will have severe problems with them. Also, some months may be more of a problem than others. No one knows for certain what causes PMS. It does appear that a woman must have ovulated (thus have both estrogen and progesterone in her system). Yet the levels of these hormones are normal. Since we currently do not know what is causing PMS, no one knows what the best treatment is. Right now, there are many different approaches including dietary and vitamin therapies. Some approaches work for some women, others for other women.

Many woman are now using PMS as an excuse for their complaints. There are other things that can cause many of the same symptoms, including fibrocystic changes in the breast, endometriosis, and emotional problems (especially depression and stress). Women need to consider the effects that an overemphasis on PMS might have. If too many abuse this as a rationalization for not being responsible for their actions, then women will again be seen as at the mercy of their hormones—and not to be trusted with jobs and careers of importance or danger or responsibility.

Do women truly go crazy when they go through the change of life? Can older people still have sex? No! Yes! The process of going through menopause (cessation of menses and the dropping of the hormone levels) may cause a woman to go through periods of being more irritable (like just before a period) or to have hot flushes or flashes. These are brief episodes when the woman will feel very warm and often will perspire profusely. If this happens occasionally, most women are not too bothered by it, but if it happens frequently, they will often seek medical help. Since these symptoms are usually related to low estrogen levels, a woman can be given pills or shots of estrogen to minimize these side effects.

A more serious aspect of a woman "going crazy" with menopause is related to what menopause means to the woman and her family. In some cultures a woman who lives long enough to make it through the change is honored and revered. In those societies women do not have any menopause-related symptoms. In other cultures such as ours, where young, fertile women are honored, a woman may feel that as she goes through the change she has lost all purpose in life. This, along with the fact that most likely her children are grown and moving out of the home, makes her a real risk to become very depressed. Now that more women are having their own careers, we may see the women of the future accepting menopause as a normal stage to go through that will relieve them of the "hassles of monthly periods" and the concern of a late-life pregnancy.

People, especially women, can have sex as long as they want. The one thing women do notice as they get older, especially after the change of life, is that there may not be as much vaginal lubrication. Sometimes there can be so little that intercourse becomes painful. This can be treated easily with hormone creams or pills.

I have a sister who had an ovarian cyst rupture, and she had to have surgery. Now my doctor tells me I have one. Will I need surgery? Ovarian cysts are a common occurrence. In fact, during every cycle a woman makes a very small cyst as she matures the egg. Occasionally the cyst will get large; that is, it may be felt on pelvic exam or possibly cause some pain. Usually they melt away with no long-term problems. Rarely will they rupture near a blood vessel and start bleeding or get so large they need to be removed. In those cases, surgery is necessary. The most common treatment for a cyst is to wait and see if it will go away, or to prescribe birth control pills to help it melt away.

What are the symptoms of cancer of the cervix, ovaries, and uterus? Cancer of the cervix often will have few, if any, symptoms till well advanced. The earliest signs are postcoital bleeding (bleeding after intercourse) or bad vaginal discharge. It is important to remember that yearly pap smears allow a physician to discover precancer changes before they have a chance to develop into cancer. This form of cancer generally happens to women in their thirties or older, but can happen at a much earlier age. Cancer of the cervix seems more likely among women who have their first intercourse at a young age, who have a number of sexual partners, and/or who contract certain sexually transmitted diseases.

Cancer of the uterus is mostly found in women who are in their forties and older. Obese women are especially at risk. The earliest sign may be irregular bleeding and especially bleeding after menopause. Any unusual bleeding in this age group needs to be evaluated by a physician immediately.

Cancer of the ovary, unfortunately, has few symptoms. Although it is most common in women in their fifties and older, it is still common in younger women. There often are no symptoms until the cancer is far advanced. Then the woman may notice nausea and vomiting (the cancer interferes with the workings of the bowels) or bloating (accumulation of fluid in the lung). At this time there is no easy way to screen for ovarian cancer. Yearly pelvic exams may allow it to be detected earlier.

I have been having sex for a year and haven't gotten pregnant. Does this mean I never will? If one hundred couples are sexually active, by the end of a year eighty-five will be pregnant. The remaining fifteen will have some type of infertility problem. This doesn't mean they won't get pregnant, just that it may take longer, or that they may need some medical help. For a certain number of couples, however, nothing will help them get pregnant. There is no simple answer to the question. However, a woman probably should see a physician if she is truly trying to get pregnant with no success.

I started having periods five years ago. Lately I have noticed that I have more dark hair on my face and chest. I used to pluck it off, but there is getting to be too much. Should I have electrolysis or use wax treatments like my grandmother? Increased hair growth can be due to three reasons: increased male hormones, decreased female hormones, or increased sensitivity to the normal amounts of male hormones in a woman's body. It sounds like this person has hirsuitism. This means that some hairs become thicker in size and darker in color. Often the extra hair is in the same areas where men commonly have hair. This is a common problem, with over one-third of the women in the United States saying they feel they have extra hair. Usually this extra hair is due to increased sensitivity of the hair follicles to the normal levels of male hormone. This trait is largely inherited; i.e., this person's sister and mother will have the same problem. Also, after the change of life, when the estrogen levels drop, many women will get extra hair since their bodies continue to make the same amount of male hormone. If a woman is having marked problems with hair increase, she should see a doctor, since there are some hormone imbalances and some tumors that will cause this.

Treatment varies, depending on the severity of the problem. Just removing the extra hair by wax treatments or electrolysis (burning it off) is only temporary. If the underlying problem is not addressed, the hair will grow back. Often birth control pills, a certain blood pressure medicine, or other therapies can be used.

My sister has been told that she has endometriosis. What is it, and will I get it? Endometriosis is a disease in which the cells that line the inside of the uterus occur on the outside in the abdominal cavity. Since cells respond to the hormone changes they will bleed monthly also. Although it is only a fraction of a teaspoon of blood, it is enough to cause pain and sometimes scarring. This scarring can damage the tubes or, in some unknown way, interfere with the ability to ovulate normally. This in turn can cause problems with infertility. It is not known how those cells get in this abnormal site, but it is known that the tendency will run in families. It is usually treated by preventing ovulation with different drugs. Sometimes surgery is necessary.

I am pregnant and wonder if I should have an amniocentesis or an ultrasound test to be sure my baby is normal. There is no way to evaluate a baby in the uterus and be able to guarantee a normal infant. Any time a woman gets pregnant, she has a 3 in 100 chance of delivering a baby with problems, and a 1 in 100 chance that the problems will kill the baby. The types of problems are very different and complex. Although an amniocentesis or an ultrasound may rule out certain problems they do not guarantee a normal baby.

Amniocentesis involves sticking a small needle through the woman's abdomen into the bag of fluid around the baby and sucking up a few teaspoons of that fluid. Although the risks are very small, it is possible to cause an infection or a miscarriage with this procedure. It is usually done when the woman is about fifteen to seventeen weeks pregnant. By doing various tests with the fluid it is possible to diagnose a number of genetic diseases, as well as some chemical problems. It will not find all problems.

Ultrasound is a test in which sound waves are bounced off the mother and baby—

like sonar in a submarine. These are not x-rays, so as far as we know there are no dangers involved in using them. This test allows the doctor to see the baby, its internal organs (heart, liver, kidneys), many of the bones, spinal cord, and sometimes the penis, if the fetus has one. Although this test can rule in or out a number of problems, it cannot guarantee a normal baby. Thus you need to speak to a doctor to see if the risks of these tests are merited by your history. If so, you probably should have them.

PART SIX

The Future of Marriage and the Family

CHAPTER 26

Men's Roles and Relationships

Writers and various professionals have been advancing the illusion that the aware man is a very recent *discovery.* There have existed, at every stage of history, men who were not sexist, whose visions of relationships were characterized by egalitarian principles, and who shared in the responsibilities of their homes and families. There have always been men who expressed their feelings, who spent time caring for their children, and who generally espoused the values and attitudes of our own contemporary liberation movement. They were men outside time who rebuffed the stereotypes of their era—and they were the exceptions.

Any book or article with a title such as "Men's Roles," or "What Men Are Like Today" needs to be approached with caution. So many different *types* of men exist, each with diverse qualities, that generalizations (though they make interesting reading) are rarely accurate.

Yet, people can be heard talking: A twenty-three-year-old woman comments, "Men drive me crazy. They're so selfish and condescending and are after only one thing from women." A nineteen-year-old college sophomore says, "Men are just great. They're so strong and funny and great to be around . . ." Neither of these caricatures is a remotely accurate description of most men, though both ring true as stereotypes. Men differ from country to country, from neighborhood to neighborhood, and from door to door. Foolishness lies in believing that one can ever truly understand men. Having issued these caveats and disclaimers, we will discuss in this chapter men's issues nevertheless, but let's be mindful of the pitfalls.

This chapter addresses a number of loosely related topics that are united by the concept that there are countless variations and adaptations among men that can be considered healthy. A man who is the breadwinner while his wife cares at home for their children can be liberated; so can a man who does the traditionally male chores (yardwork, plumbing) while his wife does the dishes and laundry. What counts more than exactly *what* is done is one's responsiveness to another human being, a willingness to accommodate, compromise, and negotiate toward an essential sense of equality. The personal issues covered herein will affect men's lives tremendously, and we hope readers will give some thought to how they operate in their own lives. Ask at each step, What kind of man am I? Or, for women, What kind of men am I attracted to?

Social commentary on men and male roles over the past two decades has seldom been complimentary. Writing sixteen years ago in 1970, Germaine Greer stated bluntly: "Women have very little idea of how much men hate them" (p. 249).

Recently, Paul Theroux (1983) wrote: "The whole idea of manhood in America is pitiful, a little like having to wear an ill-fitting coat for one's entire life. . . . Even the expression "Be a man" strikes me as insulting and abusive"(p. 116).

What are little boys made of? Snips and snails. Research documents that from birth, boys are socialized by their parents into the behaviors that they will be criticized for twenty years later. The infancy and childhood of boys looks something like this:

- Sons are physically punished much more than daughters (Minton et al., 1971).
- When boys engage in cross-sex play (e.g., play with dolls) they are punished much more than girls are (Langlois and Down, 1980).
- Sons are encouraged to compete more than daughters, not to cry, or to express a variety of emotions (Block, 1978).
- Signs of dependent behavior among sons is discouraged vigorously by parents (Hatfield, 1967).

These and other child-rearing practices produce the spectrum of attitudes and behaviors that no man possesses entirely but which every man exhibits to some extent. These include claims that men traditionally have been insensitive, rigidly independent, work-obsessed, emotionally unavailable, authoritarian, rough. While the majority of post–World War II men have been criticized by feminists, in just the past several years there has been growing publicity about the *new male* who allegedly does not conform to the old ways.

THE NEW MALE OF THE 1980s?

Unquestionably, there is evidence that a new male is emerging in some areas of the country among *some* segments of the middle and upper-middle class. A 1984 article in the *New York Times Magazine* by Barbara Ehrenreich entitled "A Feminist's View of the New Man" describes the evolution of young, urban, affluent males. Chief among his characteristics is a resistance to commitment in intimate relationships. Marriage may be postponed indefinitely: 7.5 million men live alone (twice the 1970 figure), and the average age at first marriage has risen in recent years to about twenty-five. Ehrenreich's new man is very concerned about physical health and fitness: symbols such as jogging or membership in health clubs exemplify this concern. He is also style-conscious when it comes to food, clothes, furniture, and aesthetic aspects of culture. Perhaps most telling, there is a desire for others to perceive him as "genuine, open and sensitive."

If "liberation" for men has intrinsic meaning, it is found within the relationships they enter. The affluent, urban new males discussed above are a small segment of the adult population. Though they may eschew commitment, their situation is certainly not reflected in the national statistics: the marriage rate in the 1980s is very high (over 90 percent of all people eventually marry), and though the divorce rate is also high (approximately 40 percent), so is the remarriage rate (about 75 percent of all divorced people remarry, most within five years). One need not get married to be involved, but men who view the avoidance of intimacy as progressive are working *against* the spirit of liberation.

Conversely, it would seem that a new age male would actively seek out and create intimate relationships with both men and women. Male-male friendships have been parodied as endless variations of the "slap-em-on-the-ass-pat-em-on-the-back" sports type. Male camaraderie is stereotyped as a series of violent escapades revolving around drunkenness, hunting, and anything that excludes women. Men collectively thrill to the sight of two football players embracing after a touchdown but cringe when the same men, out of uniform, embrace on a street corner. Even among new age men, these homophobic responses make the acknowledgement of caring feelings for another man difficult.

After graduation from a small college in the midwest, two men who had been close friends during college obtained jobs in the same town and decided to buy a house together in the area. Then what happened, as reported by one of them, had a dramatic effect on the course of their friendship: "It seemed like half the people we'd encounter would shy away from us, and at first we thought it was because we were new to the neighborhood, were young, and didn't keep the grass mowed right. But then we started to get the drift. People thought we must be gay and were afraid of us. After a while, we started taking it out on each other and the friendship fell apart. We sold the house. It's so stupid: if we'd lived next door to each other, everything probably would have been all right."

Vince Lombardi's classic comment exemplifies one of the most powerful forces that makes friendship between men difficult. He said, "Winning isn't everything, it's the only thing." While covering a major sports championship, for example, the television camera pans to the victor and captures that moment of winning, of triumph. If the lens lingers on the faces of the losers, we are discomfited by the look of sadness and defeat we see there. So attention goes to the winners, and we are spared the pain of the losing side.

Competition between boys, and later on between men, erodes the quality of trust that friendship requires. Competition pushes men to strive for advancement in their careers, and with it comes mobility, a scarcity of leisure time, and a preoccupation with one's success. Friendship is not an essential ingredient of success as society has defined it.

For those men who feel lonely, severed from the brotherhood of other men's friendship, a relationship with a woman may seem the answer. Nothing is wrong with this, though it places enormous strains on the woman. If something goes wrong with this relationship, other men cannot be told, for they are by then the *competition*, with whom one does not divulge vulnerabilities and fears. Cracks in this social mask appear from time to time but are pasted over with a stiff upper lip.

Men reading this book need to consider the paths they are on. It is easy and not unusual for men to say to themselves, I'll have time for friends (or my wife and children) as soon as my career is really secure. Suddenly at age sixty-five there is no one to invite to the retirement party. Friendship among men is nourished by years of mutual concern and revelation and yields a special bond of closeness and understanding. How many of the friendships formed in college will survive to age thirty or more? Our transient, highly mobile society may soon lead to the development of video friendship services, similar to the ones now tailored to video dating.

A proverb says, Women are vain; and yet in their sometimes obsessive fear of being viewed as effeminate, men betray their own vanity. Perhaps a monumental step toward friendship is the movement away from what others want of us and toward what we want for ourselves. Thomas Szasz said it best: "In the animal kingdom, the rule is, eat or be eaten; in the human kingdom, define or be defined" (1973, p. 20).

Male-female friendships are just as problematic but for different reasons. And yet, men who have formed nonsexual relationships with women find great satisfaction in it. Why is it so difficult to maintain friendships with women for so many men? In classic style, interactions between the sexes that were intimate were meant to lead to sexual relations. If not, the interaction ceased. Once the sexual involvement itself stopped, the relationship ended. It's as if the ritual between the sexes allowed either for sex or for nothing at all. Just as often, however, perfectly good male-female friendships have been ruined by the decision to *become* sexually involved. Sometimes two good friends wake up in bed together the next morning and realize they've made a terrible mistake.

This difficulty in cross-sex friendships is not surprising. As children, despite the current wave of unisex little leagues, most activities are segregated. It is not until adolescence that boys and girls take notice of each other; but even then, it is not with the feeling of equality that friendship requires. In her book *Growing Up Free*, Pogrebin maps out the dilemma: Friendship requires equality as a precondition of its existence. True friendship, as opposed to love and sex, is founded on total mutuality. Unlike love, friendship cannot be unilateral or unrequited. Unlike sex, it cannot be imposed by force. Two people *elect* to be friends because both get satisfaction from their closeness (p. 305).

Men might reflect on their own patterns of friendship. To some it might come as a novel idea that a woman could be anything but a lover or wife. The restraints placed on relationships for men have robbed them of the feeling of connectedness with other people. Even more important, men become detached from their own feelings and impulses: any spontaneous reaching out needs to be filtered through the many parental, societal, and media messages about what is acceptable for men.

CONFLICT RESOLUTION

The evolution of men's roles is probably most significant where it affects their marriages and love relationships with women. It is in these relationships that men and women forge alliances and hammer out the meaning of the many issues this chapter discusses. The differing socialization of the sexes and the divergent expectations that each brings to a relationship give rise to a good deal of conflict. *The manner in which this conflict is resolved is the most significant aspect of men's roles and liberation.*

A decade or more ago, for a time it was fashionable for couples contemplating marriage to create elaborate contracts. These contracts covered such areas as household chores, child care, employment outside the home, leisure time, and escape clauses. Though such prenuptial agreements are still being used, to a great extent they fell from favor. The contracts were radical attempts to resolve disputes before they became pronounced, but spouses probably discovered that conflict was not avoided and that legal terminology was a poor ally. Roles and rules cannot be so clearly defined as they are in contractual arrangements; in relationships, mutual trust and a sense of cooperativeness are more useful in mediating difficulties.

Feminists have made it abundantly clear that the patriarchal system, in which men monopolized power and decision making, oppresses women as well as children. Men have been perceived as belonging to a privileged class in the realms of business, government, and the family. The thrust of the women's movement has been toward achieving equality of power. The philosophy behind this has been that real love and intimacy are not possible as long as men and women relate to each other as dominant/submissive. This has a ring of truth: mutual contempt has developed where men resent women's passivity and women resent men's arrogance. In this system, conflict has not been resolved so much as it has been dismissed by masculine fiat.

One rationale offered for why men have held so tenaciously to their authority is that men are reluctant to relinquish their superior position. Why give up a good thing, unless it stands to benefit oneself? It's interesting that writers within the men's movement have disavowed this supposed "privileged" stature. Instead, they have described how the life of a man is riddled with insecurity and alienation. Indeed, the intensity of a man's swagger and braggadocio is directly related to the strength of his underlying fears and vulnerability.

This paradox can take many strange twists. Imagine a group of men planted on their barstools discussing women and sex. "Hey man, there's nothing better than hot pussy—I can't get enough," says one. "Yeah," says another, "I get hot just thinking about it. I don't care if I have to beg, borrow, or buy it—I gotta have it." What if one of the men present objects to the tone of the conversation and says, "Hey, that's no way to talk about women"? A chorus will rise in protest: "What's the matter with you? Don't you like women?"

Learning to resolve conflict equitably is no simple matter of people deciding to do so and carrying through. Often, there is a strong conscious desire to change, and almost nothing happens. The decision to cut down or stop smoking, go on a diet, or resolve a drinking problem often begins with the announcement, I'm really going to do it this time, and a flurry of activity. After this initial period, change achieved may succumb to old habits or the anxiety that arises when one tries to change. The failure of many self-help enterprises can be attributed to this anxiety, which people are unable to tolerate.

There are qualities in relationships that also can be resistant to change. Some family therapists view marriages or families as "hydraulic systems": change or pressure applied in one area (person) tends to apply pressure and shift things in another area (person). A change in how people resolve conflicts tends to spread to other areas of the relationship. This process illustrates what are called *feedback loops*—an action by person A leads to a reaction in person B, which feeds back to A and causes another reaction, etc. An example might be a husband and wife who decide together to share the responsibility for paying bills and budgeting the family income (previously this had been the husband's job). When they sit down at the agreed-upon time, the husband proclaims in his characteristic way, "We need to pay this one first." The wife, in her usual way, argues, "But honey, I thought we were going to share this." He replies, "We are going to share it, but some things can't be changed." Instead of arguing further, the wife withdraws and the bill paying proceeds as it always has. Both spouses have reacted similarly to past episodes, despite the agreement to do things differently. And both—the husband through his dominance, the wife through her withdrawal—have ensured that things will not change.

Men's possession—and use—of power in relationships has led to the charge that their dictatorial ways alone are responsible for causing inequality between the sexes. Though it may raise the ire of some feminists, it appears that many women have learned to respond in ways that perpetuate the male's role. Many men would like to believe that they are in charge completely, but that too is an illusion. The need to be in control is central for some men, who have learned that being the competent masters of their environment means being in control, both of themselves and others. Yielding some of this control threatens them with failure and with evidence of their own inadequacy. There is also a crucial question of whether men can trust another not to abuse them if they relinquish some control and allow the other to affect them.

In this light, the resolution of conflict has a great deal to do with how men and women get their needs met. Beyond physiological needs for food and water, the need for loving and caring is paramount. This is the heart of self-esteem. To a significant extent, the way that people feel about themselves is shaped by how others feel about them. The need to feel good about oneself and to be loved is intertwined; people tend to resist or sabotage things that threaten to undermine these needs. Men are not so invulnerable to these forces as many would like to think, whether they express it or not.

Ultimately, the goal is for conflict to be resolved in ways that are acceptable to both partners. For men, this involves creating *choices*. If in fact many men have been constricted by the notion that only one way to relate exists, then men's evolution points toward expanding this repertoire. For most men, this process does not occur through joining with elements of either the men's or women's liberation movements. At talks that each of the authors presents to diverse groups of students, few men are familiar with the best-known writers in the men's movement, such as Herb Goldberg, Joseph Pleck, Warren Farrell, Mark Fasteau, Bernie Zilbergeld, and Barry McCarthy. Few of them actively participate in men's groups. For whatever reason, most men shun organized efforts in the public eye. Change in this context occurs more as the choice to adapt individually, idiosyncratically, within one's own relationships.

ANDROGYNY AND DIFFERENCES BETWEEN THE SEXES

Reaching a level of communication and understanding between the sexes means that one needs to be cognizant of the similarities and differences between them. The differences are more than genital and anatomical, though not as profound as is sometimes suggested. The potential range for emotional responses, interests, and occupations, and relationships is similar for both men and women. Mostly it is learning and socialization that produce the marked differences.

The different socialization of men and women can be expressed in some simple comparisons. For example, it's not unusual for two women to accompany each other to the women's room. One woman might say, I'm going to powder my nose, and another might say, I'll go with you. They exit together, and no one says a word. Now imagine the same scene between two men: One says, I'm going to take a leak, and a second man replies, I'll go with you. If the man were joking, he'd get a belly laugh from others at the table, and if he were serious, he'd be seen as a pariah.

Many other behaviors are not feasible for men in most settings, unless they are willing to endure ridicule or suspicion. Unattached women at dances or social functions can legitimately dance with each other, either in pairs or in a group. Men behaving in identical ways would suffer the social diagnosis of "queer." Women may walk arm-in-arm without raising an eyebrow, embrace and kiss each other, cry on each other's shoulders, and try on each other's clothes with scarcely a murmur of protest from others. Since these behaviors are not acceptable for men, men learn very early in life to be circumspect and guarded.

Thus, a well-worn cliché has emerged from the work of pop psychologists: It states, Men need to get more in touch with their feelings. The average man already believes that he's aware of his feelings. He knows when he's hungry, when he's horny or thirsty, when he's tired, and when he's angry or irritated. This is only half the human emotional constellation: feelings of sadness and despair, of vulnerability and fear, are those which men are perceived to be out of touch with. These feelings, along with those of tenderness, caring, and empathy, have been narrowly viewed as feminine—and thus undesirable for men.

Men might begin to break this cycle by making a simple acknowledgement to their families and lovers that might sound something like this: I have a lot of trouble telling you how I feel or showing my emotions. I know it frustrates you, but I was never taught how to express myself. Please bear with me and I'll try to open up a little. It is an admission of imperfection and vulnerability that men may be afraid to make; but his family will probably appreciate it more than all the paychecks in the world. My husband, my lover, or my father is a human being with thoughts and feelings! He is loveable, wonderful, and imperfect after all! Even if the man must still struggle to let himself be known, and is sometimes tempted to withdraw back into himself, his family will know that he too is affected by his upbringing and social conditioning. They will realize that he is not merely cranky, moody, or unemotional—he is a man with dreams and problems who is trying to make a good life for himself and his family.

Another solution, according to a number of writers and researchers, is for both men and women to strive toward being more like each other: to shift sex roles more toward the middle ground of androgyny. Women who have been cut off from their assertiveness and sense of competent mastery in the world would be freer to manifest those characteristics, the theory goes. And men would be able to develop their own repressed feminine natures. Writings about androgyny make for persuasive reading, and the arguments in favor of it are powerful. Many researchers have evolved different definitions of androgyny; we define it as an openness to and acceptance of one's own feminine and masculine nature. It implies an ability to be both assertive and yielding, instrumental and expressive, and to accept these qualities in both men and women. Androgynous individuals are not threatened by their homosexual fantasies or impulses and advocate the essential equality of all persons. They are at home changing a diaper, playing softball, camping, going to the opera, planting a garden or barbecuing hamburgers, and respect the sanctity of all life forms.

In practice, however, the advocacy of androgyny has led mostly to the masculinization of women. As such, it has fallen prey to the sexist tendencies of the society in which we live. For instance, among those who care for young children, androgyny has received a great deal of attention. Within day-care centers and among parents themselves, the philosophy has evolved toward letting toddlers and youngsters express their inherent abilities and interests. Thus little girls can be observed shouldering baseball bats, manipulating large blocks and toy tractors, and playing soldiers, while the approving teacher or parent looks on. What of the little boy who wants to paint his fingernails or apply makeup like little girls, or who enjoys Barbie dolls and helping mommy make beds best of all? That little boy is not granted the same androgynous license, and parent/teacher anxiety peaks in response to this "effeminate" behavior.

Androgyny, although a legitimate ideal, in practice is the same old sexist dogma repackaged. Among adults, similar trends might be observed. Women now comprise 44 percent of the total labor force, and well over 50 percent of mothers with children under age eighteen work outside the home. As women have increasingly entered the executive ranks, they have adopted a style of dress comparable to men's. They wear man-tailored suits, men's shirts and ties, and carry attaché cases. The male executives have remained unchanged in dress. In countless areas, the accommodations have been women's to male standards. Furthermore, among those mothers who do choose to work outside the home, primary responsibility for child care and domestic chores remains theirs.

The evidence to support this trend is overwhelming: Nichols and Metzen (1982) found in their study that husbands spend only several hours a week in domestic chores and child care. Women, on the other hand, are typically found to spend twenty-five to thirty hours in these activities. Study after study confirms the commonsense notion that for women a job outside the home is nearly always in addition to, and not instead of, a job in the home. Men traditionally explained their lack of involvement in the home by saying, I work hard all day while my wife is home; it's her job. It is interesting that among blue-collar workers where the cult of machismo is thought to flourish husbands tend to participate more in household work than their better-educated, white-collar counterparts. Ideologically, though college-educated men tend to favor the ERA and women's rights, they do not translate these beliefs into behavior.

Here again, among dual-career couples, the androgynous ideal has a sexist texture. Do men themselves perceive this? Perhaps not. A 1982 study by Condran and Bode found that men tend to overestimate their contribution to chores, and still another study by Russell (1978) found that men also exaggerate their participation in child-care activities. This is an apparent paradox: If men wish consciously to be involved with their families and perceive themselves to be involved, something prevents these sentiments from becoming enacted.

The *breadwinner* theory is persuasive here. The focus of men's lives has traditionally been on the triad of upward mobility, income, and success. These pursuits lead men out of the house and away from their families. In fact, men who insist on having evenings and weekends at home may not be considered to be "company men" and may be passed over for promotion in favor of those whose primary commitment is to the job. This workaholic demand is especially prevalent among younger men whose careers are relatively new. These are also the men whose marriages and children are likely to be young and in need of their attention.

SEXUAL SHARING AND RESPONSIBILITY

For decades the scene has been reenacted in countless clinics and physician's waiting rooms: A woman arrives alone, checks in with the receptionist, and when her name is called she accompanies a nurse into an examining room. Once there, she has her pelvic exam, pap smear, contraception prescribed. If, as sometimes happens, she was accompanied by a man to the place, he waited patiently in the waiting room perusing ancient copies of magazines while she endured the feminine rites.

Men have excused themselves, and have been excluded from, these proceedings. As birth rates have fallen and sex-for-pleasure has become accepted, a call for greater male participation in contraceptive and reproductive matters has grown. It is ironic that as feminists and family planning specialists have advocated greater male involvement little organized effort has been dedicated to that goal until very recently. A paper by Douglas Beckstein entitled "Highlights from Research about Men and Contraception and Sex Education" points out that the office of Family Planning of the Department of Health and Human Services (HHS) allocated only $250,000 to men's sexual health-care programs in 1978, 1979, and 1980. This represents just .2% of the total 135 million dollar allocation. The other 99.8% funded women's programs.

Although it is true that only women get pregnant and that most contraceptives are designed for and used by women, society can hardly expect wholesale male cooperation without much greater educational efforts. Recently, planned parenthood centers and other clinics have made concerted efforts to include males in sexual health and counseling. Many programs are directed to adolescent males, who are most at risk for being involved in an unintended pregnancy. The question, What are you on? (meaning, what birth control are you using) has symbolized the extent of most men's participation in this vital area (if they asked at all).

Rewritten, the above scene might read: A man and woman consult their schedules and make an appointment with the gynecologist at a mutually convenient time. They make sure (or already know) that this physician is willing to have them both in the examining room. Once with the doctor, both partners ask questions and express their concerns. Any contraception, prescriptions, or medical procedures are part of the couple's relationship, just as the sexual activity they enjoy involves them both. The expense, love, and responsibility are all shared, rather than being arbitrarily dumped on the woman's shoulders.

Besides these ideological and emotional reasons for male involvement in sexually related matters, there are some compelling practical ones. When there is a problem of infertility with a couple, the man should be tested first, because his tests are simpler and less expensive than are the ones for women. When there is a question about STDs, both partners should be tested: sometimes there is a "ping-pong" effect (partners passing symptoms back and forth between each other), and sometimes men develop symptoms when their partners are asymptomatic (see Chapter 20).

Men have remained spectators to these proceedings, and as such, intimacy with their wives and lovers has been impaired. If you believe it is manly to declare, You take care of it, you betray your own integrity and display a callous disregard for the woman's well-being. Men who are presently involved in sexual relationships may want to discuss these issues with their partner; those who are not presently involved may want to think them over anyway. This provides a rehearsal for when the awareness will be needed later on.

Sexual sharing is an essential aspect of relationships. Until Freud came along, women were not supposed to have orgasms or even enjoy sex. Then Freud began the process which legitimized sexual pleasure for women amidst a storm of Victorian controversy. Since that time women have been struggling to overcome lingering societal prohibitions and parental don'ts. Pleasure is often accompanied by guilt or fear of discovery; thus, women have been afraid to communicate their sexual desires to men, and men have been reluctant to ask.

In virtually all pornography, the man's orgasm is the goal, and the end, of sexual activity. Once he comes, fade to black. A woman's enjoyment in these productions is a serendipitous by-product of the man's sexual performance, and whether or not she reaches orgasm is beside the point. Despite the awareness of women's sexuality that has been generated in the past decades, for some men their ejaculation remains the goal and ending to sexual activity. Although it may be true, as the saying goes, that women are responsible for their own orgasms, men are decidedly irresponsible and selfish when they roll over and fall asleep without thought for the woman's satisfaction. (It's tempting to suggest that since women have been accused of being cock teasers, it's only fair to call such men cunt teasers. Both of these vulgar terms define a person who is immature and unable to give lovingly to another.)

Men who are unable to appreciate a woman's sensuality typically are cut off from their own sensual responses as well: stimulation of his nipples feels ticklish and massaging his thighs is frustrating—he wants her to get down to it. This is a deprivation of his senses and an obsession with genital performance. Perhaps he fears the acknowledgement that he enjoys cuddling and caressing is unmanly and childish. Only little boys like to curl up with a woman. But sex can be playful! It can express deep, tender feelings, passion, or occur as an ecstatic romp. Any mechanical, fixed notion that sex always has to happen one way robs the experience of its thunder and magic. A conviction that one's own pleasure is more important than another's is the hallmark of egotism.

Certainly, not every sexual experience has to be prolonged. Sometimes a brief, vigorous encounter is the most satisfying for either the man, woman, or both. Unzip and it's all over in five minutes. Not every meal has to be a gourmet meal. Men for whom quickies are the total repertoire, however, are likely to be involved in sexually dysfunctional relationships. They might be attached to a woman who is willing to endure the label *frigid* to salvage the man's sense of potency, but she is simply the symptom bearer in a hurried, anxious sexual relationship.

These are among the attitudes with which men are raised, however, and they are not easily dispelled. The media, particularly television, communicate the following messages to men about sexuality, according to Mark Gerzon (1983):

Affection should be shown only when connected to sex.

If women get pregnant by accident, it's their fault.

Real men have powerful passions that are beyond control.

Men are supposed to try to score regardless of the woman's feelings.

The images of sensationalism and exploitation pervade our consciousness and are purveyed in megadoses (according to the latest estimates, the TV is turned on for over six hours each day in the average American household). One cannot have a relationship with a television, and the tube won't pay for a divorce or for child custody when the images it presents help to engender attitudes among men (and women) that promote discord in love.

At the same time as there are tremendous pressures on men to accept these stereotypical images, there exist contradictory messages that present men with alternatives (such as are contained in this chapter). The choices that men make in their lives have a profound effect on all their relationships and on their own levels of self-esteem.

FATHERS AND CHILDREN

Advice to men on their fatherhood abounds, but nobody has a fresher viewpoint than Letty Cotten Pogrebin, who wrote in *Growing Up Free* (1980), "Don't be the man you think you should be. Be the father you wish you'd had."

The concept of *maternal instinct* has long been held as the rationale for women assuming the major portion of child-rearing and care. Research and countless testimonials from mothers, as well as men who partook in the care of their children, illustrate that there is no biological or gender-based reason for this. Apart from breast feeding, which many mothers no longer experience, men and women are equally capable of raising and caring for an infant.

Fathers who do not develop early relationships and rapport with their children have the most difficulty establishing close ties later on. By being involved with the infant from the beginning, fathers are increasingly discovering the joys and satisfactions of sharing child care with their wives. Fathers can participate in prenatal care and prepared-childbirth (Lamaze) classes and be present at the delivery of their child. By diapering, feeding, and holding the infant, an early, primal bond is formed. The child becomes familiar with the father's scent and voice, the feel of his hands and body, the texture of his clothing, all of which are different from the mother's manner of handling the child. The father's involvement helps the child accept and learn a variety of stimuli and appreciate the role of the father, even if he is removed from the situation at work all day.

As the child develops and matures, the father will have a much more natural, spontaneous basis for relating to the child than if he waited for the child's first words, day at school, or even graduation.

The average father, however, is a passive figure in the home environment, and it has been estimated that he spends an estimated 37.7 seconds per day in direct one-to-one interaction with his infant son or daughter (Rebelsky and Hanks, 1971). Many children report that they grow up hardly knowing their fathers. Despite the very real demands of providing for his family, fathers should set aside a certain amount of time each day to be spent with each child. Just fifteen minutes a day alone, especially with younger children, can have a big impact on their lifelong relationships. Teenagers might prefer longer blocks of time on a less regular basis. Taking turns allowing the child to plan how the time is to be spent will complement the activities planned by the father. The father's influence in teaching, disciplining, and playing with the child will supplement and enhance the mother's role. Fathers can imagine a wide range of experiences from chess and checkers, political discussions and talks of sports, friends, school, to spontaneous, unstructured, playful fun.

It is vital for children to learn that fathers, males, can be affectionate, display warmth, share their feelings and thoughts, and be loving and giving. The father can be a role model and confidante without relinquishing his disciplinary function or giving the impression that dad is a friend who can be taken advantage of.

During the course of these exchanges, fathers can create opportunities to discuss issues pertaining to family life, sex education, and other areas of interest to the child. It is vital for fathers not to relegate this responsibility to their wives. Children benefit from *both* parents' perspectives, and mothers usually resent the father's lack of involvement. Despite their own sexist upbringings, fathers need not convey those same sexist messages to their children. Comments such as, Act like a man, That's the way women are, and Girls don't do things like that, are not helpful to the child. Fathers can also create handicaps for their daughters by sheltering them, while at the same time encouraging their sons to explore the environment. Fathers have a great opportunity, however, to help children of both sexes develop their own special capabilities and understand their sexuality in positive, self-affirming ways.

The quality of love and caring between the parents is the most significant aspect of children's sex education. Yet, fathers can create numerous other opportunities for teachable moments in the sex education of their children. Before the age of five many fathers shower with their children or bathe them, using the occasions to discuss issues related to physical maturation and positive feelings about one's body. Many parents enjoy having their children join them in bed on weekend mornings for some playful wrestling and conversation. Around the age of five, most children develop their own sense of privacy and will curtail the activities.

It is important for fathers to understand that silence on issues of human sexuality teaches children as much as openness does—but in a negative way. Fathers can get discussions going by talking about their own childhood and adolescent feelings and experiences. What better way for a child to learn than to hear of his or her father's first experiences in love? Without necessarily revealing the sexual details of his life, a father can transmit the message that sexual feelings cross all generation gaps and enter into all lifestyles and age groups.

Fathers need to be aware that they don't have to be great lovers or totally comfortable about sexual topics to be good sex educators. Even if their own parents didn't sex-educate them or they occasionally experience guilt or sexual dysfunctions, fathers can still be effective, healthy role models for their children.

Usually, around the time the child enters school, fathers begin to fear expressing affection for both their sons and daughters. They fear that the sons will mature to be effeminate or homosexual; they worry lest their daughters may develop an erotic sexual attraction for the father as the male figure in her life. Thus, the children are left bewildered and hurt at their father's withdrawal of affection and not unnaturally attribute it to something they (the child) did wrong. Over time they may come to see it as simply being the way dad is. The father's fears of negatively influencing the sexual development of his children are unfounded. There is no evidence to support the theory that sons with affectionate fathers become homosexuals, or that daughters will compete for the father's sexual attentions with the mother. Some girls love to flirt and play seductive games with their fathers, which is simply a way of affirming their attractiveness and father's love. Boys who enjoy their father's affections will, if anything, grow up to be less inhibited about themselves, their bodies, and their relationships with others of both sexes.

The fear of expressing warmth and physical attentions to children may also derive from the father's fear of becoming sensually and sexually stimulated. It is not uncommon to feel somewhat aroused by the wrestling and contact with one's children, but fathers often feel guilty and embarrassed to acknowledge these feelings. This may cause the father to be firmly reinforced in his convictions that it is preferable to withhold all physical intimacies from his children. Fathers *can* relax and enjoy the love of their children without feeling compelled to translate these into specific sexual behavior.

In the great majority of families, fathers have no direct sexual encounters with their children. Fathers are apt to experience warm, mildly erotic feelings similar to the ones their wives encounter in breast feeding or holding and playing with children. These interchanges help teach children to be sensual and loving when they grow up. Studies have shown that infants and children who are deprived of being held, cuddled, and loved tend to grow up with a variety of personality disorders, neuroses and/or sexual-identity problems.

A growing number of men are taking more interest in their children. A broad range of individual interpretations and changes have been effected, some minor and some startlingly innovative. Some men who are self-employed or unemployed or who maintain offices in their homes have found that caring for their children full-time has been one of the most rewarding experiences of their lives. Between this optimum situation and the father who invests little or no energy in his home life lie a variety of ranges or responses.

Society's views of roles within the family are altogether too narrow and confining. Some men are more "mothering" than their wives and have no cause for feeling strange in their behavior. The father may be the one who routinely asks children about their health, bowel activity, food intake, etc. Perhaps he does most of the housework because his wife absolutely hates it, and he also tucks the kids in at night.

As more and more women become seriously involved with their careers, the very nature of family decisions is changing. It used to be assumed (and sometimes still is) that when the male received a promotion to a better job in another city, the family unquestioningly moved. Now the father is more likely to ask his family if they *want* to move. More and more men are rejecting promotions tied to relocations if moving is contrary to the family's welfare. Today it is not unheard of for the family to move for the wife's career advancement.

Men pay a price for the roles imposed on them. They are often unaware of what is going on in their own families because "you can't tell your father about that." Research has established a connection between tension and such conditions as ulcers and heart disease—a connection we feel is even stronger than research suggests. There is no question of difference in longevity: women live an average of five to seven years longer than men do.

Dire predictions abound regarding the current liberation movement. According to them, we can look forward to emasculated husbands, children confused over their gender identity and sexual orientation, and women more unhappy than ever once deprived of their historic homemaker role. One need only visit a home where opportunities are equal, work is shared, and children are raised without rigid enforcement of sex-typed activities to see that these predictions are not valid. If anything, there is an exciting atmosphere of involvement with each other and a dynamic sense of motion and creativity. The husband and wife *talk to each other* and discuss issues unhampered by anyone else's expectations of how a family should be managed. Fathers, especially, report that a huge weight has been lifted from their chests once freed of the compulsion to wear a great stone face in order to be *macho*.

We'd like to close this chapter by examining the term *macho* and what it has come to represent. In English, it signifies a man who is a sexual bully, who sees women as objects for his sexual satisfaction, and who goes out drinking or fighting to prove his masculinity. A macho man is domineering, insensitive, and tough.

In Spanish, however, the language the term derived from, it has very different connotations. Men of all nationalities, including the Latin, have twisted the meaning around. The term originally described a man who was strong and able to handle the problems of life, poverty, and suffering. Macho was often used in a family context for men who took the responsibility of being good fathers and husbands, who were respectful of others, and who treated their women and children with love and respect. Above all, the word originally meant a sense of the man's own dignity.

The liberated man today is giving his family and marital relationship *priority*. He is willing to consider changes that make his family happier and that are essentially in his own self-interest.

REFERENCES

Beckstein, D. *Highlights from Research about Men and Contraception and Sex Education.* Washington, DC: Center for Population Options, 1981.

Block, J. H. "Another Look at Sex Differentiation in the Socialization Behaviors of Mothers and Fathers." In J. Sherman and F. Denmark (Eds.), *The Psychology of Women: Future Directions of Research.* New York: Psychological Dimensions, 1978.

Condran, J., & Bode, J. Rashomon. "Working Wives and Family Division of Labor: Middletown, 1980," *Journal of Marriage and the Family,* 1982, **44** (2), 421–426.

Ehrenreich, B. "A Feminist's View of the New Man." *New York Times Magazine,* May 20, 1984, 36–48.

Gerzon, M. "Let's Have Some New Heroes: Thoughts on Sexuality and Masculinity." *Television and Children,* 1983, **6,** (4), 33–36.

Greer, G. *The Female Eunuch.* London: Paladin, 1970.

Hatfield, J. S., Ferguson, L. R., & Alpert, R. "Mother-child Interaction and the Socialization Process." *Child Development,* 1967, **38,** 365–414.

Langlois, J. H., & Down, A. C. "Mothers, Fathers and Peers as Socialization Agents of Sex-typed Play Behaviors in Young Children." *Child Development,* 1980, **51,** 1237–1247.

Minton, C., Kogan, J., & Levine, J. A. "Maternal Control and Obedience in the Two-year-old Child." *Child Development,* 1971, **42,** 1873–1894.

Nichols, S., & Metzen, E. "Impact of Wife's Employment upon Husband's House-work." *Journal of Family Issues,* 1982, **3** (2), 199–216.

Pogrebin, L. C. *Growing Up Free.* New York: McGraw-Hill, 1980.

Rebelsky, F., & Hanks, C. "Fathers' Verbal Interaction with Infants in the First Three Months of Life." *Child Development,* 1971, **42,** 63–68.

Russell, G. "The Father Role and Its Relation to Masculinity, Femininity and Androgyny." *Child Development,* 1978, **49,** 1174–1181.

Szasz, T. *The Second Sin.* Garden City, NY: Doubleday Anchor, 1973.

Theroux, P. "The Male Myth." *New York Times Magazine,* November 27, 1983, p. 116.

CHAPTER 27

The Women's Movement

All women—and men—grow up with the women's movement in one form or another, and to some extent it shapes their view of the world. Whether one is adamantly pro-feminist, anti-feminist, or middle of the road, the messages and nuances that comprise the movement are inescapable in American culture. Its origins date back many generations, and thus it is an integral part of people's collective experience.

Chapter 26 discusses a ground-breaking movement that only in the past decade or so has been intruding into people's consciousnesses. This chapter on women's economic, political, sexual, and personal issues is more of an update on the movement. The polemics on both sides of women's issues have tended to create polarities of opinion (e.g., either for or against the Equal Rights Amendment), which spawn divisive political skirmishes. Although it may have once been true that nonfeminists (traditionalists, conservatives) could be easily distinguished from feminists (liberals) the lines between these allegedly separate camps have been blurring, at least in some areas. It would be difficult, for instance, to locate many conservatives who don't support at least one of the major tenets of the contemporary women's movement.

Though this chapter discusses many social and political issues, these impact in a profound way on people's personal lives. Bear in mind as you read how they might affect your relationships and plans for the future. It does make a difference in personal lives when almost all women work before, and most work after, marriage, and most work even after they have children. While striving to improve the quality of men's and women's relationships, the women's movement has initiated a kind of healthy skepticism in raising these issues and has served as a social conscience for our society.

It has become fashionable in some quarters to find fault with the women's movement as a whole and to see it as just another partisan political action group. One such attack came early in 1985 in an article by John Gordon entitled "What *Else* Do Women Want?" published in *Playboy* magazine. In the article, the author asserted that the women's movement had deteriorated into a single-minded lobby that advocated only that which is favorable to women; by implication they oppose all that may benefit men. As evidence it was claimed that proponents of the movement oppose equity in child custody cases and yet wish to prosecute men who default on child-support payments after they lose custody to their wives in our still-sexist judicial system. Further, the author charges that the movement has not challenged the male-only military registration policy in the United States, which obviously discriminates against men.

In revolutions of behavior and ideology, there are excesses, some hypocrisy, and wrong turns. Those cited by John Gordon in his article may be injustices on men perpetrated by women in their quest of justice for themselves. Movements of powerful social change must bare themselves to criticism and dissent, lest they become insensitive and autocratic. *Nevertheless*, though the women's movement may commit its share of injustices and its rhetoric at times may seem strident, those who support in principle its major goals may want to consider whether these faux pas are sufficient justification for abandoning the movement altogether.

In considering this issue, it remains true that the women's movement is not a monolithic force in which everyone who supports it agrees on all the details. Many reject the exaggerated, perhaps hostile, assertion that all men are potential rapists and child molesters. Many women and men within the movement disagree on other issues, and this contributes to its growth and vitality. For instance, although most proponents of the movement support the ERA, some disagree on the strategies that should be employed; others believe that the pro-choice issue deserves the movement's highest priority rather than the ERA. Among other elements of the movement, women have demonstrated against pornography and lobbied for laws that would make it illegal. Some feminists, however, do not support the antipornographic segment of the women's movement.

Individuals sometimes rationalize that they cannot support the movement because some of its members are lesbian or apparently antimale. Supporters of a cause or principle need to keep their eye on the overall goal that is sought. In-fighting over the details and protocol is what brought the Democratic party to its knees in the early and mid-1980s. In the end, those who support the ideal of *human equality* will succeed not by attacking each other but rather by working purposefully for the common good.

What does the women's liberation movement stand for and what are its goals? A panoramic view of the numerous women's issues might condense them into equal opportunities for decision making, career choices, use of leisure time, and equal pay for work of equal value. These things impact on both men's and women's lives in profoundly personal ways. The concept of decision making, for example, sounds abstract until people in relationships together wrestle with who's in control or who has the power.

Two researchers, Spence and Helmreich (1973), created a questionnaire called the "Attitudes Towards Women Scale" (AWS). One of the statements on it, to which people are asked to respond, states: It is insulting to women to have the "obey" clause remain in the marriage service. The "obey" clause traditionally meant that in decision making husbands ruled the home. Wives typically exercised control over the domestic concerns of what to have for dinner, when to do laundry and cleaning, etc., and men were the authorities, the patriarchal heads of families. During the years that men held the lion's share of power, women weren't expected to experience sexual pleasure, work for pay, vote, hold public office, or challenge their husband's authority.

Many women today—even those who do not overtly support the women's movement—have developed some nontraditional female values and behaviors, among them assertiveness, ambition, competitiveness, and self-reliance. Current rates of divorce and female-headed families attest to the fact that women are choosing to live independently of men if it suits their personal values, or if their relationships were unsatisfying. (Many women also are abandoned and find themselves alone not by choice.) It is not uncommon to hear women saying things similar to the following quote from a thirty-six-year-old woman: "I've been tempted to marry only one time, and I called it off because I realized that my lover, in the end, would be unable to treat me with mutual respect. I know that he loved me, but I wasn't able to compromise my needs in order for him to be in charge of my life. I'm at the age now of '36 and desperate,' and yet it's just as important for me to maintain my self-dignity as it is to love someone."

Decision making in relationships means an essential balance between partners—not a rigid equilibrium in which scores are kept but rather a sense of justice that evens out over time. Within relationships, a basic sense of trust in this area allows partners to feel that their opinions and needs will be understood and listened to when they are expressed, even if they are not immediately gratified. The need to have one's own way, to exaggerate one's position, and to be pushy, aggressive, or stubborn among both men and women is likely to be less intense when there is a general feeling in the relationship that one's partner will listen to one's point of view and that it will all work out evenly in the end.

In 1970, Germaine Greer wrote: "Women are contoured by their conditioning to abandon autonomy and seek guidance" (p. 90). In a sense, they would be expected to relinquish their power at the altar and snuggle under the protective wing of their husbands. This fantasy of male domination and female submission still has its proponents, though as a cultural norm it has faded from prominence and allegedly still exists in the "heartland," where rural, blue-collar types continue its traditions. Even there, however, the images of women have been metamorphosing: witness the powerful roles portrayed by women in such movies as "Places in the Heart" (Sally Field), "Silkwood" (Meryl Streep), "The China Syndrome" (Jane Fonda), and "Country" (Jessica Lange).

The women's movement and individual women who actively support it have at times taken a great deal of criticism for their supposed aggressiveness (trying to make women just like men) and contempt for marriage and the family. The revolution among women has drawn more than its share of such attacks, many of them based on rhetoric or false evidence: many years ago, stories circulated widely about "women's libbers" who were allegedly burning their bras in public spectacles. When the excitement died down and the facts were collected, it has emerged in the years hence that not a single instance of bra burning could be documented.

WOMEN, MEN, CAREERS, AND MONEY

One area of perhaps greater agreement is the economic livelihood of the American family. At one time, years ago when men "wouldn't let their wives work," there was little support outside the movement for such concepts as equal pay for equal work, or the more recent equal pay for work of equal value. The economic realities of the time permitted women to remain at home raising children and perform household tasks without an outside source of income. Since that time, however, a revolution in working trends has occurred. Women now comprise approximately 45 percent of the entire labor force, and well over half of women with children under eighteen years of age work at jobs outside the home. High interest rates, inflation, and skyrocketing costs of homes and mortgages all have pushed women to obtain paid employment whether this coincides with their personal values or not.

Once in the labor force, women continue to earn less for their efforts than men do: On the average, women earn only $616 for every $1000 earned by men. This figure, however, conceals some crucial reasons for this discrepancy. One of the major ones is that many women interrupt their careers to bear children and raise them. When they reenter the job market, many women work part-time for years. Thus, their advancement is slowed down in comparison to men who remain in their careers without interruption.

Among single people, the disparity in wages narrows dramatically (though there is still a significant difference): Single women earn $867 for every $1000 earned by men. Within some professions, women are now represented in greater proportions, and their wages have closed in on men's as well. In 1973, for instance, women represented just 5.8 percent of all lawyers. In 1983, 15.3 percent of all lawyers were women, and they received $710 for each $1000 going to men. Women physicians accounted for 12.2 percent of the total in 1973; ten years later, that had risen to 15.8 percent and women's pay was $809, compared to the $1000 for men. During the same period, the proportion of women engineers has more than quadrupled, and women occupy nearly twice the percentage of managerial and administrative positions as they did in 1973. (The above data were taken from *U.S. News & World Report,* 1984, and the *New York Times Magazine,* 1984.)

Economic well-being is one of the most fundamental struggles facing women and, to a lesser extent, men. These struggles are magnified by the crises facing dual-career couples and the sacrifice of baby versus career confronting many women. Policies that support women in their child-bearing roles and support couples in their transition to parenthood are lacking in this country. Paid or unpaid pregnancy leaves for women or men, when they exist at all, tend to be short (four to six weeks), sometimes with no guarantee that the job will still be there when the parent returns after delivery. Options such as flex-time (allowing people to work four 10-hour days or to work during the afternoons and evenings) and job sharing (which might allow two employees each to work halftime at a single full-time job), are available to a tiny number of women.

Perhaps more than any other obstacle, a critical shortage in quality day care hinders women from pursuing their careers successfully. The United States government, as well as the private corporate sector, have made only token provisions for the care of children while parents work (especially when compared to the programs in effect in other major industrialized nations). In the United States, approximately 10 percent of all care for children while parents work is in day-care facilities. The rest is provided by babysitters and relatives; in most instances, parents struggle to maintain quality care for their children that they can afford. Part of the dilemma is that prekindergarten day care and nursery school teachers are paid a pittance, even if they have extensive training and education in the field. It's not surprising that most of these teachers are women, and their pay reflects a national tragedy: the low priority placed on excellence of care for infants, toddlers, and young children. It is ironic that pay scales for teachers increase as they teach older children. By the time a child is older, however, he or she may not respond to even the best of teachers *if* there was poor stimulation and education at an earlier age. In a sense, the pay ratios are upside down: teachers of younger children should be paid more. This would undoubtedly be the case if more males became involved in teaching young children.

RELATIONSHIPS

Despite the disparities in wages, approximately 11 percent of women earn more money than their spouses. It has been found that these marriages are more likely to end in divorce and that the situation engenders goodly amounts of insecurity and arguments. Money equals power in some relationships, and control of finances is a key area in which equality may be tested. In seeking to help people cope with feelings of inadequacy that may develop in these situations, the women's movement has encouraged partners to work toward respect for each other's intelligence and dignity and to create an empathic bond between partners that can endure the struggles their lives together create.

At its most personal level, men and women have the opportunity to talk with each other and to share feelings and experiences. This allows for spontaneity and nurturance as couples explore the meanings of their lives with and apart from their spouses and lovers. Along the way, elements of dissension will surface and be addressed. It has traditionally been assumed, for instance, that difficulties in couples' sexual relationships most often were due to a wife's lack of desire. Research conducted by Dr. Joseph LoPiccolo, a well-known sex therapist and educator, found that early in 1970 women accounted for 70 percent of all cases in therapy where a low sex drive was the presenting complaint. By 1982, however, *men* experienced a low sex drive in 60 percent of the couples who said that lack of desire was a problem for them (*New York Times*, 1985). The numbers of men with a lack of interest in sex has not supposedly increased in the ten years between these two studies; rather, more men are seeking treatment (in addition, it is likely that fewer women are taking the rap for what may be the man's problem).

Inequities such as these crop up in other areas of loving relationships. Robert Sternberg, a psychologist at Yale University, reported in 1985 that many women continue to believe it is their own unselfishness that is crucial to the success of their relationships. In other words, if they didn't try harder and shoulder more than their share of the responsibility, women believed that their relationships would end. A further finding (which may surprise some men) is that women report loving their best friends even more than their lovers (Coleman, 1985).

The "battle of the sexes," as these dilemmas have been referred to, has created some secondary quandaries for both men and women. How can feminist women reconcile political consciousness and sexual desire for men without compromising either one? How can men reach for egalitarian goals and not feel that in doing so they are emasculated (at least by societal norms)? The truce lies in discovering together that the "battle" is really a metaphor for the quest of love and intimacy and that in the process both sexes will benefit.

A fascinating perspective on loving relationships was presented in *Ladies' Home Journal* (1985), in which 74,000 readers' answers to a questionnaire were reported. Though theirs was not a scientific study, it was revealing, nonetheless, of women's views of "traditional men," the "new man," and "macho men." It was found in general that both "traditional" and "new" men appeared to be more acceptable mates than "macho men." For instance, as lovers, both traditional and new men were rated as "excellent," while the macho man was rated as "good." Both traditional and new men are less likely to use pornography or to have an affair and are more likely to remember birthdays and anniversaries. New men were different from the other two categories mainly in the degree of their involvement in domestic tasks and in their belief that men are not superior to women. "Macho men" were more likely to spend time away from their families with male friends, and their wives do not want their sons to grow up to be just like dad.

WOMEN, MEN, AND IDENTITY

Years ago, when the title Ms. began to replace the more traditional Miss, some people questioned why such an outcry was being raised about this single syllable. The answer runs deep in American culture and concerns the ways in which women have been perceived and have perceived themselves. Ms. is a neutral title that makes no reference to a woman's marital status, just as Mr. accomplishes the same task for men. Both Miss and Mrs. identify a woman according to her attachment—or lack thereof—to a man, the same as Mr. and Mrs. John Doe obscures the woman's own first name and identity apart from her husband.

Although the great majority of women are delighted to present themselves in public as married, many also wish to be seen as differentiated from their spouses, as separate, whole persons. The cultural perception of women in this light has a broad impact on how they are treated and responded to and how their status is reflected in judicial and legislative decisions. The public image of women, their bodies, their appearance, and persona, is the other crucial aspect of identity with which the women's movement has been concerned. Women in general are accustomed to having themselves assessed largely in terms of their looks and sexual appeal. Women who met some imaginary criteria for beauty were described as real lookers or knockouts, and those whose looks fell short of the current ideal of beauty were jokingly referred to as a great dancer, a good personality, or the life of the party. These sarcastic euphemisms belied the fact that women were being evaluated mainly for their appeal to men.

A surprising slant on this women-as-sex-objects issue was presented by Gloria Steinem in her 1985 article in *TV Guide* "In Defense of Playboy Bunnies." In the article, Steinem reveals that for several weeks in 1963, she worked as a Bunny as part of a journalistic assignment for *Show* magazine. She writes that rather than condemning Playboy Bunnies all men, as well as women, should have a profound empathy for them. Collectively, they are assaulted with the "woman as piece of ass" mentality with which *all* women struggle, whether they are housewives, bus drivers, or fashion models. Among the Bunnies at the club, there existed a camaraderie and protectiveness of each other and an empathy for how difficult it was to make a living as a glorified waitress working all day in three-inch high spike heels. Coming to the defense of Bunnies, Steinem argues, is simply rallying to the defense of all women. "Empathy," she writes, "is the single most revolutionary emotion I can think of."

Women will want to explore how they perceive their body images, their self-esteem, and their identities. The women's movement has sought to create the not-so-radical image of women as more than stylized, cosmetic, sexual beings. Men who have tended to conceive of women mainly in these stereotyped ideals will find that their own identities are affected as the result. Men's and women's identities have a reciprocal influence on each other, as those in intimate relationships soon discover. As women have questioned their identity in the recent past, so too have men begun the process of examining themselves. Changes among both sexes mutually affect each other and change the nature of both individual and collective identity with which people are raised.

WOMEN AND PERSONAL GROWTH

The women's movement has also served as a catalyst for many aspects of the self-help movement. The burgeoning interest in health care emerged from an earlier concern with spiritual, political, and emotional care of oneself. The pursuit of such activities as aerobics, nutrition, exercise, self-defense, and sexuality awareness is a natural extension of what came before.

Women's body image has also been shaped by the degree of their involvement in sports. Until recently, elementary and secondary schools devoted just 2 percent of their athletics budget to girls' activities, and fewer than 300,000 girls were involved in interscholastic high school sports. Though funding still is not equitable between the sexes, the numbers of high school girls involved in sports has at least quintupled since 1970. This is due in large part to the passage of Title IX, which mandated that schools must provide equal equipment, coaching, academic tutoring, facilities, and publicity (but not necessarily equal money) for both male and female sports.

Women have been raised generally with the impression of their bodies as frail, feminine, and in need of protection. Thus, since they lacked the brute physical strength of men and were socialized not to see themselves as athletic, women tended to avoid sports. Today, though there remains a gap between men's and women's peak perform-ances, the gap is less than would have been expected. Women's sports such as college basketball are beginning to attract some attention with sportscasters; women's body-building has been accepted as legitimate and competitions now appear regularly on Saturday afternoon television specials. Telecasts of olympic events provide nearly equal coverage for men's and women's events in response to the public's interest. In events requiring extended endurance—such as a 50-mile marathon, for instance—it is believed that women's performances may eventually overtake men's. Even so, the focus is not on who wins or technically is "better"; how marvelous it is that women are becoming freer to celebrate their physical abilities, as men have done for centuries.

The struggle among women has been to develop a healthy, self-accepting sense of self and of one's body. The obsessional pressure on women to appear beautiful and slender has led to at times fanatical (and unnecessary) dieting and to a variety of psychiatric and behavior disorders. Chief among these are anorexia and bulimia, which in the past several years have been very well publicized. These are eating disorders: In anorexia, a person (almost always a young woman) virtually starves herself out of a (usually mistaken) belief that she is fat. Such women often become dangerously ema-ciated and may begin losing their hair and teeth because of malnutrition. Extensive medical and psychiatric care is often required, and one's future health may be compro-mised if the anorexia endures long enough.

Bulimia is also known as the binge-and-purge syndrome. In it, people (again, predominantly female) gorge themselves on large amounts of food and then either induce vomiting or take a strong laxative so that they will not gain weight. Karen Carpenter, the well-known singer, died at a young age of causes believed to be related to anorexia, and Jane Fonda admitted that for years she was afflicted with bulimia. When these syndromes are established, the most important elements of life may revolve around bathroom scales and mirrors, and no amount of reassurances from family or friends may convince a woman that she is not, in fact, obese. Neither anorexia nor bulimia help women attain the attractiveness they desire; nor is there peace of mind once the goal of being slender has been reached.

Some advances germinated by the women's movement have been more subtle, less easily traced across time. At one time, it wasn't unusual for males' disparaging comments about women to escape comment: e.g., women are hysterical, giddy, gossipy. Although some men continue to make such statements, they are more likely to encounter objections, raised eyebrows, and protests against sexism. People in general are more aware of the ways in which women are portrayed in advertisements, commercials, and the media, spoken about in conversations, and considered in political, judicial, and legislative action. People are more keenly attuned to the nature of equality in relationships and to the liabilities and benefits of being a man in today's world. What was once taken for granted in these many dimensions is now open to question and scrutiny.

Men and women are different—even we've noticed that. But what has that got to do with equal opportunities in the areas of work, leisure, and decision making? The debate rages on concerning whether there exist biological distinctions in the sexes' relative abilities in mathematics, logical and spatial reasoning, and language skills. The difficulty in answering whether males are genetically superior in math and spatial abilities and women in verbal ones is that from birth each sex is socialized and shaped to conform to these stereotypes. How can scientists determine whether biology, the environment, or a combination of both account for the differences often measured on such instruments as standardized tests (e.g., SAT, GRE)?

Although it may eventually develop that there are some biological differences, Alice Sterling Honig, a prominent child development specialist, commented: "Some of these differences reflect a bias toward expecting males to be agentic—to be active, decision-makers, and achievers—and expecting girls to be nurturant, submissive, and interpersonally sensitive to others. What is needed is a rethinking of the best wishes for human actualization of both sexes. *Adults need to do more to help both sexes toward achievement and tenderness*" (1983, p. 68). Honig states that although biological differences and cultural preferences between the sexes may exist for a long time, care givers and parents need to celebrate competence among both males and females in whatever form it appears.

William Sloane Coffin, Jr., Chaplain of Yale University, has observed: "The woman who needs liberation in this country is the woman in every man, and the man who most needs liberation is the man in every woman."

This chapter is intentionally brief. Personal and political issues under this part's rubric "The Future of Marriage and the Family" have been spread among the three chapters. Once, all this material would have been confined to a single chapter for women—it was, after all, considered to be of concern only to them.

REFERENCES

Enos, C., & Enos, S. F. "The Men in Your Life." *Ladies' Home Journal,* 1985, **52** (3), pp. 99–101; 180–183.

Goleman, D. "What is Love? Researchers Finally Probing Affairs of the Heart." *Syracuse Herald-Journal,* February 11, 1985, pp. B5–B6.

Gordon, J. "What *Else* Do Women Want?" *Playboy,* 1985, **32** (3), 66–68; 156–157.

Hacker, A. "Women vs. Men in the Work Force." *New York Times Magazine,* December 9, 1984, pp. 124–129.

Honig, A. S. "Sex Role Socialization in Early Childhood." *Young Children,* September 1983, pp. 57–68.

New York Times. "Bigger Sex Drive for Women." January 12, 1985.

Steinem, G. "In Defense of Playboy Bunnies." *TV Guide,* 1985, **33** (8), Issue #1665, 14–15.

U.S. News & World Report, August 6, 1984, pp. 46–51.

CHAPTER 28

The Emerging New Family

The emerging new family is going to be better than its traditional predecessor mainly because of the influence exerted by the women's liberation movement.

A certain *price* accompanies every important revolution in history. Often the price involves a longing (among those who are paying it) for a return to the "good old days." The women's revolution has created a great deal of turbulence in our society. We see it as a welcome, healthy, exciting, and enriching opportunity for both men and women. The movement is the best approach to preventing family life from "self-destructing." In fact, the problem is *not* that women have become aggressive, do not want children any more, refuse to cook and clean, and are sexually insatiable now that they realize their multi-orgasmic nature, in contrast to the resulting pathos of the premature-ejaculating male.

The problem results from the resistance of society—both males and females—to the legitimate demands of an increasingly large number of women, supported by a growing number of men. The demands are both simple and straightforward: equal opportunity in decision making, career choice, and leisure-time activities, and equal pay for work of equal value. This statement captures the substantive meaning of the women's liberation movement.

Working at home or outside it, having children or not, or being single or married have absolutely nothing to do with being a "liberated" person. These days more women certainly appear aggressive, especially when their legitimate rights are not met. Many more women have become assertive. In fact, the energy for the newly emerging egalitarian family comes from this assertiveness.

I, Sol Gordon, did not understand any of this when Judith became my wife thirty years ago. Judith, a busy professional working full-time, did all the cooking, cleaning, washing, shopping, cleaning, cooking, shopping, taking care of our child, shopping, cleaning, washing. I was busy. Until one day not too far along in our marriage, my wife said to me, "Hey, I'm busy, too. How would you like to have a divorce?" It took me five minutes to rearrange my schedule.

I still don't like to help with the cooking, cleaning, and shopping, but I'm doing it. I'm doing it because I have an assertive wife. I didn't want her to become aggressive. (I must admit that our relationship has become much more mature and better—more fun—as a result of our sharing.) I especially hate to clean. I remember thinking that women were born cleaning ladies. Now I know that women don't like to clean. I'm spreading around the rumor these days that if you like to clean, you have a cleaning disease. (People who like to clean are preoccupied with dirt.)

The emphasis on working women and freedom from household drudgery has placed "guilt trips" on women who stay at home in care giving roles and those who get others to take care of their children while they go off to work. Women have a hard time no matter what they decide to do these days.

No credible evidence exists, about which we know, proving that children in day care grow up more disturbed than those whose parents stay at home to take care of them. Many studies imply this proposition. However, none has been able to document the fact that children cared for during the day by nursery schools, grandparents, etc., are in any way harmed by the process. In fact, we know personally many such situations where children have grown up healthy, mature human beings. There are also many instances of children whose parents took care of them and never worked outside the home: in some of these cases the children didn't fare too well. It seems strange that the very people who fuss about how important it is for parents to stay at home often themselves are career women who can afford expensive babysitters and housekeepers.

A much more significant fact concerns the close to 2 million cases of child abuse in this country each year. Parents brutalize 100,000 of these children so severely that they require hopitalization. Furthermore, about 4000 children are murdered by their parents every year (Williams and Money, 1980). Most of these child-abusing parents stay at home to take care of their children.

Violence can be seen as an important by-product of a family life that stresses traditional roles with a focus on the authoritarian male and submissive female. The frustration and anxiety sometimes generated by these forced roles often lead to family violence, both among spouses and children who become innocent victims of suppressed rage.

- *Each year* 1.8 million American women are beaten by their husbands. About one-fourth of these women are raped in the process.

- 250,000 men are beaten by their wives.

- Family members, often a spouse, kill one-fourth of the people murdered annually in the United States.

- Twenty percent of all Americans condone physical violence in marriage (Strong et al., 1983).

Before we continue with our argument in support of egalitarian relationships, let's look at a few current trends in American family life. Our views are based on statistics available from the U.S. Census Bureau.

The family is by no means dead. About 90 percent of all Americans eventually marry, although a majority will not do so until their middle twenties. A total of 2,444,000 couples married in 1983, which represented a drop of 3 percent from 1982 and the first drop since 1976. About 40 percent of all marriages end in divorce; 1,179,000 couples divorced in 1983, which represented a decline for the second straight year. About 75 percent of divorced people remarry, most within five years. The divorce rate has been relatively stable since 1977, though in both 1979 and 1981 the rate hit all-time highs (NCHS, 1984). At a glance, it appears that both the marriage and divorce rates have been relatively high during the 1980s.

Seventy-eight percent of all noninstitutionalized children under the age of eighteen live with two parents. Sixty-three percent of these reside with both natural parents of a first marriage. Nineteen percent live in one-parent families (Population Reference Bureau, 1983).

More than 50 percent of all women with children now work outside the home. The good old American family consisting of a working father and a mother staying at home and caring for two children accounts for only 7 percent of the total. Altogether, only about 17 percent of the households in this country consist of a wage-earning father and a mother at home with one or more children. Twenty-eight percent of American households include two working parents and one or more children living at home. Finally, although about 5 percent of all couples do make a rational decision not to have any children (Strong et al., 1983), the average man and woman still have two children.

Of course, the period of transition from traditional to egalitarian family through which we now are passing will exact a price. Families, and especially women, will pay this price. Not all women will be able to manage successful careers and, at the same time, have good marriages. It is no accident that the women's movement feels it needs to deal with the dilemmas posed by "baby and career" as it faces the 1980s. How will a woman achieve equality with men in the working place, yet, if she chooses, also have children?

Many such dilemmas face women these days. Many professions to which women have gained access over the past few decades simply are not structured for those who want to have children and take responsibility for their care and upbringing. Some jobs place such heavy demands in time and energy on a woman that she simply cannot see her way clear to considering the possibility of having children in the first place. A cruel choice faces women of approximately thirty-five years of age who have spent the past ten years building a profession or career for themselves and who now are on the verge of achieving a position of status or power. They fast approach the age when it becomes less safe to bear children. Do they sacrifice children or career? Another dilemma concerns the career woman who must face leaving for a different city or state to advance her husband's professional position.

It needs to be stressed that liberation has nothing to do necessarily with a career. A homemaker can be liberated. A career woman may be working out of economic necessity and may not feel herself "liberated." For many women in blue collar and low-paid service industries, calling their job a career would appear to them laughable.

Furthermore, there is nothing inherently objectionable about traditional marriage—the husband with most of the authority and the wife with a role limited to pleasing her man—if it works for them. However, there is a gradual shift away from this orientation these days. Although an overall decline in the number of divorces has been noted lately, it is no accident that a rising number occur among middle-class individuals, even in long-standing marriages, some of which are no doubt initiated by women fed up with traditional marriage.

We have spent a considerable amount of time observing young people, especially college-age youth. These young men and women now marry more for love than for status, sex, financial gain, or parents' desire. This is especially true among those influenced by the women's movement. Also, a significant number live together before marriage. Contrary to the thinking of traditionalists, some evidence exists to show that such living together before marriage contributes to more stable relationships later on in life. Research in this area has not resulted in an ability, however, to make definitive statements.

Egalitarian marriage is characterized by genuine respect for each other. This has little to do with being equal. Instead, each person maintains a respect for the other's qualities and imperfections. Egalitarian marriage involves an equality of opportunity to develop one's own potential.

Although the double standard remains a pervasive force in this country, many changes have occurred. We examined articles in *The Ladies Home Journal* from twenty-five years ago and then compared them to articles in the same magazine from this year. Formerly, the articles concentrated on how women should make their husbands happy. The following words of advice are typical of the articles surveyed:

Love him. Unconditionally and with devotion. You chose him. He must be wonderful. . . . If your brain, instead of your heart, pilots your emotions, there must be regrets. You *cannot* trust your brain. You *can* trust your heart. . . . You are a woman with a thousand little pockets in your being where you can tuck away little pains until tomorrow. A man hasn't got these pockets. His emotional system isn't quite as vast a labyrinth as yours. He is simpler, straighter than you are. (January 1954, p. 36)

In contrast, one now finds much more of a balance. Both the husband and wife have roles in making a marriage work. Both man and woman share in sexuality, birth control, and pleasuring. This is what equality is all about. Traditional roles and expectations are changing. Although men and women *are* different, it seems apparent that there exist many more significant similarities than divergencies.

All major social evolutions are accompanied by a certain degree of resistance among segments of the population. This is evident in the failure of the Equal Rights Amendment (ERA) to achieve ratification. The fears of those who oppose it are intense and are reflected in the sometimes irrational arguments brought against it. For instance, some fear that the ERA mandates unisex bathrooms and women forced into military combat positions. It is abundantly clear that these developments will not come to pass, and yet opponents of the ERA use their possibility to prey on the fear of the uninformed public. For those who are unfamiliar with what it says, following is the full text of the ERA:

> Equality of rights under the law shall not be denied or abridged by the United States or by any State on account of sex.

Perhaps some people want to go back to the "good old days." Large numbers of older Americans know better and have many memories of the worldwide poverty of the 1930s. Sixty years ago women didn't vote. Less than 10 percent of all high school graduates went to college. Today, the figure is over 50 percent. Margaret Sanger was arrested for urging people to use birth control. Thousands of women died as a result of compulsory pregnancy. The list could go on and on.

On the contrary, many people welcome the fact that the American family is losing the traditional character of the "good old days." Accustomed to attributing the decline of the traditional family to increased technology (mobility and television), to affluence (money to pay for our loose morals), and to the unpopularity of the Protestant work ethic, we have neglected to appreciate other more significant factors.

The patriarchal, or extended, family, which often preoccupied itself with a grim struggle for survival, opposed the egalitarian strivings of both women and children, as well as those of men. Although the father may or may not have enjoyed an authoritarian role, his dominance more often than not created a wall between him and the rest of the family. The romanticized notion of the strong, orderly Victorian family still exists but mainly in the wishful fantasy of novelists and the memories of a very few people.

With all its supposed attributes, the traditional family more often than not enslaved women. It reduced her to a breeder and caretaker of children, a servant to her spouse, a cleaning lady and at times, a victim of the labor market. In reacting to the impossible demands of being seen and not heard, not to mention grim child employment, children often ran away from home or married early, thus effecting what they perceived as an escape.

Organized religion maintained political power over people's public activities but began to lose its influence on private behavior. People simply paid lip service to expected conformity and went about their secular business. Thus, churches and synagogues contributed more to guilt than to faith and operated on the assumption that the less people knew, particularly in the area of sexuality, the more moral they would be.

It is no accident that in the 1970s the very same people whose ideas represent the forces that perpetuated the authoritarian family and the myths of its sanctity, indissolubility, and charm are joining the religious right in attributing our social ills to sex education, the pill, homosexuality, masturbation, pornography, and the feminist movement.

Currently, about two-thirds of American families live "comfortably." Women need no longer be burdened by more children than they want. They are engaged in a full-fledged revolution that demands equality in decision making and career opportunities. Children express their own opinions and have the right to be educated and protected. At last, men can relax, if they choose to break old sexist taboos.

Most organized religions today emphasize a thoughtful and progressive attitude toward sexuality and the family. Many religions support birth control and the dignity of women, viewing sex as a celebration rather than a necessary evil.

We are beginning to notice glimmerings of the excitement, the joy, and the power of family life, based fundamentally on the fact that the husband and wife marry, not for political or economic reasons, not for escape, sex, or pregnancy, but because they love each other. Women and men respect each other, and if they decide to have children, it is because they want them. They can spend time having fun together.

Many are even beginning to discover that religion need be neither a burden nor a farce, but a faith, a ritual, and an affirmation of the spirit that brings comfort, joy, and relaxation to a hectic, complex life.

Children now discuss their ideas with parents, who no longer feel that the less a child knows about sexuality and other "adult" pleasures, the safer he or she will be. Parents communicate with their children, devoid of demands that consist entirely of don'ts accompanied by no rationale.

Those of us who believe in and like the idea of the family look forward to a new generation of egalitarian, nonsexist children who are not threatened by, and can respect, those who have developed alternative lifestyles (for example, single, gay, gray). These children will become the future antagonists of forces that want to return us to the hypocrisy of yesterday, the idealization of ignorance, and the breeding of nonorgasmic females and impotent males.

We reserve our highest praise for the pro-family people: millions of couples who remain married (even for years) and who still care for each other and who are not ashamed to acknowledge it; millions of children who remain nonplused by the fact that their parents are basically nice people; families who respect each other's ideas, impulses, and idiosyncrasies without copping out for the sake of tradition; and egalitarian marriages, both "open" and "closed," all relating to an intimate network of friendships and perhaps to an extended family as well. Hurrah for the self-actualizing family!

We believe that the emerging new family will contribute strongly to the following trends.

FREEDOM FROM SEXUAL STEREOTYPING

Cultural definitions of masculinity and femininity provide the key to sexual stereotyping. Our culture has insisted that men be aggressive, worldly, strong, rational, and dominant. Women must be passive, weak, domestic, emotional, and submissive. The achievement of honest human relationships of any kind will require the destruction of these stereotypes.

People also have been led to believe that heterosexual love exists as the only legitimate and normal kind of love. Society needs to recognize that homosexuality, lesbianism, bisexuality, and trans-sexuality are also valid sexual behaviors. We must guarantee everyone's right to reveal or not to reveal sexual interests and tendencies.

A broad range of alternative lifestyles have emerged in the past twenty years, most notably "living together," which has increased in dramatic proportions in the past decade. There are many expressions and arrangements between people who are in love that need to be legitimized, at least as far as civil rights and courtesy are concerned. Other candidates for validation are such unconventional pairings as an older woman with a younger man, elderly couples, and couples who decide not to have children.

FREEDOM FROM SEXUAL OPPRESSION

The exploitation of women for the purpose of selling products and services reduces all women to sexual objects and creates narrow, stereotypical standards of beauty. Women are also exploited as workers, being underpaid for most jobs, and receive little recognition for being housewives and mothers. People need to become aware of this exploitation on all levels—economic, social, educational, and sexual—before any two people can relate with sexual honesty.

Men are also exploited because of the roles they supposedly play in society. For example, men who are not interested in sports or who like housekeeping are ridiculed and often deprived of economic opportunities because they do not fit into a company's image of what constitutes a male role.

Women, too, exploit men and expect them to fulfill roles such as provider, daddy, or stud.

FREEDOM OF INFORMATION

Access to basic information must be guaranteed to all regardless of age, sex, or intelligence. In the case of mentally handicapped people, special efforts must be made to give them the information they need and in a way that they can understand. Freedom of information should also include the right to read literature that has been subject to societal restrictions. Only complete freedom of information can ensure an educated populace.

FREEDOM FROM SEXUALLY IGNORANT PARENTS

Young people must realize that many parents do not have adequate information about sexual behavior or, if they do, are often unable to communicate it to their children. Even parents who present the basic facts often find it difficult to deal with a child's feelings about his or her emerging sexuality. Perhaps because of their own fears and misconceptions, many parents overreact to their children's questions or sexual behavior. Although parents are a good source of moral values and attitudes, we must recognize the possibility of their passing on misinformation, prejudices, and personal problems concerning sexual matters. What is needed more than school programs is a massive sex education program directed at parents and newlyweds. Our feelings and knowledge about sex become exceedingly important when we realize that we may pass on unhealthy attitudes to our children.

FREEDOM FROM RESEARCH NONSENSE AND SEX MYTHS

Access to accurate information is crucial to a healthy sexuality. Unfortunately, not everything in print qualifies as reliable information. Some research proves extremely valuable for debunking sexual myths. In this regard, the work of Masters and Johnson is exceptional: however much it is fashionable to criticize them for not being perfect, they were, after all, pioneers. They didn't have to be proved entirely correct. The same can be said for Freud who made even more errors than they did. A flood of popular articles on sex in magazines and newspapers actually creates new myths. We must create a sane perspective on research based on common sense and the basic facts about sexual behavior.

FREEDOM TO CONTROL ONE'S OWN BODY

Individuals must be free from legal controls of their own bodies. This freedom would prohibit legislation restricting medical abortion, voluntary sterilization, consensual relations among adults, contraceptive information and devices for minors, and privacy of sexual expression. Also implied would be the right to choose one's own lifestyle and sexual partners. Inherent, too, would be the right to proper medical care and access to contraceptive devices for anyone who wants them.

FREEDOM TO EXPRESS AFFECTION

Until we overcome our fear of expressing our affection for one another, regardless of gender, we cannot achieve full sexual adjustment. Many people now suffer great anxiety even about *touching* another person (hugging, holding hands, etc.). The freedom to touch other people, even a member of the same sex, without fear of critical diagnosis is especially important with children, who want and need to enjoy physical affection from adults.

FREEDOM OF SEXUAL EXPRESSION FOR THE DISABLED

We must recognize and facilitate sexual expression among the developmentally disabled, emotionally disturbed, and physically disabled. Special educational efforts should be directed to helping these people find appropriate sexual opportunities.

Although these freedoms exist as a necessary precondition for healthy sexuality, they are not without their corollary responsibilities. These moral or ethical standards apply to all persons, regardless of life situations.

- No one has the right to exploit another person's body, either commercially or sexually.
- No one has the right to bring an unwanted child into the world.
- No one has the right to spread sexually transmitted disease.
- No one has the right to exploit children sexually or take advantage of mentally or physically disabled people.
- No one has the right to impose his or her sexual preferences, including when and with whom to have sex. Sexual choices must be voluntary.

No constitution can guarantee these freedoms and responsibilities. Instead, they will evolve gradually as people's consciousness about sexuality changes. The most important factors to effect this change will be a willingness to communicate openly and to explore preconceived notions about sexuality. Complete access to information will facilitate this process.

Eventually, society will come to realize that any two adults have the right to voluntary, nonexploitative sexual relations. Ideally, their relationships should lead to and enhance each other's personal growth. Through responsible sexual behavior and honest communication, there is a healthy and sane approach to sexuality within the context of the emerging new family.

It goes without saying that much of the success of the emerging new family depends on the quality of the relationship shared between husband and wife. This point was made earlier in our book, and here we would like to provide a more detailed discussion of an important topic we mentioned earlier: the ten most important things in a marriage.

1. Love: caring, intimacy, loyalty, and trust during good times and bad, holding strong in the face of illness or stress. This includes such simple things as remembering birthdays, anniversaries, and ordinary courtesies, offering to help without being asked, and saying I love you.

2. Learning how and when to laugh: having a sense of humor and keeping it tuned. You had one when you were little. Where did it go? If living were a series of traumatic episodes, laughter would not be practical. There simply wouldn't be time. But there are very few real traumas in life. It isn't necessary to be downcast much of the time. Learn to laugh. Practice. Find something funny in a situation that doesn't look funny at all. Watch and listen to a two-year-old baby laugh. If that doesn't get you started, have a checkup.

3. Making interesting conversation: being sensitive to the interests of your partner and sparing him or her the office gossip as well as the traffic situation on Interstate 80. The key here is willingness to communicate. Don't be afraid of hurting your partner's feelings or of revealing your own. Express your own point of view. If your partner doesn't share it, nothing is lost. If he or she explains why, so much the better.

4. Together, a passionate sense of mission or purpose about something(s): an involvement with other people's lives as a means of enhancing your own. It can be anything—a cause, your religion, the environment, or politics.

5. Friends together and separately: sharing time and talk with people you both enjoy and being sensitive to the negative chemistry between your partner and some of your dearest friends. Learn to cherish some space, privacy, interests, hobbies, and even an occasional vacation of your own.

6. A promise: you will not compromise the person you want to be. You yourself are not negotiable. Do what it pleases you to do. This category may not be nearly as large as you might at first think. If you want to have children and stay home with them while they're small, if you would rather work away from home, or if you want to balance work and family, *do it* and with no apologies. If someone else shows disapproval and says you're wasting your time, it's not your problem unless you agree. In this respect it might not be a bad idea to declare a moratorium on analyzing. If you are reasonably happy with whatever you do, why look for reasons to reconsider?

7. Tolerance: for an occasional craziness, irritableness, tiredness, clumsiness, memory lapses, human error, disagreement, argument, and very contrary points of view.

8. Willingness to accept each other's style: active in some respects, passive in others. Don't be bound by fixed or predetermined notions that X is always a female prerogative or Y a male imperative. A man can change diapers, tend sick puppies, and respond with pleasure to a woman's sexual initiatives. A woman can change a tire, bring home the biggest paycheck, and get the first (or only) Ph.D. in the house. Everyone is entitled to have important friendships with members of the same sex without incurring strange glances. The list is endless.

9. Sexual fulfillment: not measured in terms of orgasmic frequency or quality but as an abiding expression of shared intimacy. People who are sex machines may never learn to like each other. Yet, caring partners can learn to overcome their sexual difficulties by relaxing and by foregoing intercourse for a while in favor of simple touching, truthful talk about what gives pleasure, a shower or two, and listening to music.

10. Sharing household tasks: I clean, you cook, I fold, you iron, I mow, you rake. Next week, reverse it, or not, as it suits you both.

Of course, very few marriages are in an optimal state all or even most of the time. Ebbs and flows, ups and downs are part of the human condition. Marriage might best be seen as a journey in which two people together, and at times separately, discover all the other things in life they cannot offer each other. There is a growing sense that the past is past and that life is not a meaning but an opportunity for meaningful experiences. Although traditions, rituals, observances, and flexible roles can give marriage structure and purpose, they can never substitute for loving, caring, kindness, loyalty, and having fun together.

We think it appropriate to end this section with the manifesto adopted by the early proponents of women's rights who met at Seneca Falls, New York in 1848.

Resolved, That such laws as conflict, in any way, with the true and substantial happiness of woman, are contrary to the great precept of nature and of no validity, for this is "superior in obligation to any other."

Resolved, That all laws which prevent woman from occupying such a station in society as her conscience shall dictate, or which place her in a position inferior to that of man, are contrary to the great precept of nature, and therefore of no force of authority.

Resolved, That woman is man's equal—was intended to be so by the Creator, and the highest good of the race demands that she should be recognized as such.

Resolved, That the women of this country ought to be enlightened in regard to the laws under which they live, that they may no longer publish their degradation by declaring themselves satisfied with their present position, nor their ignorance, by asserting that they have all the rights they want.

Resolved, That inasmuch as man while claiming for himself intellectual superiority, does accord to woman moral superiority, it is preeminently his duty to encourage her to speak and teach, as she has an opportunity in all religious assemblies.

Resolved, That the same amount of virtue, delicacy, and refinement of behavior that is required to woman in the social state, should also be required of man, and the same transgressions should be visited with equal severity on both man and woman.

Resolved, That the objection of indelicacy and impropriety, which is so often brought against woman when she addresses a public audience, comes with a very ill grace from those who encourage, by their attendance, her presence on the stage, in the concert, or in feats of the circus.

Resolved, That woman has too long rested satisfied in the circumscribed limits which corrupt customs and a perverted application of the Scriptures have marked out for her, and that it is time she should move in the enlarged sphere which her great Creator has assigned her.

Resolved, That the equality of human rights results necessarily from the fact of the identity of the race in capabilities and responsibilities.

Resolved, therefore, That, being invested by the Creator with the same capabilities, and the same consciousness of responsibility for their exercise, it is demonstrably the right and duty of woman, equally with man, to promote every righteous cause by every righteous means; and especially in regard to the great subjects of morals and religion, it is self-evidently her right to participate with her brother in teaching them, both in private and in public, by writing and by speaking, by any instrumentalities proper to be used, and in any assemblies proper to be held; and this being a self-evident truth growing out of the divinely implanted principles of human nature, any custom or authority adverse to it, whether modern or wearing the hoary sanction of antiquity, is to be regarded as a self-evident falsehood, and at war with mankind.

Resolved, That the speedy success of our cause depends upon the zealous and untiring efforts of both men and women, for the overthrow of the monopoly of the pulpit, and for the securing to woman an equal participation with men in the various trades, professions, and commerce.

Seneca Falls is the birthplace of the women's movement in the United States. Its organizers—Elizabeth Cady Stanton, Amelia Bloomer, Mary McClintock, and Jane Hunt—published the first feminist newspaper there and held the first Women's Conference at the Wesleyan Methodist Church. The church, along with four other historic sites in the town, has been dedicated as the first Women's Rights National Park.

REFERENCES

Monthly Vital Statistics Report. National Center for Health Statistics. Vol. 32, no. 13, September 21, 1984.

Strong, B., DeVault, C., Suid, M., & Reynolds, R. *The Marriage and Family Experience*. New York: West Publishing Co., 1983.

Thornton, A., & Freedman, D. *The Changing American Family*. Washington, DC: The Population Reference Bureau, 1983.

Williams, G. J., & Money, J. *Traumatic Abuse and Neglect of Children at Home*. Baltimore: The Johns Hopkins University Press, 1980.

Books For Recommended Reading

LOVE AND INTIMACY

Buscaglia, L. *Loving Each Other.* Thorofare, NJ: Slack, 1984.
Colton, H. *Touch Therapy.* New York: Zebra Books, 1985.
Fromm, E. *The Art of Loving.* New York: Bantam Books, 1956.
Jampolsky, G. *Love Is Letting Go of Fear.* New York: Bantam Books, 1980.
Ramey, J. *Intimate Friendships.* Englewood Cliffs, NJ: Prentice-Hall, 1976.

THE RELIGIOUS PERSPECTIVE

Borowitz, E. B. *Choosing a Sex Ethic: A Jewish Inquiry.* New York: Schocken Books, 1969.
The Catholic Theological Society of America. *Human Sexuality: New Directions in American Catholic Thought.* New York: Paulist Press, 1977.
Clapp, S. *The Third Wave and the Family: The "Church Family" Braces for Change.* Champaign, IL: C–4 Resources, 1984.
Goergen, D. *The Sexual Celibate.* Garden City, NY: Doubleday, 1979.
Gordis, R. *Love and Sex: A Modern Jewish Perspective.* New York: Farrar, Straus & Giroux, 1978.
Keane, P. S. *Sexual Morality: A Catholic Perspective.* New York: Paulist Press, 1977.

Nelson, J. *Between Two Gardens—Reflections on Sexuality and Religious Experience.* New York: Pilgrim Press, 1983.

Scanzoni, L. D. *Sex Is a Parent Affair.* New York: Bantam Books, 1982.

Scanzoni, L. D. *Sexuality.* Philadelphia: The Westminster Press, 1984.

Sullivan, S. K., & Kawiak, M. A. *Parents Talk Love: The Catholic Family Handbook about Sexuality.* New York: Paulist Press, 1985.

FAMILY SEXUALITY EDUCATION

Briggs, D. C. *Your Child's Self-esteem.* New York: Dolphin Books, 1975.

Brown, L. (Ed.). *Sex Education in the Eighties: The Challenge of Healthy Sexual Evolution.* New York: Plenum Press, 1981.

Calderone, M. S., & Johnson, E. W. *The Family Book about Sexuality.* New York: Harper & Row, 1981.

Calderone, M. S., & Ramey, J. W. *Talking with Your Child about Sex.* New York: Random House, 1982.

Gordon, S., & Gordon, J. *Raising a Child Conservatively in a Sexually Permissive World.* New York: Simon & Schuster, 1983.

Pogrebin, L. *Growing Up Free: Raising Your Child in the '80s.* New York: McGraw-Hill, 1980.

HOMOSEXUALITY

Bell, A. P., & Weinberg, M. S. *Homosexualities: A Study of Diversity among Men and Women.* New York: Simon & Schuster, 1978.

Boswell, J. *Christianity, Social Tolerance, and Homosexuality.* Chicago: The University of Chicago Press, 1980.

McNaught, B. *A Disturbed Peace.* Washington, DC: Dignity, 1981.

McNeill, J. J. *The Church and the Homosexual.* New York: Pocket Books, 1976.

SOCIAL ISSUES

Carnes, P. *The Sexual Addiction.* Minneapolis: CompCare Publications, 1983.

Copp, D., & Wendell, S. (Eds.). *Pornography and Censorship.* Buffalo, NY: Prometheus Books, 1983.

Blum, G., & Blum, B. *Feeling Good about Yourself.* Available from: Feeling Good Associates, 507 Palma Way, Mill Valley, CA 94941.

Buscaglia, L. *The Disabled and Their Parents.* Thorofare, NJ: Slack, 1983.

Butler, R., & Lewis, M. L. *Love and Sex after Sixty: A Guide for Men and Women for Their Later Years.* New York: Harper & Row, 1977.

Dickman, I., with Gordon, S. *One Miracle at a Time: How to Get Help for a Disabled Child—Advice from Parents.* New York: Simon & Schuster, 1986.

Finkelhor, D. *Child Sexual Abuse—New Theory and Research.* New York: Free Press, 1984.

Neistadt, M., & Baker, M. F. *Choices: A Sexual Guide for the Physically Handicapped.* Boston: Spaulding Rehabilitation Hospital, 1979.

The Report of the Commission on Obscenity and Pornography. New York: Bantam Books, 1970.

Sex and Disability Project. *Who Cares: A Handbook on Sex Education and Counseling Services for Disabled People.* Austin, TX: PRO-RD, 5341 Industrial Oaks Boulevard, 78735.

PREVENTION AND WELLNESS

Albee, G., Gordon, S., & Leitenberg, H. (Eds.). *Promoting Sexual Responsibility and Preventing Sexual Problems.* Hanover, NH: University Press of New England, 1983.

Barbach, L. *For Each Other: Sharing Sexual Intimacy.* Garden City, NY: Doubleday Anchor, 1982.

Boston Women's Health Book Collective. *The New Our Bodies, Ourselves.* New York: Simon & Schuster, 1984.

Carrera, M. *Sex: The Facts, the Acts and Your Feelings.* New York: Crown, 1981.

Heiman, J., LoPiccolo, L., & LoPiccolo, J. *Becoming Orgasmic: A Sexual Growth Program for Women.* Englewood Cliffs, NJ: Prentice-Hall, 1976.

Kelly, G. *Good Sex: The Healthy Man's Guide to Sexual Fulfillment.* New York: Harcourt, Brace, Jovanovich, 1979.

Kitzinger, S. *Woman's Experience of Sex: The Facts and Feelings of Female Sexuality at Every Stage of Life.* New York: Penguin Books, 1983.

Lauerson, N., & Stukane, E. *Listen to Your Body: A Gynecologist Answers Women's Most Intimate Questions.* New York: Simon & Schuster, 1982.

Lumiere, R., & Cook, S. *Healthy Sex and Keeping It That Way.* New York: Simon & Schuster, 1983.

Mass, L. *Medical Answers about AIDS.* New York: Gay Men's Health Crisis, Box 274, 132 West 24th St., New York, NY 10011.

Masters, W. H., & Johnson, V. E., with R. J. Levin. *The Pleasure Bond: A New Look at Sexuality and Commitment.* Boston: Little, Brown, 1975.

McCarthy, B., & McCarthy, E. *Sexual Awareness: Enhancing Sexual Pleasure.* New York: Carroll & Graf, 1984.

Zilbergeld, B., & Ullman, J. *Male Sexuality.* Boston: Little, Brown, 1978.

MEN'S AND WOMEN'S ROLES

Bernard, J. *The Future of Marriage*. New York: World, 1972.

Cassell, C. *Swept Away—Why Women Fear Their Own Sexuality*. New York: Bantam Books, 1985.

Freidan, B. *The Second Stage*. New York: Summit Books, 1981.

Levine, L., & Barbach, L. *The Intimate Male: Candid Discussions about Women, Sex, and Relationships*. Garden City, NY: Doubleday Anchor, 1983.

Macklin, E. D., & Rubin, R. H. (Eds.). *Contemporary Families and Alternative Lifestyles*. Beverly Hills: Sage Publications, 1983.

Steinem, G. *Outrageous Acts and Everyday Rebellions*. New York: New American Library, 1983.

GENERAL INTEREST

Baker, R., & Elliston, F. (Eds.). *Philosophy and Sex*. Buffalo: Prometheus Books, 1975.

Ellis, A., & Harper, R. *A New Guide to Rational Living*. North Hollywood, CA: Wilshire Book Co., 1977.

Frankl, V. E. *Man's Search for Meaning*. New York: Touchstone, 1984.

Gordon, S. *When Living Hurts*. New York: Union of American Hebrew Congregations, 1985.

Hazelton, L. *The Right to Feel Bad—Coming to Terms with Normal Depression*. Garden City, NY: The Dial Press, 1984.

Hettlinger, R. *Your Sexual Freedom: Letters to Students*. New York: Continuum, 1981.

Kelly, G. F. *Learning about Sex: The Contemporary Guide for Young Adults*. Woodbury, NY: Barron's Educational Series, 1977.

Nass, G. D., Libby, R. W., & Fisher, M. P. *Sexual Choices: An Introduction to Human Sexuality*. Monterey, CA: Wadsworth, 1984.

Olds, S. W. *The Eternal Garden: Seasons of Our Sexuality*. New York: Times Books, 1985.

Peck, M. S. *The Road Less Traveled–A New Psychology of Love, Traditional Values and Spiritual Growth*. New York: Touchstone, 1978.

For a listing of books and audiovisual materials in the area of human sexuality write to: Ed-U Press, P.O. Box 583, Fayetteville, NY 13066.

Index

Granuloma inguinale (Donovanosis), 201
Greer, Germaine, 276, 293
Growing Up Free, 278–279, 286
Guilt, 4, 90–96

H

Hair growth, 270–271
"Happy Anniversary Ray . . . Love, Brian",
    85–87
HcG hormone, 257, 261
Hematocoele, 237
Hepatitis, 198–199
Hernia, 237
Herpes, 199–200, 261–262
Heterosexual behavior, compulsive,
    18–19
"Highlights from Research about Men and
    Contraception", 284
Hirsuitism, 271
The Hite Report, 5, 224
The Hite Report on Male Sexuality, 224
Hite, Shere, 5, 224
Hobson, Laura, 83
Homophobia, 80, 277
Homosexual(s). *See also* Homosexuality.
    behavior, compulsive, 18–19
    children, 80–83
    discrimination against, 78
    fantasies, 76
    in heterosexual marriages, 79–80
    if you think you're a, 76–78
    parents, 80, 83–84
    relationships, 79, 85–87
Homosexuality, 17–18, 73–89. *See also*
    Homosexual(s).
    American Psychiatric Association's view
        on, 74–75
    Catholic thought on, 74
    cause of, 84–88
    constitutional, 13
    latent, 82–83
    transitional, 88
Honig, Alice Sterling, 299
Hormones
    female, 235

Hormones—*Cont.*
    male sex, 234–235
    menstrual cycle and, 256–257
    pregnancy and, 257, 261
Hostile-dependent relationship, 21
How to Say No to a Rapist—and Survive,
    110–111
HTLV-III (human T-lymphotropic virus
    type III), 196–197. *See also* AIDS (Ac-
    quired Immune Deficiency Syndrome).
*Human Sexuality—New Directions in Ameri-
    can Catholic Thought*, 36–37
Human Sexuality: A Preliminary Study, 35–
    36
Humane Vitae, 37
Hunt, Morton, 178
Husband beating, 303
Hydrocoele, 237

I

Immature guilt, 14
Immune globulin, 199
Impotence, 215, 216, 220–222
In a Different Voice, 66
"In Defense of Playboy Bunnies", 297
In vitro fertilization, 53–54
Incest, 117. *See also* Child sexual abuse.
Infantilism, 151–152, 230
Infertility, 53–54, 239–242, 256, 270. *See
    also* Fertility.
    causes of, 261–262
    male, 240–241
Infidelity. *See* Extramarital sex.
Inguinal hernia, 237
Inhibited Sexual Desire (ISD), 222–224
Institute for Sex Research, 74, 129
Intermarriage, 29, 38–39. *See also*
    Marriage.
International Conference on Population,
    156
Intimacy, 5–9
Intimate networks, 50
Intrauterine device (IUD), 191, 265–266
Introceptive, reflex erection, 246

Penis, 233–234
  injury during intercourse, 250
  rings, 246
  self-examination of, 238
  size, 16, 248–249
Performance anxiety, 243
Periods. *See* Menses.
Personal hygiene and disease prevention, 186–188
Perversions, 18, 226–227. *See also* Paraphilia.
Phimosis, 247–248
Physically abusive relationships, 96
Physician's Desk Reference, 251
Pituitary, 256, 257
Placenta, 257, 261
Pleasuring, 207–208
Pogrebin, Letty Cotten, 278–279, 286
Politics of abortion, 61–65
Politics of Rape, 132
Population growth, 155–156
Pornography, 128–135
  banning, 130–131
  child, 131
  children seeing, 172
Postgonococcal urethritis (PGU), 194
Precocious puberty, 260
Pregnancy, 239, 260–261
  ectopic (tubal), 255–256, 261, 265–266
  hormones and, 257
Premarital sex, 11–12, 35
  teenagers and, 174–175
Premature ejaculation, 219–220, 243–244
Premenstrual syndrome (PMS), 268–269
Preorgasmic woman, 216–218
Priapism, 247
"Pro-kit" for prevention of sexually transmitted diseases, 189–190
Progesterone, 256, 257, 266, 268
Prolactin, 235
Promiscuous sexual behaviors, 94
Prophylactics. *See* Condoms.
Prostaglandin, 268
Prostitution, 150–154
Psychoanalysis, 99

Psychodynamically oriented therapy, 99–100
Psychotherapist. *See* Therapist.
Psychotherapy. *See* Therapy.
Puberty
  female, 257–260
  precocious, 260

R

Rape, 107–112, 302
  acquaintance, 108
  and the disabled, 136–137
  date, 108
  prevention, 110
  sexual functioning after, 109–110
  trauma syndrome, 109
  victim
    reaction to, 110, 111–112
    treatment of, 108–109
Rational Emotive Therapy (RET), 99–100
Refractory period, 242–243, 246
Relationships, 10–11, 295–296
  decision making in, 293
  Ladies Home Journal questionnaire, 296
  men's, 275–289
Religion, 40
  organized, 305–306
  and sexuality, 33–42
  and the women's liberation movement, 37–38
Religion and sexism, 37
Religious Values and Peak Experiences, 42
Renshaw, Dr. Domeena, 239
Reproductive organs
  female, 254
  female (*illus.*), 253, 255
  female (*illus.*) 233, 236
Reproductive years, female, 260–263
Retarded ejaculation, 216, 247
Rhythm method, 264
Right-to-Life, 63
Role playing, 17
Romero, Joan Arnold, 37
Rupture, 237
Russel, Dr. Diana, 117, 132

S

Sadism, 18, 229
Sadomasochism, 229
Safe Counsel, 56–57
Salpingitis, 255–256
Scabies, 202
Scrotal pain, 235–236
Scrotal sac, self-examination of, 238
Self-hatred, 94
Self-pleasuring. *See* Masturbation.
Semans method, 219
Seminal fluid, 239
Seminoma, 237
Seneca Falls manifesto, 311–312
Sex
  and alcohol, 249
  of a child, methods for choosing, 244
  drive, 296
  education
    age for, 164–165, 170–171, 176
    in churches, 40–41
    common questions about, 170–175,
      170
    and the disabled, 141–142
    parents as educators, 159–181
    in public schools, 175
    in synagogues, 40–41
  extramarital, 35, 46, 50–52, 95,
    210–213
  and friendship, 5–6
  love and, 21–23
  in marriage, 25–26
  objects, 29, 297
  premarital, 35
  saying yes when meaning no, 91–92
  surrogates, 154
Sexes, differences between, 281–283
Sexual abuse
  and the disabled, 136–137
  of children. *See* Child sexual abuse.
Sexual addictions, 18–19
Sexual assault, 107–112. *See also* Rape.
Sexual behavior
  abnormal, 13
  Kinsey's categories of, 74

Sexual behavior—*Cont.*
  normal, 13
  promiscuous, 94
Sexual communication, 204–210
Sexual deviation, 18
Sexual dysfunctions, 17, 214–224
  caused by prescribed medication, 251
  and emotions, 250
  situational erectile, 250
Sexual experiences:
  first, 19
  and guilt or anger, 90–96
Sexual fantasies, 68–69
  homosexual, 76
  women, 71–72
Sexual harassment, 112–115
Sexual identity of children, 168–169
Sexual responsibility, 284–286
Sexual revolution, 3–9
Sexual sharing, 284–286
Sexual thoughts, 13–14
Sexuality
  appreciating our, concepts, 13–19
  coming to terms with your own, 10–19
  concepts for parents, 167–170
  and the disabled, 136–143
  educators, parents as, 159–181,
    287–288
  religion and, 33–42
  repressed, 16–17
Sexually transmitted disease(s), 185–203,
  254
  causes of infertility, 261–262
  descriptions of, 191–202
  examination and treatment, 202–203
  prevention, 186–191
Shigellosis, 198
Siegman, Henry, 64–65
Single parent, 175–181.– See also Parents.
  children's reaction to new sexual relation-
    ships, 178–179
  income, 180
Singlehood, 49–50
Situational erectile dysfunction, 250
Sleep tumescence, 245
Speculum, 262

Sperm, 245
  in sequence of pregnancy, 260–261
Spermatic cord, self-examination of, 238
Spermatocoele, 237
Spermicidal agents, 264
Spitz, Reneé, 58
Squeeze technique, 220
Steinem, Gloria, 297
Sterilization, 267–268
  and the disabled, 141
Sternberg, Robert, 296
Stop-start masturbation, 219
Storaska, Fred, 110–111
Strategic therapy, 100
Structural therapy, 100
Sublimation, 16–17
Suppositories, 264
Swedish Institute, 135
Synagogues, sex education in, 40–41. *See also* Religion.
Syphilis, 191–193
  prevention, 187
Szasz, Thomas, 278

T

Teenage pregnancy, 4
Television, parents' concerns about, 169–170
Testes, 235–238. *See also* Testicles.
Testicles, 235–238
  cancer of the, 237–238
  losing one, 245
  painful, 235–236
  self-examination of, 238
  tumors of the, 237
  twisting of the, 236
Testosterone, 234–236
Therapist
  certifying organizations, 100–101
  choosing, 100–101
  /client sexual interactions, 101–102
  defined, 99
Therapy, 97–103
  behavioral, 100
  conjoint, 102

Therapy—*Cont.*
  modality, 99–100
  psychoanalysis, 99
  psychodynamically oriented, 99–100
  Rational Emotive (RET), 99–100
  strategic, 100
  structural, 100
Torsion, 236
Transitional homosexuality, 88
Transvestites, 228
Trichomoniasis, 195, 254
Tubal (ectopic) pregnancy, 255–256, 261, 265–266
Tubal sterilization, 267–268
Tumors, of the testicles, 237
Tunica albuginea, 233
Twisting of the testicle, 236

U

Ultrasound test, 271–272
United Church of Christ, 35–36
United Nations Children Fund, 63
United States Commission on Obscenity and Pornography, 129–130
United States Supreme Court decision on abortion, 61
Urethra, 234
Urolangnia, 230
Uterus, 254–255
  cancer of, 270

V

Vagina, 254
Vaginal lubrication, 270
Vaginal spermicidal contraceptives, for prevention of sexually transmitted diseases, 190
Vaginismus, 218–219
Vaginitis, 194–195, 254
van Den Haag, Ernest, 132
Varicocoele, 241
Vas deferens, self-examination of, 238
Vasectomy, 240–241
Vasovasostomy, 241

Venereal disease. *See* Sexually transmitted
 disease(s).
Venereal warts, 200, 216–262
Vibrator, 217
Violence
 pornography and, 132
 family, 302–303
Voyeurism, 18, 227

W

Warts, venereal, 200, 216–262
Withdrawal method, 249, 264
Women
 body image, 298–299
 careers, 294–295, 304
 friendship, male-, 278–279
 identity, 297–298
 personal growth, 298–300

Women—*Cont.*
 preorgasmic, 216–218
 sexuality workshop, 217–218
 sports, 298
 wages, 294–295
Women's conference at Seneca Falls,
 311–312
Women's liberation movement, 11, 14,
 291–300, 301
 goals, 292–293
 and religion, 37–38

Y

Yeast infection, 195, 254

Z

Zoophilia, 230